PILGRIMAGE AND FAITH

PILGRIMAGE AND FAITH

BUDDHISM, CHRISTIANITY, AND ISLAM

Edited by Virginia C. Raguin and Dina Bangdel
with F. E. Peters

Serindia Publications
Chicago

Published in 2010 by Serindia Publications in association with the College of the Holy Cross, Worcester, Massachusetts

Serindia Publications, Inc.
PO Box 10335
Chicago, Illinois 60610 USA
info@serindia.com
www.serindia.com

Hardcover ISBN: 978-1-932476-47-7
Softcover ISBN: 978-1-932476-48-4

Designed by Format Limited, Hong Kong
Printed and bound in Hong Kong

Front Cover: (Left) Devotees taking *darshan* of Dipankara, see page 90, Fig. 6; (Middle) Scala Santa (Holy Stairs) Rome, see page 9, Fig. 5; (Right) Male pilgrims wearing Ihram clothing on the plains of Arafat, see page 30, Fig. 18

Back Cover: (Left) Mahabodhi Temple, Bodhgaya, see page 59, Fig. 6; (Middle) Santiago, a UNESCO World Heritage Site, see page 218, Fig. 2; (Right) Dome of the Rock, Jerusalem, see page 284, Fig. 8

Frontispiece: The Church of the Holy Sepulcher, see page 215, Fig. 12

Library of Congress Cataloging-in-Publication Data

Pilgrimage and faith : Buddhism, Christianity and Islam / edited by Virginia C. Raguin, Dina Bangdel and F.E. Peters. -- 1st ed.
p. cm.
Includes bibliographical references and index.
ISBN 978-1-932476-47-7 (hardcover : alk. paper) -- ISBN 978-1-932476-48-4 (softcover : alk. paper)
1. Pilgrims and pilgrimages. 2. Buddhism. 3. Christianity. 4. Islam. I. Raguin, Virginia Chieffo, 1941- II. Bangdel, Dina. III. Peters, F. E. (Francis E.)

BL619.P5P517 2010
203'.51--dc22

2010000013

Note on Diacritics and Transliteration:
Diacritic marks have been avoided to facilitate easy reading. All Sanskrit terms are transliterated in the standard phonetic system ("a" for ā; "sh" for ś and ṣ; "d" for ḍ; "ch" for c; "ri" for ṛ; "th" for ṭh). Similarly, Tibetan terms and proper names are given in their phonetic forms, unless otherwise indicated in the text.

Contents

Preface

Virginia C. Raguin

Pilgrimage and Faith: Buddhism, Christianity, and Islam focuses on fundamental issues of the three religions and the many ways that their practices converge in the pilgrimage experience. The pilgrim's goal is the holy site and its approach involves both physical and temporal expense, beginning through detachment from the familiar. The process to, participation in, and reflection on the experience can deeply alter the sense of self and of community for the believer. The hoped-for result is a sense of humility: the smallness of the self and the greatness of the divine and the need to reform one's life and bring it more into harmony with the good. Paramount, however, is the injunction to exercise charity to others and also in humility to accept charity from others.

All three religions evidence a deeply felt motivation to affect the life of the believer through transformative experience. Pilgrimage creates a liminal situation within which the believer is neither in the realm of the mundane nor yet within the sacred. The juxtaposition, in this study, of religions whose beliefs and practices are so often seen as incompatible in a contemporary world reveals profound similarities in their efforts to bring the individual the attainment of the sublime. Shared goals of personal development and communal solidarity are exemplified through religious objects of great age and beauty as well as modern ephemera. Although often rare and beautiful, art also functions as a vital part of social systems that cement the bonds of community, as well as support the role of religion in transcending human limitations. All three religions structure an intersection of the individual with both natural and built environments, ritualized behavior, and tangible objects. These tangible objects may range from a gilt bronze and bejeweled statue venerated at a national shrine to the commonly available chromolithograph tacked on the wall of one's home.

The goals of this study are not only to see profound similarities in such pilgrimages, but also to transform our way of looking at "works of art" from these cultures, too often exhibited without their animating context. Participants on pilgrimages saw objects of supreme artistic skill (Islamic glazed tile, Christian enameled reliquaries, or Buddhist bronze statues) mingled with mass-produced objects (lead pilgrimage badges, terracotta souvenirs, or paper mementos) and personal acquisitions such as stones or soil from the holy place. These objects all share the same purpose: to make more tangible the ephemeral experience and thus enable the owner to intensify memories of spiritual commitment and social interaction. They also demonstrate continuity of the past and the present and the shared motivations and experiences of persons of all social strata.

The practices of Buddhists, Christians, and Muslims

testify to a desire to believe in a sacred made more accessible at a holy place. As described by Toni Huber in his essay, this vital "sacred power" or "blessing" is known to Tibetan Buddhists as *chinlab* (*byin rlabs*). The Christian historian Peter Brown eloquently described the tombs of saints as possessing *praesentia*, the physical presence of the holy. Charity to the pilgrim can be seen as a sharing of the sacred power, the holy. For Muslims, charity is one of the Five Pillars of Islam, and acts of charity are imbedded in the *hajj* ritual, as explained by Anisa Mehdi in her essay. Krisadawan Hongladarom speaks of receiving well wishes and material help in the form of food and money during her pilgrimage in Tibet from many people, including Han Chinese and westerners. The last chapter of the 12th-century *Pilgrim's Guide to Santiago de Compostable* discusses charity to be offered to travelling pilgrims.

A pilgrimage seeks to purify, connecting the inner process with the exterior physicality, especially ascent and circumambulation. Most pilgrimages involve long days of journey across often arduous terrain (Figs. 1-2). But even with the goal attained, Buddhists mount the steps of a temple, Christians climb the stairs to embrace the statue of St. James in Compostela, and Muslims circumambulate the Ka'ba. They carry amulets: prayer scrolls rolled within cylinders worn in Iran, the Tibetan Gau with its small objects of blessing and memory, and Christian pilgrimage badges, as discussed here by Jennifer Lee. These tangible manifestations of commitment are directed inward as much as outward. We are fragile beings; our attention wavers and our energy fails. Reminders are necessary; and whether they are for attention to scheduled hours of prayer, communal hearing, or recitation of holy texts, or the wearing of a particular form of dress or adornment, all serve to connect the individual to a tradition and a desired mode of behavior.

Pilgrimage sites are fluid; they transform to meet their transcending purposes. First, they live in the memory of those who have experienced the physical journey to the site itself. But, in many instances, pilgrims experience extended

Fig. 1
Pilgrimage in Spain, Camino of Santiago, June 2008: leaving El Cebreiro, the highest part of the route.
Photograph Virginia C. Raguin

Fig. 2
Pilgrimage in Tibet from Nyethang to Samye, May 2007; end of the day, camping at the side of the road.
Photograph Meu Yontan

lives in replication. The Bodhisattva of Compassion, Avalokiteshvara, has widespread devotion across Asia (Fig. 3). Known in Japan as Kannon, the Bodhisattva is chiefly honored through a pilgrimage in Saikoku ("Western Provinces"). In her essay, Elizabeth ten Grotenhuis notes that the Saikoku Pilgrimage was replicated at 230 additional sites throughout Japan. Christians created replicas of varying exactitude of the Holy Sepulcher, enabling those who could not journey to the Holy Land to revere in a special way the tangible moment of Christ's death and earthly resting place before his Resurrection. Muslims rarely replicate Mecca, or the holy sites associated with the Hajj, yet in many ways the daily routine of prayer, turning toward Mecca, is a gesture of physical attachment to the geography of community. With the demise of pilgrimage opportunities in the birthplace of Buddhism in India, sacred sites became associated with other landscapes, as Dina Bangdel explains in her essay on Nepal. For the true adept, however, the voyage becomes entirely sublimated, subsumed into the soul, a mediation to transcend physical limitation.

But for the here and now, the vast majority of those seeking pilgrimage have recourse to the material. The preparation of one's clothes, conversation with companions, or the interaction with those passing by are mentioned by Najah Bazzy, Anisa Mehdi, and Krisadawan Hongladarom. Souvenirs, such as the mass-produced wood block print, or even mementos as mundane as used airline tickets, serve to recall the actuality of the place and to encourage successive reflections on the meaning of the experience. Most vividly, as seen in reflections throughout these essays, the pilgrim seeks self-improvement. Reflection becomes a way of confirming to the self a continued commitment to that purpose, as well as a means of sharing with others. This is a global phenomenon that as enacted by a community of real, living beings, ineluctably meshes with politics. The present, shared use of the Holy Sepulcher in Jerusalem among the Latins, Armenians, and Greek Orthodox can become both visibly and orally disjunctive. Public performance of ritual in areas of religious/ethnic tension has confronted opposition. Hongladarom's pilgrimage of full prostration to the Tibetan monastery of Samye was cut short because of visa restrictions. The management of the Hajj and the development of the new urban Mecca have, for some, presented tensions between the traditional purpose of the journey and contemporary tourism.

Indeed, the worlds of religious expression and of secular pursuits can often seem at odds. Yet are the goals of pilgrimage completely estranged from many aspects of

Fig. 3
Avalokiteshvara, the Bodhisattva of Compassion
Tibet, second half of the 13th century
Cast copper alloy with silver and gold inlay, 6½ in. (16.5 cm)
The Newark Museum, Purchase 1979, The Members' Fund, 79.442
Photograph The Newark Museum

Fig. 4

Palestinian school children visiting the Dome of the Rock, 1996

Photograph David H. Wells/*Saudi Aramco World*/ SAWDIA

Fig. 5

Scala Santa (Holy Stairs) Rome; Pilgrims mounting stairs on their knees.

Photograph Michel Raguin

modern tourist travel? For the Palestinian children visiting the Dome of the Rock in Jerusalem, do we need to differentiate or even separate the various goals of religious obligation, cultural heritage, or artistic admiration? (Fig. 4). In Rome, we can still find people visiting the *Scala Santa* (Holy Stairs) and mounting them on their knees. The twenty-eight marble stairs have been associated with the steps that Christ climbed to face trial before Pontius Pilate, and their transference to Rome is credited to St. Helena (Fig. 5). Yet, these same devotees will assuredly visit the church of St. John Lateran just across the road, and look at some of the most revered works of Rome's medieval and Renaissance artists (Fig. 6).

An iconic image of pilgrimage, and of art, is Caravaggio's *Madonna di Loreto* (1604-1606), also known as the *Madonna dei Pellegrini*, or pilgrims, in the Roman church of Sant'Agostino (Fig. 7). The barefoot Virgin and naked Child appear to two peasants whose calloused feet are at the spectator's eye level. The setting is not celestial, but a doorway of a building with flaking plaster. The onlookers that I have observed have spent almost half an hour before the image, standing to the right, instinctively aligning themselves with the peasants gazing at the apparition. What are they thinking? Certainly, there is a mesmerizing effect of the image set within its shallow chapel. Are they pondering the Virgin and her Son, or traditions of depictions of the Virgin in Italy's many shrines, or possibly Caravaggio's personal struggles and artistic legacy? Perhaps they have accomplished the "Caravaggio circuit" of Rome, the Villas Borghese and Doria Pamphilj, depictions of saints Peter and Paul in Santa Maria del Popolo, and the chapel in nearby San Luigi dei Francesi with its magical *Calling of St. Matthew*, followed by the Apostle's Gospel writing and martyrdom. Do these works left by Caravaggio, certainly a man enmeshed in passions, function as "Bodhisattvas" helping all who gaze on

Fig. 6
St. John Lateran (San Giovanni in Laterano), Rome, 13th-18th centuries.
Photograph Michel Raguin

them empathize with the human condition, that ocean of sorrows (*samsara*)? In three-dimensional presence, sculpted by dramatic light, and intruding apparently into our own space, they embody the encounter of the commonplace with the divine. The discovery received with surprise as well as joy, as seen on the faces of the peasants, is that the divine actually is the ordinary. Concepts of separation are illusionary. Is this not the message of the Buddha? Are Mary and her Son not people like us? For those who have gazed, is this not that intense act of sacred viewing (*darshan*) that is vital to Buddhist pilgrimage? This process of engagement with materials, image, intention by the creators, and reception by fellow pilgrims seems not far removed from specified religious goals such as alleviating suffering and sharing joy. Faintly, but surely, the Buddhist dedication prayer resonates.

> *I dedicate happiness to all sentient beings without exception;*
> *May happiness spread in the air;*
> *I take on the sufferings of all sentient beings without exception;*
> *May the ocean of suffering be dry.*

Fig. 7
Caravaggio, *Madonna di Loreto* (1604-1606) Sant'Agostino, Rome.
Photograph Michel Raguin

Origins and History of Pilgrimage for Christians, Muslims, and Buddhists

F. E. Peters and Dina Bangdel

Whan that Averylle with his shoures soote
The droghte of March hath perced to the roote, ….
Thanne longen folk to goon on pilgrymages,
And palmeres for to seeken straunge strondes
To ferne halwes kouthe in sondry londes,
And specially from every shyres ende
Of Engelond to Caunterbury they wende,
The holy blisful martir for to seke,
That hem hath holpen whan that they weere seeke.

Chaucer, Prologue to *The Canterbury Tales*
Variorum Edition of the *Works of Geoffrey Chaucer*, 1993

It is springtime, and the season of the year has stirred Chaucer's "palmers," Christian pilgrims bearing the identifying palm frond, to set out for those "ferne halwes," the distant saints and their holy places (Fig. 1). In Chaucer's case the goal is the shrine of Thomas a Beckett at Canterbury, but elsewhere in England and across the European continent there were other pilgrims heading for more distant shrines, and indeed even greater numbers of the pious in the Middle East and Asia were embarked on similar pilgrimages for similar reasons.

PILGRIMAGE DEFINED, DESCRIBED

A pilgrimage is a personal passage from this place to that. As in all passages, this place, the starting point, is your place, where you are. But what sets the pilgrimage off from other journeys from here to there is that the "there" of pilgrimage is a holy place like Canterbury, and it is precisely its holiness that draws the pilgrim to that place. If the pilgrimage is a journey, it is also a visitation, a going forth and a returning thither, as opposed to resettlement in or immigration to a holy place, which is a related but different phenomenon.

The pilgrimage is a journey in real time and across real space, and is thus distinguished from other imaginary, mystical, or metaphysical voyages to real, intentional, or cosmic holy places. Thus they differ from the exalted experiences of saints, mystics, and shamans of all religious traditions. Neither are they mere transports, the like of which carried Ezekiel before the throne of God or Jesus to the pinnacle of the Jerusalem Temple, or Muhammad by night from Mecca to Jerusalem, "the distant shrine"; or monk Mogallyayana's visitation to Bodhgaya, the place of the Buddha's enlightenment, where he acquired a shoot of the sacred Bodhi tree so that it could be replanted at Jetavarna Monastery.

While such Buddhist narratives of miraculous transport to the sacred sites are familiar themes in the early canons, the notion of pilgrimage as journey is emphasized by the Sanskrit term *dharma yatra,* "journey of the Dharma", *or tirtha yatra,*

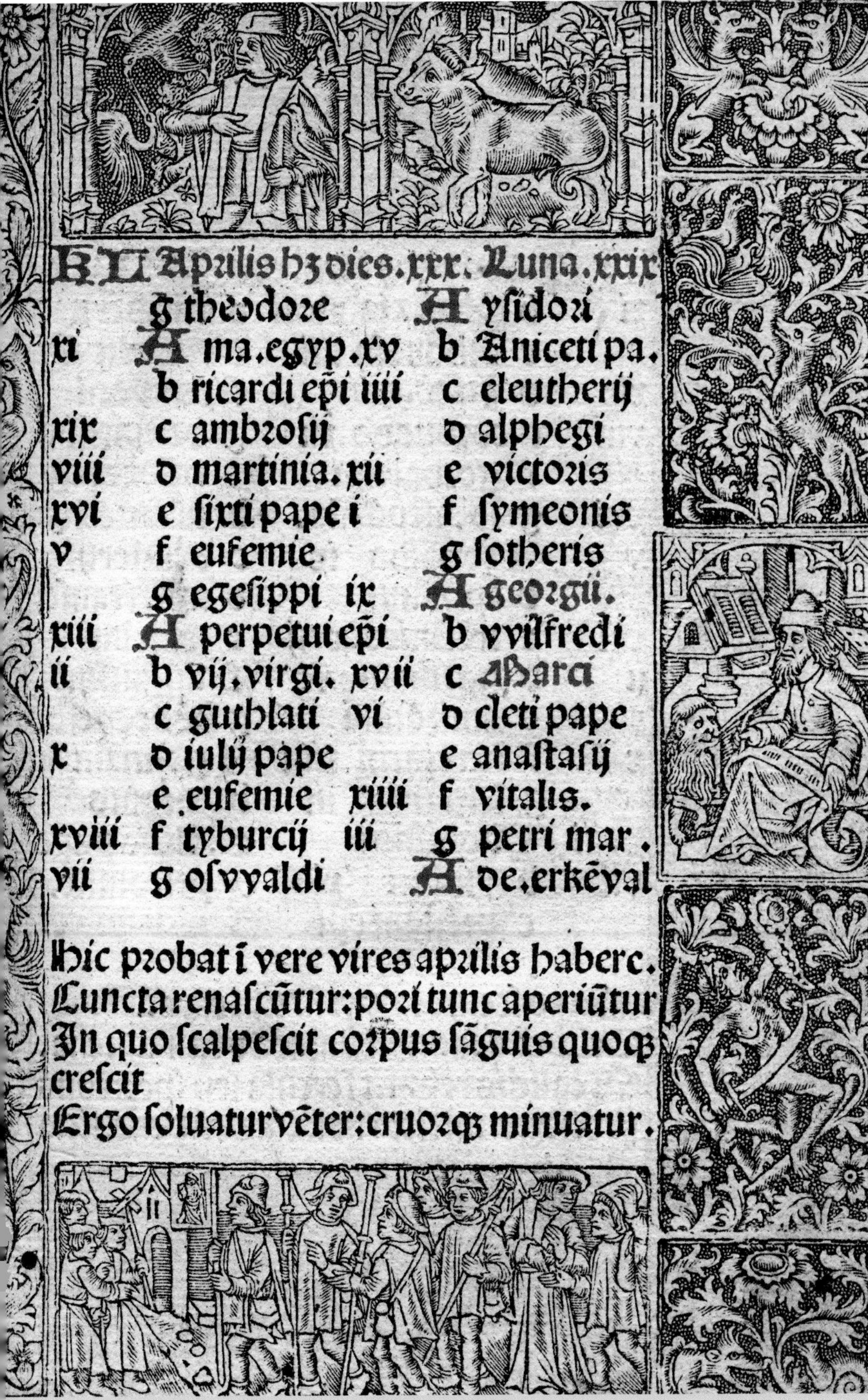

Fig. 1

Calendar Page for April: Labor of the Month Hawking and Zodiac Sign of the Bull. At the bottom, pilgrims: All wear hats with scallop shell badges and carry staffs. The first carries a banner. To the right, an onlooker gives charity to a pilgrim (shown with patched leggings) who lifts his hat in thanks.

Book of Hours, Use of Sarum (English usage)

Printed in Paris by Simon Vostre, 1512

Stonyhurst College, Lancashire, S.3/3.fol.3.

meaning "journey to the crossing/ford," with the idea that one goes forth to the crossroads, the liminal spaces that afford communion with the divine. In the Indic religious systems, a pilgrim is a *yatri* or *yatrika*, "journeyman," who departs with the right motivations and an attitude of veneration (*sraddha*), with mental and moral discipline to travel to these distant places, expecting the journey to require fortitude of mind and body, and finally returns home transformed and touched by the experiences of the holy. The pilgrimage thus becomes a process of purification of corporal and mental states, and in Buddhism, *dharma yatra* as pilgrimage is a meritorious journey that provides liberation from the lifetimes of karmic defilements. The *Rigveda*, composed around 1000 BCE, and predating Buddhism, contains one of the earliest references to the spiritual wandering of a pilgrim in the context of South Asian religions:

Flower-like the heels of the wanderer,
His body groweth and is fruitful;
All his sins disappear.
Slain by the toils of his journeying.

Aitreya Brahmana. Rigveda, III. vii. 15.

Pilgrimage may be looked at from a number of perspectives: that of the person performing it, his or her condition, intentions, or experiences; the voyage or the passage, its route, manner, and the places and persons encountered along the way, as Chaucer so vividly describes; the social experience at the holy place, since sanctity draws crowds and famous sanctity, very large crowds indeed; and finally, the goal, the holy place to which the pilgrim is tending. We start with this latter perspective, which is both the *arche* and the *telos* of pilgrimage, its originating and final cause.

THE HOLINESS OF PLACE

Holiness, like its opposite, impurity, is a quality that various religious traditions recognize as inherent in both persons and places. Indeed, both qualities have an almost physical presence. Holiness is discernible as an aura or light, for example – the halo is its reduced signature – or by a pleasant odor: the odor of sanctity is a commonplace in religious

Fig. 2
Tomb of David, Jerusalem. Since the 12th century the former Byzantine church of Hagia Zion was believed to contain the tomb of the Jewish king David on the ground floor, and on the upper floor, the room in which Christ shared the Last Supper with his disciples.

Ermete Pierotti, *Jerusalem Explored: Being a Description of the Ancient and Modern City*, Thomas G. Bonney, trans. London: Bell and Daldy, 1864, pl. XLV.

traditions. Impurity or evil also smells, usually of burning or decay. The physical quality of both sanctity and impurity is graphically illustrated by the fact that it can be transmitted by touch – it is contagious! – and it can often be removed by the physical act of washing.

If a decaying corpse is generally avoided in most religious traditions, the dead holy man or woman is quite another matter. Whatever their view of the afterlife, most cultures are convinced that the powerful in life continue to possess that power after death, and that it is possible for the living to access that power from beyond the grave. The powerful in a religious culture are the sanctified, the saints, and their sanctity both persists beyond death and is accessible by the living. The tomb-shrine is a common feature on almost all religious landscapes (Fig. 2). The grave merely houses the dead; the tomb signals its enshrinement by the living and that latter act directs our first step toward and understanding of a holy place.

THE HOLY MAN AND WOMAN

Before there was the tomb, there was the saint. People are regarded as holy by their own or later generations for a variety of reasons. Some are not of their own making, like those sacralized by their office. The priestly castes of the Jews and the Hindus are examples of those who are born into a sacred state but who are also expected to maintain that state through a life remote from all impurity. Others may volunteer for or be pledged to such a sacred office, like the sacerdotal clergy of Christianity or the Roman vestal virgins, and if the office itself sacralizes them, they are nonetheless expected to live an appropriately sanctified life. It is only rarely that a sacralizing office does not carry with it a sacralizing lifestyle. The deification of Roman emperors appears to have been such at the outset: their divine office had no connection with their conduct (Fig. 3). But as time passed this office too began to develop a patina of sanctity in the form, if not of a moral life,

Fig. 3
Procession of Roman Imperial family, officials, and priests: Ara Pacis Augustae.
Rome, 13 BCE
Photograph Michel Raguin

then at least of a highly ritualized one.

Sacred offices are but a minor contribution to personal holiness. The overwhelming number of those thought to be holy in religious cultures are those who have borne witness to the religious faith that informs them. The Greek word for "witness" is *martyros* and the Arabic *shahid*, and among both Christians and Muslims the word conveys the notion that the person in question has borne witness to the faith by dying for it, generally in the Christian instance by choosing death over denial, and in the Muslim one by dying in defense of the faith. But in both traditions martyrdom by no means exhausts the category of personal sanctity. Many more Christians and Muslims have "witnessed" their faith by their manner of life rather than by dying for it. They have manifested their faith in the first instance by their heroic "observance" of the mandates of the faith, and then, inevitably, by going far beyond the great body of the faithful not only in their observance – whose voluntarily assumed supererogatory practices may be generally characterized as "asceticism" – but even more persuasively by their progress along the path of spiritual perfection. Though the ascetical practices of holy men and women may be visible to all, spiritual perfection is an inner state. Holiness becomes public, however, when it is manifested by the saint's ability to perform wonders or miracles, and what may have been a merely local reputation can quickly become religious fame.

As a non-theistic religion without a universal God, Buddhism has as its ultimate goal this spiritual perfection, the self-transformation and awakening that can only be attained through the prescription of "asceticism" and meditation. And, for the lay and monastic communities of Buddhism, the moral, ethical, and physical codes of discipline, practiced both individually and collectively during pilgrimage, serve as the ingredients of *communitas* in this pious journey. As exemplified by the Buddha, who left his home to journey to unknown places in his quest for spiritual understanding, the life of Shakyamuni Buddha becomes paradigmatic for the faithful (Fig. 4). For the monks and nuns, this means leading the life of renunciation to follow the ideal path of a wandering ascetic in search of the truth – a pan-Indic practice that is religiously mandated as the last phase of the four-fold life stages (*ashrama*). For the Buddhist laity, "asceticism" is to be achieved as a way of life through religious ordinances, through faithful observances of the Eight Ethical Precepts, in which merit (*punya*) acquired through pilgrimage benefits not just the individual but all living beings. As the principal "witness" of the faith, it is Shakyamuni Buddha – the model of the Buddhist holy individual and the teacher *par excellence* – and all things associated with this extraordinary individual during his lifetime and beyond that become the core elements of Buddhist pilgrimage.

After Shakyamuni's death, relics and relic-monuments developed as the archetypal model for Buddhist pilgrimage. Textual accounts of the legendary "war of the relics" immediately after the cremation of the Buddha and its division into eight equal parts among the Vijjian Republic in 5th-century BCE India emphasize the potency of relics as a symbol of power. About two hundred years after the death of Shakyamuni, it is precisely these original relics that the Emperor Ashoka in the 3rd century BCE redistributed throughout India in his mission to establish Buddhism as a state religion. What resulted was the ideal model of the Universal Monarch (*chakravartin*) as the pious pilgrim, who visits the holy places of Buddhism as protector of faith. Ashoka not only visits the four places associated with the key events of the Buddha's life – the birth, enlightenment, first teaching, and death – but also thirty-two secondary places of pilgrimage. Hence, even from the earliest moments of Buddhist history, this association of authority and relic possession is critical in the transmission of Buddhism from its homeland in India to other regions in East and Southeast Asia. A case in point is the Sacred Tooth Relic in Sri Lanka, which became a strong symbol of temporal and spiritual power, since it was believed that whoever held the relic also held the power of governance in the country. Similarly in Japan, relics served as the legitimization of Buddhist rule in the medieval imperial courts.[1]

The holy in Buddhism focuses on the relic. Like the Christians in their classification of relics, the Buddhists recognize a three-fold hierarchy. The bodily relics (*sharira*) of bones or teeth found among the cremated ashes are the most potent of Buddhist relics, since they are believed to embody the physical essence of the enlightened being. These are most often enshrined in relic structures such as *stupas*, and thus become the first-class relics. The second-tier relics are *paribhogika*, literally "places of pleasure," implying the places of action and objects of use designated as the relics of the Buddha. And lastly, images and representations called *uddeshaka*, meaning "point to" or "illustrate," constitute "reminder relics" of the Buddha. Pilgrimage places in Buddhism therefore become principal places of relic veneration, whose significance is realized in the earliest of the Buddhist canons.

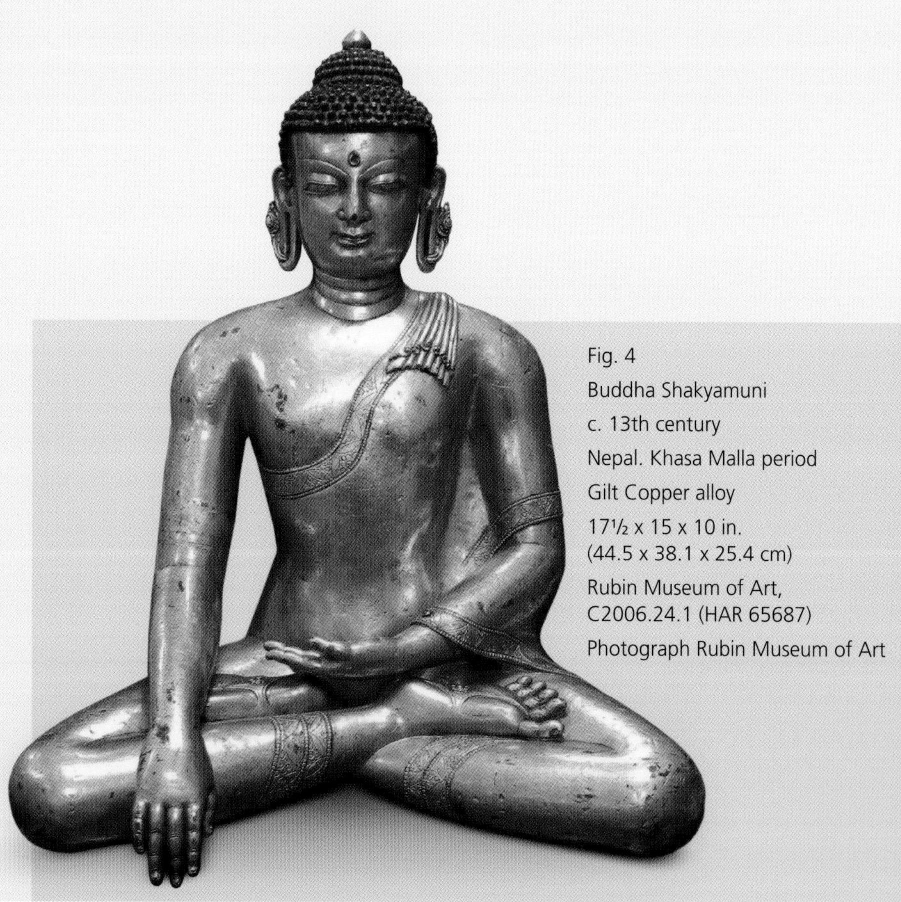

Fig. 4
Buddha Shakyamuni
c. 13th century
Nepal. Khasa Malla period
Gilt Copper alloy
17½ x 15 x 10 in.
(44.5 x 38.1 x 25.4 cm)
Rubin Museum of Art,
C2006.24.1 (HAR 65687)
Photograph Rubin Museum of Art

*"Because of the glory of his [relics], this great earth is embellished by excellent offerings. Thus the all-seeing Buddha's bodily relics are well-honored by those who are most honored; they are worshipped by the lord of the gods; the lord of serpent-*nagas *and the lord of the men… bow down with folded hands… for it is difficult indeed to meet a Buddha through hundreds of aeons."*

Digha Nikaya. 2:167-68 (*oral transmission written down in the 1st century BCE*).

SAINTS AND THEIR SHRINES

Miracles testify to a special power possessed by an individual and are an obvious sign of God's favor, and the saint is recognized through them. And, as has already been said, no one was inclined to think that the saint loses that power, much less God's favor, after death. But it is at this point that a certain tension sets in. Christianity is a *redemptive* religion, in the sense that the believer is saved for eternal life principally through the merits of the God-man Jesus' death on the cross. Whether those merits were earned or applied was profoundly debated for at least a millennium in Christianity, but Christians on both sides of that debate believed, at least down to the Reformation, in the power of *the intercession of the saints*: those whom God had favored in life could and would intercede after their deaths for the rest of the faithful. Hence, there were intercessory prayers to the saints throughout Christendom and special rituals at their tombs, which were soon made into shrines.

Judaism and Islam do not share in this redemptive theology, and they formally deny the intercessory powers of the pious departed. Indeed, the corpse of the departed, whether pious or not, is regarded as a rich source of ritual impurity: the dead must be buried, of course, but they also contaminate. But what the theologians and lawyers formally deny, the Jewish and Muslim faithful often and effectively affirm. In their eyes the tomb of the saint shares the sanctity of the dead saint within[2] (Fig. 5). Thus Israel has its share of tombs for biblical heroes – those of Abraham and the other patriarchs and their wives at Hebron are probably the most

Fig. 5

View of the Valley of Jehoshaphat showing tombs, among them the tombs of Absalom and Zacharias, and also the Jewish cemetery.

Ermete Pierotti, *Jerusalem Explored: Being a Description of the Ancient and Modern City*, Thomas G. Bonney, trans. London: Bell and Daldy, 1864, pl. XLIX

spectacular – and the Jewish landscape of Galilee is crowded with the tomb shrines of departed saintly rabbis. Who or what now lies within is irrelevant: the place itself has become the sanctified surrogate of the saint. The "Abode of Islam" is likewise dotted with tomb shrines, from the modest domed *qubbas* of North African holy men to the gorgeously more ornate shrines of Sufi saints in India to the largest tomb of them all, Muhammad's own sarcophagus within its ornate aedicule inside the enormous mosque of Medina (Fig. 6).

Although Buddhism does not offer redemption, forgiveness, or heavenly hope, but instead emphasizes moral ethical behavior and self-effort as the spiritual goal, the concept of a Bodhisattva is directly analogous to that of the Christian saints, whose powers of intercession help the faithful in their communion with God. The Bodhisattvas are fully enlightened beings who have transcended worldliness and, free from suffering themselves, continue to manifest in various realms of existence to minister to the diverse beings still caught in the painful endless cycle of rebirth and death. The celestial Bodhisattvas are exemplars of the goals that should be attained along the path to enlightenment (Fig. 7). These compassionate beings aid all who are far from liberation, not only in the mundane aspirations of everyday life, but most importantly in achieving the qualities necessary for the attainment of self-realization. These Bodhisattvas may also take human form, like the Dalai Lama, who, for the Tibetan Buddhists, is the Bodhisattva of Compassion, now in his 14th incarnation, as he promises to be continually reborn to guide all beings in the Buddhist teachings until all have attained enlightenment. A Buddhist pilgrim must also take a Bodhisattva vow to perform the pilgrimage with this aspiration of altruistic compassion for all.

Fig. 6
Medina: Distant View of the Mosque
Photograph Abdullah Y. Al-Dobais/*Saudi Aramco World*/SAWDIA

Fig. 7
Bodhisattva Manjushri with Attendants
China, Liao Dynasty, 10th-11th century
Marble, 23 x 24¼ in. (58.4 x 61.6 cm)
Metropolitan Museum of Art, Purchase, The Vincent Astor Foundation Gift, 2002 (2002.440)
Image © The Metropolitan Museum of Art/ Art Resource, NY

Most beloved is the Bodhisattva Avalokiteshvara, the embodiment of universal compassion, and by extension, his female aspect, Tara, who was created through his tears and is known as the Bodhisattva of Mercy and savior from the Eight Great Perils (fire, water, lions, elephants, snakes, thieves, disease, and wrongful imprisonment). Because the types and needs of sentient beings are infinite, there is no end to the forms and ministrations that Bodhisattvas might adopt in order to empty the realms of the physical world (*samsara*). Each Bodhisattva embodies unique cultural characteristics of a region in its sacred history, manifestations, iconography, and practice. As Buddhism moved out the holy land of India and into Asia, sites and shrines associated with the great Bodhisattvas gradually increased in importance as popular pilgrimage places, and often as self-arisen hierophanies – in mountaintops, caves, or waterfalls – hence giving a distinctly Buddhist identity to the physical landscape. In Nepal, Avalokiteshvara is known as Karunamaya, "The Compassionate One," and his annual festival attracts hundreds of pilgrims when his image is brought into the city in a festival cart from his remote shrine, and for a month the sacrality of the urban landscape is vivified by the presence of the Bodhisattva. In Tibet, the Potala Palace, the home of the Dalai Lamas, is appropriately considered as Potalaka, the paradise of Avalokiteshvara (Fig. 8); while in China, Avalokiteshvara is transformed into the Goddess Guanyin, with Putuoshan as her sacred mountain. In Japan, hundreds of thousands of pilgrims go on a popular Buddhist pilgrimage circuit, the Thirty-Three Stations of Avalokitesvara in Saikoku (the Western Provinces) (Fig. 9).

Fig. 8

Shadakshari Lokeshvara with Deities and Monks

Tibet, late 15th century

Gold, ink and color on cloth, 40³/₈ x 31¹/₄ in. (102.6 x 79.4 cm)

Gift of Margery and Harry Kahn, 1985

The Metropolitan Museum of Art, 1985.390.3

Image © The Metropolitan Museum of Art/ Art Resource, NY

Shadakshari Lokeshvara is a manifestation of Avalokiteshvara, the Bodhisattva of Compassion

Fig. 9

Woodblock print of the Thirty-Three Forms of Kannon from the Saikoku Pilgrimage, detail. Late 19th century. 16 x 5³/₈ in. (40.6 x 13.7 cm)

Elizabeth ten Gotenhuis

Photograph Michel Raguin

THE PILGRIMAGE AND THE PIOUS VISIT

Muslims distinguish between a *hajj*, a mandated and defined set of rituals in and around Mecca that every capable Muslim must perform at least once in a lifetime, and a *ziyara*, a pious visit to a holy place, an act that would include most of what we would generally defined as a pilgrimage. In the strict sense, there have been only two authentic Hajj in the monotheistic tradition: the Muslim one to Mecca and the Jewish pilgrimage to Jerusalem and its Temple. Both acts were mandated by religious law to take place at a specific place and a specific time when and where the pilgrim was to participate in a defined ritual. The Jewish *hag*, as it was called, required adult males resident in the Land of Israel to come to Jerusalem to celebrate there the festivals of *Pesach* or Passover, *Shavuoth* or Weeks, and *Sukkoth* or Tabernacles (Deut. 16:16). And although both the city and the land remain holy for Jews, the obligatory *hag* has been moot since the destruction of the city and its Temple. Jewish visits to Jerusalem, like those of Christians and Muslims, are now just that, pious visits or *ziyaras*.

Visits too, in that same technical sense, are all those journeys to other holy places, what may be called *secondary sites* like the tomb shrines of saints and the locus of apparitions. When Muslims have completed the ritual Hajj in Mecca, they finally turn aside to make a *ziyara* to the tomb of Muhammad at Medina, 275 miles to the north, and Christian pilgrims go to their primary holy sites in Jerusalem spread out across the Middle East to visit secondary shrines, ranging from the spot where Paul was secretly lifted onto the walls of Damascus after his conversion to the places connected with the Holy Family in Egypt. Ashchi Dede gives a moving account of his visit to Muhammad's tomb (see essay *The Prophet's Tomb in Medina*).

Fig. 10
Mount Kailash in Western Tibet
Photograph Toni Neubauer

HOLY PLACES

If people are judged holy by their acts, then places, which have no moral ground in action, become holy for quite different reasons. We have already seen one such: the presence of the tomb of a holy person, a numinous presence that extends from the remains of the saint to the place of his interment. Haifa is sacred to the Bahai'I because Baha Allah is entombed there, and Najaf is sacred to the Muslims by reason of Ali's tomb in that city. But a place can also become holy if it is identified, at least in the personalized religions,[3] as the site of a theophany, a divine self-manifestation, like that to Moses at Sinai and to Jacob at the more appropriately named Bethel, or, more recently, the apparitions of the Virgin to believers at Lourdes or Guadalupe (see essay *Paths through the Desert: Hispanic Pilgrimage Experiences in Mexico City and Chimayó*) or Fatima.

A complementary phenomenon in Buddhism, in particular, is the re-creation of surrogate pilgrimage sites

Fig. 11
Kumbha Mela, India, 1992
Hindu Pilgrims bathe in the Ganges River
Photograph permission Swami Nardanand, Siddha Ashram

as a focal point of holy places. For Buddhists in regions far from the sacred center of India, there was little possibility of visits to the core places of Buddhism; the landscape of the region, however, could be reconstructed symbolically to create surrogate pilgrimage sites. Many among these are natural sites that are believed to be tangible expressions of the sacred. Often, these natural features are in remote places, and the rigors of travel to these distant places become central to the pilgrimage experience. In addition, important pilgrimage locations have often been abodes of indigenous spirits and deities that are incorporated into Buddhist cosmology. These are especially true of mountain pilgrimages, and the sites are often syncretic in nature, such as the sixteen pilgrimages to Adam's Peak in Sri Lanka, sacred to Hindus, Buddhists, Christians, and Muslims. Similarly, the remote Mount Kailash (Fig. 10) in northwest Tibet is considered the center of the Buddhist world system, but the site is equally important as a sacred pilgrimage to Hindus, Jains, and animistic Bon practitioners. One of the earliest writings capturing the physical harshness of Mount Kailash was written by the Italian Jesuit missionary Ippolito Desideri (1684-1733) in 1715, appropriately exemplifying traits for deeply transformative pilgrimage: "… a mountain of excessive height and great circumference, always enveloped in cloud, covered with snow and ice, and most horrible, barren, steep and bitterly cold."[4] Almost 150 years later, another westerner, Lama Anangarika Govinda, described an experience that transformed the barren landscape into a very different pilgrimage experience: "Just as a white summer cloud, in harmony with heaven and earth, freely floats in the blue sky from horizon to horizon following the breath of the atmosphere – in the same way the pilgrim abandons himself to the breath of the greater life that… leads him beyond the farthest horizons to an aim which is already present within him, though yet hidden from his sight."[5]

A further extension of this hierophany of sacred space is sacred time, during which ordinary space is transformed into a pilgrimage experience. An unparalleled example is the twelve-year pilgrimage cycle of the Kumbha Mela at Prayag, India – the confluences of the sacred Ganges and Yamuna rivers – that marks the sacred place where the gods and demons had churned the nectar of immortality in the cosmic sea. This special astrological configuration, which occurs every twelve years, is sacred to all Indic religions of the Hindus, Buddhist, and Jains; and the Kumbha Mela pilgrimage offers the largest congregations of pilgrims in the world in a specific time and place (Fig. 11). Mark Twain's wonderful eyewitness account of the Mela in 1895 still holds true of this event today, which in the most recent pilgrimage of 2001 witnessed upward of 70 million pilgrims in the great river deltas of the Ganges. Twain writes:

> *These pilgrims had come from all over India; some of them had been months on the way, plodding patiently along in the heat and dust, worn, poor, hungry, but supported and sustained by an unwavering faith and belief; they were supremely happy and content, now; their full and sufficient reward was at hand; they were going to be cleansed from every vestige of sin and corruption by these holy waters which make utterly pure whatsoever thing they touch, even the dead and rotten. It is wonderful, the power of a faith like that, that can make multitudes upon multitudes of the old and weak and the young and frail enter without hesitation or complaint upon such incredible journeys and endure the resultant miseries without repining. It is done in love, or it is done in fear; I do not know which it is. No matter what the impulse is, the act born of it is beyond imagination….*[6]

Finally, holiness also accrues to a place when some event of deep religious significance has taken place there. This is true, as we shall see, of the Jerusalem churches built to commemorate Gospel events in the life of Jesus, and those shrines on the Temple Mount associated with Muhammad's Night Journey, and the journey to the eight great pilgrimage sites associated with the life of the Buddha. Karbela in Iraq is doubly sacred to Shi'ite Muslims (Figs. 12-13). First, it was the site of the 680 CE ambush and slaughter of Ali's sacred son Husayn and the protomartyr of Shi'ite Islam,[7] an event that is marked there, and elsewhere, by its annual reenactment. And then, to compound its sanctity, the city is also the site of Husayn's now richly enshrined tomb. Prayers are not only offered at the tomb shrines, but can also be inscribed as texts that are carried on the body in amulets for remembrance (Figs. 14-15).

THE HOLY CITY

Karbela, like Jerusalem (Fig. 16), Mecca, Benares, Bodhgaya, and Kyoto, is a holy city. The notion of a holy city is somewhat counterintuitive since there is a broad register of religious tradition that makes the city the epicenter of sin. Sodom and Gomorrah are merely the first in a long line of reprobate cities. What then makes a city holy? One might attempt to give a purely functional definition: a holy city is one where the principal holy place is of such magnitude or allure that it dominates the city, changes its institutions and creates its own, and draws to the city numbers of people and types and amounts of investment that would not normally be found in an urban settlement of that size or in that place.[8] Holy cities double or triple their population during times of pilgrimage; a touristic windfall, no doubt, and a boon to the local economy, but often a mixed blessing for the host settlement, which must cope with a great many attendant social and political problems.

Fig. 12

Shi'ite Muslims cherish the practice of praying by touching the forehead to a small piece of clay called a *Mohr* or *Turbah* from the Holy City of Karbela. These small tablets of pressed clay vary in shape but generally carry some inscription. This tablet is decorated with blessings and the names of Muhammad, Ali, Hasan, and Husayn with bands of repetitive pattern. For Shi'ites it is a symbolic gesture of never forgetting the battle of Kerbela and the death of Husayn.

Private Collection

Photograph Michel Raguin

Fig. 13

Imam 'Ali with Hasan and Husayn

19th century

Opaque watercolor and gold on paper

14⅛ x 9⅜ in. (35.9 x 23.8 cm)

Harvard Art Museum, Arthur M. Sackler Museum, Alpheus Hyatt Purchasing Fund, 1958.137

Photograph Imaging Department © President and Fellows of Harvard College

Fig. 14
Amulet box
Iran, probably 19th-20th century
Silver, 4 x 1 in. (10.2 x 2.5 cm)
Containing a scroll with Prayers from a Shia text: 36 in. (91.4 cm)
Blue, red, and black ink on paper; the black texts are of litanies each to a different subject; the colors introduce the subjects.
Private Collection
Photograph Michel Raguin

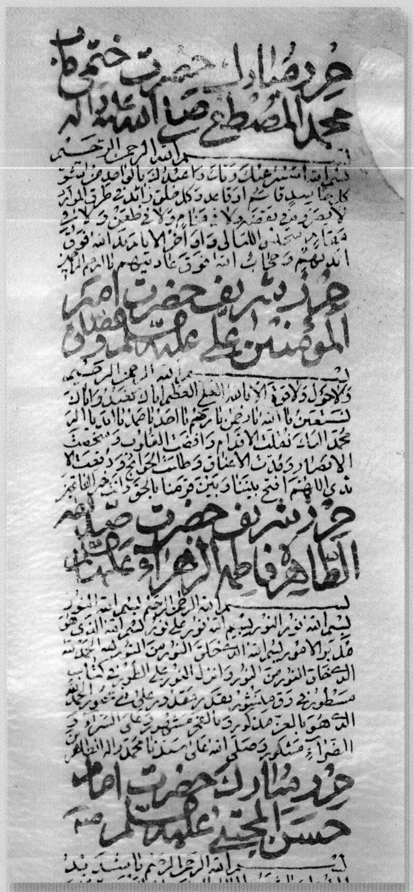

Fig. 15
Amulet box, Detail of scroll
Iran, probably 19th-20th century
Silver, 4 x 1 in. (10.2 x 2.5 cm)
The blue title is in celebration of the Prophet Muhammad; the red is for Ali (his son-in-law and also 4th caliph, and 1st Imam of the Shia); the 2nd blue is for the Prophet's daughter Fatima; the prayers then progress to Hasan, then Husayn (the two grandsons of the Prophet) and then in succession the Shia Imams.
Blue, red, and black ink on paper
Private Collection
Photograph Michel Raguin

ENSHRINEMENT

Explosive population changes are not the only problems raised by holy cities. They also create difficulties for their rulers who are, in a sense, in competition there with an authority higher than themselves. As a result, the rulers of holy cities prefer to govern them from elsewhere. David and Solomon's experiences in Jerusalem were not happy ones, and their successors preferred other seats: Herod in comfortably pagan Caesarea-by-Sea, Constantine in the distant city of his own making and bearing his name, and Salah al-Din in Damascus or Cairo. The Muslim experience is similar. Beginning with Muhammad himself, who chose to stay in Medina, and continuing down to the Saudis, who prefer to rule from Riyadh, Mecca has not been an attractive political capital or residence. Caesar and God do not make compatible roommates.

It is those same rulers, however, who significantly contribute to the conversion of an urban settlement into a holy city. If a ruler does not want to compete with the sacred, he is quick to acknowledge and celebrate its presence. Generosity toward the local holy place reaps rich political rewards, as every ruler from Solomon to the Saudis has quickly understood. That generosity translates as investment, and the investment into the visible evidence of architectural enhancement. The site is adorned, enriched, enlarged, all in a quite public fashion that testifies not only to the importance of the site but also to the piety of the ruler who has spent his, and the polity's, treasure on it. And royal or imperial generosity is contagious. Relatives, successors, and grandees of the realm can compete for a share in the political benefits by contributing their own assets to the enshrinement of the holy place.

Fig. 16

View of "Mosque of Omar" and the Dome of the Rock, Jerusalem.

David Roberts, *The Holy Land: Syria, Idumea, Arabia, Egypt and Nubia*. From Drawings made on the Spot by David Roberts, with Historical Descriptions by the Rev George Croly, Lithographed by Louis Hage. London, F. G. Moon, 1842-1849.

John J. Burns Library of Boston College

Photograph Michel Raguin

In the Buddhist experience, no site exceeds Bodhgaya in witnessing vicissitudes of religio-political shifts in its history. From the 9th to the 12th centuries, with the lavish patronage of the Pala kings of northeastern India, Bodhgaya was extensively refurbished, the shrine and site expanded with the royal donations. At its peak, Bodhgaya saw thousands of pilgrims from the far reaches of the Buddhist world gathered to bear witness to the sacred place where the Buddha has attained enlightenment. After the annihilation of the Pala dynasty in the 13th century, primarily due to the Muslim invasions of north India, the last surviving stronghold of Buddhist lands disappeared, and what followed was the ultimate demise of Buddhism in its homeland. Subsequent pilgrimage accounts to Bodhgaya are virtually nonexistent, with no more than sporadic visits of intrepid travelers, and the once-glorious history of the site was only a distant memory. For almost six hundred years the temple fell into ruin, prey to looting and destruction that also took the surrounding monasteries, until its ultimate takeover by Hindu sects. It was not until the 19th century that the site would witness a Buddhist revival, largely due to the efforts of Burmese and Sri Lankan Buddhists, and Bodhgaya's special character as the "Buddhist Jerusalem" would reemerge.

Fig. 17

Mecca, Aerial View of the Mosque, Haram, and Ka'ba.

Photograph Abdullah Y. Al-Dobais/*Saudi Aramco World*/ SAWDIA

Fig. 18

A human chain of pilgrims encircling the Chadur holy mountain in Amdo, Eastern Tibet.

Photograph Toni Huber

HOLINESS AND PILGRIMAGE

If we can identify a holy place by external signs like its architectural enshrinement, and even discern the causes of holiness in a place, the measurement of the quality or intensity of the holiness that is thought to reside there is a more difficult project. One index is what we might call the *haramization* of the place, that is, the strength and extent of the taboos surrounding it. The Jerusalem Temple, we know, and particularly the later Second Temple, was rather precisely tabooed: the Holy of Holies was probably such from the outset, but the outer courts were also marked as progressive taboo zones. Compare this to the Ka'ba at Mecca (Fig. 17), which, like the Jerusalem Temple, has a taboo zone or *haram* surrounding it, but whose interior enjoys no special taboo protection: any and all Muslims may enter it without distinction. Or compare to the Temple the synagogue or indeed the mosque, which by this index are not holy places, while traditional Christian churches, with their clearly delineated sanctuaries and their secondary taboo characteristics as recognized asylums, clearly do qualify.

In the Buddhist contexts, the taboo zones surrounding the sacred space often have to do with special ritual purifications or obligations of conduct or worship. Buddhist monuments like *stupas* or temples, like the previous examples, contain the clearly defined makers of the sacred. In these cases, actions of viewing, touching, and circumambulation (Fig. 18) are signifiers of the holy, and progressive taboo zones are delineated in which the central shrine is the holiest of the holy but can still be accessed by the pious. In the natural landscape, for example, the visitation to the summit often is taboo, while shrines at the base and along the circuit become conduits of veneration. In these cases, the movement is almost always clockwise circumambulation. For example, at Mount Kailash, as at Mount Sinai, the proscription against accessing the summit is strictly followed; the physical act of circling the mountain as the pilgrim meditates and prays along its thirty-two-mile circumference becomes the ideal meritorious activity. By walking the circuit in one day, or by performing full-body prostrations around the mountain, which even for the very fit generally takes four days, the pilgrim attains spiritual benefits for all living beings. In other cases, as in the Japanese Shikoku pilgrimage to the Eighty-Eight shrines, pilgrimage evokes memories of the ideal pilgrimage of a saint or teacher. Behavioral codes of conduct are strictly observed, such as "ascetic training in the form of standing before the gates of strangers and asking for alms… every day at about twenty-one houses, following the example set by the [Kobo] Daishi."[9] The pilgrims symbolically walk along with the monk-pilgrim Kukai in a reenactment of the transformative sacred journey that this great teacher had undertaken in the 9th century.

There is, however, another index to the holiness of a place, the phenomenon called pilgrimage. Pilgrimage, which is, as we have seen, the visitation of a place by reason of its holiness, is a visible activity, an act that unfolds in time and space and so is at least theoretically quantifiable; though, as we all know, ancient sources are not the best place to look for trustworthy numbers. In the large sense, pilgrimage is a manifestation of sacred magnetism: the believers are *drawn* to the place by reason of its sanctity: though not always and not entirely. That magnetic sanctity is sometimes leavened by other considerations, when the magnetism of sanctity is first diluted by a more secular wonder, and finally yields to mere curiosity, and the pilgrim has been transformed into the tourist.

PULLING AND PUSHING THE PILGRIM

But another preliminary and rather obvious distinction warns us not to proceed too quickly with the notion of magnetic attraction as the unique operating principle in pilgrimage. The Muslim sorting out of journeys to a holy place into Hajj, pilgrimage as a ritual requirement, and *ziyara*, pilgrimage as a pious visit, quickly reminds us that some pilgrimages are voluntary. Some pilgrimages, however, are obligatory, that is, the believer *must* perform the act: he is being pushed, not pulled, to the holy place. These latter acts, what may be called *juridical* pilgrimages, are no small matter. At some point before the redaction of Deuteronomy, Jewish pilgrimage on the three great holy days became just such an obligation, and more, was directed to this place to the exclusion of all other places (Deut. 12:5-14). So too was the Hajj to Mecca, and this on the authority of the Quran itself (22: 26-30). Even Christianity knows this phenomenon of the obligatory pilgrimage. Pilgrimage to the Holy Land was not uncommonly assigned by medieval confessors as a penance in remission of the temporal punishment connected with homicide. Nothing is attracting the Christian felon: he is being unceremoniously pushed, slouching, toward Jerusalem.

But we should not be misled. All three of these cases represent *interventions*. A recognized authority, the Jewish priesthood or the Jewish king, the Prophet Muhammad, the Church, has for its own purposes converted – or perhaps subverted – a voluntary reaction to the holy place into an obligation. Surely the Israelites were drawn to make *hag* to Jerusalem – and earlier to a variety of other places[10] – before they were *pushed* there by the twelfth chapter of Deuteronomy. We know it is true in the Meccan case: both the Hajj and the *umra* or "Lesser Pilgrimage" were popular festivals in Mecca before Muhammad intervened and converted one into an obligation and the other – oddly, the more Meccan of the two – into a work of supererogation.[11] And finally, the Medieval Latin Church was accustomed to assigning pilgrimage to Jerusalem as a penance for the grave sin of homicide. But even so, there were likely far more voluntary pilgrims than homicides embarking at Jaffa en route to Jerusalem, and millions go to Mecca, we can be certain, for reasons other than the discharge of a legal obligation. Even in an obligatory pilgrimage there remains the residual attraction of the holy place that draws the pilgrim hither.

In Buddhism, given the absence of a centralized figure of power in religious office or the authority of a single holy scripture, pilgrimage is foremost a voluntary pulling of faith and veneration. Even though in theory the Buddha himself recommended the pilgrimage to the places directly associated with his life as highly meritorious (see essay *Tracing the Footsteps of the Buddha: Pilgrimage to the Eight Great Places* (Ashtamahasthama)), pilgrimage in the Buddhist understanding is fundamentally a reminder to the pious of the goals of Buddhism, and the travails of this journey are highlighted through the exemplary lives of the great teachers and saints in search of self-realization. Hence, pilgrimage, directly and indirectly, reenacts these narratives, and, ideally, by extension the experience. While individual motivations of the archetypal pilgrim-monk may vary, Buddhist pilgrimage accounts reinforce key aspects of this tradition that the faithful should consider emulating: India as the holy land (*punya bhumi*) of pilgrimage (and by extension, the need for recreating the surrogate sites outside of the homeland), and pilgrimage as a meditative and transformative experience that is as much mental as it is physical. In 8th-century Tibet, for instance, the Tantric Buddhist master Marpa becomes legendary; accounts talk about his long and arduous pilgrimage to India to receive teachings from the Indian teachers, and to gather Buddhist scriptures to take back with him to Tibet. Similarly, Ennin, the Japanese Buddhist teacher of the Tendai School, goes to China in 838-847, and his accounts of his nine-year pilgrimage sojourn in his diary subsequently become Japanese Buddhists' inspiration for pilgrimage for the centuries to come. Additionally, the places established by or associated with the pilgrim-monks are quickly recognized as holy, such as the circular pilgrimage to the Eighty-Eight Stations of Shikoku, which came into prominence because of the vivid pilgrimage accounts by Kukai (774-835 CE), the founder of the Shingon sect, in the 9th century (see essay *Saikoku Pilgrimage: Japanese Devotees Search for Kannon*). This familiar pattern continues in 17th-century Japan, when the work of Zen master and *haiku* poet Basho, *The Narrow Road to the Deep North*, an account of his pilgrimage journey, becomes a metaphor for inner transformation.[12]

THE ATTRACTIONS OF THE HOLY PLACE

The attraction of the holy is a generic concept that is spelled out in different ways in the minds and hearts of the believers. Different religious traditions understand the holy in different ways, and these differences are reflected in the intentions and the actions of the faithful with respect to the particular holy place that is the goal of pilgrimage. Judaism, for example, in the matter of the holiness of place, as opposed to the moral condition of the believer,[13] places more emphasis on the absence of impurity than on the nature of holiness that is thought to reside there, which is simply parsed as the presence of God. Thus, the Jewish approach to a holy place is tentative and guarded. Moses was invited up to the summit of Sinai and into the presence of God, but the Israelites, who were ordered to purify themselves at its base, were warned not to set foot on the holy mountain itself under pain of death.

For Jews the holy is undoubtedly taboo, something dangerous and restricted. The Jerusalem Temple, the primary locus of the holy for Jews, was divided into zones of relative taboo, with the greatest license allowed at the greatest distance from the center and with progressively more strict purity regulations as one proceeded to the central holy place, the Holy of Holies, where the divine presence was thought to be focused. Gentiles were limited to the outer courts and then, proceeding inward, female Israelites, ordinary male Israelites, and finally, in the innermost court, the purified elite, the priests of Israel. No one could proceed beyond that and into the Holy of Holies save the high priest alone, and he only on a single day of the year, Yom Kippur or the Day of Atonement.

Islam shows many of the same attitudes as Judaism in the matter of purity. The Ka'ba, the House of God in the center of Mecca, is surrounded by a *haram*, a taboo zone, and the city itself is surrounded by a much larger Haram zone from which non-Muslims are banned (Figs. 17-18). Traditional Christianity, on the other hand, bears only vestigial remains of such haramization. The sanctuary area of a church where the altar is situated is clearly separated from the rest of the building by a screen or rail and was restricted in the past, if not to the clergy alone, then certainly to males.

Taboo and power with holy places of a different degree are particularly relevant in the esoteric Buddhist traditions, where images, shrines, and Tantric Buddhist practices are only open to those who have been given the special teachings and ritual empowerment. Entrance and access into these shrines and the viewing of these "secret" images are strictly prohibited, and it is precisely because of the restrictions of access that the shrines acquire their potency (see essay *Pilgrimage Traditions in Nepal*). Pilgrimage places associated with Tantric Buddhism often embody this aura of danger – physically and spiritually – as many are found literally in "dangerous" liminal places for humans, located between the boundaries of sacred and profane worlds, such as cremation grounds, confluence of rivers, or high mountain passes. These are places considered to be particularly effective in

Fig. 18

During the Hajj, male pilgrims wearing Ihram clothing, a white two-piece seamless garment, on the plains of Arafat, 1974

Photograph S. M. Amin/*Saudi Aramco World*/SAWDIA

bringing about internal transformations as one is confronted by the horrors of the physical reality, where myriads of beings, benevolent and negative spirits, hungry ghosts, and demons, may be. In Nepal, the secrecy and taboo of the Chakrasamvara at Shantipur is precisely what makes it one of the most powerful places of Buddhist pilgrimage. Or, for instance, the shrine of Pehar Gyalpo, the chief protector of the State in Tibet, is considered both dangerous and sacred, and must be approached with the proper attitude of veneration and respect. Most popularly, the hagiographies and imagery of the Eighty-Four Mahasiddhas ("great adepts") in Tantric Buddhism abound with the imagery of taboo, danger, and power, where normative categories of pure and impure are reversed. These Mahasiddhas are the great accomplished masters of the esoteric Tantric tradition, and the loci of their miracles and magical feats often become major pilgrimage places.

THE ATTRACTION OF THE HOLY

But if the holy place is protected from defilement, it also draws the believers to it by reason of the blessings that it confers on those who approach it. Or so it is thought. It is not at all clear, from those communications from on high that are called revelations, that the deity in fact wishes to be approached. The Bible, as already indicated, is filled with advice to the contrary, and the Quran gives no indication that God is approachable by any means except the telecommunication called prayer.

But the believers are drawn nonetheless physically to approach those places where the numinous is thought to dwell, either primarily and immediately, as in the Jerusalem Holy of Holies, or by association, as is the case with the Meccan Ka'ba. Though this latter is called the "House of God" and is the *qibla* or focal point of Muslims' prayer wherever they are in the world, it is not thought to be the actual dwelling place of the deity. This becomes clear from the absence of a higher degree of haramization – as opposed to reference of veneration – than that of the area around it;[14] or, finally, when the numinous is manifested in secondary subjects, in the holy men and women who, as we have seen, bear the divine seal and share the deity's power, even beyond the grave.

One of the most evocative references to the Buddhist spiritual journey and attractions of the holy places is found in the last chapter of the *Avatamsaka Sutra* called *Gandavhyha*, "Flower Garland," often described as the "*Pilgrim's Progress* of Buddhism." Composed in stages from the 2nd century CE onward, it retells the story of the young boy Sudhana Kumara's pilgrimage, as he travels in search of enlightenment from teacher to teacher, eventually seeing fifty-three teachers as he visits these sacred places, where miraculous events take place. Each teacher deepens his awareness, and at the end, the reader is left with a vision of Sudhana as a fully Enlightened Buddha, who through this transformative journey is able to travel the Buddhist heaven-world as he desires, without hindrance. Indeed, this text is one of the earliest extant illustrated printed books from China.[15] These popular narratives continue to provide didactic models for pilgrimage in the Buddhist context.

THE POWER OF THE HOLY

The believers are drawn not only to approach the locus of the sacred but even, in despite of all the warnings to the contrary, to *touch* it. The paradigm incident is perhaps the Gospel account of Jesus' encounter with the hemorrhaging woman (Mk 5:24-34 and parallels). She, with her flow of blood, is in a high state of ritual impurity and so she and her fellow Jews would normally keep a safe distance between them lest there be a contamination. And yet she identifies and is drawn to the power of the numinous in Jesus to the point that she does the unthinkable: she reaches out and deliberately touches him. And her faith is justified: she is immediately cured, while Jesus, for his part, is aware that "power has gone out from him."

Jesus' power to cure, by touch or at times even simply by a word, is manifested throughout the Christian gospels. But the power is not his alone: it is shared by his associates. Miracles are coming in the early Christian church and they are sometimes brought about in a manner that makes clear that the holy is, like the impure, a contagious thing. The ill and the diseased are carried to a place where the Apostle Peter will pass by and his shadow draws upon them and cures them (Acts 5:15); and, in a foreshadowing of Christian relics, Paul's "handkerchiefs and scarves," which had been in contact with his skin, were carried to the sick, who were cured of their diseases (Acts 19:11-12).

In Buddhism, blessing or spiritual merit (*punya*) is conferred by the very act of sacred "viewing" (*darshan*), which means not only to see and be in the presence of the holy, but most importantly to touch the object of sacrality. For instance, this may include viewing bodily relics, or touching the "handprint" of the great Tibetan teacher Padmasambhava in the Pharping caves, or simply being in the physical proximity of pilgrimage shrines that were established to commemorate the site of a miracle. In this regard, the cave at Zuthal Puk, "Cave of Miracles," at Mount Kailasha is particularly powerful, as it recalls the site of the miracles of the great Tibetan teacher Milarepa. Each pilgrim to Mount Kailash makes a mandatory stop to reflect and to "witness" the place of this miraculous happening. In general, miracle stories are directly associated with Buddhist teachings and spiritual realization, and the paradigms of such miracles are Shakyamuni's four great miracles that demonstrated his nature as a perfected being. These four sites of the miracles become added to the initial four places of Buddhist pilgrimage to constitute what is known as the "Eight Places of Wonder" of Buddhism. Similarly, miraculous events as part of the deeply transformative pilgrimage experience are standard narratives in the literature. Even the modern biography of the iconoclastic Tibetan Buddhist monk recounts the following experience of pilgrimage sojourn to India from 1934 to 1946:

"At a few holy places very great miracles occurred. From them, he directly encountered Kasha Phagpa [image of Avalokitesvara at Lahul, northwest India] and burst out crying uncontrollably. As Gendun Chophel cried, when he looked up through his tears, elixir came out from the body of the Kasha Phagpa, after which it was completely wet."[16]

THE PILGRIMAGE OF PETITION

These incidents reveal a larger aspect of pilgrimage. One reason that people make pilgrimages, why they undertake a journey to the holy place, is to gain a favor, either in the form of the well-advertised spiritual blessings that attach to visits to holy places, what the Christians call "favor" (*gratia*) or, somewhat more specifically, "forgiveness" or "remission" (*indulgentia*);[17] and the Muslims call a "blessing" (*baraka*). If this is divine favor parsed generally, there are also more specific favors sought by the pilgrim. The *pilgrimage of petition* is a common religious phenomenon, particularly in connection with secondary holy places like the shrine-tombs of saints or numinous apparition sites. The pilgrim's aim is to gain from the saint a quite specific favor, commonly a cure or the gift of fertility or occasionally enlightenment in a life choice. And the petitions are not entirely random: certain sites (and their saints) are associated with specific favors. Motivations for Buddhist pilgrimage are similarly connected with a "vow" or "promise" (*vrata*) to visit a sacred shrine, and *ex voto* offerings are left at the shrine as a seeking of blessing, or taken back as reminders of the fulfillments of a vow. Throughout Asia, these objects constitute a significant part of the pilgrimage accouterments, such as the clay *tsa tsas* in the Himalayan contexts, the talismanic amulets in Thailand, or *ex voto* paintings and sculptures left at the site. *Vrata* as the devotional rites to the chosen deity are seen as commitment to follow the Buddhist way of life. Special days of prayers and worship of Buddhist deities that may occur at the specific pilgrimage sites and shrines are recognized for efficacy, both in the mundane and supramundane contexts.

What is socially interesting about such pilgrimages and petitions to secondary shrines is the often dominant presence of women. For a variety of reasons there is a tendency to exclude women from the more highly institutionalized forms of religion: the higher clergy, for example, and the canonical rituals. One result is that women's devotions seek other outlets in secondary forms of worship, like pilgrimages to tomb-shrines or even their presence at the graves of less notable holy men in Muslim cemeteries. Women's participation in Buddhist ritual celebrations is dramatically visible during pilgrimage festival days in specific localized shrines. Communicating the experience of *communitas* through shared motivations and codes of conduct, women, during these special festival days, often undergo the restrictions of "asceticism" through prayer, meditation, special dietary restrictions, and even dress, following closely the fundamental Buddhist values of Five Ethical Precepts.

THE PILGRIMAGE OF FULFILLMENT

If pilgrimage is often made to a holy place to *ask* for a favor, it is equally customary, particularly among Christians, to make the same type of pious visit in *thanksgiving* for a favor bestowed. Often this type of pilgrimage is made in fulfillment of a formal vow, the "martir for to seke, That hem hath holpen whan that they weere seeke," as Chaucer says. If the petition or favor is granted, the devotee solemnly promises, I shall make a pilgrimage to your shrine. And so it is done, and the pilgrim leaves at the shrine a formal symbol of the vow fulfilled. This object, which is called an *ex voto* or "from a vow," is frequently in a form that memorializes the exact favor: a pair of crutches or eyeglasses or, in other instances, models of limbs and organs, or even paintings or photos that depict the favor granted. Similar *ex voto* objects, found literally by the thousands in pilgrimage shrines, are the clay votive offerings in the Himalayan regions, which are among the most visible reminders of the pilgrimage motivation as the fulfillment of a vow (Fig. 19). Elsewhere, unusual Buddhist offerings have included cooking utensils, such as pots and pans, or mirrors as a popular offering. These are personal mementos that commemorate the personal favor or promise fulfilled. In the case of Japan, the most popular manifestation of such vows is seen in the form of the Daruma dolls, which actually represent the Zen patriarch Bodhidharma. Each new year, hundreds of pilgrims come to the Takasaki Shorinzan Daruma temple where they purchase Darumas without eyes. At the end of the year, if the wish has been granted, the eyes are painted on and the dolls are brought back to the temple to be burned.

Fig. 19
Tsatsa of Thousand-Armed Avalokiteshvara
Tibet; 18th century
Clay, 11½ x 8⅞ x 1¼ in. (29.2 x 22.5 x 3.2 cm)
Rubin Museum of Art, F1996.18.5 (HAR 700012)
Photograph Rubin Museum of Art

PILGRIMAGES OF PARTICIPATION AND REENACTMENT

Petition and fulfillment are characteristic motives for pilgrimages to secondary holy shrines. The major pilgrimages of Christianity and Islam are driven by quite different intentions, however. Chief among them is participation in a ritual that is proper or even unique to that place. The instance is clearest in the case of Islam, in which a mandated formal pilgrimage, the Hajj, is in effect a ritual, or rather a set of rituals, one Meccan and the other in its near vicinity

Fig. 20
Holy Sepulcher Tomb
Church of the Holy Sepulcher, Jerusalem
Ermete Pierotti, *Jerusalem Explored: Being a Description of the Ancient and Modern City*, Thomas G. Bonney, trans. London: Bell and Daldy, 1864, pl. XXXV.

(Mina and Arafat), of which the pilgrim is the primary celebrant.[18] The Meccan ritual is a twofold reenactment, first of Abraham's original acts while that patriarch was at Mecca with his son Ishmael and the boy's mother Hagar. The Quran thus identifies Abraham not only as the builder of the post-Flood Ka'ba (Quran 2:127)[19] but as the Institutor of the pilgrimage (Quran 22:27). But more, the Muslim is retracing the steps and practices of Muhammad himself, who in the last year of his life made his first and only purely *Muslim* pilgrimage when, by the prophet's own example, the Hajj was shorn of its pagan accretions and returned to its pristine Abrahamic form.

At Jerusalem, too, the earliest Christian pilgrims went to the city not so much to view the Jesus sites as to participate in the liturgies that had sprung up around them. Christians were thus engaged in the liturgical reenactment of the events of Jesus' last days in Jerusalem. The celebration of Christmas in Bethlehem was an afterthought; it was the liturgical reenactment of the events of Jesus' passion, death, and resurrection that drew pilgrims to Jerusalem, and precisely during the calendrical Holy Week, when those events had originally taken place (Fig. 20). Christian pilgrimage to Jerusalem was, like the Muslim Hajj, tied from the beginning to both specific sites and specific times. For Christians and Buddhists, however, both evolving image-rich religions, representations of these holy places soon became symbolic as well as literal. Bethlehem, for example, the place of origin of the Savior, became represented by a glittering city, and the

Fig. 21
Celestial Jerusalem, summit of Good Samaritan Window
Cathedral of Sens, 1207-13.
Photograph Michel Raguin

faithful depicted as the sheep of Christ's flock, as seen in the 9th-century mosaics of Rome's Santa Prassede (Fig. 22). Jerusalem became conflated with the Heavenly Jerusalem foreseen in St. John's vision (Revelations 21). Invariably it was the celestial city portrayed in art and in morality tales (Fig. 21).

The liturgical reenactment of major religious events marks the Buddhist religious calendar, as well, when pilgrims make special efforts to visit the sacred sites in order to participate in the ritual activities. The full-moon day in the lunar month of Vaisakh (April-May) is special for all Buddhists, as it commemorates the birth of the Buddha as well as his Great Renunciation. Pilgrimage and worship at Lumbini and Bodhgaya; the places of his birth and enlightenment are considered exceptionally auspicious during these occasions. Local festivals, similarly, are reenactments of the sacred Buddhist history of the region, and are of special import to the cultural underpinnings of the religion. Despite the Chinese takeover of Tibet after 1957 and the crackdown on Tibetan Buddhism, Tibet's Shodon festival is one such example that has retained its integrity for the last six hundred years. Each year, hundreds of pilgrims come to Lhasa to celebrate this "Great Yogurt Banquet," which traditionally marked the end of the monastic meditation retreats. Pilgrims come to take blessings of the giant embroidered painting of the future Buddha Maitreya, 3,200 feet square, which is displayed only once a year for the five days, and placed on the rocky slopes Nyima Hill at Drepung Monastery. Likewise, in Japan, during the summer festival

Fig. 22
The faithful depicted as the sheep of Christ's flock, leaving Bethlehem
Apse mosaic, Santa Prassede, Rome, 9th century
Photograph Michel Raguin

of the dead (*obon*), special pilgrimages to the Thirty-Three Stations of Avalokiteshvara along the Saikoku route, or the Eighty-Eight Stations of Shikoku, including the pilgrimage of Mount Koya, are performed. In such cases, the participation in a ritual celebration becomes the principal motivation of the pilgrimage.

BEING THERE

Petition for a favor and fulfillment of a vow for favor received are two motives of pilgrimage. Participation in a ritual is another and, in the case of the Muslim Hajj, is the principal reason that the pilgrim journeys to the holy places. But there are other powerful forces drawing the believer to the *sacrum*. History is one of them. Jerusalem's holy place rituals were, as we have already seen, reenactments of historical events connected with the life of Jesus. Likewise, the actions of Muslim pilgrims on the Hajj are meant as reenactments connected to the lives of Abraham, Ishmael, and Hagar.[20] But the pilgrim requires neither ritual nor reenactment to engage him or her in the site. Judaism, Christianity, and Islam are all *historical* religions in that their foundation story is read not as allegory but quite literally as history. The pilgrim, then, is cast, in a sense, as a historical tourist, a visitor whose gaze is cast forth upon the actual sites from the historical past. But that history is a crucial element in the divine economy and a chapter in the history of salvation; and so the tourist is also a pilgrim and one who is also sacralized by his physical presence at the site. To a large extent, Buddhism follows this paradigm of a *historical* religion, with the life of a persona of Shakyamuni at the core of this non-theistic tradition. In its soteriological emphasis, the personas of myriads of Buddhist deities and Bodhisattvas unite the mundane and supramundane into a complex structure of Buddhist cosmology. It is in this sense that for Buddhists the physical pilgrimage is also virtual; highly philosophical, meditative exercises of visualization ensure that advanced practitioners experience the journey as mental.

Hence, the macrocosm of the external world is believed to be identified in the practitioner's body, as succinctly stated in the words of Saraha, one of the Eighty-Four Great Adepts:

"Here, within this body, is the Ganges and Jamuna... here are Prayaga and Benaras – here the sun and moon. Here are the sacred places, here the pithas and upa – pithas. I have not seen a place of pilgrimage and an abode of bliss like my own body."[21]

In these higher practices, the *mandala* meditation and visualization therefore becomes the archetypal practice of a virtual pilgrimage, in which the deities of the mandala are literally stamped into the natural landscape, thus through this mental pilgrimage collapsing even further the dichotomy of macrocosm and microcosm.

1 Richard Karl Payne, *Jewel in the Ashes: Buddha Relics and Power in Early Medieval Japan* (Cambridge, Massachusetts: Harvard University Asia Center, 2000).

2 And even, of course, if the tomb is empty, as Jesus' in Jerusalem must be for Christianity to make any sense.

3 Behind these appearances of a personalized deity lie older animistic traditions of a numinous spirit that is thought to inhabit a tree, a mountain, or a spring, like the source called Zamzam at Mecca, which may have been the original ground of the sanctity of that place.

4 *An Account of Tibet: The Travels of Ippolito Desideri of Pistoia, S. J., 1712-1727* by Filippo de Filippi, ed. 1937; reprinted New Delhi, 2005.

5 Anagarika Govinda, *The Way of the White Clouds* (Woodstock, New York: Overlook Press, 2006).

6 Mark Twain, *Following the Equator: A Journey Around The World*, vol. 2 (Hartford, Connecticut: The American Publishing Company, 1901), 163-64.

7 Husayn is another example of sanctity *ex officio*: he was the designated inheritor of the mantle of the *Imamate*, the Shi'ite defined headship of the Muslim community.

8 F. E. Peters, *Mecca and Jerusalem: The Typology of the Holy City in the Near East* (New York, New York University Press, 1987), 3.

9 As quoted in Simon Coleman and John Elsner, *Pilgrimage* (Cambridge, Massachusetts: Harvard University Press, 1995), 184.

10 There was *hag* dancing in the vineyards of Shiloh before the more sacerdotally controlled ritual was transferred to Jerusalem; Judges 21:19-21.

11 See both pre-Islamic festivals in F. E. Peters, *The Hajj* (Princeton, New Jersey: Princeton University Press, 1994), 31-38.

12 M. Basho, *The Narrow Road to the Deep North and Other Travel Stories*, Nobuyuki Yuasa trans. (Harmondsworth: Penguin Books, 1966).

13 Though here too the moral goodness of the believer, the choice of the moral over the immoral, is matched by a rather precise set of rules for the avoidance not of sin but of even inadvertent ritual impurity.

14 The interior of the Ka'ba is ritually the same as its exterior, and all Muslims may enter it without distinction, though the wardens of the place have tended to grant permission to do so as a political gesture or reward.

15 Jan Fontein, *The Pilgrimage of Sudhana: A Study of Gandavyuha Illustrations in China, Japan, and Java* (The Hague: Paris, Mouton, 1968). See also Anne Elizabeth McLaren, *Chinese Popular Culture and Ming Chantefables* (Leiden, Brill Academic Publishers, Sinica Leidensia vol. 41, 1998).

16 As quoted in *The Guide to India: A Tibetan Account by Amdo Gendun Chophel*, Toni Huber, trans. (Dharamshala: Library of Tibetan Works and Archives, 2000), 11.

17 The remission, that is, of the afterlife punishments due to their sins, even those confessed and absolved in this life.

18 One of the major differences between Christianity and Islam is that the clergy of the latter are, like the rabbis of post-Temple Judaism, essentially legal experts, while in the former they are, like the *kohens* of Temple Judaism, ritual celebrants who perform liturgies on behalf of the believers.

19 According to Muslim tradition, there had been an earlier building on the same site constructed by Adam.

20 The difference between the two is that the Jerusalem Pilgrim was reenacting the site-tied events that constitute a consecutive narrative in the Gospel texts, while the Abrahamic moments of the Hajj are discrete events that derive from a large extra-biblical tradition of uncertain origin.

21 As quoted in Molly Emma Aitken, ed. *Meeting the Buddha: On Pilgrimage in Buddhist India*, (Riverhead Books, 1995), 8.

BUDDHISM

Details of Fig. 18

Relics, Pilgrimage, and Personal Transformation in Buddhism

Susan L. Huntington

INTRODUCTION

The veneration of relics is a major component of Buddhist practice and a key motivation for pilgrimage. Traceable in India soon after the death of Shakyamuni Buddha in the 5th century BCE, the practice of Buddhist relic veneration spread as the religion traveled to the Himalayas, Southeast Asia, and North and East Asia, including Mongolia, China, Korea, and Japan. More recently, Buddhist ideals and practices, such as relic veneration, have extended to Europe, the Americas, and Australia, among other places. Beyond literary references to the importance of relics and pilgrimage, such as an often-cited passage in the *Mahaparinirvana Sutra*, these practices are best understood through a study of the actual objects. These include the relics themselves as well as reliquaries and reliquary monuments housing them at virtually every site of Buddhist practice in the world.

RELICS AND PILGRIMAGE

In Buddhism, the term for relic is *dhatu*. The many definitions of this term include element, characteristic, and nature, all of which convey the notion of an essence or innate quality. In most forms of Buddhism, all sentient beings are said to have Buddha-*dhatu*, meaning that each of us has within us the Buddha nature, or the essence of Buddhahood, which we must recognize and develop to its fullest potential. This element is present in every pore and cell of our bodies and, in turn, persists in our bodily remains even after we have passed away.

The most important type of Buddhist relic is, not surprisingly, a bodily relic (*sharira dhatu*). Bodily relics can include such things as a tooth, a hair, or a fingernail collected from the living individual; or items retrieved after cremation, such as ashes, fragments of bone, and crystallizations (such as kidney and gallstones). The most revered bodily relics are those of Shakyamuni Buddha himself, but bodily relics of many of his disciples and followers are also preserved, enshrined, and honored. Such relics are particularly cherished because they derive from the body of a revered person and thereby contain the essence (*dhatu*) of that individual.

In addition to the bodily relics are secondary relics that arise through physical contact with an individual, including everything that the person touched or used and every place that the individual visited. In Buddhism, the most revered secondary relics, called *paribhogika dhatu*, are also those of Shakyamuni Buddha, but, as is the case for *sharira dhatu*, secondary relics associated with important Buddhist personages are also revered. Thus, for example, every chair upon which His Holiness the Dalai Lama has sat may be considered a *paribhogika* relic.

A third type of Buddhist relic, called *uddeshaka dhatu*, does not derive from the physical body or contact with that body, but, rather, is a reference to or reminder of an individual. In Buddhism and Buddhist art, a portrait, whether naturalistic, stylized, or abstract, and whether painted, sculpted, photographic, or otherwise created, is an example of an *uddeshaka* relic.

While each category of relics is separately defined, different types can be combined to provide opportunities for complex, multileveled veneration. For example, the sculpted image of a renowned Buddhist teacher, which is an *uddeshaka* relic, might have a *sharira* or bodily relic enclosed within it. When the sculpture also contains objects that the individual had used, such as a set of counting beads, a ritual implement, or a piece of cloth from a robe, the image would also function as a container for a *paribhogika* relic. Its veneration would provide devotees with a focus made powerful by the rich, overlapping roles of the object.

By virtue of their association with Shakyamuni and other revered exemplars, Buddhist relics are considered to embody and generate unsurpassed power. The opportunity to be in the presence of any or all of these three types of relics therefore provides a major impetus for pilgrimage, aiding individuals in their quest for progress along the Buddhist path. Pilgrimages to relic sites may be undertaken alone or in groups and by members of the monastic and lay communities alike. Pilgrimages may be relatively short, consisting of only a few days, or may involve extended periods of time that necessitate long leaves of absence from day-to-day responsibilities.

Because the most important relics are those associated with Shakyamuni Buddha, pilgrimage to places associated with him is of principal importance. As the founder of the Buddhist monastic system and the individual whose teachings (the *dharma*) are at the core of all Buddhism, Shakyamuni is above all others in the religious tradition. His relics then, those of his body (*sharira dhatu*), things that he used (*paribhogika dhatu*), and his representations (*uddeshaka dhatu*), along with his teachings, which are often considered relics, are the centerpieces of Buddhist veneration. The Buddha himself is said to have instructed his followers on the manner in which his bodily relics should be treated

Fig. 1

Sculpture showing the distribution of Shakyamuni Buddha's relics.

Gandhara region of Pakistan. 2nd-3rd century. Schist. 4⅜ x 6½ x 1½ in. (11.1 x 16.5 x 3.8 cm). Los Angeles County Museum of Art. Purchased with Harry and Yvonne Lenart Funds. AC 1992.58.1.

Photograph © 2009 Museum Associates/LACMA/Art Resource, NY

Fig. 2

Buddhist relic caskets in the form of jars.

Stone with *sharira* bone relics. From Piprahwa. India. National Museum, New Delhi.

Photograph John C. Huntington

Fig. 3

Buddhist relic casket in the form of a *stupa*.

Metal. From Gandhara region of Pakistan. Karachi Museum, Pakistan.

Photograph John C. Huntington

after his death, but even he could not have imagined the extent to which his relics and those of his followers would be venerated, nor the hardships pilgrims might undertake in order to be in their presence.

Following Shakyamuni's death, a war ensued among various Indian kingdoms over possession of the relics, and a compromise was reached by dividing them among eight competing groups, each of which enshrined the relics in a type of reliquary monument known as a *stupa*. A ninth *stupa* was created to house the jar that had held the cremation ashes, as it had become a *paribhogika* relic by virtue of its contact with the Buddha's ashes. A 2nd-century sculpture from the Gandhara region shows the division of Shakyamuni Buddha's *sharira* relics into eight portions after his cremation (Fig. 1). The central figure in the sculpture is a Brahmin named Drona who, according to Buddhist texts, divided the ashes into eight portions, shown on the table in front of him. The container that had held the ashes is represented at the lower center of the relief. Flanking Drona are seven of the representatives of the eight kingdoms, who have come to claim the relics; an eighth figure has broken off from the sculpture at the far left. Each figure holds a container to carry away his kingdom's share of relics.

Fig. 4
Buddhist relic casket (*chorten*) in the form of a *stupa*.
Tibet. c. 16th-17th century. Private collection.
Photograph John C. Huntington

Sharira relics are irreplaceable, and, given their treasured status, are preserved in one or more special reliquary containers. Through recent archaeological excavation and, alas, some treasure hunting, many examples of ancient Buddhist reliquaries have come to light. Of great variety, they are often of high aesthetic value. The simplest ones have round, often jar-like forms (Fig. 2). The examples shown are made of stone, but reliquaries are commonly made of metal, including gold, and may also be made of other precious materials such as crystal and gemstones. Reliquary containers vary from simple cylinders to replicas of structures that reflect the architectural styles of the various Buddhist regions. An example from ancient Gandhara in what is now Pakistan is shaped into the form of an architectural *stupa* of a type commonly found in the region (Fig. 3). Examples from Tibet (Fig. 4), China, Japan, and other Buddhist regions also demonstrate the use of local architectural forms in the creation of reliquaries.

Yet, no matter how lavish, interesting, or artistically beautiful, Buddhist reliquaries were almost invariably buried, most often within a *stupa*. The expectation was that the reliquaries would never be seen again and that the relics contained within would never be disturbed. Although not visible to devotees, relics empower the site and all who live there or visit.

Little is known about the locations and forms of the eight *stupas* originally created to enshrine Shakyamuni's ashes. Remains believed to belong to this early phase of *stupa* construction have been found at Vaishali, Piprahwa, Rajgir, and Kushinagara. However, all of the early remains were later encased in brick and even stone overlays, making it difficult to determine the form of the original core. Excavations at Vaishali suggest that they were simple mud mounds.

Fig. 5

Relief showing royal figure (possibly Ashoka) on elephant and carrying a reliquary. This scene may show the actual procession that carried Shakyamuni Buddha's relics for enshrinement at this very *stupa*. Bharhut, India. c. 2nd century BCE. Indian Museum, Kolkata.

Photograph John C. Huntington

Fig. 6

Stupa 1 (Great Stupa) at Sanchi, Madhya Pradesh, India. The core of this *stupa* belongs to the period of Ashoka but the monument achieved its final form c. 10-25 CE.

Photograph John C. Huntington

Following the enshrinement of Shakyamuni's cremated ashes in the eight original *stupas*, there is a gap in our knowledge of the practice of relic veneration. However, Buddhist texts record that some two centuries later the first great Buddhist emperor, Ashoka, retrieved the relics (although not the jar) and re-enshrined them in eighty-four thousand *stupas* that he erected throughout his vast Indian empire. A 2nd-century BCE sculpture on the *stupa* railing from Bharhut shows a royal figure riding on an elephant while holding a reliquary in his left hand (Fig. 5). Because this monument was likely founded by Ashoka to house a portion of the Buddha's ashes, the representation may show the emperor himself bringing relics for enshrinement in the *stupa*.

With Ashoka's redistribution of the relics, Shakyamuni's Buddha-*dhatu*, or essence, and the accompanying talismanic power, were disseminated throughout the Buddhist world. Over the millennia, additional bodily relics of Shakyamuni and locations where he was believed to have made miraculous visits were identified, resulting in a proliferation of the

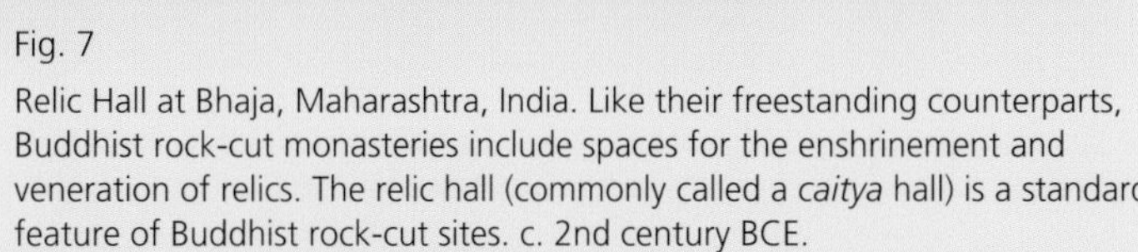

Fig. 7

Relic Hall at Bhaja, Maharashtra, India. Like their freestanding counterparts, Buddhist rock-cut monasteries include spaces for the enshrinement and veneration of relics. The relic hall (commonly called a *caitya* hall) is a standard feature of Buddhist rock-cut sites. c. 2nd century BCE.

Photograph Cathleen A. Cummings

Fig. 8

Svayambhu Mahachaitya. Kathmandu, Nepal.

Photograph John C. Huntington

number of relics and associated sacred sites throughout Asia. Countless numbers of representations of him fashioned in metal, stone, wood, and other materials also became part of the relic veneration practices associated with Shakyamuni. Added to these innumerable relics of Shakyamuni, the relics of his disciples and followers were also revered. The material record thus documents the pervasiveness of relics, reliquaries, *stupas*, and other reliquary monuments in Buddhist art and architecture, and in practices associated with them, as a core element in Buddhism. It may therefore be suggested that relic veneration is one of the most ubiquitous and consistent features of Buddhism, wherever it has traveled.

Although the number eighty-four thousand may have been metaphorical rather than literal, archaeological evidence shows that the cores of numerous *stupas* in India and Nepal date from the time of Ashoka's redistribution of the Buddha's relics. Over time, these *stupas* were enlarged and redecorated and in other ways modified, making it very difficult to know what a true Ashokan-period *stupa* would have looked like. The so-called Great Stupa at Sanchi in central India, also known as Stupa 1, is believed to have housed a portion of Shakyamuni's redistributed remains (Fig. 6). However, even this monument was later enlarged and encased in stone. The mound's hemispherical shape and enclosure within a railing are characteristic of the early Indian monuments from the 2nd to 1st centuries BCE. The four gateways, one facing each of the cardinal directions, and a central pole indicating the center of the Buddhist universe, endow the *stupa* with cosmic symbolism.

A nearby *stupa* at Sanchi, called Stupa 2, contains a grouping of relics of various Buddhist luminaries who lived and died at different times. The practice of mingling relics of different individuals in a single monument suggests that the *stupas* had commemorative, not funerary, roles. In other words, the remains from individuals who may have died at different times were collected for enshrinement at a later date. Also notable is the fact that reliquaries found at nearby

sites contained portions of some of the same individuals found in Stupa 2. Thus, the idea of spreading important relics to empower multiple places appears to have been an early element in Buddhist veneration.

Although most of the material record of early Buddhist monasteries is lost to us, by the time monastic sites appear in the artistic remains of India, *stupas* are an integral and necessary element of every known monastery. In addition to freestanding *stupas* at sites like Sanchi, rock-cut monasteries dating as early as the 2nd century BCE also document the centrality of relic veneration. Always present at the early Buddhist rock-cut sites are *stupas*, whether as an individual elements or enshrined in special halls as the main objects of veneration, as seen, for example, in the relic hall at Bhaja (Fig. 7).

Over time, and as Buddhism moved to new regions, the style and form of the *stupa* changed. Although such monuments became complex, symbolic forms, with elaborate structures and iconography, the foundational purpose and meaning of the *stupa* as a reliquary remained. *Stupas* in Nepal are often similar to the hemispherical Indic mounds, as seen in Nepal's most important Buddhist monument, Svayambhu Mahachaitya (Fig. 8). Examples from regions as far flung as Tibet and Indonesia demonstrate the complex symbolism of the *stupa* representing Mount Meru, the center of the Buddhist cosmos, in a geometric layout known as a *mandala*. Multiple levels symbolize the devotees' ascent to higher levels of spiritual attainment. For example, the *stupa* at Gyantse in Tibet is notable for its square lower storeys, each diminishing in size as they rise higher, while at the top is a Tibetan-style *stupa* (Fig. 9). The storeys suggest the levels of Mount Meru. Doorways on each level lead to chambers with sculpted and painted iconographic programs. The *stupa* of Borobudur in Java, Indonesia, is ten storied, each storey referring to a level of Mount Meru (Fig. 10). Sculpted panels and imagery on the various levels provide an iconographic program meant to be didactic as well as inspirational.

The East Asian *stupa* of China, Korea, and Japan takes the form of the pagoda, incorporating the meaning and symbolism of the Indic reliquary monument with the stylistic

Fig. 9
Stupa at Gyantse, Tibet
Photograph Eric R. Huntington

Fig. 10
Borobudur Stupa. Java, Indonesia. c. 800.
Photograph John C. Huntington

and structural elements of a multistoried watchtower. The 7th-century pagoda at the Horyu-ji is the earliest surviving pagoda in Japan (Fig. 11). While often unacknowledged in Buddhist art history, its relics demonstrate that it is a functional reliquary, rather than simply interesting architecture. While the form of most East Asian pagodas does not suggest their role as *stupas*, examples belonging to the Shingon sect of Buddhism in Japan, such as that at Koyasan, sometimes incorporate the Indic *stupa* form within the pagoda design.

Aside from the existence of uncountable *stupas* throughout the Buddhist world, the importance of *sharira* relics and veneration to them is so important in Buddhism that the art of Buddhism is notable for its many representations of devotees paying homage to *stupas*, or, more specifically, to the relics housed within them. Examples include some of the earliest surviving Buddhist art, such as the relief carvings from the Great Stupa at Sanchi (Fig. 12), which date from around 10 to 25 CE. Such scenes commonly show not only the revered object but also the act of veneration by pilgrims and other devotees, including respectful gestures (*anjali mudra*), bowing, the act of adorning a *stupa* with garlands, and circumambulating the object of veneration. Although many scholars exclusively associate such representations with early Indian Buddhism, these devotional compositions are widely depicted in the 2nd- to 3rd-century art of Gandhara (Fig. 13), in the early 9th-century relief carvings of Borobudur *stupa* (Fig. 14), and in artistic renderings from virtually every other Buddhist region of Asia. Further, veneration of *stupas* and the relics they contain has never waned in Buddhism, as may be seen in a recent photograph showing circumambulation and veneration at the Svayambhu *stupa* in Nepal (Fig. 15).

In addition to the preservation of bodily relics in reliquaries and reliquary monuments, the secondary, or associated, relics of Shakyamuni Buddha are also central to the core practices in Buddhism and to the impetus for pilgrimage. The most celebrated secondary relic (*paribhogika dhatu*) is the *bodhi* tree at Bodhgaya in India, under which the Buddha meditated and achieved enlightenment. An

Fig. 11
Pagoda at Horyu-ji. Nara, Japan
Photograph John C. Huntington

Fig. 12
Relief showing veneration of a *stupa*. Stupa 1 (Great Stupa) at Sanchi. Madhya Pradesh, India, c. 10-25 CE.
Photograph John C. Huntington

Fig. 13
Relief showing veneration of a *stupa*. Although scenes venerating non-figurative objects are commonly said to have died out after around the turn of the Common Era, such depictions have remained popular in many Buddhist artistic traditions to the present day.
Gandhara region of Pakistan. 2nd-3rd century. Peshawar Museum, Pakistan.
Photograph John C. Huntington

Fig. 14
Relief showing veneration of a stupa. Borobudur stupa. Java, Indonesia. c. 800.
Photograph John C. Huntington

Fig. 15
Veneration of Svayambhu Mahachaitya. Kathmandu, Nepal.
Photograph John C. Huntington

Fig. 16
Veneration of the Bodhi Tree at Bodhgaya, India.
Photograph Eric R. Huntington, 2007

offshoot of the original tree is enshrined at the site today (Fig. 16). This "tool," or object of use, led Shakyamuni to his highest achievement and, even today, Bodhgaya is the premier *paribhogika* destination for Buddhist pilgrims. Like *stupas*, the *bodhi* tree and other trees associated with Shakyamuni, such as the tree under which he was born, are frequently depicted in art as objects of reverence (Fig. 17). Such practices are not only depicted throughout the Buddhist world over time, but may be seen as present-day devotees at Bodhgaya repeat the time-honored tradition (Fig. 16). Like the scenes of devotion to *sharira* relics, representations of *paribhogika* relics almost invariably show individuals performing acts of devotion and making gestures of respect.

The so-called reminder relics (*uddeshaka dhatu*) are the least studied and most poorly understood of the various categories of relics. One of the most important *uddeshaka* relics in Buddhism is the image now housed in the main chamber of the temple at Bodhgaya (Fig. 18). Although not likely to be the original image in this temple, this sculpture, which shows the Buddha in the moments prior to his enlightenment, has become an archetype for Buddha imagery throughout the world. Such images are, of course, of great value to scholars of art for their historical, stylistic, and iconographic importance, but at the most fundamental level they are reminder relics to Buddhist practitioners. Veneration of figurative images, like veneration of *sharira* and *paribhogika* relics, constitutes a critical component of Buddhist practice (Fig. 19).

RELICS, PILGRIMAGE, AND PERSONAL TRANSFORMATION IN BUDDHISM

To understand the value of relics of Shakyamuni Buddha and his followers, it is important to examine the basic goals and principles of Buddhism itself. Foundational to Buddhist practice are two interdependent concepts: *samsara* and *karma*. *Samsara* is the cycle of transmigration to which all living beings are subject. Simply, Buddhists hold that while each of our lives ends in death, death in turn results in rebirth. This is true not only for humans but for all sentient beings. What determines the form of the new birth is the *karma* that one has performed in the previous life. *Karma* ("action"), from the verbal root *kr*, which means "do," refers to everything one has thought and done, whether virtuous or not, including, most fundamentally, adherence or non-adherence to the teachings of Shakyamuni Buddha.

The preliminary goal of most Buddhists is to continually improve one's *karma* to help ensure a higher rebirth until, like Shakyamuni, one reaches the awakened state of *bodhi*, or enlightenment. In turn, enlightenment provides the opportunity to attain *nirvana*, or extinction from the realm of continuing *samsaric* rebirths. Shakyamuni Buddha is the exemplar *par excellence*, having himself gone through uncountable numbers of births until his last life, when he achieved enlightenment (*bodhi*) and, subsequently, extinction (*nirvana*). A Buddhist's life is thus a quest to perform more good *karma* than bad and to offset bad *karma* by doing good. Although in some schools of Buddhism meritorious *karma* is thought to be transferable from one individual to another, for the most part individuals are responsible for expiating their own bad *karma* and for accruing the good. Indeed, the *samsara/karma* world view puts enormous responsibility on the individual to take action regarding his or her own *karma*.

Improving one's *karma* is not a simple matter. Indeed, it is difficult enough for individuals to think, say, or do the right thing even when the "right thing" is clearly defined. The matter is even more difficult because Buddhism does not codify a simple list of "dos" and "don'ts." Instead, Buddhist practice demands extraordinary effort by each individual in terms of both interpretation and execution. The Buddhist practitioner must constantly ask whether his or her actions and thoughts are directed correctly. Such a need for interpretation is nowhere clearer than in the so-called Eightfold Path, one of the most fundamental teachings of Shakyamuni Buddha.

The Eightfold Path may be translated in the following way:

1. Right Views
2. Right Intention
3. Right Speech
4. Right Action
5. Right Livelihood
6. Right Effort
7. Right Mindfulness
8. Right Concentration

Fig. 17

Veneration of a sacred tree. Stupa 1 (Great Stupa) at Sanchi, Madhya Pradesh, India. c. 10-25 CE

Photograph John C. Huntington

Fig. 18

Image of Sakyamuni Buddha in the main shrine of the Mahabodhi Temple at Bodhgaya, Bihar, India. Stone. The image dates from the 10th century but the painting and adornment are recent.

Photograph John C. Huntington, 2007

Fig. 19

Veneration of Bodhisattva image. At Mahabodhi Temple, Bodhgaya, Bihar, India.

Photograph Kerry Brown

At first glance, the list appears to be an easily memorized and easily implemented code. Yet these precepts contrast sharply with the specificity, for example, of the Ten Commandments of the Abrahamic traditions in which an adherent finds little room for doubt about the precept "thou shall not kill." But what, for example, are Right Views and how do we know if and when we have them? Right Action could, theoretically, include the idea of not killing, but is this a precept to which there might be an exception? Could there be a circumstance under which a Buddhist would take a life – human or other – and still have this considered Right Action? Does Right Speech mean that you hold your tongue and never say a negative word about someone or never rise up in protest? What is Right Livelihood? Obviously, being a hired assassin would not likely qualify as the right way to make a living, but is it a violation to be a farmer or a builder of tract homes who, by virtue of performing his job, destroys the natural habitats and therefore the lives of animals? If you earn part of your livelihood by investing in the stock market, can it be considered an infringement of Right Livelihood to own shares of stocks in companies that produce weapons of mass destruction? And, finally, it is safe to say that Buddhists do not believe in being untruthful, something that is not explicitly listed in the Eightfold Path, but which may be inferred not only from Right Speech but also Right Action, Right Intention, and other items on the list. But we all know that a lie can be an act of great kindness and that dispensing the truth can be the ultimate cruelty. The challenge is to know when to do what – and to desire to do the right thing.

In other words, Buddhism is about choice, not rules: There is no rule to which a Buddhist devotee can subscribe that covers all situations. A Buddhist must consciously choose his or her actions to suit each situation as it arises. Buddhism thus requires the individual both to select actions and to be responsible for the karmic retribution that will result. Simply following a list of rules – the thou shalls and though shall nots – is not sufficient for an individual to do good *karma*, for simple compliance is not the goal. Instead, Buddhism is emphatically about the individual's quest to become better and better, until, in fact, a state of absolute moral, ethical, and spiritual perfection is attained. This state, called *bodhi* – awakening or, commonly, enlightenment – in turn consists of Perfect Wisdom and Perfect

Fig. 20
Votive Plaque with the Buddha.
India (Bihar) Pala period, 9th century CE
Terracotta, 7 1/16 x 2 1/2 in. (18 x 6.4 cm)
The Metropolitan Museum of Art, Rogers Fund 1933 (33.50.10)
Image © The Metropolitan Museum of Art/ Art Resource, NY

Compassion. Perfect Wisdom enables the individual to always make the right decision free from the tyranny of self-interest. Perfect Compassion enables the individual to transform such wisdom into love and care for all living beings above his or her own selfish pursuits. Whether the attainment of perfection comes in a single lifetime or develops over myriad lifetimes, the goal of Buddhist practice is, simply put, not only to meet the minimum standards prescribed by a moral society but to achieve the highest level of personal goodness. This process of self-perfecting in Buddhism requires the directing of one's thoughts, speech, and efforts toward the goal.

As a religious system that is about personal transformation, Buddhism's activities and practices for members of the monastic community and the laity are directed at helping the individual achieve this goal. Activities supportive of gaining merit and achieving perfection include learning from Buddhist teachers; performing good actions (*karma yoga*), such as showing charity and compassion to all sentient beings; meditating; and being in the presence of exemplars.

This last practice in particular might lead a Buddhist devotee to undertake a pilgrimage to receive teachings from a living master or visit a relic site of a deceased exemplar, such as Shakyamuni. Such personal experience establishes or reinforces a link between the relic or person and the individual who is showing reverence. During such an encounter, a devotee may be said to be "taking *darshan*." The term *darshan* literally means "seeing," and refers to the physical act of seeing an important person, image, tree, relic, or other worthy object. This includes being in the presence of the sacred relic or person even when it is hidden, as when enclosed within a *stupa*.

Pilgrims who visit important Buddhist places, not surprisingly, commonly return with mementos or what might be termed "relics of the reliquary places," serving both as *paribhogika* relics of the site and as *uddeshaka* reminders. Small ceramic plaques available at sacred sites may have served as pilgrimage souvenirs (Fig. 20). Still, undertaking a physical pilgrimage is not always feasible. Poor health, inaccessible sites, or financial constraints, among other reasons, might prohibit such a journey. However, there are numerous ways in which a Buddhist might undertake a surrogate pilgrimage. These include a meditational pilgrimage aided by a work of art, such as a *mandala*, or a visit to a surrogate site. From the 12th through the 18th centuries, when the site of Bodhgaya was inaccessible to Buddhist visitors due to the political dominance of the Muslim rulers in northern India, surrogate Bodhgaya temples were erected in Thailand and Burma to help fulfill the needs of Buddhist practitioners. The intentionality of the experience, then, can be as important as the actual journey in terms of aiding a devotee on the Buddhist path, and the definition of relic veneration and pilgrimage in Buddhism must include what might be called virtual as well as actual journeys.

RELICS, PILGRIMAGE, AND THE PERSONAL EXPERIENCE: CONCLUDING REMARKS

Although this essay focuses on Buddhism, I suggest that relic veneration is not simply a religious practice, Buddhist or otherwise, but rather arises from a very fundamental human desire to have a physical connection with and a first-hand, eyewitness experience relating to an important being, whether living or dead. Indeed, the concept of the *sharira* relic is universally expressed when we visit the gravesite of a loved one or keep an urn with the ashes of a deceased family member in our homes. We also cherish the *paribhogika* relic, whether by keeping a treasured antique handed down from generation to generation or revisiting the place where an important life event, such as a birth or a wedding, took place. Such devotion to *paribhogika* relics is evident from a notice in *People* magazine, which read: "Busloads of people drive up to storefronts, and they want to touch a chair [Barack] Obama sat in and take a picture." And, certainly, particularly since the advent of photography, images also serve as reminders or *uddeshaka* relics of those whom we admire and cherish.

From this shared human perspective, we may contextualize the role that relics and pilgrimage play in Buddhism. On the most personal level, such activities provide the devotee with a first-hand experience that establishes or reinforces a connection with Shakyamuni or his disciples. Through this experience, the devotee's karmic record is forever changed.

See further reading on page 338

Details of Fig. 7

Tracing the Footsteps of the Buddha: Pilgrimage to the Eight Great Places (*Ashtamahasthana*)

Dina Bangdel

"There are four places, Ananda, that a pious person should visit and look upon with feeling and reverence.... And there will come, Ananda, to such spots, believers, monks, nuns of the Order, or devout men and women, and will say: 'Here was the Tathagata born!' or 'Here did the Tathagata attain the supreme and perfect insight!' or 'Here was the kingdom of righteousness set on foot by the Tathagata!' or 'Here the Tathagata passed away in that utter passing away which leaves nothing whatever to remain behind!'

And they, Ananda, who shall die while they, with believing heart, are journeying on such pilgrimage, shall be reborn after death, when the body shall dissolve, in the happy realms of heaven."[1]

This well-known passage from the *Mahaparinirvana Sutra* establishes the centrality of pilgrimage as a recommendation prescribed by the Buddha himself to his followers. It evokes the experience of pilgrimage as an emotive and meritorious journey, through the pilgrims' desire to visit the places most closely associated with the life of the Buddha and to recall the events that took place at these sacred sites. Although the initial list was limited to the four key events – birth, enlightenment, first teachings, and death – an extensive network of sacred places gradually expanded with the spread of Buddhism outside its place of origin in northern India. Homage to the remains (relics) of the Buddha Shakyamuni was the impetus for Buddhist pilgrimage, principally through the dissemination of his bodily relics (*sharira dhatu*) and the establishment of the eight *stupas* immediately after the death of the Buddha in c. 420 BCE. Gradually, another type of relic cult came into existence that commemorated places of activity or the defining "life events" (*paribhogika*, or "place of enjoyment") of Buddha Shakyamuni as secondary pilgrimage sites.

The earliest historical evidence of Buddhist pilgrimage is attributed to the 3rd-century BCE Mauryan emperor Ashoka, when he made his "*dharma* journey" (*dharma yatra*) to the established places associated with the Buddha's relics. The inscription of a pillar at Lumbini in southern Nepal commemorates Ashoka's imperial visit to the place of Shakyamuni's birth (Fig. 1). His biographical narrative in the *Ashokavadana* (dating to c. 2nd century BCE) expresses poignantly his pilgrimage experience:

> *Upagupta took [Ashoka] to the Lumbini Grove, and stretching out his right hand he said: 'In this place, great king, the Blessed One was born.'*

Fig. 1
Ashokan Pillar at Lumbini, Nepal
Photograph Lain S. Bangdel

Fig. 2
Map of the Eight Great Places of the Buddha. Drawn by Norma Schulz and Toni Huber. Reprinted from Toni Huber, *Holy Land Reborn*, fig. I.I.

And he added:

This is the first of the caityas
of the Buddha whose eye is supreme
Here, as soon as he was born
The Sage took seven steps on the earth,
Looked down at the four directions,
And spoke these words:
'This is my last rebirth
I'll not dwell in a womb again.'

Ashoka threw himself at Upagupta's feet and getting up, he said, weeping and making an *anjali* [gesture of the veneration]:

They are fortunate and of great merit
those who witnessed
the birth of the Sage
and heard his delightful voice. (Aikens, 33-34).

Over the next two or three centuries, many other places were added to the original list of four, namely his birth at Lumbini, the enlightenment at Bodhgaya, the first teaching at Sarnath, and his final cessation (*parinirvana*) at Kushinagara. As the legends grew, so did the variety and locations of the pilgrimage sites, some even far outside the homeland of the Buddha himself. Such relics, both objects and places, were referred to as "traces" and functioned as the locus of local pilgrimage traditions (Huber 2008, 20). Over time, secondary sites were added to the original four, as evidenced in the accounts of the early Chinese pilgrims (Faxian, Xuan Zang and I-Ching) and by the 4th to 5th centuries CE, several Buddhist texts describe a network of eight sites as a group. This became known variously as Ashtamahasthana ("Eight Great Places"), highlighting the primacy of location, or as Ashtamahapriharya ("Eight Great Miracles"), emphasizing the actual events that took place in these sacred sites. These four secondary places and events are as follows: the great miracle (*mahapratiharya*) in Jetavana Monastery at Shravasti, the descent from Trayastrimsha heaven at Sankashya, the taming of the wild elephant Nalagiri at Rajagriha, and the gift of honey by the

monkey at Vaishali (Fig. 2). By the 8th to 9th centuries, the eight events and sites were further codified as a group of stand-alone surrogates for the entire life of the Buddha, and were formalized in pilgrimage practice, text, and art.

In India, specifically during the Pala period (c. 850-1200), the cult of the Eight Great Miracles (*ashtamahapratiharya*) developed as a popular devotional practice centering on images and *stupas*. Indeed, a single image with the eight main events symbolically served as a visual reminder of the life of Shakyamuni, an *uddeshaka* relic or tangible memento of the pilgrimage experience. Like a *mandala*, the image could stand for a mental pilgrimage to the eight sites. The image type usually displays the central Buddha at the moment of enlightenment in Bodhgaya, with the other events surrounding the central figure. A c. 10th-century example from Nalanda Monastery in Bihar represents the standard iconographic form of the Pala Ashtamahapratiharya prototype (Fig. 3). At the center is large figure of Shakyamuni Buddha in the earth-touching gesture, representing his defeat of Mara and his enlightenment at Bodhgaya. The seven events are arrayed around the stele. Clockwise from the lower left are the birth at Lumbini, the descent from Trayastrimsha at Sankashya, the great miracle at Shravasti, the final cessation (*parinirvana*) at Kushinagara (top), first sermon at Sarnath, taming of the elephant at Rajagriha, and the monkey's gift of honey at Rajagriha.

This visual codification of eight life events of the Buddha into this iconographic scheme gained popularity at a time when pilgrimage to Bodhgaya was at its peak. Pilgrims were coming to India from across the Buddhist world. Portable sculptures and votive plaques commemorating these sites were commonly brought home with pilgrims as sacred mementos of their pilgrimage journeys (Fig. 4). The small size of the votive stele, less than four inches, suggests that this image had most likely traveled as a personal devotional souvenir. Furthermore, votive plaques produced in Southeast Asia, especially from Myanmar (Burma), began to employ the Pala iconographic convention, and were exported to other

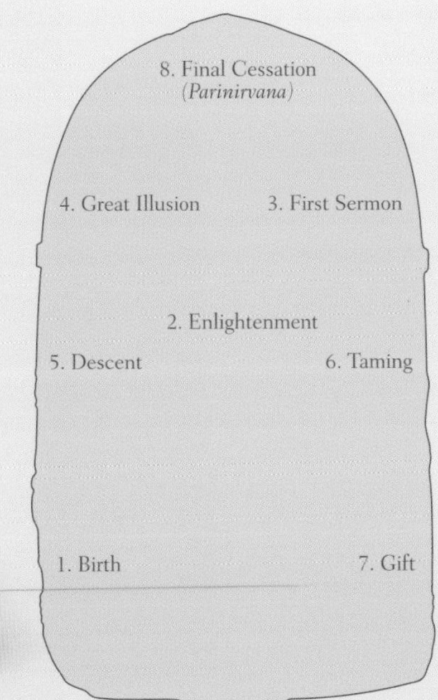

Fig. 3
Stele Representing the Eight Life Events of the Buddha (Ashtamahapratiharya)
India, Pala period, c. 10th century
Nalanda Site Museum, Bihar India
Photograph John C. Huntington
Courtesy of Huntington Archive

regions in Asia, such as Tibet and Sri Lanka. These plaques were again tangible reminders of the sacred heartland of Buddhism. An 11th- to 12th-century Burmese plaque from the Rubin Museum of Art illustrates the distinctive iconographic convention popular in Southeast Asia, as an indicator of its provenance (Fig. 5). Following the standard Pala convention, it represents the eight great events in a complicated array of figures arranged in columns and rows. The life scenes depicted around the rim of the plaque in the top three rows surrounding the central figure of Shakyamuni. Starting at the top left side are represented the offering of the monkey, the first sermon, and the taming of the elephant. On the right side, from the top, are the descent from Trayastrimsa, the miracle at Shravasti, and the birth at Lumbini, with the final cessation placed at the usual top center position. However, unlike its Indian counterparts, the Burmese stele displays six additional Buddha figures, arranged in two columns, immediately surrounding Shakyamuni. These Buddhas represent the seven stations the post-enlightening events during the seven weeks after Shakyamuni attained enlightenment at Bodhgaya. At each place around the sacred site, the Buddha is said to have meditated before his first teaching Sarnath.

The strong connection between Myanmar (Burma) and the seven post-enlightenment meditation sites at Bodhgaya may be attributed to the Burmese interpretation of the post-enlightenment narrative. As described in the *Nidana Katha*, on the last day of the seventh week two merchants, Tapussa and Bhallika, came upon the Buddha as he sat meditating. Realizing that they were in the presence of a great man, the two offered the Buddha food. This was the first food the Buddha took after his forty-nine days of fasting during the period after his enlightenment. In Myanmar (Burma), it is believed that these merchants were traders from the city of Rangoon, and that the merchants converted to Buddhism after providing him with this gift of food. In appreciation for the gift of food, the Buddha gave them the hair and nail relic that is now enshrined in the Shwedagon Stupa in Burma (Myanmar).

Fig. 4
Plaque with Scenes from the Life of the Buddha
India (Bihar or West Bengal), Pala period, 12th century
Mudstone, 3 15/16 x 2 15/16 in. (10 x 7.5 cm)
The Metropolitan Museum of Art, Purchase, Anonymous Gift, 1982 (1982.233)
Image © The Metropolitan Museum of Art/Art Resource, NY

Fig. 5
Buddha Shakyamuni
Myanmar (Burma). c. 11th-12th century
Stone, 6 1/2 x 4 1/2 x 1 1/4 in. (16.5 x 11.4 x 3.2 cm)
Rubin Museum of Art
C2005.4.2 (HAR 65388)
Photograph Rubin Museum of Art

BODHGAYA: CENTER OF THE BUDDHIST UNIVERSE

No other place of Buddhist pilgrimage is more sacred than Bodhgaya, the site of Shakyamuni's enlightenment. The main focus of the site has always been the sacred tree that sheltered Shakyamuni when he attained enlightenment and that now marks the location of that pivotal event. Variously known as the *vajrasana,* "adamantine seat," or *bodhi manda,* "seat of enlightenment," the seat on eastern side of the tree represents the exact center of the Mount Meru world system in Buddhist cosmology, where the Buddhas of the past, present, and future realize enlightenment (Fig. 6). Although the adamantine seat and Bodhi tree are both foci of veneration for all Buddhists, it is the Mahabodhi Temple that substitutes for Bodhgaya as a site (Fig. 7). Numerous copies of miniature Mahabodhi temples serve as surrogates of the main temple.

Although the present Mahabodhi Temple is a 19th-century British reconstruction of a much-ruined temple, a small clay plaque from Kumrahar, Patna, with a 2nd- to 3rd-century Kharoshti inscription, provides one of the earliest representations of the Mahabodhi Temple (Fig. 8). Because of their ephemeral nature, these clay plaques, known as *saccha* (Tibetan *tsa tsa*), were popular votive offerings and were inexpensive, practical, and portable souvenir objects that pilgrims could easily carry through their travels. These could even be consecrated or vivified with relics when the clay was prepared, as it continues to be today in the Himalayan tradition. The Kumrahar plaque is very probably a souvenir of a visit to the Bodhgaya site by a pilgrim of the time. The plaque depicts the distinctive multitiered superstructure of the Mahabodhi Temple, with the image of Shakyamuni enshrined at the center. Surrounding the temple enclosure are votive *stupas* and buildings surrounding the monastery, and what appear to be figures around the temple

Fig. 6
Mahabodhi Temple.
Bodhgaya, Bihar, India.
Photograph John C. Huntington

Fig. 7
Mt. Meru
Tibet, c. 19th century
Pigments on cloth, 38¾ x 25¼ in. (98.4 x 64.1 cm)
Rubin Museum of Art C2006.63.11
Photograph Rubin Museum of Art

Fig. 8

Clay plaque depicting the Mahabodhi Temple

From Kumrahar, Bihar, India. Terracotta. $4\frac{3}{16}$ in. (10.6 cm)

Patna Museum, India

Photograph John C. Huntington

Fig. 10

Model of the Mahabodhi Temple

Nepal, c. 19th century

Copper alloy with gilding,
H: 41 in. (104.1 cm)
W: $19\frac{1}{8}$ in. (48.6 cm)
D: $19\frac{5}{16}$ in. (49 cm)

The Field Museum, Chicago (1905.907.89146)

Photograph The Field Museum

Fig. 9

Model of the Mahabodhi Temple

Eastern India, c. 11th century

Stone (serpentinite), $6\frac{13}{16}$ in. (17.3 cm)

On long term loan from the Nyingjei Lam Collection

Rubin Museum of Art L2005.9.91 (HAR 68417)

Photograph Rubin Museum of Art

Fig. 11

Shakyamuni Buddha with Life Scenes and Jatakas

Tibet, c.18th century

Pigments on cloth,
28 x $19\frac{3}{4}$ in.
(71.1 x 50.2 cm)

Rubin Museum of Art, C2006.66.217 (HAR 264)

Photograph Rubin Museum of Art

complex, referencing the seven stations of meditations of the post-enlightenment events.

A very special and common pilgrimage souvenir was a model of the Mahabodhi Temple itself (Fig. 9). These models serve as accurate portrayals of what the temple may have looked like before its destruction in the aftermath of the Islamic conquest in the 13th century. Such small stone models of the Mahabodhi Temple, most likely produced in Bihar as pilgrimage souvenirs, have made their way from the homeland in eastern India to Nepal, Tibet, Sri Lanka, and Burma (Guy, 362). Increasingly, with the loss of the Buddhist homeland and with the perils of travels, these models have become even more critical reminders of pilgrimage to these sacred places. In addition, full-scale Mahabodhi replicas were built in various places in the Buddhist world, and this relocation of the sacred center from the homeland recreated a surrogate pilgrimage in the localized landscape. The Nepalese model (Fig. 10) is one such example of a surrogate replica, as it closely approximates both the Mahabodhi Temple at Bodhgaya and its Nepalese reconstruction – Mahabuddha Temple at Patan built in the 16th century by the Newar pilgrim Abhayaraj Shakya after his three-year sojourn to Bodhgaya.

Even though popular pilgrimage to the Buddhist homeland virtually came to a standstill with the decline of Buddhism in the 13th century, the eight life events of Shakyamuni continued to be commemorated through paintings and sculptures. Especially for the Tibetans, India remained as the premier "sacred land" (*arya bhumi*), the source of the pure Dharma. In one sense, works of art not only became representative of Ashtamahapraharya veneration,

Fig. 12
Painting Depicting the Eight Stupas
Tibet, c.19th century
Pigments on cloth, 23 x 17½ in. (58.4 x 44.5 cm)
Rubin Museum of Art, C2006.66.126 (HAR 73)
Photograph Rubin Museum of Art

but also came to serve as didactic reminders of the paradigm of Buddhist enlightenment through the life events of Shakyamuni. The 18th-century Tibetan painting from the Rubin Museum of Art (Fig. 11), for instance, depicts the familiar events and places related to the eight pilgrimage places. Clockwise from top left are depicted the taming of the elephant at Rajagriha, defeat of Mara and the moment of enlightenment at Bodhgaya, the first sermon at Sarnath, and the *parinirvana* at Kushinagara. Additional events included are his miraculous cremation, with this image surrounded by a rainbow of flowers and an altar with eight *stupas* containing his bodily relics.

The cult of Eight Great Places continued to hold a significant place in the Tibetan tradition, as we know through extant Chinese and Tibetan translations of original Sanskrit texts, such as the 10th-century *Ashtamahapratiharya Sutra* and *Ashtamahasthana-chaitya Sutra*. The texts described not only the veneration to the Eight Great Places, but also the honoring of the eight *stupas* located at these sites. In the Tibetan tradition, *stupas* of eight different forms are associated specifically with the eight places and events of the life of the Shakyamuni. Representations of the eight *stupas* in painting (Fig. 12), sculpture, and architecture hence symbolically reify the centrality of place and pilgrimage in the Buddhist tradition. Coming full circle, travel to the eight great sites has once again been revived in the contemporary context as the core pilgrimage to the Buddha's homeland.

See further reading on page 338

1 *Digha Nikaya* II, 16, *Mahaparnibbana Sutta*, Ch. V, 140.

Pilgrimage Traditions in Nepal

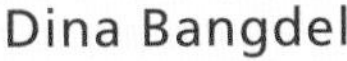

Dina Bangdel

As Buddhism spread outside its homeland in India to the rest of Asia and transformed into a religion that accommodated indigenous practices, local sites of worship, and pre-Buddhist belief systems, pilgrimages similarly developed as expressions of distinctive regional traditions. Yet, the goal of pilgrimage invariably emphasizes the fundamental tenets of Shakyamuni's teachings, that is, self-transformation through the cultivation of morality (*shila*), contemplation (*samadhi*), and insight (*prajna*). To attain these qualities, Buddhism focuses on the ideal moral code of the Five Precepts and the Six Perfections or Virtues (*paramita*) in order realize enlightenment. Pilgrimage motivates the faithful to cultivate these qualities through devotion (*sraddha*) while at the same time providing opportunities for one to earn religious merit (*punya*) through direct experience with the sacred. What we find among the Newar Buddhists of Nepal is uniquely localized pilgrimage that articulates the sacred geography of the Kathmandu Valley. Pilgrimage is therefore deeply embedded in the religious lives of Newar Buddhists, as a collective experience of the community in formalized ritual settings.

PILGRIMAGE AND SACRED NARRATIVE

The Buddhist origins of the Kathmandu Valley are associated with the miraculous appearance of the Self-Arisen Light Form (*svayambhu jyotirupa*) from the thousand-petalled lotus on the sacred lake that was the home of the *nagas*. Prior to this event, the Manushi Buddhas (seven mortal Buddhas of the past) had made pilgrimages to this place. Realizing its inherent power, the first Buddha Vipashvin had sown a lotus seed from which emerged the formless primordial Buddha as five-colored rays of light. At a later time, the Bodhisattva of Wisdom Manjushri, gaining insight into this extraordinary occurrence, left his abode at Mount Wutai in China and arrived with his two wives to take *darshan* of the primordial Buddha. Seeing that the sacred Valley was filled with water, the Bodhisattva cut the lake with his sword and drained it, thus making the auspicious locations (*tirthas*) in the Valley accessible to all sentient beings who wished to venerate them. In this way, the Kathmandu Valley was created, and through the ages the faithful came to the Valley to receive *darshan* of the Primordial Buddha. After all seven Manushi Buddhas, including Shakyamuni, had make pilgrimages to the Valley, the Light Form came to be encased in the form of the *stupa* that we know today as Svayambhu Mahachaitya, "Great Self-Originated Stupa" (Fig. 1).

Because of its association with the origin myth, the Great Stupa is the premier locus of Newar Buddhist religious life and pilgrimage. On the *stupa*, the five-colored light rays are associated with the Five Buddhas (*pancha jina*) as a

three-dimensional mandala. Veneration begins with an arduous climb up a steep flight of stairs leading to the summit, literally ascending to the top of Mount Meru (the center of Buddhist cosmology) until one is finally in the presence of the primordial Buddha. Reaching the top, the faithful begin circumambulation from the east side, as if meditating on a two-dimensional mandala. Moving clockwise, they venerate the shrines of the Five Jina Buddhas and their female embodiments, who are aligned with the cardinal directions and intermediate points (Fig. 2).

Localized pilgrimages and festivals developed around the sacred history of Svayambhu. The *Svayambhu Purana* begins as a series of conversations between either Shakyamuni and his disciple Ananda, or Emperor Ashoka and his minister Upagupta, who extol the virtues of the Valley before embarking on a pilgrimage. The narrative clearly incorporates indigenous traditions of Newar culture, specifically the cult of the *nagas* (serpents) and *matrika* (mother goddesses) integrated into a distinctive Buddhist framework. As a result, pilgrimage sites designated by the *Svayambhu Purana* often overlap with Hindu places of worship, as a shared acknowledgement of the power of the site rather than an indicator of sectarian domination. This accommodation of indigenous beliefs and acceptance of multivalent identities is found in pan-Buddhist contexts, since Buddhism's special character is to subsume local practices, deities, and holy places and to transform these aspects to fit a doctrinal Buddhist construct. For instance, in Tibet, indigenous Bon and Buddhist practices are conflated, as are

Fig. 1
The Great Stupa of Svayambhu
Photograph John C. Huntington

Fig. 2
Buddha Amitabha on the west shrine at Great Stupa of Svayambhu is the focus of lay devotion at the site, because of the association with rebirth in his Land of Bliss (Sukhavati) paradise.
Photograph Dina Bangdel

Daoist and Buddhist practices in China; while in Japan, Shinto sites and practices are shared, as illustrated in the Kumano Nachi pilgrimage (see essay *Saikoku Pilgrimage: Japanese Devotees Search for Kannon*).

THE HOLY MONTH OF GUNLA

More formalized pilgrimages to the Great Stupa are often connected with the ritual calendar. For example, during the holy month of Gunla (July-August), devotees observe daily purification rites, such as fasting, bathing, and abstinence from meat and alcohol. They visit the *stupa* daily for prayer songs and to make gifts of charity. Offerings of jewelry, cloth, food, and money for the maintenance of the monument are also given, while prayer flags and whitewashing of the *stupa* are offered as expressions of honor and faith. Very often, as part of the merit-making activity, votive *stupas* may be offered at Svayambhu as well as in the courtyards of the four-hundred-plus Buddhist monasteries in the Valley. During this time, the *Svayambhu Purana* is recited daily in the homes, thereby reifying and affirming the sacred origins of the monument.

Another important religious activity, also performed during Gunla but especially for women, is the ritual of creating a hundred thousand (*laksha*) miniature clay *stupas* over a period of four weeks, beginning the day after the new moon of Gunla. The process of performing the Laksha Chaitya ritual observance and making the miniature *stupas* is described, albeit with varying details, in the *Vrata Avadana Mala* and *Chaitya Pungava*. On the day of the ceremony, different kinds of clay are gathered, preferably the dark clay found in riverbeds. The *stupas* are made of this clay mixed with milk, yogurt, ghee, cow dung, and cow urine, the five offerings ritually made at the *stupa*. During kneading, the clay is further purified by twenty-one recitations of the Vairochana mantra, and is finally fashioned into *stupas*. As the community gathers to make the hundred thousand such *stupas*, an empowerment ceremony of merit dedication is performed and ultimately the clay miniatures are dissolved in the river. In this way, ritual and pilgrimage emphasize the transitory nature of worldly existence.

One of the most popular texts recounting the merits of making clay *stupas* is the *Shringabheri Avadana*, "Buffalo Horn-Blowing Tale" (Lewis, 39). As a requisite for the Laksha Chaitya observance, the story is recited daily for a month during Gunla, and the culmination of the ritual is heralded at Svayambhu with musical accompaniment from a buffalo horn and other traditional instruments. As the text suggests, the horn-blowing ritual is one of the most meritorious acts that can be performed by the laity to ensure rebirth in a celestial realm. Indeed, according to Newar legend, the Laksha Chaitya was also performed by the Manushi Buddha Vipashvin during his visits to the sacred Valley. Later, Shakyamuni himself is said to have performed this ritual in honor of the Great Stupa, and the horn-blowing tradition continues to be a central aspect of the pilgrimage ritual experience at Svayambhu during Gunla (Fig. 3).

Fig. 3
Horn-blowing festival at Svayambhu during the holy month of Gunla, as part of the localized monthly pilgrimage to Svayambhu.
Photograph Sanu Bajracharya

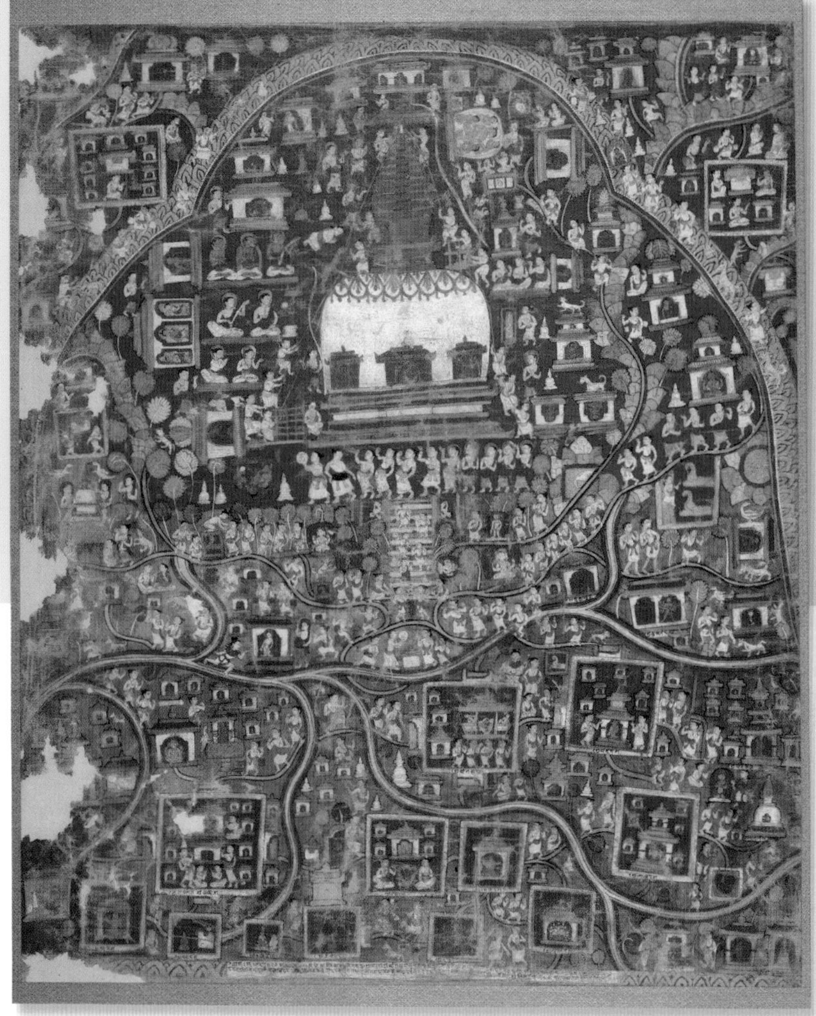

Fig. 4
The Great Stupa of Svayambhu and Sacred Sites of the Kathmandu Valley
Nepal, dated by inscription, N.S. 685 (1565)
Opaque watercolor on cloth
45 x 36 in. (114.3 x 91.4 cm)
The Robert A. and Ruth W. Fisher Fund
Virginia Museum of Fine Arts, 2000.15.
Photograph Virginia Museum of Fine Arts

Sculptures and paintings are often commissioned to commemorate the completion of a ritual or pilgrimage. Inscriptions record the patrons and their religious intentions, reiterating that the benefits of meritorious actions are earned not only by the individuals performing the acts, but by all sentient beings. A rare painting dated 1546 from the Virginia Museum of Fine Arts depicts a kind of "pilgrim's map," centering around the Great Stupa of Svayambhu (Fig. 4) during its renovation. The representation of identifiable holy sites of the Valley suggests that the sacred landscape and pilgrimage circuits visited by contemporary pilgrims were already well-established by the 16th century.

Another elaborate visual map from the Philadelphia Museum of Art illustrates the pilgrimage route to Gosainkunda Lake, a site that is sacred to the Hindus, Buddhists, and local shamanistic traditions (Fig. 5). Located in the Langtang Valley outside the Kathmandu, the lake is considered an important *tirtha* associated with Shiva in his form as Nilakantha (Blue-Throated Lord), recalling the place where he drank the cosmic poison to save the world, while the Buddhists make pilgrimage to Nilakantha as one of the twelve forms of Avalokiteshvara. The painting identifies by inscription the sacred topography of Hindu and Buddhist sites, beginning with the Red Avalokiteshvara temple at Bungamati in the far left; the Great Stupa of Svayambhu; and the cityscape of Patan, with the sculpture of King Yoganarendra Malla that was erected in 1693 (Vergati, 98). Male and female pilgrims, ascetics practicing yoga, and other devotees make their way through the holy places of the Valley, finally reaching Gosainkunda at the far right of the scroll (Fig. 6). Other pilgrimage sites outside the Valley are recorded, such as Devighat in Nuwakot district, with the representation of the Prithvi Narayan Shah's distinctive palace that was built in 1762. This presence of the Shah king's palace and the inclusion of Devighat pilgrimage suggests that this painting may have been commissioned after the Shah overthrow of the Malla kings in 1768.

Fig. 5
Pilgrimage from Kathmandu Valley to Gosainkund Lake
Nepal, probably Bhaktapur
Late 17th or early 18th century
Opaque watercolor on cloth, 33 x 171½ in. (83.8 x 435.6 cm)
Purchased with the Stella Kramrisch Fund
Philadelphia Museum of Art, 2000-7-3.
Photograph Philadelphia Museum of Art

Fig. 6
Detail of painting, depicting pilgrims traversing mountains and rivers, and ascetics performing yoga.

VENERATION OF MANJUSHRI

Manjushri the Bodhisattva of Wisdom is the patron deity of Newar Buddhism because of his close association with the Buddhist origins of the Valley. Manjushri is believed to have come to the Valley from his abode in China's Wutaishan Mountain in his human manifestation as manjudeva, and to have made it habitable by draining the great lake. Elevated from his status as one of the Eight Great Bodhisattvas to a fully Enlightened Buddha, he is regarded as the Lord of Speech (Vagishvara) and the embodiment of enlightenment. Quasi-historical and historical accounts of pilgrimage to Manjushri's abode at Wutaishan in China spiritually connect the sacred history of the Valley and China, and Manjushri's iconography symbolizes his identity with the "Five-Peaked" mountain of Wutaishan. Hence, paintings and sculptures of Manjushri became popular offerings of merit in Nepal, Tibet, and China (Fig. 7). Conceptually seated in his abode at Wutaishan, four-armed Manjushri holds in his right hand the Chandrahasa sword with which he drained the Valley, while in his left he displays the Perfection of Wisdom text atop a lotus. His principal hands bear a bow and arrow, symbolizing the defeat of egoism. His two-armed form as Arapachana Manjushri, named after his mantra A RA PA CHA NA, is especially important to Newars, as he becomes the primordial teacher of the esoteric Tantric meditations, such as the Chakrasamvara Mandala. Rituals, festivals, and acts of faith centering around Manjushri, such as the daily chanting of the *Namasangiti* text, reiterate the significance of this deity to Newar Buddhists.

Fig. 7
Tikshna-Manjushri, the Bodhisattva of Wisdom
China, Ming dynasty, Yongle period (1403-1424 CE)
Gilt bronze; H. 7½ in. (19.1 cm)
Rogers Fund, 2001
The Metropolitan Museum of Art, 2001.59
Image © The Metropolitan Museum of Art/Art Resource, NY

His preeminence in Nepal is especially highlighted during the annual festival Shri Panchami (January or February), when thousands make a special visit to the Manjushri shrine at Svayambhu to receive his *darshan*. (Fig. 8). Here devotees touch the footprint relic (Manjushri Pada) that is displayed only during this festival (Fig. 9). Every year, Manjushri promises to return to the Valley from Wutaishan and reside at Svayambhu for two months to expound on the extraordinary qualities of the Great Stupa. Further, he teaches the esoteric meanings of his root text, *Namasangiti*, "Chanting the Names of Manjushri." On the festival day, both Hindus and Buddhists converge at this holy site, the Hindus conflating Manjushri, the Bodhisattva of wisdom, with Sarasvati, the Hindu goddess of learning. In this case, the representation of the feet allows for the fluidity of multivalent religious identity, similar to what is seen in other cultural contexts. For instance, Shri Pada, the "Sacred Footprint" mountain in Sri Lanka, is important to four major world religions: Hinduism, Buddhism, Christianity, and Islam. The Buddhists regard this as the *paribhogika* relic of Shakyamuni Buddha, left during the time when he visited the island nation, while the Hindus worship the site as the footprint of Shiva. For the Christians, the footprint is believed to belong to St. Thomas, who first brought Christianity to Sri Lanka. Also popularly known as Adam's Peak, the site is considered by Muslims to contain the footprint of Adam, at the place where he stood on one foot for a thousand years of penance after being expelled from Paradise. In the case of the Manjushri Pada, it becomes a popular cult object as a symbol of Manjushri's enlightened qualities, yet is venerated for the more mundane aspirations of material benefit, success in education, business, and all new endeavors.

Fig. 8
Manjushri festival during Shri Panchami, (January-February) at Svayambhu.
Photograph Dina Bangdel

Fig. 9
Main shrine object, depicting footprints of Manjushri (Manjushri Pada) during Sri Panchami festival.
Photograph Dina Bangdel

Fig. 10
Plaque with footprints of Manjushri (Manjushri Pada). Silver.
Photograph Dina Bangdel

Portable Manjushri padas, with the Bodhisattva's "eyes of knowledge" (*jnana chakshu*), are the focus of lay devotion (Fig. 10). Similarly, in Tibet and China, handprints and footprints often became pilgrimage mementos, as seen in the woodblock print from the Rubin Museum of Art, which was most likely acquired as a souvenir during a pilgrimage to Wutaishan (Fig. 11).

PILGRIMAGE AND POWER-PLACES

Although pilgrimage inherently seeks to emphasize higher aspirations and to further the individual on the spiritual path, such power-places are often associated with the more mundane needs of the here and now. This is case of Shantipur, one of the five "cities" (*pura*) that symbolize the five elements (earth, air, fire, water, and space/ether). Believed to be a complex network of subterranean caves, Shantipur is the secret Tantric shrine *par excellence*, and houses the esoteric Tantric deity Chakrasamvara. Only two priests are ever allowed to enter the inner shrine (Fig. 12). Shantipur, however, is invoked for state protection through its rainmaking powers and association with *nagas*. In historical and quasi-historical accounts, the kings of the Valley have entered Shantipur during times of drought, famine, and other physical disasters.

The most detailed account of such a pilgrimage is attributed to the Hindu king of Kathmandu, Pratap Malla (r. 1641-1674). A 1658 inscription at the site describes the king's efforts to bring back the Naga Mandala drawn in the blood of the Eight Naga Kings, together with the *Mahamegha-sutra*, in order to produce rains for the Valley. The inscription speaks of Pratap Malla's pilgrimage map, now lost, but extant in copies. A 19th-century representation of this historic event is based on the inscriptional narrative and shows multiple, labeled levels, beginning with the following (Fig. 13): "His Majesty, King of Kings, Lord of Poets, Jaya Pratap Malla Deva entered with *puja* materials, a fish, black *soya* beans and cow's milk." In the center of the second level is a mandala where the king encountered Mahasamvara, whom he worshipped, and found the *Samvara Tantra* "concealed in a copper

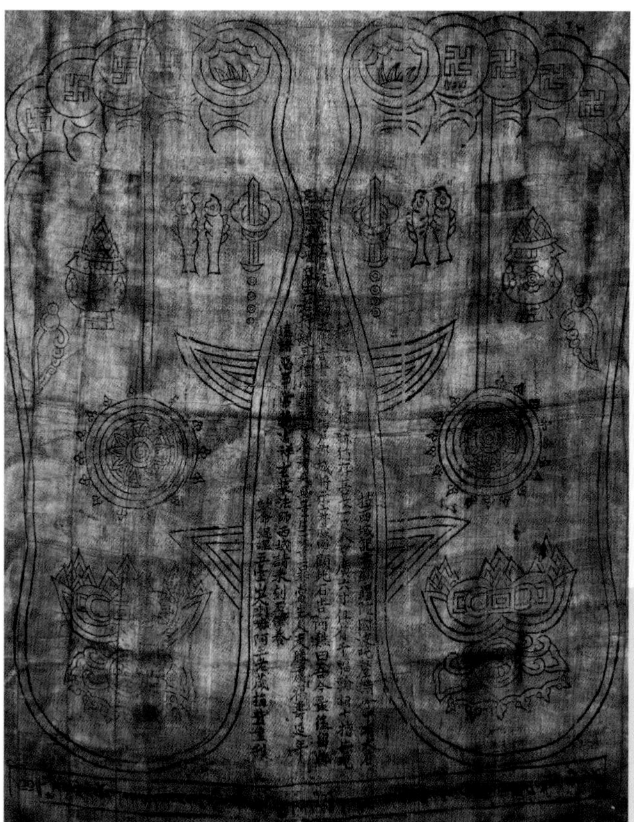

Fig. 11
Footprints of the Buddha (Buddhapada) as Pilgrimage Souvenir
China. 19th century
Ink on cotton. 22½ x 17½ in (57.2 x 44.5 cm)
Rubin Museum of Art, C2006.66.438
Photograph Rubin Museum of Art

Fig. 12
Interior of Shantipur, the esoteric shrine dedicated to Chakrasamvara. At Svayambhu.
Photograph Sanu Bajracharya

milk-pail." (Slusser 1979, 80). The king's perilous journey is described in vivid detail: "bats as large as kites or hawks came to kill the light." In the second room, "ghosts, flesh-eating spirits, and hungry ghosts came to beg. If you are unable to pacify them they clutch at you." The third room was filled with snakes: "If you cannot pacify the snakes by pouring out milk they chase and bind you. Having pacified them, you can walk on their bodies." Finally, in the central room, he met the great Tantric teacher Shantikaracharya, "who had become a *siddha*, sitting in meditation. He was alive with no flesh on his body. He gave the King instruction, and here the King found the mandala, written in the Naga Kings' blood, which he took out to make rain." By bringing the text out of the cave and completing the ritual, King Pratap Malla caused the Valley to receive the much-needed rains. Pratap Malla is also said to have made a second entry into Shantipur in 1667. Tradition attributes his sudden death in 1674 to having made that subterranean pilgrimage without performing the required preliminary rituals.

This narrative points to elements of secret ritual characteristic in Vajrayana Buddhism. Places of power related to Tantric (esoteric) pilgrimages are *pithas*, literally self-arisen "seats" that occur naturally in the landscape. Through rituals, individuals can link the self and the universe, the microcosm and the macrocosm, and the internal and external. Such sacred seats are located in the periphery, in the dangerous liminal spaces between the sacred and the profane. Often at the confluence of rivers or cremation grounds, they mark the outer boundaries of protected space. To realize the inseparability of the internal and external journeys of pilgrimage, practitioners use a cosmogram or mandala. The mandala paradigm thus functions as an element in the construction of both pilgrimage and landscape.

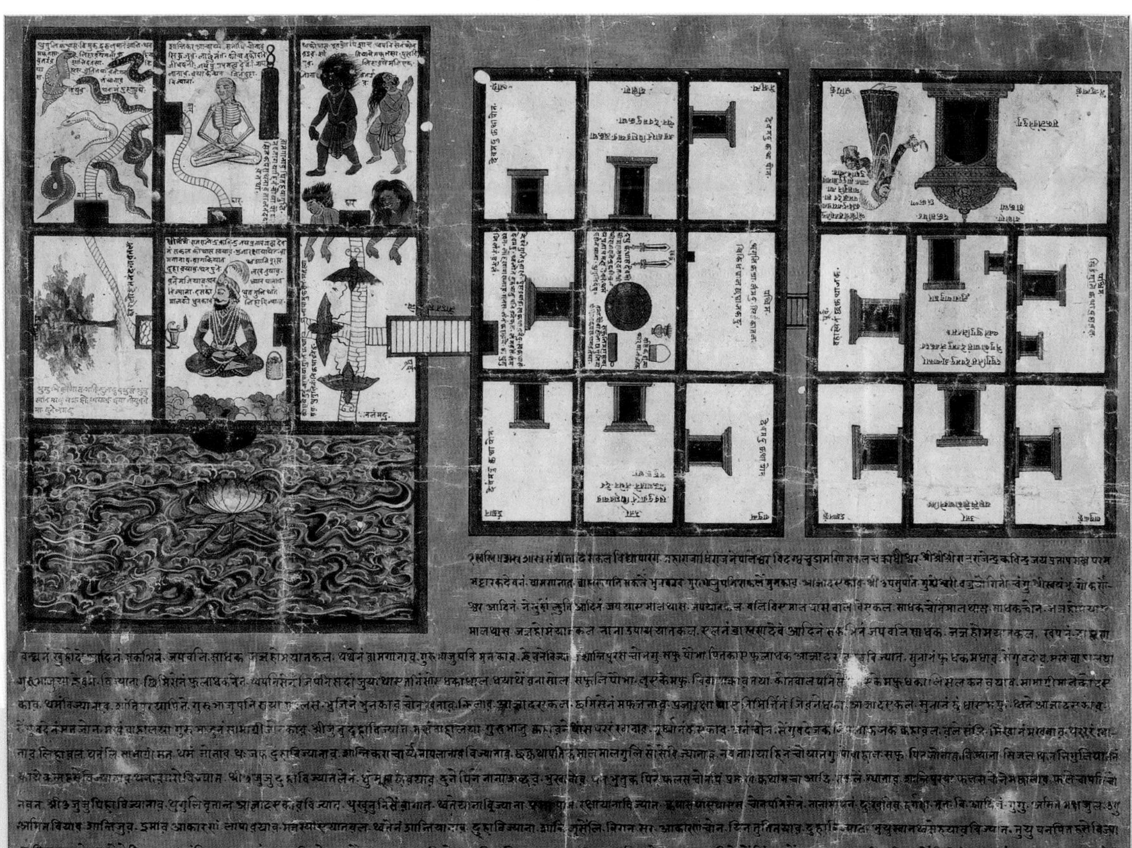

Fig. 13

King Pratap Malla's descent into Shantipur

With inscription in Newari, in Devanagari characters

19th century

Opaque watercolor on cotton. 25 x 19½ in. (63.5 x 49.5 cm)

Copy of an original in the possession of a Kathmandu family

Private Collection

Photograph Ian Alsop

SACRED GEOGRAPHY AND PILGRIMAGE OF THE VALLEY

By the 15th century, texts such as the *Gunakarandavyuha* and the *Svayambhu Purana* refer to the Valley as the Nepal Mandala, defining the geography in a mental mapping. This notion of a lived space that is both conceptually and physically constructed is foundational to South Asian religions. This space is, most often, conceived of as a mandala or *yantra*, literally a cosmogram, in which the sacred environment radiates from a central point. In the case of Newar Buddhism, this conception is articulated through the mapping of sacred places for pilgrimage in the natural landscape. And, as a mandalic arrangement, deities appear in sets of four, eight, twenty-four, sixty-four, etc. A common characteristic is that these sites are very often self-arisen power-places, that is, rocks, caves, natural springs, rivers, or mountains. These are most often autochthonous places, later shared by Buddhist and Hindu traditions.

In Newar Buddhism, this construction is continually reified during liturgical practice. Vajracharya priests recite verses of offering, a practice known as the "great gift" (*adya mahadana*), in which the offerer makes the statement of intent (*sankalpa*). The passages enumerate geographic locations in the Valley: "the place of the Great Stupa of Svayambhu, presided by Goddess Guhyeshvari [Secret Goddess] Prajnaparamita [Perfection of Wisdom], in the land presided by Manjushri, in the Nepal Mandala that is in the form of Chakrasamvara Mandala." The ritual text also locates the key pilgrimage sites: Twelve Tirthas (confluences or bathing places); Eight Vaitargas ("Passionless Ones"), dedicated to the eight Bodhisattvas; Four Sacred Mountains; Four Sacred Rivers; and Four Yogini Pithas (Fig. 14). Pilgrimage practice in this context is collectively referred to as *tirtha seva*, "service at the confluence."

Twelve Tirthas

These holy sites at the confluence of rivers are sacred to both Buddhists and Hindus (T1-T12 on map). Both inauspicious (polluting rituals related to birth, death, and purification) and auspicious rituals are performed at these liminal places. As cremation grounds, these *tirthas* are the places where the rituals such as the *sraddha* and *pinda*, offerings for the ancestors, are performed. By dying or being cremated at a *tirtha*, the individual gains merit that will help to improve his or her rebirth in the next life. Stories of Tantric *siddhas* attaining spiritual and magical powers are often associated with the cremation grounds. These dangerous places are the residences of the Tantric goddesses, such as the Eight Mother Goddesses, who provide the practitioner with the *siddhi* powers. Moreover, the cremation ground not only serves as the outer boundary of the mandala, but also becomes the quintessential meditational space of Tantric *siddhas*. On the other hand, ritual purification by bathing in these places gives one merit (*punya*). *Tirthas* therefore symbolize the location of a realm in which both purifying and impure rituals take place. Pilgrimage and ritual offerings at the Twelve Tirthas are specified in religious texts. Each site is specified for certain offerings (flowers, incense, jewels, color, cloth, fruits, gifts, etc.), evils to be abandoned, and states of mind to be cultivated.

The annual bathing pilgrimage is most widely performed in conjunction with the fasting observance (*uposadha vrata*) to Amoghapasha Lokeshvara, the six-armed form of Avalokiteshvara. Each of the Twelve Tirthas is visited once a month in a year-long cycle, starting from the month of Shravan (July-August), beginning with the Punya Tirtha at Gokarna and ending with the Jaya Tirtha at Nakhu in Patan. Each site is associated with a specific form of Avalokiteshvara, and at the end of the year, the devotees have encircled the entire Valley. For those pilgrims not capable of the year's cycle, there is an abbreviated version in which the Twelve *Tirthas* are visited during the month of Karttika (September-October). This cycle starts with the full moon (*Sakimila Punhi*) and ends with the next full moon (*Thila Punhi*). In addition, pilgrimage to the Twelve Tirthas is closely associated with death rituals, in which the sites are visited and *sraddhas* (offerings to the dead) are performed in order to accrue merit for the deceased. These sites are circumambulated in a conceptual clockwise direction, as the actual locations of the sites do not conform precisely to a circular layout. During this pilgrimage worship, the sacred history and significance of each site is recited at each *tirtha*, with the Valley's sanctified landscape thus reaffirmed.

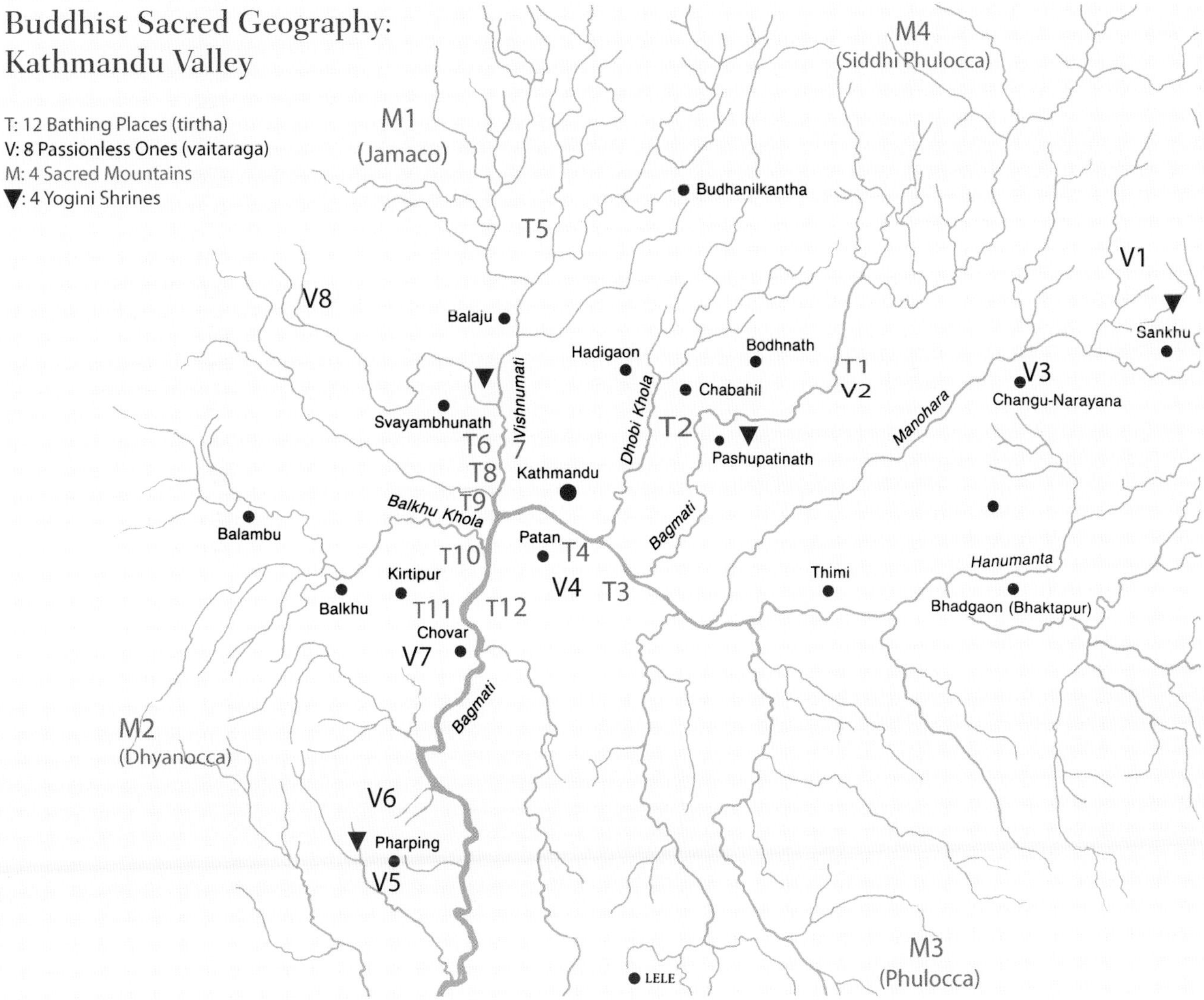

Buddhist Sacred Geography: Kathmandu Valley

T: 12 Bathing Places (tirtha)
V: 8 Passionless Ones (vaitaraga)
M: 4 Sacred Mountains
▼: 4 Yogini Shrines

Fig. 14
Map of Major Pilgrimage circuits around the Kathmandu Valley
Drawing Dina Bangdel

Eight Passionless Ones

Eight sacred sites called Vaitaragas, or "Passionless Ones," are dedicated to the Eight Great Bodhisattvas, the enlightened beings who have mastered their passions and, because of their immense compassion, now choose to manifest themselves at these locations for the benefit of all sentient beings. These sacred sites, however, are temples of the Hindu God Shiva, and the shrine object (*linga*) is identified with one of the Eight Great Bodhisattvas (V1-V8 on map). Thus, these sites function for both Buddhists and Hindus. Pilgrims offer *ex voto* plaques at the successful completion of their pilgrimage cycle. Here, each Bodhisattva is symbolized by one of the eight auspicious forms (*ashtamangala*). Similar to pilgrimage to the Twelve Tirthas, visits to the Eight Vaitaragas is also associated with the observance of Amoghapasha Lokeshvara and is performed throughout six months of the year, beginning in the month of Shravan (July-August) and ending in the winter month of Magha (January-February). Each site has a specific type of offering, text to be recited, *naga*, and benefit associated with it.

SACRED GEOGRAPHY AND YOGINI MANDALA

The esoteric pilgrimage to the Four Yogini Pithas is a tradition open only to the members of the community who have received higher Tantric initiation. In Nepal, *pithas* are invariably associated with goddesses at self-arisen sacred sites. Four important *pithas* are located on mountain tops, where the esoteric goddesses related to the Chakrasamvara Mandala reside: Guhyeshvari, Vajrayogini (Fig. 15), Khadgayogini, and Vidyadhari. These *pithas* are the clearest example of a place of power that is propitiated by both Hindus and Buddhists. For example, Guhyeshvari as an open spring is identified by the Hindus as Guhyakali or Kubjika and attended by high-class Hindu Newar priests (Karmacaryas). This same site is equally significant for the Newar Buddhists, and Guhyeshvari is a Tantric Buddhist *yogini* who is equated with Prajnaparamita, the Mother of All Buddhas and the progenetrix of Newar Buddhism. At Puran

Fig. 15
Prayer flags offered at the Vajrayogini Shrine, Pharping
Photograph Kim Masteller

Fig. 16
Main object of veneration at Guhyeshvari *pitha*, the shrine dedicated to the Secret Goddess.
Photograph Dina Bangdel

Guhyeshvari, the object of veneration is an open spring, embellished with a silver lotus covering, and devotees come daily to venerate the goddess (Fig. 16). These shrines have enjoyed extensive royal patronage, as the goddesses are also associated with state protection, as seen in the Khadgayogini Temple in Shankhu.

Newar Buddhists see the Valley as a living mandala, and this view enables them to interact productively with two-dimensional mandalas as visualization tools. The purification of the Body, Speech, and Mind integral to Tantric meditation traditions is reified during pilgrimage to the sacred sites and by the conceptual circumambulation of the Valley. In short, by identifying the landscape (macrocosm) with the individual (microcosm), purification and mental transformation of the practitioner can occur. By conceptualizing the sacred geography of the Valley during the liturgical process, the priest invokes the sacredness of the Valley before him. By calling forth the sacred pilgrimage sites, he visualizes the Nepal Mandala and performs the mental pilgrimage. Like the devotee who physically participates in the process, the priest purifies his mind through this internalized pilgrimage process.

A painting dated 1822 depicts the Yogini Mandala of the Valley, with Vajravarahi, the female aspect of Chakrasamvara, at the center (Fig. 17). Vajravarahi, identified by her sow's head behind her right ear, holds a skull cup and knife as she dances atop the corpse. Surrounding her are the eight cremation grounds, the ideal places for meditation in the Tantric context. In the corners are four Yoginis of the Valley. At the top left is blue Guhyeshvari, who, among the group of four, is the most important as the divine source of the Newar tradition, according to the *Svayambhu Purana*. At the top right is Vajrayogini from Pharping; at the bottom left is Vidyadhari, or Akasha Dakini, with her legs-up posture; and on the lower right is Khadgayogini at Shankhu. Below are the four male and female donors, whose names are inscribed, suggesting that they had commissioned the painting after the completion of the pilgrimage to the Yogini Pithas. Directly above Vajravarahi is the root teacher Vajrasattva, while the six-angled star mandala of Vajravarahi is directly below her.

Fig. 17
Yogini Mandala of the Kathmandu Valley
Nepal. Inscription date 1822
Opaque watercolor on cotton. 15 x 11 in. (38.1 x 27.9 cm)
Rubin Museum of Art, C2006.66.46
Photograph Rubin Museum of Art

SACRED LANDSCAPE: INNER AND OUTER PILGRIMAGE

Tantric meditation practices imagine a parallel, subtle (*sukshma*) body consisting of energy centers (*chakras*) through which the practitioner purifies the inner self. Pilgrimages are often associated with the visualization practices of the subtle body, in which the practitioner maps the deities of the mandala, in this case the mandala of Chakrasamvara, onto both the natural landscape and the physical body (Fig. 18). Referred to as *pitha seva*, "worship at the seats of the goddess," or *purva seva*, "preparatory service," this pilgrimage is restricted to the Buddhist castes of the Vajracaryas and Shakya, and specifically to those who have received the initiation of Chakrasamvara. In the physical mandala of the Valley, the goddess shrines conceptualize the sacred mandala of Chakrasamvara, with four inner yoginis as the four goddess *pithas* of the Valley: Vajrayogini of Pharping, Khadgayogini of Shankhu, Akasha Yogini of Bijeshvari, and Guheshvari Yogini. Furthermore, the pilgrimage entails visits to twenty-four *pithas* in three concentric rings, corresponding to the Body, Speech, and Mind circles of the Chakrasamvara Mandala (Fig. 19).

In meditational practice, the twenty-four male and female deities of the Body, Speech, and Mind circles correspond to the twenty-four places on the practitioner's body, which protect and prepare him or her for the transformative meditation that is to take place (Fig. 20). In the texts relating to Chakrasamvara the twenty-four deities are seen as universally present in the physical world, residing in *pithas*, literally "seats" across multiple geographic locations (Dawa-Samdup, 26). Texts offer different lists of these twenty-four *pithas* throughout South Asia, but local traditions, such as the one found in Nepal, attribute the sacred sites within the localized landscape. For example, in the Tibetan tradition, there is a pilgrimage route from central Tibet to Zanskar, Kashmir, Kulu, Hazra, and Swat, that pertains to the twenty-four *pithas* presided over by the deities of the Chakrasamvara Mandala. In mapping the sacred landscape, the individual's body is thus identified with Chakrasamvara, and, as the generator of the mandala, manifests the material (phenomenal) world. In this manner, the identity of the microcosm with the macrocosm is both mentally and physically reified, with the twenty-four meditational deities transferred to the physical *body* of the natural landscape.

In Nepal, the twenty-four *pithas* are associated with the Eight Mother Goddesses of the Valley, whose antiquity goes back to the pre-Buddhist roots in the Valley. Located near cremation grounds or the confluences of rivers, these "seats"

Fig. 18
Mandala of Chakrasamvara
Nepal. Inscription date 1822
Opaque watercolor on cloth. 28 x 27 in. (71.1 x 68.6 cm)
Rubin Museum of Art, C2006.66.44
Photograph Rubin Museum of Art

The Kathmandu Valley as Chakrasamvara Mandala

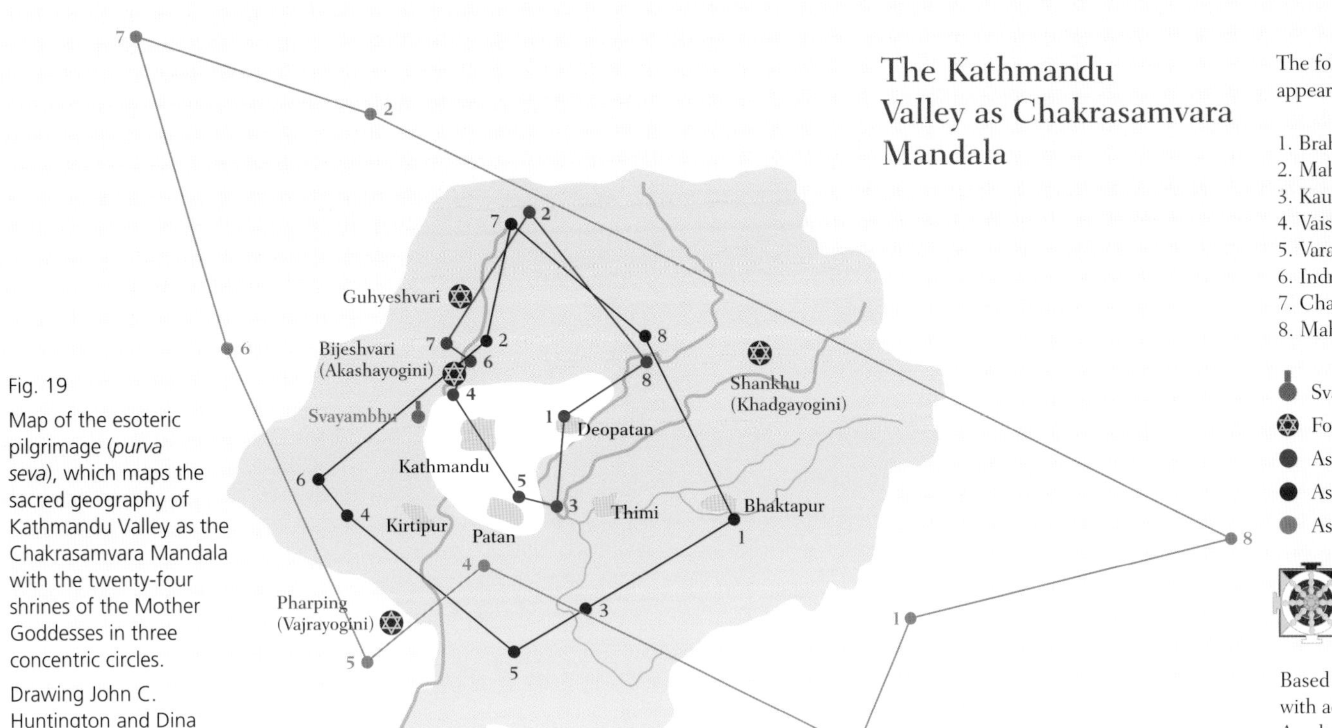

Fig. 19
Map of the esoteric pilgrimage (*purva seva*), which maps the sacred geography of Kathmandu Valley as the Chakrasamvara Mandala with the twenty-four shrines of the Mother Goddesses in three concentric circles.
Drawing John C. Huntington and Dina Bangdel

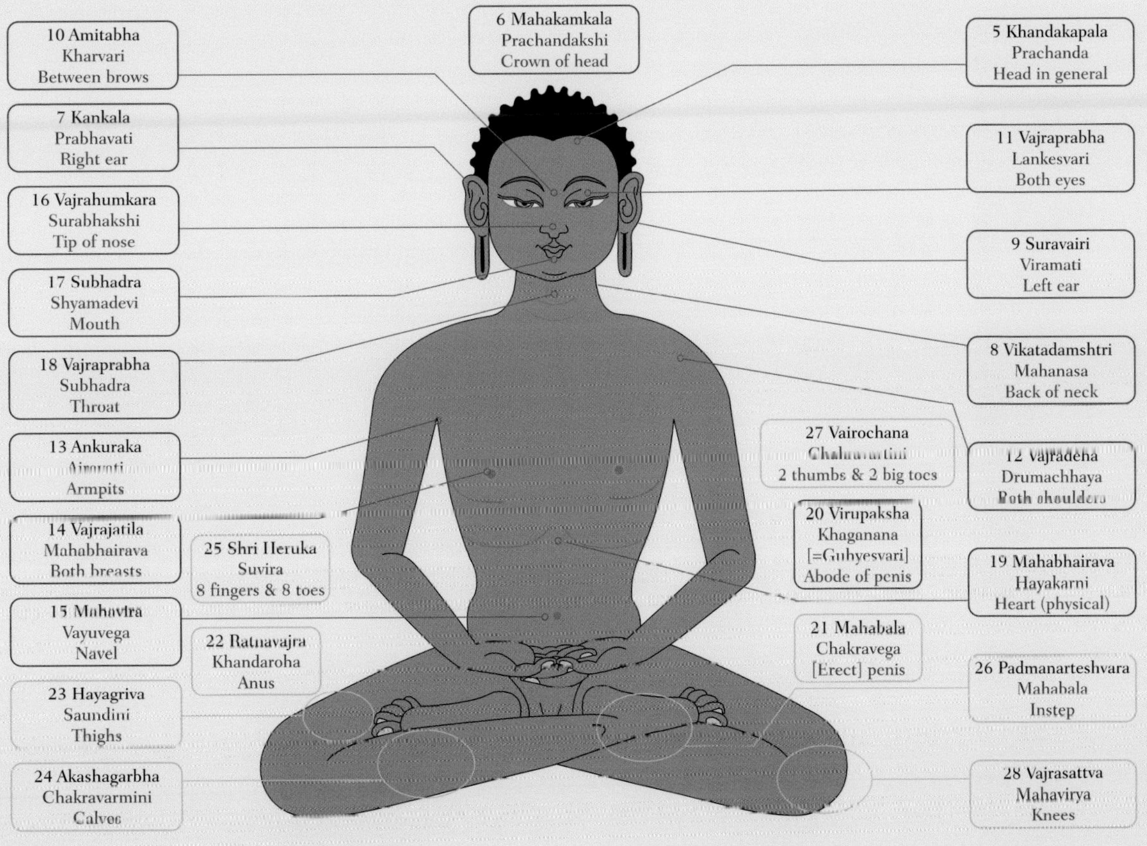

The following Ashtamatrika appear once in each chakra

1. Brahmayani
2. Maheshvari
3. Kaumari
4. Vaishnavi
5. Varahi
6. Indrayani
7. Chamunda
8. Mahalakshmi

- Svayambhu/Shantipur
- Four Yoginis
- Ashtamatrika Pithas of Chitta Chakra
- Ashtamatrika Pithas of Vak Chakra
- Ashtamatrika Pithas of Kaya Cakra

Formalized arrangement of the Chakrasamvara Mandala

Based on Gutschow and Bajracharya, with additions and corrections.
An alternate set of 24 pithas are also in practice.

Citta Chakra
Vak Chakra
Kaya Chakra

10 Amitabha
Kharvari
Between brows

7 Kankala
Prabhavati
Right ear

16 Vajrahumkara
Surabhakshi
Tip of nose

17 Subhadra
Shyamadevi
Mouth

18 Vajraprabha
Subhadra
Throat

13 Ankuraka
Airavati
Armpits

14 Vajrajatila
Mahabhairava
Both breasts

15 Mahavira
Vayuvega
Navel

23 Hayagriva
Saundini
Thighs

24 Akashagarbha
Chakravarmini
Calves

25 Shri Heruka
Suvira
8 fingers & 8 toes

22 Ratnavajra
Khandaroha
Anus

6 Mahakamkala
Prachandakshi
Crown of head

27 Vairochana
Chakravartini
2 thumbs & 2 big toes

20 Virupaksha
Khaganana
[=Guhyesvari]
Abode of penis

21 Mahabala
Chakravega
[Erect] penis

5 Khandakapala
Prachanda
Head in general

11 Vajraprabha
Lankesvari
Both eyes

9 Suravairi
Viramati
Left ear

8 Vikatadamshtri
Mahanasa
Back of neck

12 Vajradeha
Drumachhaya
Both shoulders

19 Mahabhairava
Hayakarni
Heart (physical)

26 Padmanarteshvara
Mahabala
Instep

28 Vajrasattva
Mahavirya
Knees

Fig. 20
Subtle body of the Tantric practitioner, with the mapping of the twenty-four *pithas* (seats).
Drawing John C. Huntington

of the goddesses are considered powerful, yet dangerous. In these shrines, the goddess manifests herself in her primordial nature, as natural rock outcroppings and unhewn stone. To vivify the image, ritual paraphernalia, such the silver crown, flowers, and vermillion powder, are offered (Fig. 21). Hence, her identity is fluid and is ultimately realized through the practitioner's own religious identity. Regardless of sectarian identifications, she is always *ajima*, the primordial "grandmother," a term of respect and affection, reflective of both the antiquity of the site and the great importance of the goddess in Newar tradition. The emphasis on goddess worship for Newar pilgrimage suggests autochthonous practice, going back to the earliest layers of Nepalese religious history.

For the practitioners, the sacrality of the Valley emerges through the presence of these self-arisen *pithas*, and, in this context, their arrangement is not seen as a human construct of spatial ordering, but one that is inherent to the landscape.

Fig. 21
Pitha goddess as natural outcropping of rock. Mhepi Ajima, Kathmandu.
Photograph Dina Bangdel

Encircling the Valley, the twenty-four goddesses not only sanctify and protect the sacred space, but also generate the ordered existence of the urban dwellers. Through the performance of pilgrimage and circumambulation of the Valley, the practitioner physically and in a literal way identifies with the universe. In the more esoteric context of Chakrasamvara meditation, through the awakening of the deities that reside in various parts of the body, the individual visualizes the macrocosm within himself. In this way, mapping of a specific religious identity on a physical landscape becomes an experiential process, reinforced through pilgrimage.

PILGRIMAGE TO THE AVALOKITESHVARA SHRINES

While the pilgrimage of Chakrasamvara is restricted, the most popular form of pilgrimage for the laity is the Karunamaya Vrata, in which the major Avalokiteshvara shrines are visited in a monthly cycle, generally begun on the eighth day of the bright half of Karttik (October-November). Pilgrimage associated with Avalokiteshvara, the Bodhisattva of Compassion, is indeed pan-Buddhist. Tibetan Buddhists understand the Dalai Lama to be the corporeal manifestation of the celestial Bodhisattva, who through his immense compassion desires to be reincarnated until all sentient beings have attained Enlightenment. In China, Mount Putuo is sacred to Avalokiteshvara and considered to be his mountain paradise of Potalaka, while the thirty-three temples at Saikoku in Japan formalize an elaborate pilgrimage circuit (see essay *Saikoku Pilgrimage: Japanese Devotees Search for Kannon*). In Nepal, he is called Karunamaya, "Compassionate One," and his cult is conflated with that of the Hindu Natha Yogi tradition. In that case he is also referred to as Matysendranath, the teacher of the famed Gorakhnath, and the patron saint of the Hindu Shah kings who ruled Nepal until 2009.

Four major shrines are dedicated to Avalokiteshvara. The principal deity is Red Avalokiteshesvara of Bungamati and Patan, known as Bungadyo, "God of Bunga." He resides in the urban landscape of Patan for six months and in the rural beauty of Bungamati for the remaining six months

(Fig. 22). The other three Red Avalokiteshvara are Shrishtikanta Lokesvara of Nala, Anandadi Lokeshvara at Chobar, and the White Lokeshvara of Jana Baha in Kathmandu. Coinciding with the full moon of Vaishakh (March-April) when Shakyamuni attained enlightenment, the chariot festival of Red Karunamaya is one of the most elaborate festivals of the Valley, to which hundreds of pilgrims come to take *darshan* of the clay image. The chariot of Red Karunamaya itself journeys from his home in Bungamati in the outskirts to the city center, ritually circumambulating the medieval kingdom of Patan. Taking *darshan* of Karunamaya for the duration of the month-long festival is considered highly efficacious, and will remove past karmic defilements and help one accrue merit (Fig. 23). The more mundane benefit of venerating Karunamaya is to ensure satisfactory monsoon rains, necessary for rice planting. A pair of rare Newar textiles, inscribed in embroidery with the dates 1899 and 1900, depicts the chariots of Bungadya and Minnath and was most likely commissioned as an offering to Avalokiteshvara (Fig. 24), and used to decorated the *ratha*.

Such types of festival ceremonies also have political implications. Buddhist festivals incorporate the aspects of mapping the sacred landscape through ritual circumambulation. Similar to the Red Karunamaya, White Karumanaya in Kathmandu (Fig. 25), although in a less elaborate celebration, has his annual chariot festival that demarcates the sacred environs of the city proper. Pilgrimage therefore is not merely a pious act to accrue merit. By means of a conscious construction of sacred geography, pilgrimage affirms one's religious identity, in this case a Buddhist identity among a largely Hindu majority. Through large public pilgrimage festivals or individual efforts, visits to holy places in the Valley reinforce the specific experience of *communitas* within this localized community.

A magnificent painting dated to 1850, now at the Rubin Museum of Art, depicts Red Avalokiteshvara along with an illustrated narrative of the life of the Buddha highlighting the key events that are associated with Buddhist pilgrimage sites in India (Fig. 26). At the center is an elaborate multistoried temple, undoubtedly a visual reference to the Karunamaya's temple in Patan, built by Srinivas Malla in 1670s. Enshrined within is the red form of the Bodhisattva of Compassion.

Fig. 22
Shrine image of Red Avalokiteshvara, Bungadya, Nepal.
Photograph Dina Bangdel

He holds his characteristic lotus with his left hand while displaying the gesture of giving with his right hand. Flanking him is the wrathful form of Hayagriva, red in color and identified by the green horse's face protruding from the top of his head. A kneeling figure with his hands in the gesture of respect is at his feet, and is most likely the patron who commissioned the painting. Above this group in the second storey of the temple is yellow Shakyamuni flanked by two of the five Jina Buddhas: Vairochana and Amoghasiddhi. The top tier completes the set of the Jinas, with Ratnasambhava, Amitabha at the center, and Akshobhya.

The top six registers depict the life scenes of Shakyamuni Buddha, with each episode visually separated by a tree, a visual convention popular in Newar painting after the 15th century. Beginning at the top left, the narrative represents his conception by Queen Mayadevi;

Fig. 23
Chariot of Red Avalokiteshvara during Macchindranath Jatra.
Photograph Dina Bangdel

Fig. 24
(left) Chariot festival of Red Avalokiteshvara (Macchendranath), Minnath, and Krishna Temple, Patan.
(right) Two urban scenes with temples and houses showing various architectural types
Dated by inscription: 1900 (left) and 1899 (right)
Newar. Kathmandu Valley, Nepal
Cotton embroidery.
37½ x 14 in. (95.3 x 35.6 cm) (left);
30 x 14 in. (76.2 x 35.6 cm) (right)
Private Collection
Photograph Ian Alsop

Fig. 25
Shrine image of White Avalokiteshvara from Jana Baha
Photograph Dina Bangdel

Fig. 26
Rato Macchendranath Temple
Nepal, dated 1850
Pigments on cloth, 63 x 56½ in. (160 x 143.5 cm)
Rubin Museum of Art, C2006.42.2
Photograph Rubin Museum of Art

his birth at Lumbini with Indra and Brahma in attendance; the declaration of the baby Siddhartha as Universal Ruler (*charkavartin*); the presentation to sage Asita; the marriage followed by the scenes of marital bliss; the Great Departure, with Prince Siddhartha on a horse led by his Chandaka; the Renunciation, at which Prince Siddhartha becomes an ascetic; return of the charioteer to the palace; gift of rice milk by Sujata before his meditation at Bodhgaya; his resolution to attain enlightenment at Bodhgaya; the temptation of Mara's daughters; the victory over Mara as the moment of enlightenment, with the demon Mara's army attacking him; his First Sermon (although Shakyamuni here makes the gesture of enlightenment, rather than of teaching); and finally, a uniquely Newar iconography of the Return to Lumbini, in which Shakyamuni visits his home in Lumbini and is welcomed by the host of gods and celestial beings.

Finally, in the lower five registers are male and female devotees, including children, who have their hands in the gesture of respect (*anjalimudra*) as they participate in an elaborate ritual to Red Avalokiteshvara that is officiated by a Vajracharya priest. Even today, pilgrimages to the four major shrines of Avalokiteshvara often entail fasting and worship, and are generally conducted as large community activities. Among the popular ritual observances to Avalokiteshvara carried out by the laity is the Ashtami Vrata of Amoghapasa Lokeshvara. *Vrata*, literally "religious vow," is especially associated with pilgrimage in the Newar Buddhist context, and involves certain formal liturgical practices such as bathing in the river; fasting or abstinence from food or water, or specific food restrictions; offerings of foods favored by the deity; pilgrimage to a holy site or city; chanting and reciting Buddhist verses; some form of self-denial, penance, or austerity; and participating in priest-led rituals.

In ancient India, the practice of *vrata* was an obligatory ritual performed in order to atone for one's sins. As popular Hindu traditions developed, *vratas* were seen as a means of drawing the attention of the deity to what one desires, in a form of a reciprocal promise on the part of both the devotee and the divine. For the devotee, the promise is the vow of worship; from the deity, some form of service/devotion (*seva*) in response to the desired wish, be it spiritual or mundane. Pilgrimage practices therefore incorporate this intensely personal relationship between the devotee and the holy. Sacred objects, such as paintings and sculptures, are often made as *ex voto* offerings, given in fulfillment of the vow, in gratitude, or as meritorious offerings for blessing. The façade of the Adinath Lokeshvara shrine in Chobar, for example, is covered with votive offerings of a distinctive type: pots, pans, water jugs, and all categories of cooking utensil made of brass or copper.

KATHMANDU VALLEY AND TIBETAN PILGRIMAGE

When the great Buddhist centers in northeastern India were destroyed by the Islamic takeover, pilgrimage travel in India came to a standstill and gradually almost all traces of Buddhism disappeared. As the inheritor of the Sanskrit Buddhist tradition via the Indian teachers fleeing from the destroyed monasteries, Nepal became an interface between India and Tibet after the 13th century. From the earliest layers of Tibetan Buddhist history in the 7th century, the Kathmandu Valley was a place of significance. Later, Indian teachers such as Padmasambhava (c. 8th century), Atisha (c. 11th century), and Vanaratna (c. 15th century) lived and taught in the Valley, thus influencing the development of Tibetan Buddhism. Throughout the history of Tibetan Buddhism, Tibetan teachers made regular pilgrimages to the Kathmandu Valley, especially the Great Stupa at Svayambhu. They also made significant offerings for the restoration and expansion of sacred shrines and, through the centuries, developed a distinctly Tibetan type of pilgrimage. Among its directions, special ritual attention was given to natural topography, especially mountains, lakes, and caves, where great Indian teachers were said to have meditated.

Pilgrimage to distant places, such as India and Nepal, was important for the collection of texts and teachings. For example, in his biography, the 13th-century Tibetan monk Dharmaswamin describes his pilgrimage to the Valley, where he stayed at Svayambhu for eight years. After traveling to India and discovering that monasteries and holy places were in ruins, he sought Nepal where he studied the *mandala-sadhanas* such as the *Guhyasamaja* and *Vajravali* under the

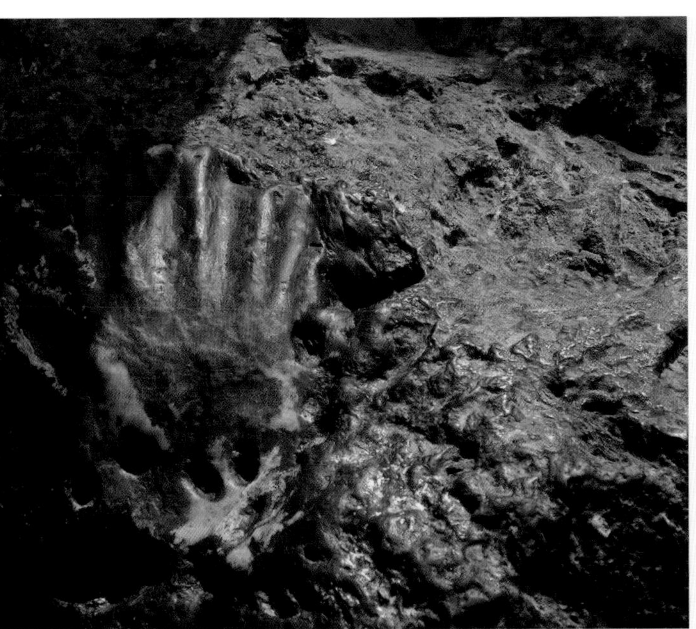

Fig. 27
Rock imprint of Padmasambhava's hand at the Asura Cave in Pharping, Nepal.
Photograph Wonderlane

Fig. 28
Buddha Footprints
Tibet (possibly Mongolian), c. 19th century
Pigments on cloth, 31½ x 21½ in. (80 x 54.6 cm)
Rubin Museum of Art, C2003.37.1
Photograph Rubin Museum of Art

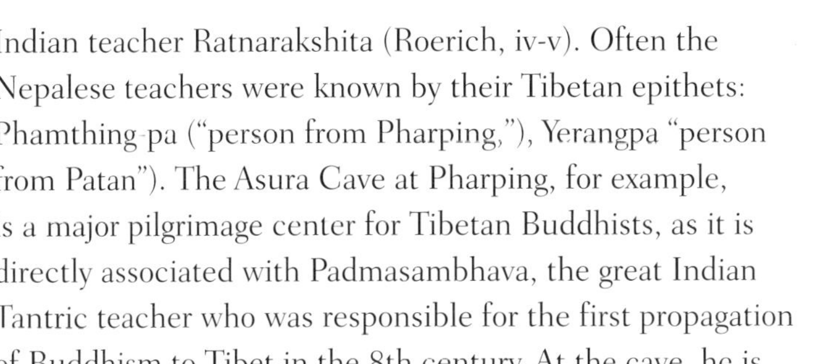

Indian teacher Ratnarakshita (Roerich, iv-v). Often the Nepalese teachers were known by their Tibetan epithets: Phamthing-pa ("person from Pharping,"), Yerangpa "person from Patan"). The Asura Cave at Pharping, for example, is a major pilgrimage center for Tibetan Buddhists, as it is directly associated with Padmasambhava, the great Indian Tantric teacher who was responsible for the first propagation of Buddhism to Tibet in the 8th century. At the cave, he is said to have acquired the meditative technique to subdue the nonhuman supernatural forces in the Valley. At Pharping, his handprint on the rock surface serves as a reminder for the faithful of his eternal presence (Fig. 27). This is the place where he is said to have realized the Vajrakila meditations, especially important to the Nyingma tradition. Pilgrimage souvenirs often included woodblocks or paintings that depict handprints and footprints of great teachers as a form of portable relic (Fig. 28).

Several Tibetan texts enumerate pilgrimages of the holy sites, describing the sacred history and the meritorious benefits of such sites. These accounts present the Great Stupa of Svayambhu as a place of great significance, since Tibetan teachers had time and again since the 11th century reconstructed the *stupa* or offered major gifts. Because the Buddhist homeland of India was out of reach, Tibetans transferred the identity of the Buddhist sites to shrines in Nepal. For example, Kimdol Hill is referred to as the Vulture Peak, a pilgrimage place in India where Shakyamuni is said to have taught the *Prajnaparamita Sutra*. In the mid-13th century, the Sakya abbot, Phagpa, donated fifty ounces of gold to refurbish Svayambhu, and also invited the Newar artist Aniko and eighty others to embellish the Sakya Monastery in Tibet. Funds for another restoration were given in 1750 by the 13th Karmapa Lama (1733-1797). Similarly, Situ Panchen (1700-1774), the renowned Kagyu teacher, stayed at Svayambhu and translated a short version of the *Svayambhu Purana* into Tibetan in 1748. The Tibetan pilgrimage guides of the time assess merit for visiting the Great Stupa as thirteen billion times more efficacious than that gained from visiting any other site in the Valley.

Since 1951, with the exile of thousands of people from Tibet and their resettlement in Nepal, pilgrimage to the

Valley has become even more important. Of key significance is the *stupa* at Boudha, known to the Newars as Khasti Chaitya. Historically a major center of Tibetan pilgrimage since at least the 7th century (Fig. 29), it is the largest *stupa* in the Valley. Pilgrims come to Boudha to have direct encounter with the object of power, as the *stupa* is said to contain the bodily relics of the past Buddha Kashyapa. Tradition narrates that the relics were given to a poor widow, Djazima, and through her meager resources, she built a *stupa* to house them. Because of her meritorious actions, Djazima's three sons are said to have been subsequently reborn as the Tibetan king Tisong Detsen (r. 755-797) and the Indian teachers Shantarakshita and Padmasambhava, who are credited with having established Buddhism in Tibet. Historically, Boudha has continued to be patronized by Tibetans and texts often mention miraculous visions of Tibetan masters that occurred at the Bouda Stupa. Because Boudha was linked to Tibetan trade routes through Shankhu, this was the first entry to the Valley by Tibetan traders, and the monument naturally grew into a major center of pilgrimage for the travelers. Today, pilgrims perform the full-body prostrations around the *stupa* and make special

Fig. 29
Boudha Stupa
Photograph Dina Bangdel

Fig. 30
Painting of Boudha Stupa, Nepal
Tibet, c. 19th century
Opaque watercolor on cotton, 38½ x 23 in. (97.8 x 58.4 cm)
The George Crofts Collection
Royal Ontario Museum, 2005_1597_4
Photograph Royal Ontario Museum

offerings of butter lamps, prayer flags, and whitewash to the *stupa*, especially on the full moons. A 19th-century painting of Boudha from the Royal Ontario Museum wonderfully captures the essence of pilgrimage activities and veneration, with the faithful circumambulating the *stupa* by performing full-body prostrations (Fig. 30).

PILGRIMAGE AND PROTECTION: TARA, SAVIORESS OF PERILS

Like Avalokiteshvara, Tara becomes the patron saint of travelers from an early date in the Indic tradition. As a fully Enlightened Buddha and universal savioress, she provides protection from perils: drowning, fire, disease, captivity, thieves, snakes, wild elephants, lions, and evil spirits. For pilgrims, who are making perilous journeys often for months or even years through the harsh Himalayan climate, Goddess Tara is especially propitiated to protect against these so-called Eight Great Dangers. The earliest known artistic representation dates from the 7th century, when Buddhist pilgrimage to India was flourishing, as indicated by the accounts of the Chinese pilgrim Xuan Zang. Tibetan Buddhist pilgrims often carry a talisman (*tsa tsa*) or mantra in the portable shrines (*gau*) for protection again physical and mental perils. Tibetans who make pilgrimages to the Valley will frequent the shrine of the Talking White Tara, who is believed to have flown to the Valley from her home in Tibet. More recently, the self-arisen Tara at Pharping major has a growing cult following (Fig. 31). Indeed, offerings to Tara are among the most popular expressions in Buddhism, often given in gratitude at the completion of a long pilgrimage, as seen in the example of the painting dedicated to Green Tara, offered by Newar Buddhists living in Tibet (Fig. 32).

See further reading on page 339

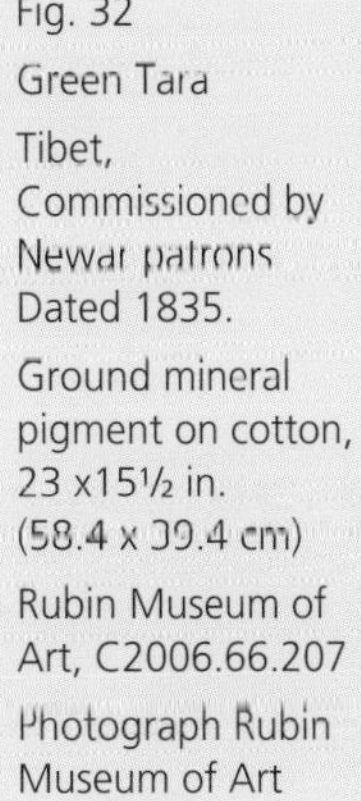

Fig. 31
Self-arisen Tara shrine inside cave at Pharping, Kathmandu Valley
Photograph Wonderlane

Fig. 32
Green Tara
Tibet, Commissioned by Newar patrons
Dated 1835.
Ground mineral pigment on cotton, 23 x15½ in. (58.4 x 39.4 cm)
Rubin Museum of Art, C2006.66.207
Photograph Rubin Museum of Art

Details of Fig. 8

Pilgrimage and Gift-Giving in Newar Buddhism

Kerry Lucinda Brown

Cultivation of nonattachment through selfless giving (*dana*) and merit-making (*punya*) are foundational principles of all three Buddhist traditions – Theravada, Mahayana, and Vajrayana. While each tradition has distinctive philosophical and sectarian emphases, the two practices are universally acknowledged as essential for the individual's path toward personal liberation. Of the six perfections (*paramita*) to be cultivated as a means of self-transformation, the virtue of generosity and alms-giving is foremost, followed by morality, forbearance, diligence, meditation, and wisdom. *Jataka* stories recounting the Buddha's past lives, as well as the events of his last rebirth as Siddhartha, describe the merits gained by such altruistic actions. For example, it was a gift of rice milk by the young woman, Sujata, just before the Buddha's enlightenment, which gave him the strength necessary to defeat the forces of Mara and attain enlightenment beneath the Bodhi Tree. Moreover, after the enlightenment, the offerings of food from two merchants provided the Buddha with sustenance to begin his career as a teacher. In return for their generosity, the merchants became the first converts to Buddhism and were given relics to bring back to their homeland. This reciprocity of gift exchange establishes *dana* as an ideal religious action between the lay Buddhists and monastics. Gifts made of pure faith and devotion generate immense merit. The ultimate effect of this action is to humble the donor and to align his/her moral compass with virtue rooted in the Buddhist teachings. Offerings of food, clothing, monetary support, and even land gifted to monastic communities are common in Buddhist texts and contemporary practice. In return, the lay community receives teachings, blessings, and merit that support them on their own journey to enlightenment. Such reciprocal gift exchanges embody the Buddhist pilgrimage experience, since the offering of *dana* at sacred sites to the monastic community, the poor, or infirm accrues even more merit.

The Buddhist model of gift exchange is especially associated with Dipankara Buddha, the first in the series of historical (*manushi*) Buddhas. In an important narrative of Shakyamuni's previous life, the Buddha-to-be was born a young Brahmin named Megha. Upon meeting Dipankara, Megha offered him a simple gift of flowers and spread his hair and cloak over a muddy road so that the Buddha would not dirty his feet. Witnessing such an act of pure faith (*sraddha*), Dipankara predicted that this young Brahmin would one day attain enlightenment in a future rebirth and be called Shakyamuni Buddha. For Buddhists, this event serves as a paradigm for their own progress toward enlightenment, and artistic representations of this narrative appear in India as early as the 2nd century CE. In Nepal,

the cult of Dipankara continues to be actively practiced as the paradigmatic reenactment of gift-giving (*dana*), as evidenced by the presence of Dipankara images in the major monasteries of the Kathmandu Valley (Fig. 1).

The Dipankara (Dipankha) *yatra*, "the journey of Dipankara," is an important pilgrimage related to this practice. It commemorates the visit of Dipankara to the Valley, when he taught the Dharma, ultimately leading to the acceptance of Buddhism among the indigenous Newar community. This pilgrimage only occurs at the moment when five astrological signs align, making it a highly auspicious event (Allen, 133-37). Positive actions at this time are multiplied, making any act of gift-giving a powerful spiritual one. During the event, which takes between twenty-four and thirty-six hours, participants walk to the shrines of the gods and goddesses of importance to the Newar Buddhist community. The pilgrims carry with them offerings for all those they will visit during the journey, ultimately making a long and circuitous path across the Valley (Fig. 2). Some believe that the path taken by the pilgrims is the same as that taken by Dipankara when he came to the Valley to spread the Dharma, but there are other explanations of the route (Allen, 134). Popular belief sees this pilgrimage as the same route as that taken by Shakyamuni Buddha in his previous rebirth as a blue-horned ox who wandered across the Valley in search of Dipankara to receive his teachings. The sculpture of the blue-horned ox at Nag Baha in Patan is said to have miraculously appeared from the bones of the dead animal; hence the pilgrimage begins and ends at this location (Fig. 3). The most recent Dipankara pilgrimage occurred on October 17, 2005, after a thirty-eight-year hiatus. Conservative estimates suggest that more than 150,000 people participated in the pilgrimage, traveling

Fig. 1
Dipankara Buddha
Nepal, c. 17th-18th century
Patan Museum
Photograph Dina Bangdel

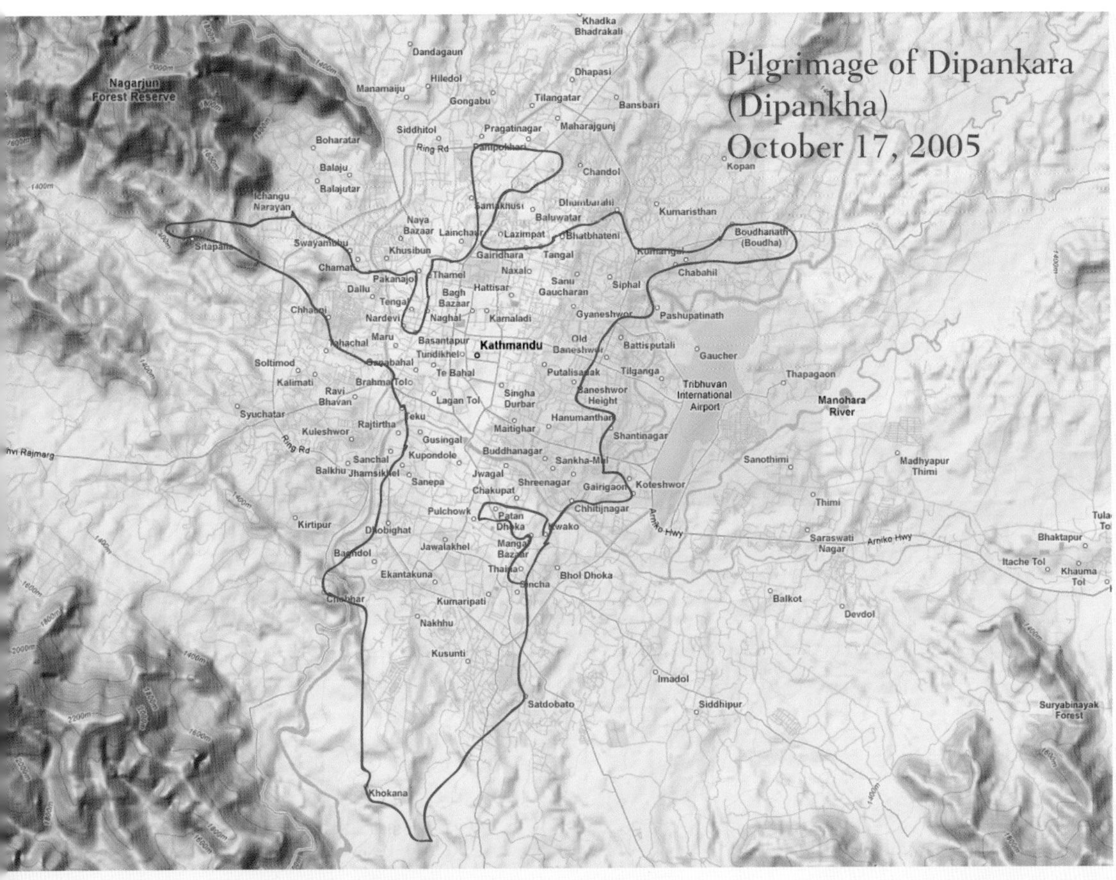

Fig. 2

Map of the pilgrimage route during the Dipankha Yatra "Journey of Dipankara" in 2005

Drawing Dina Bangdel

Fig. 3

Offerings being made to Dipankara Buddha by the lay community during the Samyak festival of Patan. 2008

Photograph Kerry Lucinda Brown

Fig. 4

Pilgrims during the twenty-four-hour pilgrimage around the Valley during Dipankha Yatra. 2005

Photograph Sanu Bajracharya

Fig. 5

Shakyamuni Buddha in his previous rebirth as a blue-horned ox, Nag Baha. Patan

Photograph Sanu Bajracharya

Fig. 6

Devotees taking *darshan* of Dipankara images during Kathmandu Samyak, 2003

Photograph Dina Bangdel

Fig. 7

Red-faced Dipankara Buddha walking in procession through Kathmandu with the "dancing" *yasti* pole next to him.

Kathmandu, Nepal. 2005

Photograph Kerry Lucinda Brown

thirty-seven miles and visiting approximately 140 shrines and monasteries (Fig. 4). The event serves as a powerful statement of the strength of the Newar Buddhist community, affirmed through a long history of elaborate festivals, localized pilgrimages, and daily devotional acts.

Yet another example of the Newar utilization of pilgrimage is that during the alms-giving festival known as Samyak Mahadana "the Great Gift-Giving festival" (Fig. 5). During the Samyak festival, Dipankara Buddha images are ceremoniously brought in procession from their monasteries to the city center. As the lay Buddhist community takes *darshan* of the Buddhas, the members of each monastery receive alms of grain, food, or money as the ultimate act of *dana* and merit-making (Fig. 6). Each of the three major cities of the Valley – Kathmandu, Patan, and Bhaktapur – has specific religious organizations (*guthi*) in charge of organizing Samyak. However, due to the organizational complexity and financial responsibility of the festival for areas involved, Samyak occurs in different yearly intervals. Bhaktapur, the smallest of the cities, celebrates Samyak every year. Patan organizes this festival in a grand manner every four years, while Kathmandu observes it in a twelve-year cycle. In Patan and Kathmandu, more than one hundred images of Dipankara are paraded around the city, with each image representative of a specific monastery. The festival images, some more than six feet tall and weighing more than eighty pounds, consist of large gilt copper repousée heads and hands attached to a wooden body armature draped in silk robes (Fig. 7). Once assembled, these images travel in procession to the event site, aided by a man who climbs inside the wooden body to assume the legs of the Buddha. For the next day, the entire community comes to offer the "great gift" (*mahadana*) to the Dipankara Buddhas. Through their selfless acts of generosity, they hope for a prediction of their future enlightenment.

A Nepalese painting of Dipankara from the Rubin Museum of Art highlights the significance of the gift-giving ceremony at the Samyak festival (Fig. 8). Dated to 1853, the painting was commissioned by a Buddhist merchant, Bhaju Ratnasingha Tuladhar, and his family of Jadhunche in Ashokamandapasthan, located in Kathmandu, and documents the family's participation in the Kathmandu Samyak. The central figure is Buddha Dipankara, standing on a lion throne flanked by two monks carrying staffs and bowls, with the donor figures located below the central triad. Above the central image is the Great Stupa of Svayambhu, where a small figure of Dipankara, shown in profile, is teaching at the site. The narrative moves clockwise with a group of devotees welcoming the Buddha into the city gates in a ritual typical of Newars, called *lasakusa*. Dipankara Buddha wears elaborate robes, jewelry, and a crown, displaying the hand gestures (*mudras*) characteristic of Newar iconographic conventions. His right hand presents the fear-not gesture (*abhaya-mudra*) while his left displays the gift-giving gesture (*varada-mudra*), alluding to his role in Newar Buddhism as the bestower of fortuitous rebirths and the predictor of enlightenment (Brown, 33-7). Framing the central figure to the left, right, and below are rows of small houses, where members of the monastic community are accepting offerings from the lay community. The crowns and long garments worn by the standing figures in each building indicate their monastic status, representing the Vajracharya priests. These events illustrate the main activity of gift-giving as the central focus of Dipankara veneration, such as Samyak and Pancadana "Five Gifts [of Grain]." For some, the immediate aspirations for their gifts may be mundane, but ultimately these actions will contribute to improved physical and mental states along the path to enlightenment.

The movement of images of the gods and goddesses throughout Kathmandu during the Samyak transforms mundane space into a localized sacred landscape. Rituals take place in the fields below the Great Svayambhu Stupa on the western edge of the Valley. As seen in the painting, performers play music announcing the Buddha's arrival, celestial *apsaras* carry garlands decorating the space, and Buddhas and Bodhisattvas appear in the sky above. Kathmandu is transformed into a sacred realm where all participants can see Dipankara, make offerings to him, and reaffirm their Buddhist vows. The clockwise action of the painting around the central Buddha image suggests that while the participants make offerings to the monastic community they are also circumambulating Dipankara in the process. During the days that the Samyak festival is celebrated in

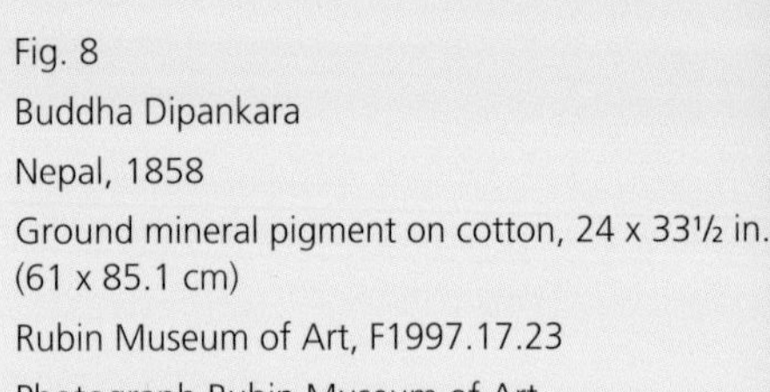

Fig. 8
Buddha Dipankara
Nepal, 1858
Ground mineral pigment on cotton, 24 x 33½ in. (61 x 85.1 cm)
Rubin Museum of Art, F1997.17.23
Photograph Rubin Museum of Art

Fig. 9
Samyak festival in Kathmandu. Nepal, 2005
Photograph Kerry Lucinda Brown

Kathmandu, the mundane spaces of daily life are transformed into a sacred realm where individuals can engage with the Buddhas and other assorted deities in attendance. In this painting, the central Dipankara figure accepts the offerings of the faithful while providing them with a promise of enlightenment in return.

Even during contemporary celebrations of the Samyak festival in Kathmandu, it is the reenactment of seeing Dipankara and offering him gifts that is the dominant focus of the festival. In Kathmandu, flags and banners line the streets; musicians play drums, horns, and cymbals while singing songs welcoming the Buddhas. Once all the images arrive, they ceremoniously walk in procession through town to the fields below the great Svayambhu Stupa (Fig. 9). Here, the images, along with the members of the monasteries they are from, receive a wide variety of offerings from the Buddhist communities. Thus, through such public events of pilgrimage and gift-giving, the Newar community expresses a shared sense of *communitas* that is vital to their Buddhist faith and identity.

See further reading on page 339

Details of Fig. 5

Pilgrimage in Tibet

Toni Huber

INTRODUCTION

The main historical religions of Tibet, namely Tibetan Buddhism and Bön, both exhibit features that are similar to those of many organized religions elsewhere throughout the world. Thus, to many outsiders who visit Tibet or the high Himalaya, the presence of pilgrims worshipping at relic shrines and temples or travelling to holy mountains may be something quite familiar, perhaps a point of recognition between cultures. But superficial similarities often mask quite profound cultural differences, and we might all too easily misinterpret Tibetan religious life in terms of European meanings and categories.

Compared with other dimensions of religious life in Tibet, pilgrimages are in fact quite easy to observe and even participate in. Pilgrimage is one of the more common public religious activities in Tibetan societies, and one that can be undertaken at any time by worshippers, either as individuals or in groups. It is also an egalitarian practice. Pilgrimage is open to all worshippers regardless of their gender, age, or social status, and it does not require the mediation of any religious specialists, such as monks or priests. Its only real requirements from a Tibetan point of view are that the pilgrim be able-bodied enough to undertake the ritual journey involved and possess the appropriate motivation for doing so. Both the nonspecialist character and the open status of pilgrimage in Tibet may be partial explanations for its popularity as a ritual among Tibetans.

TIBETAN CONCEPTS OF PILGRIMAGE

We use the word "pilgrimage" in Western languages to translate two closely related Tibetan terms, *nékor* (*gnas skor*) and *néjel* (*gnas mjal*). These terms can be more literally translated as "going around (*skor*) a *né*" and "meeting/direct encounter with (*mjal*) a *né*." Thus, for Tibetans a pilgrimage is conceived of as the circumambulation of a "holy place" or *né* (*gnas*), and perhaps even as a circular journey there and back, as well as the need to have some direct and personal contact with the object of pilgrimage at the destination. The term *né* simply means an "abode" or the place where something dwells or exists. As the object of pilgrimage or "holy place," *né* specifically refers to the location or residence of a Buddha or an enlightened being, or one of the other powerful nonhuman beings in the Tibetan pantheon or cosmos. The concepts of both circumambulation and direct encounter conveyed in *nékor* and *néjel* were originally derived from the ancient Indian ritual models of circumambulation (*pradakshina*) and sacred viewing (*darshana*). We know that before the Tibetans converted to Buddhism, they had no ritual method equivalent to pilgrimage. Thus, pilgrimage was originally a foreign ritual that was adopted by the Tibetans,

and one that they later developed in their own specific ways.

According to the formal teachings of both Buddhism and Bön, a person who goes on pilgrimage to a holy place with pure motivation or faith will earn religious merit. Accumulation of this merit can increase the moral or "karmic" status of the pilgrim and hence contribute to the person's attainment of salvational goals: improved rebirths in the next life, and, ultimately, enlightenment and a complete end to rebirth and the suffering it inevitably entails. However, this classical theory is not only abstract, but also represents a rather distant horizon for the attainment of religious benefits or goals. Not surprisingly, Tibetans also explain their ritual life as pilgrims in much more tangible and embodied terms.

Any Tibetan "holy place" or *né* is always defined as the "abode" or place where a Buddha or other powerful beings exist in the world. The presence of such enlightened or powerful beings is associated with a vital "sacred power" or "blessing" known as *chinlab* (*byin rlabs*). *Chinlab* is thought of as a positive transformational power, one that can morally and physically improve those who come into contact with it. It is believed to be physically present in the environment of a holy place, and therefore available for pilgrims to make contact with and even harvest in various ways.

Tibetans also recognize that the human body is the primary vehicle for enacting any ritual. Thus, the pilgrim's body is the actual site where the transformative possibilities of ritual actions such as pilgrimage are both worked out and accumulated. A human being is thought of as having three psycho-physical dimensions: those of body, speech, and mind. Due to our negative actions (*karma*) in the world, both in this present life and in our former rebirths, we accumulate gross and subtle impurities in all three of our psycho-physical dimensions. These accumulated impurities are often imagined to be like shadows or stains, or even pollution, and are recognized as a kind of embodied moral status. They hinder us from developing the refined types of behavior and consciousness which are necessary for attainment of the salvational goals of Buddhism or Bön. Different types of rituals are believed to help cleanse or remove these impurities in different dimensions of the person. Tibetans classify pilgrimage as a ritual that is beneficial for purifying the body dimension. Thus, a common expression states, "Impurities of the body will be cleansed by way of prostration and circumambulation (*lus kyi sgrib pa sbyong phyir phyag 'tshal dang skor ba*)." When combined with pure intentions and motivation, it is the actual ritual work of walking around a holy place, and bowing down in prostration toward it, that generates the religious benefits for the pilgrim.

HOLY PLACES, HOLY ICONS, AND HOLY PERSONS

According to the ideas we have just presented, the range of possible holy places for Tibetan pilgrims is very great indeed. Some manifestations of the Buddha or enlightened being are believed to be present in natural topographical features, for example, at certain sacred mountains or *néri* (*gnas ri*) located in Tibet and the Himalayas. Thus, they are classified as *né* and are visited by pilgrims who circumambulate them. The mountain in western Tibet that Tibetans call Kang Tisé, but which is better

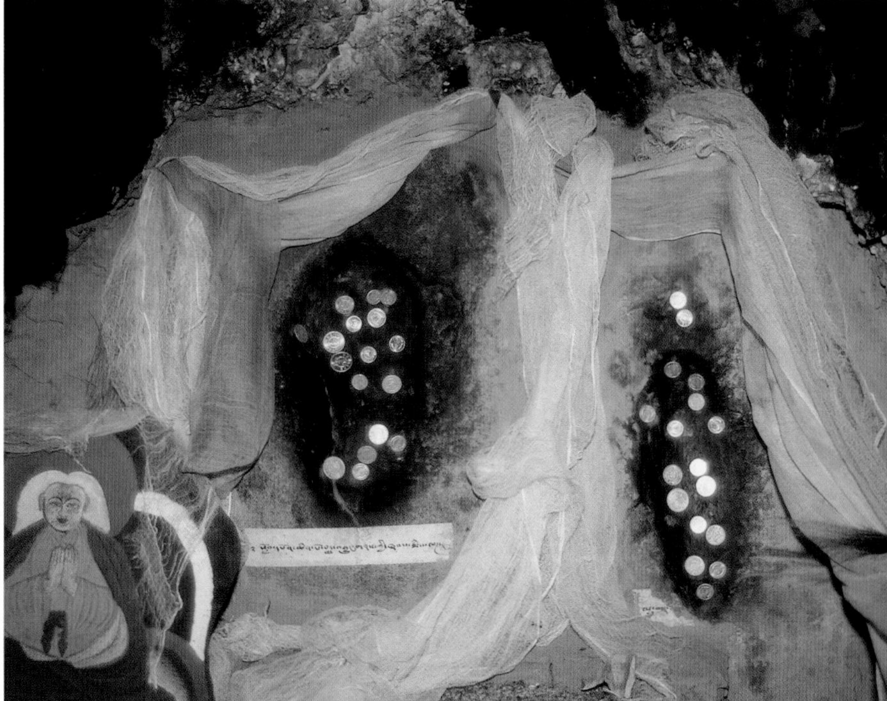

Fig. 1
Saint's footprints inside cave in Yerpa, northeast of Lhasa.
Photograph Toni Huber

known outside Tibet as Mount Kailash, is a famous example of a *néri* (see essay *Origins and History of Pilgrimage for Christians, Muslims, and Buddhists,* Fig. 10). It is considered the abode of a wrathful Heruka form of the Buddha, named Chakrasamvara, and his consort Varjavarahi, and it is a very popular destination among Tibetan pilgrims. Certain other natural features, such as lakes and caves, or even whole landscapes in Tibet, may also be valued in the same way, and thus become places of pilgrimage (see essay *Pilgrimage Traditions in Nepal*). Most natural pilgrimage destinations are full of additional local sites of ritual importance, including the meditation places of famous saints; foot or body imprints or other miraculous marks left behind upon rocks by powerful religious individuals or deities; and local spring waters and herbs or even deposits of earth all believed to have healing properties (Fig. 1). Most dimensions of the natural environment at a *né* are believed to offer the pilgrim opportunities to come into contact with and harvest its sacred power.

Any iconographical representations (*rten*), such as statues, paintings (both cloth scrolls and wall murals), portable shrines, or even the temples within which such items are housed, may also be defined as *né* or objects of pilgrimage (Fig. 2). This is because most types of religious icons in Tibet are defined as being representations of the body, speech, and mind of the Buddha. This is not merely a symbolic category for Tibetans; it also implies the presence of the vital "sacred power" or *chinlab* which is associated with any *né* or holy place. Icons can be formally consecrated by way of rituals known as *rabné* (*rab gnas*), during which the enlightened being represented by a statue or painting is invoked and invited to take up residence – even if only temporarily – in the object (Fig. 3). This transforms the icon into a *né* and a source of *chinlab*, and thus a possible object of pilgrimage.

Furthermore, particular statues or paintings in Tibetan

Fig. 2
Shrine image of Tibet's great protectress Palden Lhamo in Palalubu cave shrine at the base of Chagpori Hill in Lhasa, Tibet.
Photograph Toni Huber

Fig. 3
Chorten (relic stupa)
Tibet, c. 12th century
Copper alloy, $4^{7}/_{8}$ x $2^{3}/_{8}$ in. (12.4 x 6 cm)
Dr. Albert L. Shelton Collection, purchase 1920
Newark Museum, 20.391
Photograph Newark Museum

Fig. 4
Pilgrims performing the full-body prostration outside the Jokhang Temple. Lhasa.
Photograph Toni Huber

Fig. 5
Shrine image of Jowo Shakyamuni at the Jokhang, 7th century with later restorations.
Photograph Toni Neubauer

temples are often famous among pilgrims as a result of amazing stories or legends associated with them. Their different reputations for once having miraculously talked or gestured to visiting pilgrims, for being able to answer a pilgrim's questions, or even for having manifested by themselves, can make them very special objects of pilgrimage. Other Tibetan icons can have their status enhanced to that of pilgrimage destinations due to their mythical or historical importance. The Jokhang temple situated in the centre of old Lhasa is the most famous Buddhist shrine on the entire Tibetan plateau, and one of the Tibetans' most important places of pilgrimage (Fig. 4). At its heart resides the Jowo Rinpoche, which is a large image of the Buddha Shakyamuni at age twelve, and the most important single religious icon in Tibet today (Fig. 5). As every pilgrim visiting the Jokhang knows, the Jowo's great reputation derives partly from its alleged history, which includes its manufacture by a divine artist during the Buddha's lifetime in India, then its later dispatch to China by an Indian monarch, and its eventual arrival in Lhasa with a Chinese princess destined to marry Tibet's great founding ruler and culture hero, Emperor Songtsen Gampo. Moreover, the Jowo's history presents it as a marvelous symbol of endurance, which includes miraculously surviving numerous attempts at its destruction and removal, but most important of all for modern Tibetans, its survival, untouched, throughout the Cultural Revolution when the Jokhang served as a military barracks and a slaughterhouse, and when many other temples and their contents were razed to the ground in Tibet.

In wealthy modern societies, we tend to value Tibetan religious icons for their antiquity and hence rarity, but also especially for their aesthetic qualities. For Tibetan pilgrims, these are not at all important criteria by which to judge the value of an icon as an object of pilgrimage. Twenty years ago, I visited the temple of Trandruk in the Yarlung Valley of Central Tibet, together with a large group of Tibetan pilgrims. At the time, Trandruk housed what I considered to be a valuable collection of old and very beautiful painted and sculptured icons. However, the single-most popular image among the pilgrims – particularly the women – was a brand-new, rather unattractive statue of Lonpo Gar (Fig. 6), the minister-cum-ambassador of the Emperor Songtsen Gampo. This new icon had been recently crafted in Lhasa from clay and wood, and finished off with bright acrylic paints by modern artists. Lonpo Gar is well known to Tibetans for his role in obtaining brides for the emperor, a task entailing many adventurous travels, and, according to popular belief, for fathering a child by one of the brides-to-be during a long journey back to Lhasa. He is thus popularly associated with both marriage and fertility, and many pilgrims offered items of personal jewelry to the new image of Lonpo Gar at Tandruk, in the hope of gaining a spouse or a child.

Finally, a *né* or holy place can also be a living or dead human being. The Dalai Lama and other lamas who have a status known as "emanation body" or *tulku* (*sprul sku*) are believed to be the living, incarnate manifestations of enlightened beings, such as Buddhas and Bodhisattvas. Their human bodies are thus *né*, the abodes of enlightenment, and Tibetan pilgrims regard and treat them in exactly the same

Fig. 6
Modern statue of Lonpo Gar with pilgrims' offerings, Tandruk.
Photograph Toni Huber

Fig. 7
Famous *tulku* blessing crowds of pilgrims in Amdo, Eastern Tibet.
Photograph Toni Huber

Fig. 8
Relics of Tsongkhapa used to bless pilgrims, Ganden Monastery.
Photograph Toni Huber

ritual manner as they would any other object of pilgrimage. When pilgrims visit a famous *tulku* lama, for example, in addition to actually seeing him in person, the least they hope for is to gain a physical blessing from him by being touched upon the head or receiving a ceremonial scarf from his hands (see essay *Journey of the Heart: Prostrating on the Roof of the World*), both of which serve to transmit his sacred power or *chinlab* to the pilgrim (Fig. 7). Making visits to renowned lamas is thus a very popular form of pilgrimage in Tibetan communities all over the world.

Just as Tibetans believe that lamas who are incarnations of enlightened beings possess and transmit sacred power or *chinlab* during life, they believe that the same is also true during death. It is especially true of the mummified bodies and other physical relics of those *tulkus* and famous meditators who have passed away and left their human remains behind. The preserved corpses and other bodily relics of such persons are equally potent sources of *chinlab*, and once they are entombed within special funerary shrines or reliquaries (*gdung rten*), these too become a very common and important object of pilgrimage for Tibetans. Such beliefs are often reinforced for visiting pilgrims by the guides and caretakers at these shrines. During the mid-1980s, I visited the monastery and pilgrimage site of Ganden in Central Tibet. The entire Ganden Monastery and its most treasured sacred object, a golden tomb known as Tongwa Donden (or "Meaningful to Behold") containing the corpse of Tsongkhapa (1357-1419), the great medieval synthesizer of Buddhist teachings in Tibet, had all been destroyed during the Cultural Revolution. Reconstruction of the Tongwa Donden had recently been completed when I visited, and pilgrims were informed by the shrine-keepers that it contained a fragment of Tsongkhapa's skull that had been saved from the destruction of the site during the 1960s. The master's begging bowl, ritual scepter (*vajra*), and tea cup were also on display (Fig. 8), and pilgrims were being blessed with these objects by having them touched to the crowns of their heads. Pilgrims at Ganden were

Fig. 9
Portable relic shrine (*gau*)
Tibet, c. late 19th century
Copper alloy, glass. 6 x 6 x 2½ in. (15.2 x 15.2 x 6.4 cm)
Dr. Albert L. Shelton Collection, purchase 1920
Newark Museum, 20.405A,B
Photograph Newark Museum

also told an edifying story: when the original tomb had been smashed open during the Cultural Revolution, the vandals had been shocked to discover that the corpse of Tsongkhapa had continued to grow its hair and fingernails over the centuries, and that these were extremely long and filled the inside of the tomb. The saint's vital power was clearly believed to have lived on long after his apparent human demise. One of Tsongkhapa's teeth was also kept next to the Tongwa Donden in a small silver reliquary. Impressions of this tooth were stamped into balls of dough, and pilgrims were very anxious to obtain one of these blessed talismans and carry it off. Such portable contact relics that are collected by pilgrims at holy places are frequently deposited in small amulet-boxes (*ga'u*) (Fig. 9), to be worn around the neck or over the shoulder so that their sacred contents can continually protect the wearer from harm, illness, or bad luck, and even help ensure them a better passage to the next life when they die.

RITUAL DIMENSIONS OF PILGRIMAGE

Pilgrimage in Tibetan societies can be usefully considered as a form of asceticism that can be undertaken by all lay persons. Monks and nuns in Tibet are of course already engaged in asceticism by virtue of their special lifestyles, which ideally demand quite high degrees of self-discipline and abstention. The great majority of pilgrimage journeys in Tibet also demand certain degrees of self-discipline and abstention for the ordinary lay persons who become pilgrims. For example, pilgrims temporarily give up the comfort and security of their own homes when setting out on a pilgrimage. Pilgrimages are frequently undertaken on foot, which can entail further hardship for many. Even if modern pilgrims travel to a particular holy place by bus or truck, they will eventually abandon the vehicles and have to walk around the particular holy mountain, lake, cave complex, monastic centre, or even holy city that is their goal. Such journeys can last from several hours to several weeks, depending upon the location. Many pilgrims amplify the intensity of their personal asceticism while on pilgrimage by undertaking simple and temporary vows. These vows commonly include abstention from eating meat and drinking alcohol, strictly avoiding killing anything, or abstention from sexual relations throughout the course of a pilgrimage. All such additional forms of morally positive self-disciple are thought to increase the amount of religious merit one can accumulate from the act of pilgrimage.

There are more extreme ritual dimensions of asceticism possible during Tibetan pilgrimage, all of which also aim at increasing the religious benefits of the practice. A very common feature of Tibetan religious worship in general is a concern with the frequency of any ritual act (Fig. 10). This is a kind of "ritual arithmetic," in which Tibetans keep a careful count of the number of times they perform prostrations, chant prayers or ritual formulas, or circumambulate a holy place (Fig. 11). During pilgrimages, this is often associated with simple vows, such as a pilgrim promising him or herself, "I will not go home until I have circumambulated this holy place twelve times!" Not only does a higher number of circumambulations of a holy place yield more religious benefit, but the fulfillment of such vows is considered to be

a strong demonstration of pure motivation by the pilgrim. Without such motivation, ritual action is considered to be purely mechanical and of no particular religious value. Due to the importance of the actual number of times a ritual is performed, pilgrims can often physically record the frequency of pilgrimages. At the Bön holy mountain of Chadur, in the Amdo region of eastern Tibet, some pilgrims possess wooden tally-sticks (*khram shing*), upon which each circumambulation they perform around the mountain is marked by a notch or cut (Fig. 12). Many temple complexes in Tibet, such as the monastery of the Panchen Lamas at Tashilhunpo, are surrounded completely within high walls, and the circumambulation path for pilgrims runs right around the outside of these walls (Fig. 13). Many times when I have visited Tashilhunpo to observe the pilgrimages there, I have noticed pilgrims scratching groups of parallel lines upon the whitewashed mud walls of the temple enclosure. This is the pilgrims' simple way of keeping an accurate count of the number of circuits they have performed around the whole temple enclosure.

A more intensive method of increasing the ascetic value of a pilgrimage is to combine the normal journey on foot toward and around a holy place with the performance of full-length bodily prostrations (see essay *Journey of the Heart: Prostrating on the Roof of the World*). In this method, the standing pilgrim makes a ritual salute with both hands together and then stretches his or her body out full length on the path in front, with arms fully extended. The pilgrim marks the furthest point on the ground reached by his hands, and rising once again, steps forward to that point and begins the next prostration. Thus, the pilgrims measure out the length of the entire pilgrimage circuit with their bodies. This method greatly increases the amount of time required to perform pilgrimages. The completion of the pilgrimage circuit around the Bön holy mountain of Chadur in Amdo usually requires about eight hours walking by able-bodied pilgrims. Prostrating pilgrims I met on the Chadur circuit during 1996 told me it would take them from seven to nine days' travel to complete the same circuit.

Fig. 10
Pilgrim turning the *mani* wheels with Avalokiteshvara's six-syllabled mantra, *Om Mani Padme Hum*. The *mala* of 108 beads assists practitioners in keeping count of mantra recitations and circumambulations of the inner *kora* at the Jokhang Temple.
Photograph Toni Neubauer

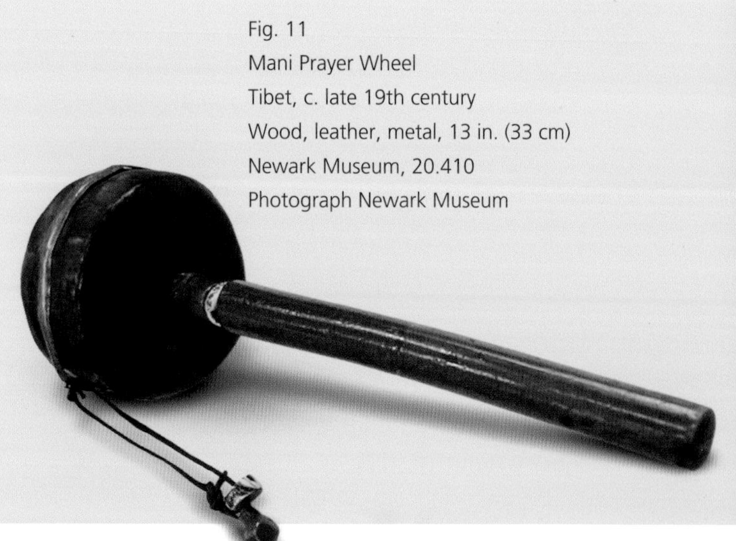

Fig. 11
Mani Prayer Wheel
Tibet, c. late 19th century
Wood, leather, metal, 13 in. (33 cm)
Newark Museum, 20.410
Photograph Newark Museum

Some prostration pilgrimages in Tibet are undertaken across truly vast distances. In the Kham region of eastern Tibet during 1999, I met a party of four young male pilgrims in their late teens or early twenties travelling along a main road. They were making a pilgrimage to the holy city of Lhasa, a distance of some 1000 km from their home place, and they were prostrating the entire way. One member of the group pulled a small handcart containing their possessions and supplies, while the other three spent up to twelve hours per day prostrating gradually toward their goal. These types of pilgrims typically wear heavy, full-length aprons and thickly padded gloves to protect themselves as they slide out along the ground with each new prostration (Fig. 14). The pilgrims from Kham hoped to reach Lhasa after about six months, and when finished there they planned to turn around and prostrate all the way back home once again, in order to complete a grand ritual circuit. The young men had invested all their personal savings in this trip, and received spontaneous donations of cash or hospitality from the Tibetan farmers and nomads whose communities they passed through.

Another form of asceticism that can commonly be found along the pilgrimage paths which surround Tibetan holy places are natural tests or challenges which pilgrims can perform. Very often these involve the pilgrims having to squeeze their bodies through tight rock crevices or crawl along narrow tunnels or passageways among boulders or

Fig. 12
Notched stick for recording a pilgrim's circumambulations, Amdo, Eastern Tibet.
Photograph Toni Huber

Fig. 13
Pilgrims circumambulating the outer walls of Tashilhunpo Monastery, Shigatse, southern Tibet.
Photograph Toni Huber

in solid rock (Fig. 15). The idea behind such tests is to measure the embodied moral status of the pilgrim. It is believed that the ability to complete such tests has nothing to do with the physical size of the pilgrims' bodies or the diameter of the openings or passages in the rock through which they must pass. The tunnels and crevices in the local rocks of the holy place will only allow those with a good moral or karmic status to pass through, whereas pilgrims who are unworthy will not be able to complete the same tests. One such rock test at the holy mountain of Kang Tisé or Mount Kailash in western Tibet is termed "Sins Black and White" (*sdig pa dkar nag*), suggesting the comparative moral evaluation that the test entails. Another similar type of challenge is the need to pass along narrow and precarious footpaths, often high upon mountain cliffs, in order to complete the circumambulation of a holy site. These potentially dangerous and frightening walkways often have suggestive names, such as "Narrow Path of the Intermediate State between Life and Death" (*bar do 'phrang lam*). The implication is that the virtuous need not fear, and that a successful passage during pilgrimage will mean a successful transit of the intermediate state between death and the next rebirth also, rather than a fall to hell.

THE INTERNATIONAL SCOPE OF TIBETAN PILGRIMAGE

So far, we have discussed pilgrimages and pilgrims as they can be found and observed on the Tibetan plateau itself. However, the geographical scope of Tibetan pilgrimage is international, and it has been so since the advent of this form of ritual among Tibetans. Tibetan pilgrims have regularly set out on religious journeys to areas that are nowadays located in Pakistan, India, Nepal, Bhutan, and China.

In western China, Tibetan pilgrims have long paid visits to the great Buddhist sacred mountains of Wutaishan and Omei Shan, which are considered the earthly abodes of the Bodhisattvas Manjushri (see essay *Origins and History of Pilgrimage for Christians, Muslims, and Buddhists,* Fig. 7) and Samantabhadra, respectively. In fact, Tibetan interest in Wutaishan dates back all the way to the early 9th century, during Tibet's imperial era. In 824 the Tibetan court made a formal request to the Tang Dynasty administration for a map of the famous holy mountain, which the Chinese duly provided. This is the earliest historically dated example of indigenous Tibetan interest in a Buddhist holy place of pilgrimage. One of the most impressive representations of the sacred topography is a six-foot-long woodblock print commissioned by a Mongolian monk in 1846 (Fig. 16). Numerous

Fig. 14
A prostrating pilgrim with protective apron and gloves, Kham.
Photograph Toni Huber

Fig. 15
Pilgrims crawling through a rock passage test, Ganden.
Photograph Toni Huber

Fig. 16
Map of Wutaishan, the earthly abode of Manjushri
Sino-Tibetan, 1846
Painted and colored xylograph, 56 7/10 x 76 7/10 in. (144 x 194.8 cm)
Rubin Museum of Art, C2004.29.1 (HAR 65371)
Photograph Rubin Museum of Art

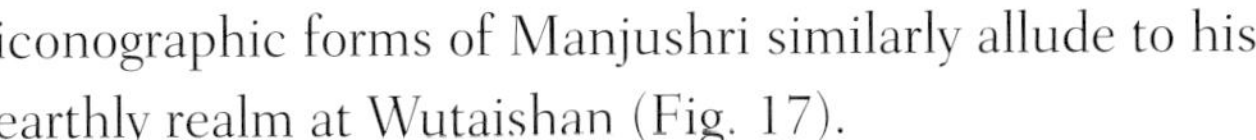

iconographic forms of Manjushri similarly allude to his earthly realm at Wutaishan (Fig. 17).

Nevertheless, it is India, as the origin place of Buddhism, that has always held the strongest attraction for Tibetan pilgrims, and they have long referred to India quite explicitly as their "holy land" (*'phags pa'i yul*). Tibetan pilgrims have regularly visited the well-known Indian sites associated with the life story of the Buddha Shakyamuni, such as the Mahabodhi Temple at Bodhgaya (see essay *Tracing the Footsteps of the Buddha: Pilgrimage to the Eight Great Places* (Ashtamahasthana)), Sarnath, and Rajagriha. With the complete demise of Buddhism in India after the 13th century, the main Indian shrines of the Buddha became abandoned, and lost to the jungle, or buried beneath the earth, only to be excavated by archaeologists and revived once again in the late 19th and early 20th centuries. During the intervening centuries of loss of the holy places of the Buddha, Tibetan lamas claimed to have rediscovered some of them again, although not in the Middle Ganges region where they were originally located, but in distant Assam, along the course

Fig. 17

White Manjushri

Tibet, c. 18th century

Pigments on cloth, 21 x 14 in. (53.3 x 35.6 cm)

Rubin Museum of Art, C2006.66.30 (HAR 846)

Photograph Rubin Museum of Art

The form of white Manjushri, known as Vimala Manjushri, is associated with the northern peak of Manjushri's earthly abode, Wutaishan "Five-Terrace Mountain," located in Shanxi Province of China.

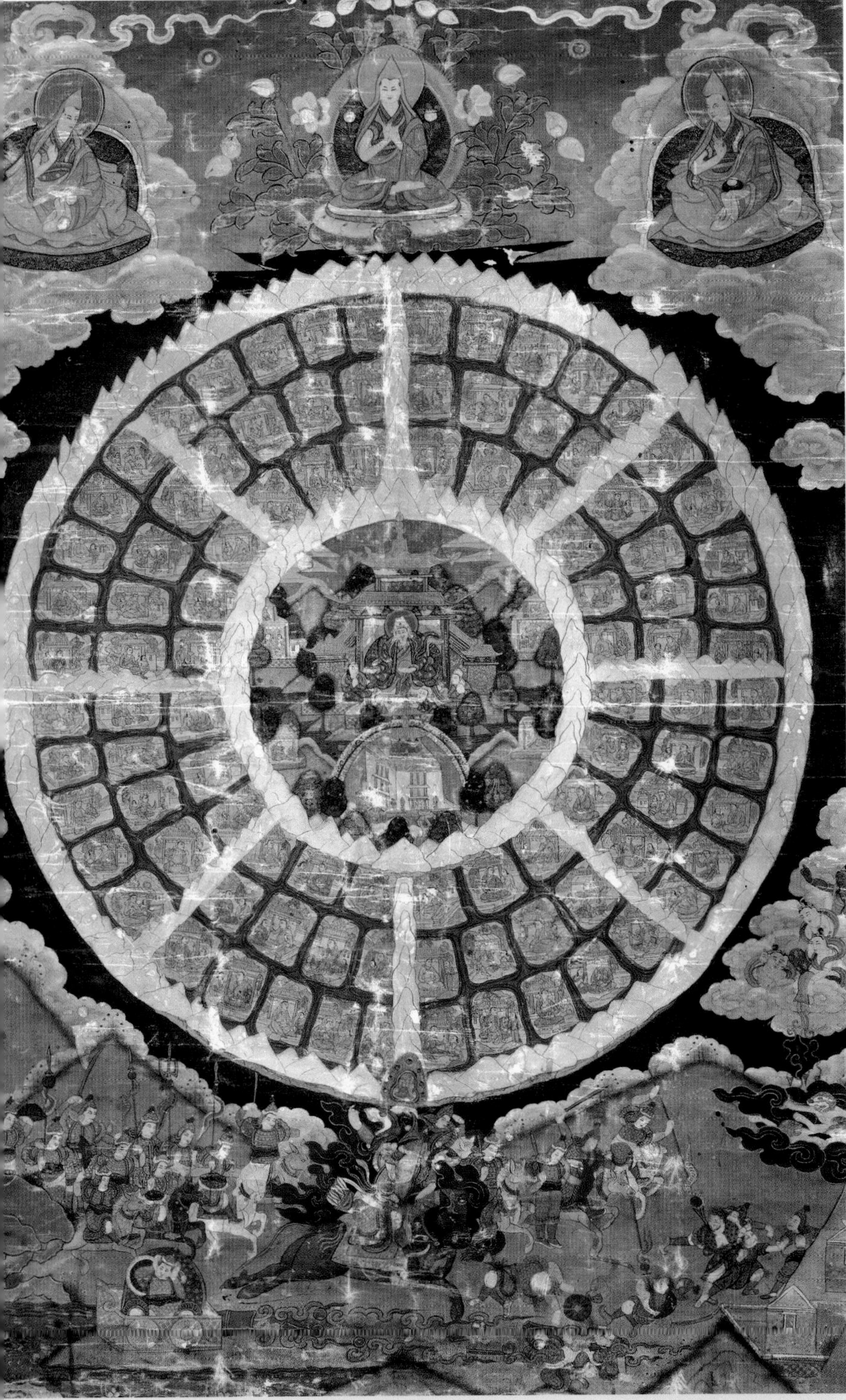

Fig. 18
Mandala of Shambhala
Tibet, 19th century
Pigments on cloth, 23¼ x 15¾ in. (59.1 x 40 cm)
Rubin Museum of Art, F1997.38.2 (HAR 563)
Photograph Rubin Museum of Art

of the Brahmaputra River in the far northeast of India. Between the 17th and the early 20th centuries, large numbers of Tibetan pilgrims visited popular Hindu shrines in Assam in the firm belief that they were in fact the original sites of the Buddha. However, once the colonial archaeologists and modern Buddhist revivalists had done their work to restore the ancient sites of Buddha in the Middle Ganges region, Tibetans gave up going on pilgrimage to Assam.

Finally, there is one distant and highly elusive pilgrimage destination that has for long fascinated the Tibetans: the great and mysterious country of Shambhala (Fig. 18). The concept of Shambhala was first introduced to Tibet in the Indian literature of the *Kalachakra Tantra*, and has been popular with Tibetans ever since. Shambhala is part of a Buddhist millennial cult that was based upon earlier Hindu myths describing the future appearance in the world of a messianic incarnation of the god Vishnu, who returns to reorder the world following an era of degeneration. In the Buddhist version of the story, the Bodhisattva king of Shambhala will come forth in the future with his army to fight a holy war that destroys all the followers of Islam, and restores the Buddhist teachings. According to a 13th-century Tibetan pilgrim's guide-book, Shambhala is a real place which the religious traveler can easily visit on foot by two alternative routes. To reach it, the pilgrim must travel well to the north of Tibet, across the Tarim Basin through Turkestan, and over the Tien Shan mountains into the heart of Central Asia. However, by the 18th century, Tibetan lamas were describing the physical journey to Shambhala as being virtually impossible, something that only the most spiritually advanced pilgrims might undertake, and perhaps only to be attempted in a Tantric visionary state. Shambhala thus became an impossible goal for Tibetan pilgrims, and came to be accepted rather as a mysterious and hidden place that will someday decide the future fate of the Buddhist world.

For a thousand years or more, pilgrimage to holy places has continued to be a vital aspect of Tibetan culture, and one in which all of the Tibetan people can freely participate. Judging by its high popularity today, pilgrimage can be expected to remain a significant part of Tibetan life and identity well into the future.

See further reading on page 339

Amitabha Buddha in Sukhavati Paradise
Eastern Tibet, 1700-99
Karma (Kagyu) tradition
Ground Mineral Pigment, Fine Gold Line on Cotton, 31½ x 19¾ in. (80 x 50.2 cm)
Rubin Museum of Art (P1994.19.1)
Photograph Rubin Museum of Art

Pilgrimages to Paradise[1]

Martin Brauen

People in crises, including Tibetan Buddhists, sometimes develop millennial dreams. Here I investigate two manifestations: belief in hidden paradise-like regions in the Himalayas to which one can escape in dangerous times, and a trance-like ceremony which enables the practitioner to attain the paradise of Buddha Amitabha through a kind of mental pilgrimage. These ideas are not completely new, but, following the 1959 exile, they have taken on a new form. Numerous writings, works of art, and oral accounts attest to beliefs in a paradise from which the final liberation from the cycle of suffering, the ultimate goal, is more easily achieved. The most famous of these paradises is that of Buddha Amitabha, called Sukhavati (opposite).[2]

Buddhist conceptions of paradise are reminiscent of those of other millennial movements, and are called, among other terms, chiliasm, cult movements, eschatological movements, *Heilserwartungsbewegung*, revitalization movements, crisis cults, and millenarianism.[3] I prefer the latter term, with the understanding that millenarianism is not confined to movements influenced by Christianity and its fixation on one-thousand-year reigns. I include as millennial movements collective endeavors to attain a paradise state even temporarily. The way leading to paradise is a sort of pilgrimage – in one case a "one way pilgrimage," as those who participate believe that they will remain for eternity in that "promised land." However, while most millennial movements claim that salvation lies in this life, Buddhists believe that paradise can only be attained in the hereafter, that is, after death. Yet in Tibetan Buddhism, conceptions of terrestrial paradises or paradise-like states are not unknown. And there are means to reach them – collectively and with the help of a leader (guru).

THE *PHOBA* CEREMONY AS "MENTAL PILGRIMAGE"

Western literature about Tibet has noted a ceremony called *phoba* (*'pho-ba*), conducted shortly after death for the welfare of the deceased. It facilitates the transference of consciousness through the aperture of Brahma, which is situated on the crown of the head at the sagittal suture where the two parietal bones articulate, and is opened by means of the yogic practice of *phoba*. Consciousness travels immediately into the pure land called Dewacan, the paradise of Buddha Amitabha. The *phoba* ceremony is, however, not only for the welfare of the deceased, but can extend to the living. This ceremony is mainly performed by specialized monks.[4] Although not a pilgrimage in the strict sense, *phoba* is included here since it is a pilgrimage that happens in the mind. The practitioner "travels" with special techniques and

with the support of a leader from this world to the other side, to a paradise. One can call it a mental pilgrimage.

My research suggests that a popularization of this *phoba* rite took place in the 1980s among Tibetans in Swiss exile when some united to practice *phoba* on a regular basis. Thus paradise has become the focus of a salvation rite for lay persons. It is a highly complex practice which, when correctly executed, places great demands on the person meditating.[5] A mental transference through the *phoba* ceremonies enables a paradise, in this case that of Amitabha, to be attained immediately. Aspects of this ritual mirror other characteristics of millennial movements; some participants – most are women – fall into trance-like states which are accompanied by rhythmic hyperventilation, moaning, whimpering, or loud sobbing, and sometimes by arm movements. For anyone accustomed to the quiet atmosphere of Buddhist meditation, these séances seem alien.[6] The *phoba* rite as performed for the living is only a rehearsal of the entrance into paradise, to become realized at the time of death. Here, experience of Amitabha's paradise is realized only during the limited time of the *phoba* ritual.

PILGRIMAGE TO PARADISIACAL HIDDEN COUNTRIES

During talks with practitioners of Nyingmapa, one of the four major schools of Tibetan Buddhism, I was told about regions in the south of ethnic Tibet which appear to be kinds of earthly paradises. Western literature rarely mentions these sites (*sbas gnas or sbas yul*).[7] Through interviews and consultation of a Tibetan text,[8] I learned that these hidden countries vary and are divided into three categories: external, internal, and secret. In some a visitor can remain for an indefinite period, whereas in others the visitor is limited to several years. The best-known *beyul* (*sbas yul*) are Pemakö, Sikkim, and Khenpalung in Nepal.[9]

Only believers who are convinced of the existence of the *beyul* and who engage without reservations can expect to be successful in their search. Seekers must also have acquired merit and have freed themselves from attachment to food, wealth, and family. They also need the help of a guidebook, or the *beyul* is unattainable. The time to enter the *beyul* is strictly regulated, given in secret oral instructions by a spiritual leader. Care must be taken, also, that instructions do not fall into the hands of unscrupulous teachers, or that careless talk does not circulate about the hidden countries.

A hidden country must be approached from one of the four cardinal points, depending on the time of the year:[10] in autumn from the east, in winter the south, in spring the west, and in summer the north. Even when these rules are observed, the path is an arduous one. A gate with so-called curtains stands at each cardinal point, and obstructions that include snow, disease, wild animals, thirst, and malicious local deities and spirits must be overcome before the *beyul* can be entered. These obstructions can be surmounted with the help of rituals, among them burning certain substances, taking pills, reciting prayers, making offerings, and piling up stones.

These hidden countries were described differently by different informants, but they are all paradise-like regions where aging is halted and life is pleasant. According to one tradition, there are caves full of *tsampa* (roasted and ground barley), other grains, and springs from which milk flows like water. Fruits such as apples and peaches in the *beyul* are at least twice normal size. Crops are not planted, but grow of their own accord. One place stores agricultural instruments; another, frying pans, grinders, and earthen pots. In the hidden countries there are different treasures (*gter*) of material goods, including salt, turquoise, weapons, seeds, and medicines, and *dharma* and wealth. There is abundant meat so long as no injury is done to the animals living in the hidden countries.

Descriptions are often quite detailed: in the center of a forest there is a blue stone with the footprints of Guru Rinpoche (Padmasambhava). Viewing it will forever cure diseases caused by the *nagas* (serpent beings), such as madness and paralysis. In a huge cave there are objects which bestow superhuman powers; a skull wrapped in a blue cloth contains a substance for attaining speed. By putting a little of that material under the sole of the foot, one can travel swiftly wherever one wishes. A whip made of *ba*-wood makes one invisible to gods, spirits, and human beings. Finally, there is a mirror wrapped in red cloth. When washed with the milk of a red cow it will reveal all major and minor elements of the universe.

In the hidden country there is no hunger or thirst. Everything good increases: one's life span, happiness, good fortune, and wealth. The *beyul* provides not only worldly but also spiritual goods. Lakes which bestow clarity of the mind and caves in which enlightenment is attained are located in the hidden country of Sikkim, which is compared with the holy places of Bodhgaya, Potala, Indra's palace, and Sukhavati. In this hidden country *bodhichitta* (Buddhahood) increases and with it clarity of mind develops; ignorance and the power of the five poisons diminishes. It is even said of the *beyul* of Sikkim that it is the "seed of Sukhavati."

> *Happiness comes spontaneously there and spiritual attainment occurs automatically. Even the bugs on the bodies of those striving to get into this hidden country will be reborn in Sukhavati. The power of this hidden country is so great that just by hearing its name great merit during countless lives is accumulated, and just by seeing the place freedom from passage into one of the three unfortunate realms is gained.*[11]

A person may leave a hidden country, but reentry is impossible, as the following story illustrates:

> *One day after stalking and shooting at an animal, a hunter, not finding his prey, set out in search of it. He happened upon a cave and, penetrating into the deeper recesses, finally came upon a kind of paradise. The hunter became very peaceful and without realizing it he stayed in this hidden country for twelve years. Upon remembering his family, however, he left. At the entrance to the cave he found his bow and arrows, which in the meantime had rusted. He himself, however, was no older than he had been on the day on which he had entered the cave. When the hunter reached the village, he saw how the inhabitants had aged and learned some had even died during the time he had been away. The hunter told the people about his experience and they, upon hearing this, demanded that he lead them to the hidden country. In spite of the*

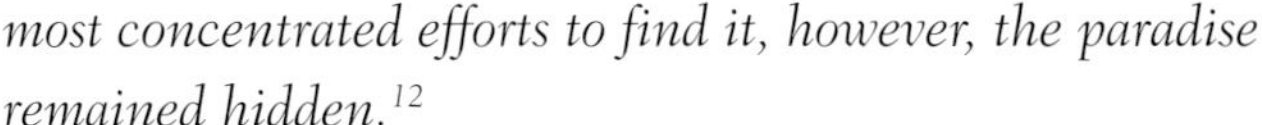
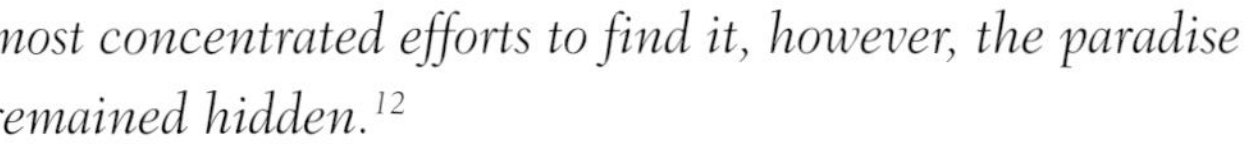

> *most concentrated efforts to find it, however, the paradise remained hidden.*[12]

THE IMPORTANCE OF THE "CRISIS" AND OF THE LEADER

Anthropological literature notes that millennial or paradise movements originate from crises, prompting some authors to refer to them as "crisis cults."[13] Regarding Tibet, is there evidence to suggest that crises, to which large groups of Tibetans have been exposed, might lead them to form pilgrim groups to search for one of the promised lands?

Beyul are first mentioned in Tibetan texts at the beginning of the 14th century. This was the period of the Mongol hegemony over Tibet, a time of political, and to some extent religious, deprivation. Further, Tibetan informants related to me that during the Dzungar war in the early 18th century, there were attempts to reach hidden countries.[14] Bacot, too, tells of a concrete, historical crisis which led to a collective search for *beyul*. According to him, a thousand families are said to have set out in search of the holy land of Pemakö in the first years of the Sino-Tibetan conflicts at the beginning of the present century.[15] Following the Chinese occupation of Tibet in 1959, according to the Tibetan refugees, the idea of the *beyul* once again gained currency. This idea seems supported by the conscious choice of an escape route which passed through the region in which the most important *beyul* lie. Refugees belonging to the Nyingmapa school also report that, before and during the flight, they focused on their leader, Dudjom Rinpoche, wondering if he would declare that the time had come to look for one of the hidden countries. When the refugees finally reached India and the crises abated, interest in the *beyul* correspondingly declined. Upon arrival, Dudjom Rinpoche is said to have declared that India was also a sort of hidden country.[16]

Even in exile, however, Tibetan thought of the *beyul* never completely disappeared. During the early, difficult years, we learn, at least one large group of the faithful followed a lama to Sikkim in order to enter a hidden country.[17] At the spot designated by their spiritual leader, they waited in the hope that boulders would open, admitting

them to the *beyul*. Due to severe weather, including an avalanche, many people died and the disillusioned survivors retreated. Later they argued that they had been led astray by a false lama.[18]

Still, the idea of the *beyul* continued. Even recently, some continued to think that their leader would announce a time for pilgrimage in search of the hidden country. This millennial dream has not only been passed down orally, but is preserved in written form in prophecies attributed to Padmasambhava, as the following example shows:

> *O great master! When the age of the five degenerations comes benevolent ways cease, harmful ways increase, bad omens occur in all the lands, great changes occur, and fighting breaks out in China, Mongolia, and Tibet instigated by the Lalos [irreligious people]. What possibilities are there to find suitable places, both big and small, for the practice of* dharma, *in order to attain the full enlightenment of Buddhahood? And by what methods can one get to these places?*

Guru Rinpoche replied: "Listen, faithful Lord, with your father, mother, sons, and whole entourage. I shall explain the methods for getting to the holy places..."[19] Another passage in the same text about the *beyul* of Sikkim names the so-called visible signs, whose appearance is a signal for the faithful to go in search of the *beyul*:

> *When Tibet is overrun by the Lalos, when the main holy places of Gtsang are destroyed... when the golden roof of the Samye Monastery falls down, when the great stupa Tsang-trang in Kham collapses, when the tip of the stupa in Yer-pa bends, when the great centers of Ü burn down....*

The incidents listed here represent crisis situations (wars, fires, floods, etc.) or are, as is the case of the destruction of the holy buildings, considered by the Tibetans as clear indications that critical times are approaching.[20] Thus, we understand that Tibetans themselves regard the paradise myths of the *beyul*, hidden countries, as particularly vital in times of crisis and danger, when the faithful are more likely to form a group of pilgrims to realize these myths.[21]

Tibetans have told me that current practice and popularization of the *phoba* ritual is also connected with a state of crisis, a deteriorating world political situation. These bad times with still worse to follow justify extending the ritual to lay persons. My informants refer to enormous, rapid changes, during which nothing is like it used to be, and we are beset by numerous wars, famines, and other great sufferings. Amitabha's paradise, once a remote goal only attainable through clerical intercession, now becomes personalized and urgent. It still demands great personal effort, under the supervision of a lama, but it is now placed well within the reach of a faithful lay person. Although the Tibetan texts leave no doubt as to the difficulty and danger of attaining consciousness transference when not practiced by someone "who has been long on probation and been found worthy,"[22] lay persons are nonetheless now allowed to conduct the *phoba* exercises, thus gaining a clerical privilege.

A great many, if not all, millennial and paradise pilgrimages are led by personalities said to be charismatic, who command the absolute trust of the members of the movement. Members are prepared to follow these leaders unconditionally. The cult movements mentioned here are inconceivable without such leaders: for the *phoba* rituals the lama has the function of a traditional Tibetan spiritual leader, that of an instructor and spiritual guide during the ritual. In the case of the *beyul* the lama is more than a spiritual leader. He also functions as Padmasambhava's envoy, or at least as his spiritual successor; he is both a prophet and a pilgrim leader who actually, not just figuratively, leads the faithful to the paradise land.

SUMMARY

These two examples display characteristics of millennial or paradise movements among Tibetan Buddhists, similar to millennial movements elsewhere. They are apparently activated whenever the faithful feel threatened; i.e., when they experience deprivation and when there is a leader who recognizes the acute need for millennial aspirations and tries to channel these wishes into collective actions. These phenomena among Tibetans, whether pilgrimages in mind or physical pilgrimages in search of a paradise-like place, have until now received scant attention. The movements have been neither very spectacular nor very disruptive, and generally, secrecy concerning some details appears inherent in the practice. Yet, these observations also challenge a common, but incorrect, notion that Buddhism and Hinduism do not give rise to millennial ideas and movements.[23] Finally, it appears that millennial behavior and ideology are particularly pronounced among the Nyingmapas, who remain on the periphery of Tibetan society and religion. This would support the thesis that millennial ideas and the pilgrimages resulting from them are likely to exist among people who are in some way politically, ideologically, religiously, or economically deprived, or who at least feel that they are.

See further reading on page 340

1 This article appeared first in *Soundings in Tibetan Civilization, Proceedings of the 1982 Seminar of the International Association for Tibetan Studies*, held at Columbia University, Manohar, 1985, with the title "Millenarism in Tibetan Religion." It was revised for the present essay.

2 For a Tibetan description of Sukhavati, see Schwieger (1978), which contains further references. The paradise is described in ornate language in the *Sukhavati-vyuha* in Müller (1894).

3 See also La Barre (1971), p. 11.

4 According to what I am told by Tibetan informants, traditional *phoba* texts for lay people also exist, though *phoba* ceremonies for larger groups of lay persons were very seldom performed; for instance, every sixth year at 'Bri-khung Monastery.

5 See Evans-Wentz (1967), p. 261ff. I have also received oral and written information from Ayang Rinpoche, etc.

6 The extraordinary effect that the *phoba* exercise can have on the practitioner is indicated in a text translated by Dawa Samdup for Evans-Wentz (1967), p. 266: "Manifest thy humble fervent faith till the very hairs of thy body stand on end and tears course down thy cheeks..." A Nyingmapa monk reported that he had never been able to observe any of the aforementioned phenomena among monks who practiced *phoba* in Tibet. Occasionally, though, a monk fainted, he said. Michael Aris told me that he observed an outbreak of religious hysteria in the village of Uchu, Paro Valley, Bhutan, while the Nyingmapa lama Pad-rgyal gling-pa bestowed the *phoba lung* on the villagers, mostly blacksmiths. About three quarters of the villagers present were affected.

7 See Bacot (1912), Aris (1975 and 1979), Reinhard (1978), and Bernbaum (1980).

8 Namely, *beyul 'bras mo ljongs kyi gnas yig phan yon dang bcas pa ngo mtshar gter mdzod*, translated with the help of Lama Lodroe Dahortsang, Rikon.

9 There seem to be two Khenpalung, one in Bhutan and one in Nepal. See Aris (1979), p. 80.

10 This and the following descriptions refer to the *beyul* of Sikkim.

11 Similar descriptions can be found in Reinhard (1978), p. 19-20, and Bernbaum (1980), p. 63ff. Another paradise no less wonderful is that of Sambhala (see essay in this volume *Tibetan Pilgrimage* by Toni Huber), which will not be discussed here, but which is supposed to lie to the northwest of Tibet. The description of the complicated path to and the structure of Sambhala reveals certain similarities with reports on the hidden countries. See Grünwedel (1915), Oppitz (1974), Damdinsüren (1977), Bernbaum (1980). The Bon-pos believe in the existence of a similar mythological country, called Ol-mo-lung-ring. According to a personal communication from Samten Karmay, several groups of Bon-pos have gone in search of this country.

12 Oral communication. See also Bernbaum (1980), p. 72.

13 See Weston La Barre (1971), and Peter Gerber (1980), p. 61ff.

14 For this information I am indebted to Tashi Tsering, Library of Tibetan Works and Archives, Dharamsala, India (1982).

15 Bacot (1912), p. 11.

16 According to Bernbaum (1980), p. 70: "When Tibetans were fleeing from the Chinese takeover of Tibet in the 1950s, a lama tried to lead a band of refugees to the safety of this valley [Pemakö]..."

17 According to Tashi Tsering from Dharamsala, this lama was Brtul-zugs glin-pa.

18 Oral communication. See also Bernbaum (1980), p. 68.

19 See n. 8 above.

20 The same text also mentions the "four external signs"– earthquakes, floods, fires and strong winds-and the "four internal signs"– fighting among beings, fighting between brothers, destruction of temples, and monks not abiding by the rules.

21 See also Reinhard (1978), pp. 16, 17, and 23; and Bernbaum (1980), p. 66.

22 Evans-Wentz (1967), pp. 254 and 257.

23 How the notion of a hidden country came to provide a mythic formula accounting for the origin of Bhutan is shown by M. Aris (1978), p. 82. This indicates that millennial myths and movements developing out of them can, under certain circumstances, acquire a political meaning. See, for instance, Talmon (1962) and Mühlmann (1961).

Details of Fig. 2

Journey of the Heart: Prostrating on the Roof of the World

Krisadawan Hongladarom

Sometimes what seems impossible becomes possible when we decide to do things according to our hearts, without considering logic or reason, when we do not worry about what others may think of us, and when we do not doubt our own ability. We only need to let faith drive and support us. When there is belief in the good, when the resolve and commitment is unshaken, a hard, seemingly impossible task then becomes easy and possible.

This was the background of one of the best journeys of my life, which took place in May 2007 on the sacred rooftop of the world in Tibet.

The journey took only eighteen days, and spanned eighty kilometers. It started in Nyethang, south of Lhasa and ended in Samye, two historic towns in central Tibet which are related to two renowned Indian masters, namely Atisha from Bengal and Padmasambhava or Guru Rinpoche from Oddiyana. The towns are also related to Tara, the Bodhisattva of Compassion. In the 8th century CE, Padmasambhava formally established Buddhism as the state religion, known as the First Propagation. More importantly, he established Samye, one of the still-extant early monasteries in Tibet, whose mandalic ground plan is said to be modeled after Indian sources. Conceived as a three-dimensional mandala, Samye has a circumambulatory path so that pilgrims can perform full-body prostrations along this path.

Even though my journey was rather short, it was deeply meaningful to my life and was impressed in my memories. This is not only because I had the opportunity to take part in the beautiful tradition of the Tibetans in prostrating on a modern, asphalt road full of fast vehicles, but also because this experience has taught me to become aware of the true meaning of "pilgrimage." It is a journey that is peaceful, both in its inner and outer aspects, and full of happiness.

Outer peace is gained by prostrating on the ground, visualizing that in front of us we see all the Buddhas and Bodhisattvas, and by being surrounded by one's fellow sentient beings who are also prostrating. Our mouths are full of prayers of refuge to the Three Jewels (the Buddha, Teachings, and Community). Our bodies lie there tranquilly amidst the great nature.

Inner peace consists of no attachment to anything, living a life of the wanderer, journeying on the selected path with only a friend to help carry the baggage. When you are tired, you take a rest in the shade of a tree alongside the road. When night comes you take the bank of the Brahmaputra River as your resting place.

Along the way the passersby, Tibetans, Han Chinese, and Westerners, stopped with greetings and well wishes. Some gave us food, candies, drinks, and a little money. Some came to greet and talk with us, inviting us to their homes.

We were full of smiles, and the children were full of laughter, their faces expressing sympathetic joy in our merit. This is a special gift, which enabled us to have more strength to go on. One afternoon, while I was prostrating through a barley field, an old man who was carrying his farming equipment gave me a thumbs-up.

However, the best gift for me was the chance to know myself and to learn how to be humble. When one prostrates, one becomes only a speck of dust. Grains of sand stuck to one's fingers, forehead, nose, and clothes remind one that humans and nature are one and the same.

I was born in a small resort town called Hua-Hin to the south of Thailand. When I was young, I loved to run with my younger brother following the yellow bright moon wherever it went. I remember how uplifted my spirit was when our feet went quickly trying to capture the seductive and illusive moon. I ran after the moon for many years until one day I realized the moon was too high to reach and it was pointless to try. I stopped running, and the special bond between the girl and the moon gradually disappeared. I became diligent in my studies until I received a first-class honors from Thailand's most prestigious university.

One day in 1983 I met a woman who introduced me to a program called "Youth Seminar on World Religions." I was selected to be a young Buddhist representative to join a group of youth from various spiritual traditions. I got to meet two Tibetan monks on that trip. I learned about Tibet for the first time through them and learned to appreciate another sect of Buddhism of which I had been unaware.

Many years after that incident, I found myself studying Tibetan, doing sociolinguistic research among Tibetan refugees in Nepal, and conducting research projects in eastern Tibet. I lived in two worlds: as a university professor and as a field researcher trying to understand the complexity of Tibetan dialects. I became fascinated by Tibet's beauty, simplicity of life, and total faith of the people, which is reflected in their eyes, voices, and daily behavior.

My research in Tibet brought me in contact with pilgrims who prostrated or walked to sacred mountains and spiritual sites. The sight of these pilgrims moved my heart. One time I did a pilgrimage with a Tibetan nun to Nagchu, a northern nomad town. On the way we met a man and two women pulling a cart full of belongings. Their determined and dark faces were hardened by days in the sun and the wind.

I looked into their eyes and found myself yearning to follow their footsteps. After we parted from them, I told my friend Yontan that I wanted to do a pilgrimage like them. He objected to it, saying that I did not have to resort to this type of basic practice. As these villagers could not read texts, they took this means of Dharma practice. But I explained to him that Dharma practice was not restricted to meditation or text recitation. Pilgrimage is a great practice in its own right. I told him if he did not want to go on a pilgrimage with me, I would not mind doing it alone. That determination softened his heart. Later on Yontan became the great supporter of that most memorable journey that I took in May 2007.

PROSTRATION ROUTE

The journey covered more than a hundred kilometers, from Nyethang Tara Temple near Gongga Airport in Lhasa, to Samye. I chose this route because of the special connections the places have with Goddess Tara and the Indian teacher Padmasambhava, respectively. Besides, the distance was short enough for me to reach the destination within one month, the period of my semester break from the university.

Tibetan pilgrims often go on a prostration pilgrimage for more than a year. They start from their hometown and prostrate their way to Jokhang or continue their journey to Mt. Kailash. It could take years to complete the route. But with devotion and faith, the daunting task could be accomplished without much difficulty.

There are two ways to reach Samye from Nyethang: by motorway and by walkway. At first, I planned to take the walkway and gradually move my way to the destination. But the old cart carrying our belongings could not make it on a country road. So I decided to prostrate on the main road. Each day I left my resting ground after sunrise and stopped around six or seven o'clock, before sunset. Yontan would carry the cart behind me. At that time, we became the happiest people on earth, with free spirits and the goodwill of passersby to nourish and sustain us.

PREPARATIONS

I did the journey without thinking about difficulties and hardships that might happen on the way. I did not prepare myself much for it, apart from biking about half an hour in the mornings two weeks before the departure and preparing some prostration gear. Yontan checked with some former pilgrims on how they prepared themselves. We were advised to take some protection, particularly for our hands and knees. He made me several pairs of wooden gloves and an apron for body protection. I chose to wear a Tibetan dress or *chupa* like a Lhasan woman and I felt proud to help preserve this ancient Tibetan custom.

THE JOURNEY

Day 1

May 1, 2007. Our group left a hotel in the city center of Lhasa, headed to Tashigong Monastery in Nyethang, around 7 AM. It was a lovely day with sunshine and a bright blue sky. I felt excited. Two hours from now till I reach Samye, I thought. I will live my life on the roads.

When we arrived at the monastery, we saw welcoming smoke coming out of a *tsang* incense burner. Sweet fragrance of burnt juniper filled the air. We went to see Kunga Sangbo Rinpoche, the *tulku* of the monastery, whom I have known for seven years. Before going there, I told him about my mission to come to Tibet. Rinpoche rejoiced in my motivation and offered to help me as best as he could. Apart from helping with the preparations, Rinpoche had performed a long life empowerment for me a few days before (Fig. 1). It was the most meaningful gift for my journey that brought auspiciousness to us.

Around 9 AM, we left for Nyethang Tara temple. It took about ten minutes to get there from Tashigong. This temple is renowned for the statue of Speaking Tara (Fig. 2) and for a *stupa* containing Atisha's relics, as well as the skull relics of the Indian adept (*mahasiddha*) Naropa.

We walked inside to pay our respects to the main shrine. When we came out of the temple gate, we checked our cart to make sure everything was ready. A friend who came to see us off suggested that we take out some things from the heavy cart. But Yontan insisted that everything was needed.

Fig. 1
Kunga Sangbo Rinpoche of Tashigong Monastery in Nyethang gives a blessing of long-life empowerment before the start of the 80-km pilgrimage journey.
Photograph Meu Yontan

Fig. 2
Speaking Tara at Dolma Lhakhang (Tara Temple) in Nyethang.
Photograph Aurapin Pochanapring

When it was time to start the journey, Rinpoche, Yontan, and I turned our faces toward the main shrine of the temple, with our hands pressed at our hearts. But only I did full prostrations on the ground. At that time, I knew my life would not be the same. All the eyes were watching me with loving kindness. I felt overwhelmed as if I were being ordained to become a nun. I requested Tara's blessings for me to reach the destination without getting sick or facing other kinds of obstacles. I felt the power of faith in my heart.

From then on, the road was to be my home; devotion would be life-sustaining nectar. All the motor sounds were like mantra singing. Spiritual masters, Buddhas, Bodhisattvas, *dharma* protectors, and *dakinis* were to be my traveling companions. Yontan would be the only earthly traveling companion, bound by *karma*.

After prostrating to Tara three times, I turned my face toward the main road. I used the wooden gloves awkwardly. We all laughed. Kusho Tseten, a monk from Tashigong, went to the temple's store and bought many pairs of cotton gloves for me. I used his gloves instead, putting aside the wooden ones for a while. The kindness of everyone touched my heart. Although I prostrated alone, all the friends' hearts were with me, including Rinpoche's.

When my body touched the main road for the first time, I could feel freedom – nothing tied my mind (Fig. 3). There were no family, pets, job, not even the foundation that I set up back home. Nothing was more meaningful at that time than having Buddhas in my heart. I recited the refuge vow:

> *Before the precious Triple Gems and Three Roots,*
> *Veins, winds and drops, Bodhichitta,*
> *Mandala of compassion, true natural state,*
> *I take refuge in the three levels of the Triple Gems till I gain enlightenment.*

I recited this verse thinking of Guru Rinpoche as an embodiment of all the teachers. I thought about Buddhas of the Past, Present, and Future and all the sacred beings that fill the vast sky. To my right was my father and on my left my mother. Surrounding me were family, relatives and friends, and those that I knew and did not know, including beings of the six realms. Before me were enemies and those to whom I owed karmic debts. I invited all beings to prostrate with me in my visualization.

Having covered five kilometers with approximately five hundred prostrations, I was asked by Yontan to finish for

Fig. 3
Wearing the prostration gear of apron and gloves, the author covers 5 kilometers, with 500 prostrations on the first day of the pilgrimage.
Photograph Meu Yontan

the day. It was around 5 PM. We selected a location on the bank of the Yarlung Tsangpo (Brahmaputra). He pitched tents and prepared our dinner while I rested under a tree's shade. I thought of my life, the curious faces of strangers who rushed to take my pictures during prostration, and the remarkable experience I had gained that day.

Day 2

7 AM. The sky was still dark. But I decided to get up and get ready for the day. Yontan went to fetch water from the river. He boiled water to make tea. We drank it with *tsampa*. About half an hour later, Kusho Tseten dropped by. He looked happy to see that we were doing well and that I was not sick. Before leaving us, he encouraged us to call him if we needed any help.

I started the prostration at the exact location where I'd finished the route the day before. We'd put a stone pile there. I prayed to Guru Rinpoche and recited the refuge prayers.

The sounds of the wooden gloves touching the asphalt road mixed with those of my own breaths, and there were also sounds of the cars passing by, and that of Yontan's cart from behind. And the sounds of the two of us praying. I prayed to the Three Jewels, while Yontan prayed to ask for blessings from the Buddhas to protect us from obstacles.

11 AM. I still could not see the kilometer mark. The pain in my arms returned. We took a rest and had some cookies before continuing the journey.

While I was prostrating some tourists got out of their bus to take photos of us. A Chinese man ran across the road, taking out a 20 yuans note and a chocolate bar. I thanked him with my palms pressed together at my heart. At that instant it occurred to me that there was neither Tibet nor China. Everybody was brothers and sisters. When you are doing the prostration and somebody takes care of you, it is a noble act of compassion that is hard to describe. It does not matter whether the one who is helping is religious or not.

A car drove by and stopped close to us. A woman got out and came toward us. She asked me with a friendly voice, "Where are you going?" "To Samye," I replied. "Wait a moment," she said, and walked to her car and returned with a loaf of bread. "Eat it up," she said.

At that moment there was no Krisadawan, a professor from Chulalongkorn University, no president of the Thousand Stars Foundation; there was only a pilgrim whose heart yearned for the teachings of the Buddha and who wanted to make the best use of her human body.

Day 3

I became better at prostrating. My mind was better concentrated. We moved past the Tsa Do village. An old lady came to Yontan.

"Where are you from?" she asked.

"Amdo," said Yontan.

"Both of you?"

"Yes," Yontan answered with a smile, thinking that she knew I was a foreigner.

"This one is also from Amdo?" she asked, pointing her finger to me.

"Actually she is not. She's from Thailand."

"Is she really?" the woman said, looking at me interestedly.

"Can she speak Tibetan?" she inquired.

"Yes. She speaks Lhasa," Yontan answered for me.

I was listening to their conversation and got a chance to take a rest.

"She is a university lecturer at home. Her university is as famous as Peking University here," said Yontan to her.

"I don't believe it. University lecturers do not prostrate like this," she said.

"Why not? Don't university lecturers want their merit?"

"They might, but lecturers might not be able to do this hard work."

The old lady asked us to move forward slowly. She wanted to bring us food. She walked across the road, while we continued on our way. Fifteen minutes later she returned with two cloth bags. One of the bags contained *tsampa*; the other had *kaptse* (crispy fried dough).

"Please keep them for yourself," I said to her, knowing that this food was valuable to the villagers.

"It does not matter. I have a lot. This is what little I can do for both of you. I am glad that young people do prostrations like this. It brings you a lot of merit," she said.

Fig. 4
Two local boys, Tenzin and Chungta, were companions for the fourth day, helping to repair the cart, fetching firewood, and setting the tents.
Photograph Meu Yontan

Fig. 5
The author practices the "walking and prostrating meditation," focusing the mind on Guru Yoga, or meditation on the teachers as embodiments of Buddhahood.
Photograph Meu Yontan

We thanked the lady with our palms pressed together. Even though the *tsampa* and *kaptse* that she gave us were old and did not taste very good, her compassionate spirit will forever remain in our memories.

Day 4

Two boys came to greet us. One had a round and playful face. His name was Chungta. The other looked more serious but had a sweet smile, with one dimple. His name was Kucho Tenzin. That's a big name meaning "Venerable Tenzin." Both were shepherds. While they were talking with us, their sheep went ahead. The two boys looked interested in my prostrations, especially Chungta, who walked alongside us (Fig. 4).

During that day the two boys remained with us, helped us repair the cart, fetched firewood for us, and helped set up our tents. We had dinner together. It was a simple meal of instant noodle with dried mushroom soup, which the boys really liked. After the dinner Yontan asked them to leave, thinking that their parents might get worried.

Then I called home for the first time and talked with my mother. I told her that I had been prostrating for four days, making tens of kilometers. I asked her to feel proud of me and think that she has been prostrating with me.

Day 5

The prostration went better, for I became used to the weather and the condition of a prostrating pilgrim. Today I started to practice the kind of meditation called "walking and prostrating meditation," mingling my mind with that of my teacher and Guru Rinpoche. Doing so incurs great benefits because it focuses the mind. No matter how noisy the traffic is, your mind is not distracted by it (Fig. 5).

I noticed that I stopped to take a rest fewer times. The people paid us less attention, but still there were those who came to give us food and water. The donations I received throughout the journey totaled around 200 yuans. Most of the donors were Chinese, but there was a group of tourists from England. Although this was not a big amount, it gave us a lot of inspiration. Later on this amount became very useful to us when I needed to see a doctor for some stomach problem. We paid for the medicine as well as the bus trip back to Lhasa.

We did not bring a lot of money to begin with, because we thought there was not much need to use it. From this experience, Yontan and I then thought that in the future, if we happened to see pilgrims doing prostrations, we would give them some money to let them know that we rejoiced in their merits, so they would have some money for emergencies.

Day 6

When I came out of my tent this morning, I found Chungta sitting in front of the tent. It was a joy to see him again after we'd met him the first time two days earlier. He had been helping Yontan to move the load onto the cart. It was a difficult job because the ground was muddy. The two of them pushed the cart back to the road. I put on my prostration uniform and continued my prostration ahead of them.

I continued the prostrations with a cheerful heart, then stopped to take a breath and drink some water. I brought my mind back to my teacher, whom I realized was inseparable from Guru Rinpoche. After two hours we came to another kilometer mark, which was located at a curve on the side of a mountain. I looked back but saw that Chungta was not there. Yontan had told him to leave because he thought Chungta came with us without asking his parents. I felt a bit sad that we had not said good-bye to each other. I knew that we might not meet each other again, because we'd made merits together only this much.

That afternoon I concentrated and visualized that I was Vajrayogini, who had great devotion to Guru Rinpoche, according to the Guru Yoga *sadhana* (visualization) that I had been practicing. The prostration that afternoon thus became another meditation. Since my mind was focused, all the aches and pains disappeared. I prostrated happily. Chinese tourists stopped by and regularly took pictures of me. Some asked Yontan if they could take my picture. That was really the only question they asked.

At six o'clock in the afternoon, a white car stopped ahead of us. I thought it was another group of tourists. But that time it was different because all the four doors were flung open at the same time and red robes were flying. I looked up from my prostration and saw Kunga Sangbo Rinpoche, the abbot of Tashigong Monastery, smiling at me. I did not know how to find words to describe my joy at that moment. Rinpoche came to visit me without telling us in advance; it was like a visit from an older relative. Even though I realized that I was making merit in front of the teacher, I still felt a bit shy, because this was the first time Rinpoche saw me expressing this great faith in Buddhism.

After taking pictures with Rinpoche, I took off my headband, the wooden slab, and the wooden gloves. I tried to become the old Kesang Dawa (my Tibetan name) and invited him to sit down and have a chat, as if the ground there were my own home.

Rinpoche called his students to bring up the boiled yak meat for us. Though he was a strict vegetarian, he still had the willingness to bring the meat to us. He said that prostrators needed a lot of food so that they had the strength. Apart from the meat he started to knead *tsampa* at that spot. He had all the ingredients – butter, cheese – as well as Tibetan tea and hot water.

Before leaving, Rinpoche said that he was very happy to see me prostrating. He said that this was the real Dharma practice. After he left, I decided to continue the prostration even though it was past seven o'clock, so that I could use the energy obtained from Rinpoche's food to the full. The sky was still bright. Cars and buses were many, and the prostrator continued her journey until the sun left the sky around eight o'clock.

Day 7

I prostrated on the road, which led to a tunnel under a mountain. It was a long and seemingly never-ending road. I stopped to rest more than four times. I kept asking Yontan how much further we had to go on that expressway. He said around one kilometer. He asked me to be patient. But it seems a Tibetan kilometer is longer than what I was familiar with. I kept prostrating but could not reach the tunnel.

It was dark and there were only dimming lights from the street. When I looked at my watch, it was already nine o'clock. I told Yontan I couldn't prostrate any longer. Since noon we had not eaten anything except for some cookies.

Yontan ran to the front to see where we could pitch our tents. He came back with a worried look on his face. He said we would not be able to go on but had to stop for a night. I was delighted to stop prostrating after having done so for six continuous hours. I put off the prostration uniform, and followed Yontan quietly. I thought of the events of the past week, the good spirits that people had shown to me, the difficulties at some points. I still could not believe that I had prostrated on the expressway leading to the airport.

Day 8

I walked back to where I'd left the prostrating route yesterday. After an hour, I arrived at the Kela Riwo tunnel. After the tunnel was built, travelers could arrive at the airport quickly. Pilgrims did not usually enter the tunnel; they walked around the mountain. But I did not know that.

Yontan and I rested in front of the tunnel. He gave me a pack of peanuts and milk. It took some courage to go inside. Cars went in quickly, leaving frightening echoing sounds. Then I decided to enter the tunnel with Yontan following me closely. I did prostrations on the dusty walkway. Yontan asked me to cover my mouth and nose. He looked concerned and kept checking how I was doing. I did not think much about the road conditions, but focused my mind on the visualization.

After four hours we exited the tunnel. I was extremely happy, as if I had done something great in my life. The gloves were torn apart. The white apron had turned brown and my body was full of smoke. Near the tunnel there was a small garden. I went there and washed my face, hands, and feet. Difficulties disappeared in an instant. But after the wash, I could not resume my journey. I asked Yontan to pitch me a tent. An hour later I felt dizzy and experienced headaches. I slept for several hours, got up to eat some food, and went back to sleep again.

Day 9

I still did not feel well and could not eat. Still, I was determined to go on prostrating. I went back to the exit of Kela Riwo and performed some prostrations there. But I could do this only twenty times. I felt exhausted. My determination gave in and I had to ask Yontan to find another spot to rest. We rested a while near some shade. Yontan looked worried about my health and the prospect of our arriving at Samye within the designated time.

As my condition did not improve, we decided to walk to the airport. I still recited the refuge prayers, though deep inside I felt sad about not being able to fulfill my promise of nonstop prostrations. Finally, we reached Gongga, a town near the airport. Yontan took me to a restaurant, thinking that I might have an appetite. It felt strange for a pilgrim to eat in a restaurant. Even though the dishes were those that I used to enjoy, I could not eat any of them.

Day 10

After good rest, I felt better and resumed my prostrations again in the afternoon. We went past some villages and met a group of friendly children, who invited us to visit their homes for tea. We asked some passersby how many more days it would take us to reach Samye. They did not have the same answers. Some said one more week. Some said one month. And some insisted that we take a ferry; otherwise, we would not reach there in two weeks.

I called my parents again. Mother sounded excited to hear that I had prostrated for many kilometers. I reminded them not to forget that they were prostrating with me.

Day 13

We met a group of English tourists with white *kataks* (auspicious scarves) around their necks today. They came in and took a lot of pictures. Their guide was a Tibetan. An Englishwoman asked me in Tibetan where I was going. I told her that I was on my way to Samye and that I was a Thai, who was following a beautiful Tibetan custom. Her friends came in and gathered around while we were talking. A man offered some biscuits, which we greatly appreciated.

We went on and took a rest on the side of the road. I looked straight ahead and saw a blue mountain range far away.

Day 14

This morning we saw three children shooting at a lizard with their slings. Yontan shouted loudly, telling them not to hurt

Fig. 6
On the banks of the Brahmaputra River, it seemed that the heaven in the sky and the paradise on earth are one and the same.
Photograph Krisadawan Hongladarom

animals. His face looked serious. The boys complied, and then they became his assistants. They helped him pull the cart, hunt for firewood, and fetch the water.

We pulled the cart off the road to prepare for lunch. At the place, a monk was already there. He came alone on pilgrimage, and had only a backpack. His face was very dark, but was radiant. Yontan talked with the monk as if they had known each other for a long time. I prepared instant noodles with mushrooms and gave some to the monk as well as to the three assistants. The boys ate so fast that we needed to prepare another pot very soon.

The monk was on a pilgrimage journey to all the important sites in central Tibet. He came from Amdo in eastern Tibet, traveling by hitching and walking. When he'd first started he had a companion, but the man fell ill on the way and had to go back. The monk traveled alone. He had already been to Samye and was walking to Lhasa. The simplicity of the monk's pilgrimage inspired me greatly. Traveling with just a few belongings brings one's life much closer to nature. That evening we were invited to stay the night in a Tibetan home.

Day 15

The good rest at the house made me feel strong again. We had *tsampa* and buttered tea with the house owner. She helped me put on my prostration uniform and helped Yontan carry his cart to the road.

The road ahead led all the way to the horizon. Blue sky contrasted with white floating clouds. I prostrated with a determined heart. With recovered strength, I thought I had nothing to worry about any longer. All day I prostrated, for five kilometers, with concentrated mind. I told Yontan that I felt my body was surprisingly light and active. While we stopped for lunch, a man drove by and stopped his car to deliver us a box full of instant noodles. It was such a generous gift. I told Yontan we would never starve.

At six o'clock we decided to stop for the day. I helped Yontan pull a cart to the bank of the Brahmaputra. The scenery at that time was striking. It was as if the heaven in the sky and the paradise on earth were one and the same (Fig. 6). That was a reward that nature gave us. I watched the sky kissing the earth until the sun left our sight. I reckoned the meaning of emptiness in vast expanse.

Day 16

It was raining all day and obstacles visited us again. This time it was not illness but a problem with my visa. My doctor friend from Lhasa called to let me know that he could not extend my visa, because of the new regulations enacted after some Americans and Tibetans planted a Tibetan flag on top of Mt. Everest earlier in the month. He urged me to go back to Lhasa by May 18, the expiration date of my visa.

I could not express my feelings at the moment – frustration, disappointment, hopelessness. But after some reflection, I regained myself and told Yontan that we would take a ferry to Samye and I would do prostrations again on the desert before we arrived at Samye Monastery. He consoled me and said that I had done my best for more than two weeks.

Day 17

We decided to give our belonging to villagers and shepherds. Although they were not of much value, the gifts were treated with sacredness, as they had been used by pilgrims.

Day 18

From the shepherd's house which we adopted as our temporary base, we rode a bus for fifteen minutes to the harbor to board a two-hour ferry to the Samye shore. There were ten or fifteen people on the boat. Many of them were Han Chinese tourists; some were modern Tibetan women in tee shirts and jeans. When we got to the shore, we boarded a minivan to the monastery.

We told the driver to drop us off soon after we caught a glimpse of the monastery. Although we could see Samye's golden roof from afar, the whole place was vast desert (Fig. 7). Yontan told the driver to stop on the desert. People in the car did not know what we were up to, or why we wanted to get off in the middle of nowhere. I put on the prostration gear one piece at a time. This was the big day, the highlight of my journey. I was happy to be able to prostrate again.

Seeing the 8th-century monastery established by Guru Rinpoche himself, I prayed to my root teacher, to Guru Rinpoche, and recited four immeasurable thoughts and refuge prayers. Then I put my hands and feet on the sand.

Fig. 7

View of Samye Monastery from the distance. The monastery was built in the 8th century by the Indian teachers Padmasambhava and Shantarakshita and is among Tibet's oldest.

Photograph Dina Bangdel

Fig. 8

On the last day of the prostration pilgrimage on Day 18, the fulfillment of a dream is so close.

Photograph Meu Yontan

Traces of a pilgrim appeared on the soil, just like those shadows in Kela Riwo. With each step I took, I prayed for peace to prevail on earth and for humans not to hurt one another and not to do harm to animals.

I prostrated to where Yontan was waiting in the shade of a tree. He wanted to wipe off the sand and dust from my face. But before doing that, he burst out laughing. "Your face is like a *yogini*, not like Kesang Dawa. Your face has changed," he said. "How?" He took a photo of me in a digital camera and showed it to me.

I saw a smiling woman leaning against a tree (Fig. 8). Her body, face, and hair were dusty. She looked different from the woman in clean Lhasa dress in front of Tara temple seventeen days ago. Her smile reflected deep happiness inside. At that particular moment, peace was in her heart. She had achieved many things and her mind was transformed. The desert ground became soft carpet. Yak dung was a jeweled ornament of the desert. Surrounding her were other sentient beings who were prostrating with her.

She continued drawing images of a prostrating *yogini* on the sand with courage, and sacred happiness filled her entire being.

Fig. 9
Dedicating the blessing of the journey to all sentient beings, the vow is now complete.
Photograph Meu Yontan

SAMYE

When Yontan and I finally arrived at Samye Temple, there was a halo around the sun in the middle of the day, an auspicious sign. When we finally entered the temple, many tourist buses were there. Loud Chinese pop music punctured the air. A man dressed in prostrating uniform like myself was begging for money in front of the Assembly Hall. I walked past him to finish my journey at an ancient inscription stone (Fig. 9). The sun was intense. I stood there and recited the dedication prayer, which I had done in cemeteries, mountains, forests, and throughout the journey.

I dedicate happiness to all sentient beings without exception;
May happiness spread in the air;
I take on the sufferings of all sentient beings without exception;
May the ocean of suffering be dry.

If I am happy,
I dedicate my happiness to those who seek it;
May happiness spread in the air;
If I am suffering,

I bear the suffering of all sentient beings;
May the ocean of suffering be dry.
May the sufferings of gods and demons be collected in me;
May my happiness be transformed into theirs.

Om Mani Padme Hum.

Details of Fig. 9

Saikoku Pilgrimage: Japanese Devotees Search for Kannon

Elizabeth ten Grotenhuis

Japanese pilgrimages are of two sorts: linear pilgrimages to one sacred site, and circuit pilgrimages in which many sacred sites are visited in a prescribed order. Most Japanese pilgrimages are associated with Buddhism, although one of the most important linear pilgrimages is to the Shinto shrines of Ise, dedicated to the sun deity Amaterasu, traditionally considered the progenitrix of the Japanese imperial family. The most famous examples of circuit pilgrimages are the Pilgrimage to the Thirty-Three Holy Places of Kannon in the Western Provinces, a fifteen-hundred-mile route commemorating the Bodhisattva Kannon (Skt. Avalokiteshvara), who appears in thirty-three different forms to save sentient beings; and the "Pilgrimage to the Eighty-Eight Temples of Shikoku," an eight-hundred-mile circuit commemorating Kûkai (774-835 CE), the founder of the Japanese esoteric Shingon sect of Buddhism (Fig. 1). Some 80 percent of Japanese pilgrimages focus on deities; the rest honor the founder or patriarch of a religious school or sect.

I will discuss circuit pilgrimages venerating Kannon, focusing on the Pilgrimage to the Thirty-Three Holy Places of Kannon in the Western Provinces (*Saikoku sanjûsan Kannon junrei*), henceforward called the Saikoku ("Western Provinces") Pilgrimage. The Saikoku Pilgrimage in south-central Honshû, the largest island of Japan, is the most famous of more than two hundred Japanese circuit pilgrimages to the Thirty-Three Holy Places of Kannon located throughout the country. I will also examine in detail the sacred site of Nachi, on the coast due south of Kyoto. The Buddhist temple Seigantoji at Nachi, whose main object of devotion is the Talismanic Wheel (*nyoirin*) Kannon, is the first stop on the Saikoku Pilgrimage.

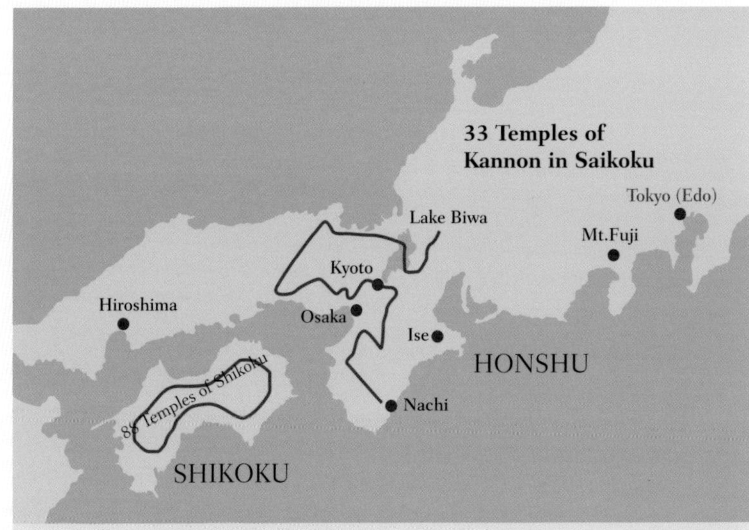

Fig. 1
Map of Japan showing Pilgrimage Routes to the Eighty-Eight Temples of Shikoku and Thirty-Three Temples of Kannon in Saikoku
Design Rachel Raguin

Victor Turner's paradigm for both the outer physical pilgrimage and the interior poetic or psychological pilgrimage is widely accepted. In Turner's view, three stages are critical for the true spiritual experience of pilgrimage. First, pilgrims must leave the specific social settings with which they are familiar. They must then undergo "liminal experiences" by means of various sorts of displacements that enable them to gain an understanding of greater or magnified truths, notably spiritual insights. Finally, they must become reintegrated into their original social structures (Rimer, 20-24). The physical journey of pilgrimage is easily imagined. This exhibition presents objects acquired on such journeys, objects that presumably contributed to the expansion of consciousness experienced by the pilgrim. These objects also enable devotees to create or recreate physical pilgrimages by psychological means once they have returned home.

PILGRIMAGES TO THE THIRTY-THREE HOLY PLACES OF KANNON

In the twenty-fifth chapter of the immensely popular *Lotus Sutra*, Kannon appears in thirty-three different forms to save all sentient creatures. This Mahayana Buddhist text presents the powerful concept that multiple emanations of individual deities manifest a unified spiritual whole. Mahayana thinkers believe in the permanent presence of the Dharma or Buddhist Law in all spheres of existence, and assert that countless Buddhas and Bodhisattvas fill the universe to assist sentient beings in their spiritual quests. Just as the historical Buddha Shakyamuni presented multiple versions of himself walking, standing, sitting, and lying down during the "miracles" at Shravasti in India, so too other deities, like Kannon, present multiple versions of themselves to inspire and save sentient beings. The thirty-three manifestations of Kannon in the Lotus Sutra include divine and human beings, male and female, and young and old. Some are of noble birth, some of humble birth (Katô, 319-27).

There is no direct correlation between the thirty-three manifestations of Kannon mentioned in the *Lotus Sutra* and the actual iconic images enshrined on the Saikoku Pilgrimage. Eleven forms of Kannon, including the Thousand-Armed Kannon and the Eleven-Headed Kannon, are venerated by devotees. Some of these images are always on view, but some – called "secret images" – are shown only one day a month, others one day a year. Eight of the "secret" Kannon images are shown only every thirty-three years, two are shown every fifty years, and nine images are never shown at all.

The Talismanic Wheel Kannon at Seigantoji at Nachi is one of six Talismanic Wheel Kannon images honored on the Saikoku Pilgrimage. The image at Seigantoji is a secret image shown annually on February 3. Seigantoji is one of fifteen temples on the Saikoku Pilgrimage belonging to the Tendai School lineage. Fifteen other temples belong to the Shingon School lineage. (The last three temples belong to the Hossô, Northern Hossô, and Honzan Shugen sects.)

Pilgrims begin the Saikoku Pilgrimage at Seigantoji at Nachi. Often a pilgrim will wear simplified garb, usually a white shirt, and will carry a sturdy staff signifying the arduous journey (Fig. 2). Sometimes pilgrims purchase the full paraphernalia: a white robe (Fig. 3), a staff (Fig. 4), and a round straw sedge hat (shaped like an inverted bowl, approximately a foot and a half in diameter). Most pilgrims carry a string of Buddhist prayer beads as well as paper prayer slips that they present to each temple along the route. These prayer slips are gathered together and eventually burned in a religious ritual at each temple.

Pilgrims also carry albums of doubled sheets of paper. These albums are blank at the beginning of the pilgrimage but full at the end: at each temple on the route, priests (for a donation equivalent to a few dollars) will certify a pilgrim's visit with vermilion stamps and with calligraphy in black charcoal ink. Priests may also stamp and inscribe pilgrims' staffs, clothing, and hats. One pilgrim's album from the Saikoku Pilgrimage (Fig. 5) is dated 1860. The number of the temple is stamped at upper right; the name of the manifestation of Kannon worshipped appears in the center of the page, written in black ink over a vermilion stamp; the date of the pilgrim's visit appears at upper left; and the name of the temple appears at lower left. In the Edo period (1615-1868), when this album was filled,

Fig. 2
Female Pilgrim at Seigantoji, Nachi.
Photograph, late 20th century.

Fig. 3
White Pilgrim's Robe with Central Inscription *Namu Amida Butsu* (Homage to Amida the Buddha) from Shikoku Pilgrimage. Dated Shôwa 52 (1977).
Robert and Marilyn Hamburger
Photograph Michel Raguin

Fig. 4
Pilgrim's Staff from Mount Kôya. Late 20th century.
Robert and Marilyn Hamburger
Photograph Michel Raguin

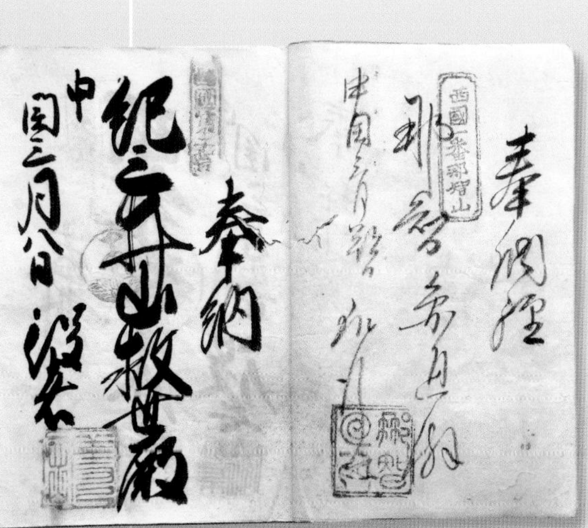

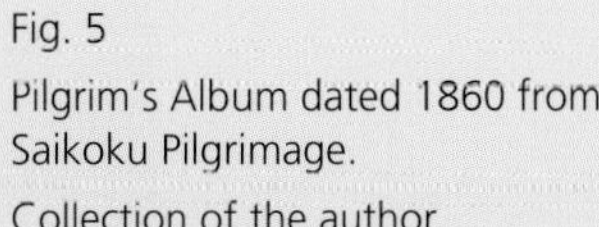

Fig. 5
Pilgrim's Album dated 1860 from Saikoku Pilgrimage.
Collection of the author.
Photograph Michel Raguin

the number of Japanese pilgrims increased dramatically. Members of the general populace had the time and means to take advantage of improved transportation. Although the government restricted travel among provinces, an exception was made for pilgrimages.

Pilgrims can also commemorate and recreate their spiritual journeys by displaying hanging scrolls with an image of Kannon surrounded by the stamps and calligraphy from each of the thirty-three holy sites. A hanging scroll (Fig. 6) dating from the mid-20th century represents the Saikoku Pilgrimage. A woodblock print (Fig. 7) shows images of the thirty-three forms of Kannon venerated on the Saikoku Pilgrimage. This memento of the spiritual journey, dating from the second half of the 19th century, was acquired at Kegonji in Gifu prefecture, the final temple to be visited on the route. The Talismanic Wheel Kannon from Seigantoji appears at the right of the register of three Kannon images at the top of the print; the name Kegonji appears at the bottom, below the Eleven-Headed Kannon from Kegonji, seen at the extreme left of the lowest register of images of Kannon. Kegonji belongs to the Tendai School lineage; its Eleven-Headed Kannon is a secret image never revealed to the pilgrim.

In the same way that multiple emanations of a single deity suggest enhanced spiritual power, multiple versions of a pilgrimage extend the potency of that spiritual route. During the Edo period, the popularity of the Saikoku Pilgrimage led to its replication: some 230 Thirty-Three Kannon pilgrimage routes were created throughout Japan, more than 30 percent in eastern Japan, close to the new capital of Edo (present-day Tokyo). The Bandô Thirty-Three Kannon Pilgrimage of eastern Japan, considered the most important replica of the original Saikoku Pilgrimage, winds through the eight provinces of the old Bandô region. Sugimotodera in Kamakura, just south of Edo, was designated the first temple on the Bandô Pilgrimage. The Saikoku and Bandô Pilgrimages were then linked to thirty-four Kannon temples on the so-called Chichibu Pilgrimage (in present-day Saitama prefecture, just north of Tokyo) to create the traditional One Hundred Temples of Kannon.

NACHI, A MULTIFACETED PILGRIMAGE SITE

Nachi is not only the first stop on the Saikoku Pilgrimage, but is also the third sacred place to be visited on the linear pilgrimage to the Three Mountains of Kumano (*Kumano sanzan*), a pilgrimage route representing Buddhist-Shinto syncretism. In 1997, officials from Wakayama prefecture, where Kumano is located, and officials of the Galician Community, signed an agreement linking the Kumano pilgrimage route to the Christian pilgrimage route to Santiago de Compostela in Spain (del Alisal, 81).

Fig. 6
Hanging Scroll of Kannon surrounded by stamps and calligraphy from Saikoku Pilgrimage. Mid-20th century.
Collection of the author
Photograph Michel Raguin

The Three Mountains of Kumano comprise three shrines: Hongû or "Main Shrine"; "Shingû" or "New Shrine"; and Nachi Shrine on the coast south of Shingû. A pilgrimage route some eighty miles long winds through beautiful forested mountains intersected by rivers along scenic coastline from Hongû to Shingû to Nachi and back to Hongû. Worship of Shinto nature deities (*kami*) probably began in this region in prehistory, and evidence of Buddhist worship dates from the 7th century: the oldest gilt-bronze image of an Eleven-Headed Kannon in Japan is a late 7th-century standing figure excavated at Nachi (ten Grotenhuis, 163). The three shrines seem to have been formally associated by the mid-11th century, when Shinto deities worshiped there came to be paired with Buddhist deities. The earliest spot where worship occurred at Nachi was very likely at the majestic four-hundred-foot-high Nachi Falls (Fig. 8). Archaeological finds of ritual objects confirm that by at least the beginning of the 8th century this waterfall was considered sacred and was venerated accordingly.

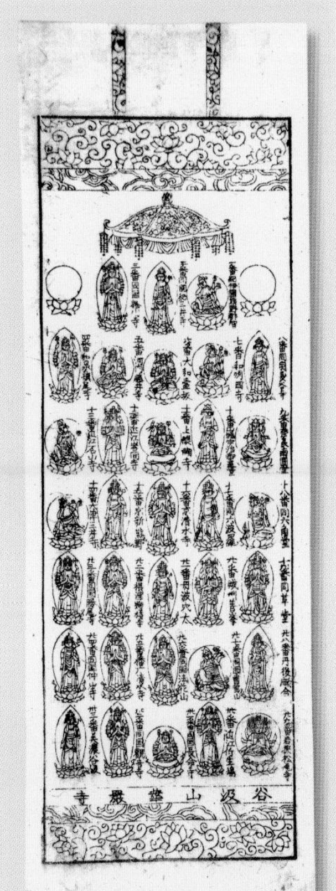

Fig. 7
Woodblock print of the Thirty-Three Forms of Kannon from the Saikoku Pilgrimage. Late 19th century. 16 x 5³/₈ in. (40.6 x 13.7 cm)
Collection of the author
Photograph Michel Raguin

In 1161 the monk Kakuchû of the temple Miidera, located just southeast of Kyoto on the shores of Lake Biwa, designated Nachi as the first stop on the Saikoku Pilgrimage. (Miidera itself is the fourteenth temple on the Saikoku Pilgrimage.) The nature deity embodied in Nachi Falls was paired with the Eleven-Headed, Thousand-Armed Kannon, and the Talismanic Wheel Kannon became the main object of devotion at present-day Seigantoji, the Buddhist temple located near the waterfall. In the *Kegon Sutra*, a boy pilgrim, Zenzai dôji (Skt. Sudhana), experiences enlightenment after walking from east to south, where he meets Kannon, an important teacher on his journey. He then walks to the west and north where he meets the primordial Buddha Dainichi (Skt. Mahāvairochana). The Saikoku Pilgrimage begins at Nachi in the east, then proceeds to temples located in the west, and finally the north. The *Kegon Sutra* may have influenced the geographical route of the Saikoku Pilgrimage just as the *Lotus Sutra* inspired the group of thirty-three temples dedicated to Kannon along the route (Usui, 36).

At the site of Nachi itself lies a linear pilgrimage beginning on the shore at the temple Fudarakusenji (Potalaka Temple), and ending at Amidaji, a Shingon sect temple dedicated to the Buddha Amida (Skt. Amitābha) on the summit of Mount Myôhô, the tallest mountain in the region. The fact that Kannon's paradise-like Pure Land, Potalaka, became identified with Nachi offers us the opportunity to explore the localizing in East Asia of sacred South Asian Buddhist sites.

Fig. 8
Nachi Falls. Photograph, late 20th century.

Fig. 9
Nachi Pilgrimage Mandala 17th century. 65 x 99 in. (165.1 x 251.5 cm).
Dr. Kurt Gitter and Ms. Alice Yelen
Photograph courtesy Dr. Kurt Gitter and Ms. Alice Yelen

THE NACHI PILGRIMAGE AND PILGRIMAGE MANDALAS

Before the 15th century, the Saikoku Pilgrimage was undertaken only by serious practitioners who had the ardor, time, and in the case of laypersons, the resources to make this long and often difficult journey. After the 15th century, the route became increasingly popular, followed partly for spiritual questing and partly for the joy of traveling. Lay priests and nuns, who could not perform official rituals but who were allowed to work in less official capacities, often solicited funds for the temples and shrines along the route. On their journeys of solicitation they would sometimes carry large representations of sacred sites painted on paper, which they would unfold and use as visual props while discussing the benefits of making pilgrimages to the sacred sites. Eleven of the thirty-three temples on the Saikoku Pilgrimage are pictured in the approximately eighty extant "pilgrimage mandalas." More than one quarter of these mandalas depict the internal, linear pilgrimage at Nachi, a much greater number than for any other site (ten Grotenhuis, 172-73) (Fig. 9).

Mandalas (Jap. *mandara*) assume many different forms in Japan, but they are all representations of sanctified realms where identification between the human and the sacred occurs. The mandala is a kind of cosmic ground plan or map, laying out a sacred realm, showing the relations among the various powers active in that realm and offering devotees a place where they can attain enlightenment. The term "pilgrimage (Jap. *sankei*) mandala" is a 20th-century term that refers to a specific kind of picture made for a popular audience primarily in the 16th and 17th centuries. Painted in what might be described as a folk or naive style, pilgrimage mandalas do not focus on depictions of deities, but rather on representations of bustling temple and shrine precincts.

Because they were used as visual aids in public lectures, pilgrimage mandalas are large, measuring three feet or more in height and four feet or more in width. Most are painted on paper, a less expensive material than the silk used in mandalas created for temple rituals. The treatment of space is often unclear, and bands of haze may be used to divide the space into cells. Bridges and stairs sometimes zigzag across the pictures in an attempt to create a sense of depth, as well as to indicate the pilgrimage route, but the compositions are generally flat, lacking convincing perspectival treatment. A round golden sun appears at the upper right and a full silver moon at the upper left, although the silver is now usually oxidized to dark gray or black. These two celestial bodies, which have a long history of representation in East Asia, are interpreted in many ways, for example, as the light that guides pilgrims to their destination, both by day and by night, and also as light that symbolizes the benefits devotees will receive in this world and in the world beyond (Bambling, 70-82).

Many Japanese make the pilgrimage to Nachi today, but they usually travel by car or bus. This is a great pity. One of the most important parts of the route, the ascent to the summit of the tallest peak in the region, is accessible only on foot. All pilgrims, however, even those who travel by car or bus, start exactly where lay priests and nuns in the past would have begun as they traced the route on a Nachi pilgrimage mandala, that is, at the seaside temple Fudarakusenji.

Looking at the Nachi shoreline from the sea (in a northwesterly direction), the pilgrim sees the actual landscape that is reproduced in the pilgrimage mandala (Fig. 10). Much of the route that pilgrims climb on foot today covers the same ground, including weathered stone steps that pilgrims trod hundreds of years ago (Fig. 11). From Fudarakusenji, pilgrims climb in a southwesterly direction until they encounter a path of stone steps. They then shift direction and climb in a northeasterly direction toward Nachi Falls, shift direction again and finally worship at the main temple and shrine complex. This fills one day of the two-day climb. The next day, pilgrims begin the ascent of the tallest mountain in the region, Mount Myôhô, located to the west some twenty-five hundred feet above sea level. The final temple to be visited is Amidaji, located near the top of the mountain. The last leg of the journey is to the Okunoin subtemple of Amidaji at the very summit of the mountain (Fig. 12). This final ascent can be made on foot only, by a climb over old moss-covered stone steps that rise precipitously. It is not surprising that a temple dedicated to the Buddha Amida is located in the west at the top of Mount Myôhô: Amida offers pilgrims who mimetically recreate the journey from this world to the next the promise of birth after death in his paradise-like Western Pure Land.

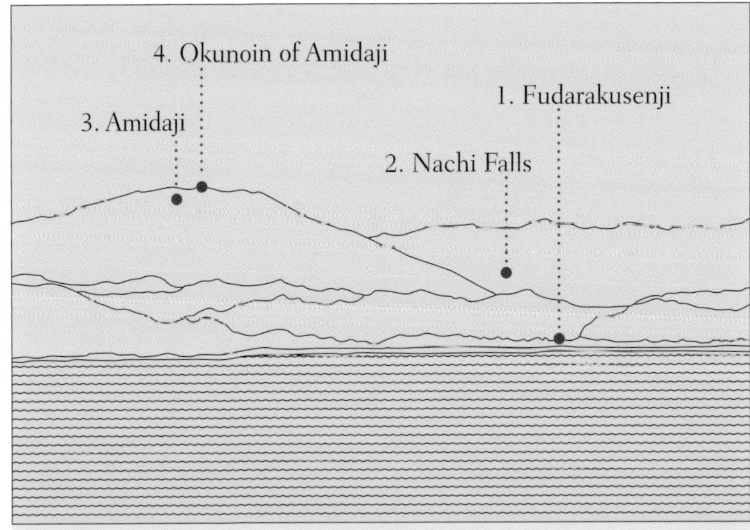

Fig. 10
Diagram: Nachi Shoreline and Nachi Pilgrimage Route.

Fig. 11
Stone Steps on Nachi Pilgrimage Route. Photograph, late 20th century.

Fig. 12
Okunoin at Amidaji, Nachi. Photograph, late 20th century.

A NACHI PILGRIMAGE MANDALA IN THE GITTER-YELEN COLLECTION

Moving from landscape to representation of landscape, pilgrims can comfortably recreate the journey mentally by contemplating a Nachi pilgrimage mandala. The Nachi pilgrimage mandala in the collection of Dr. Kurt Gitter and Ms. Alice Yelen is one of two Nachi pilgrimage mandalas in American collections, the other belonging to the Frances Lehman Loeb Art Center at Vassar College. Like most pilgrimage mandalas, the Gitter-Yelen painting is large, measuring five feet five inches by eight feet three inches, and is painted on paper with bright pigments. Despite its essentially flat appearance, the mandala presents details of the pilgrimage route quite accurately.

The pilgrimage route begins at the lower right of the mandala where Fudarakusenji is paired with the Shore Shrine, or Hama no miya. The first leg of the journey shows a gentle ascent from right to left. A pilgrim couple dressed in white is portrayed repeatedly, indicating movement through the landscape. They are the main characters who travel through the composition in the technique known in Japanese as *iji-dôzu* (different time-same illustration), the journey through time depicted on an unchanging representation of space. The fact that a man and a woman are shown in Nachi pilgrimage mandalas is significant. The presence of this couple communicates the fact that the Nachi pilgrimage is meant not only for men but also for women. In fact, Mount Myôhô has been called *nyonin Kôya*, or "women's Mount Kôya." (Mount Kôya – the site of Kûkai's Shingon-sect sanctuary – was forbidden to women until the beginning of the Meiji period in 1868.) Mountain ascetics guide the pilgrim couple at Nachi, instructing them how to worship at each sacred spot. The couple wears white clothing, which is significant. White is used to clothe corpses, but it is also the traditional color of the clothes of pilgrims, who experience a symbolic death and rebirth by their pilgrimage.

A lady dressed in aristocratic clothes of the Heian period (794-1185) appears in the center foreground of the painting just below the large curved bridge. This figure has traditionally been identified as Izumi Shikibu (lived c. 1000), the most accomplished poet of her day, who left a collection of more than fifteen hundred *waka* (thirty-one-syllable poems). Married twice, and the mistress of two imperial princes, Izumi wrote poetry that expressed on the one hand her intensely amorous nature, and on the other her longing to transcend passion through Buddhist practice (Moerman, 194-200). She made pilgrimages to Kumano and is commemorated not only in Nachi pilgrimage mandalas but also in woodblock prints such as the one designed collaboratively in 1858-59 by Hiroshige II and Toyokuni III (Fig. 13). This print is part of a series, the Miracles of Kannon (*Kannon reigenki*), which presents emblematic images from the temples on the Saikoku, Bandô, and Chichibu pilgrimages. Hiroshige II (1826-69) designed the landscapes presented on single panel screens across the top of each print in the series. In his view of Nachi, the artist juxtaposed Nachi Falls at right with a hall identified as the Nyoirindô at left (present-day Seigantoji). The waterfall spills down into the middle and lower parts of the composition, which were designed by Toyokuni III, also called Kunisada (1786-1864). Izumi Shikibu, now garbed in a 19th-century kimono, stands holding her pilgrim's staff near the Shinto *torii* gate found at the base of the falls, an attendant kneeling beside her. This print, which is soiled and was folded vertically in two at one time (probably for insertion in an album) originally was a popular, inexpensive memento of Nachi.

Having journeyed from right to left in the foreground plane of the mandala, pilgrims cross the second curved bridge and now reverse their direction to travel from left to right in the middle section of the mandala in the direction of Nachi Falls. The large architectural complex at upper left shows shrine buildings adjacent to a Buddhist temple. The Buddhist temple houses the Talismanic Wheel Kannon, the first of the thirty-three manifestations of Kannon honored in the Saikoku Pilgrimage. The painting also shows aristocrats on pilgrimage seated in the middle of the large courtyard. Perhaps these figures represent Retired Emperor Goshirakawa and his entourage, who in the 12th century made thirty-three pilgrimages to Kumano (Moerman, 163-67).

The Nachi pilgrimage continues with the ascent of Mount Myôhô, represented in the upper left edge of the Gitter-Yelen painting. This is in fact a longer journey than the journey from the shore to the main Nachi complex, but

Fig. 13
Nachi from series *Miracles of Kanno*
Hiroshige II and Toyokuni III, 1858-59
Woodblock print, 13½ x 8⅞ in.
(34.3 x 22.5 cm)
Collection of the author
Photograph Michel Raguin

because there are no major temples and shrines to visit on the way, the distance is compressed in the painting to a narrow vertical space. Stone stairs mark the approach to Amidaji. The ultimate goal of the pilgrimage is Amidaji's subtemple Okunoin at the very summit. Okunoin's funerary monuments are shown just to the left of the oxidized moon in the Gitter-Yelen mandala.

POTALAKA LOCALIZED ON THE NACHI SHORE

A characteristic feature of Nachi pilgrimage mandalas is the small boat with a large white sail, shown in the lower right of the painting. This boat represents the rudderless, oarless boats that carried enlightenment seekers searching for the Bodhisattva Kannon's offshore island Pure Land, called Fudarakusen in Japanese, Potalaka in Sanskrit. Tradition holds that, in the years between 868 and 1722, twenty-five earnest priests set sail from the port of Nachi, probably nailed into coffin-like boxes. The boats following the Potalaka-bound boat were filled with well-wishers who accompanied the religious suicide on the first part of his journey out to sea, benefiting from that association. Other well-wishers are shown on shore.

Fudarakusen/Potalaka, believed to be an actual site in India, came to be identified with actual sites elsewhere in Asia. A seaport on the Indus River called Potala may have given its name to the mountainous retreat identified as the dwelling of Avalokiteshvara/Kannon and often located on the southeastern coast of India. The most well known evocation of Potalaka today is probably the Potala Palace in Lhasa. The Fifth Dalai Lama of Tibet, considered like all dalai lamas to be an incarnation of Avalokiteshvara, began to build this palace in 1645.

Several places were localized as Kannon's earthly Pure Land in Japan. The most important are Mount Mikasa, which rises behind the Kasuga Shrine in Nara; Mount Futara at Nikkô; Mount Ashizuri on Shikoku (where the nearby temple Kongôfukuji is the thirty-eighth stop on the Pilgrimage to the Eighty-Eight Temples of Shikoku); Mount Otowa at Kiyomizudera in Kyoto, the sixteenth stop on the Saikoku Pilgrimage; and Mount Myôhô at Nachi. These sites were probably chosen because even in pre-Buddhist times they were already sacred precincts on earth. Their physical features may also have seemed to correspond to passages in Buddhist texts. The *Shin Kegon Sutra* of 695-99 CE, a Chinese re-editing of the *Avatamsakasûtra*, describes the visit of Zenzai dôji to this Pure Land, where the boy hears the Law preached by the enthroned Kannon. Zenzai dôji is told to go to "Fudaraku in the ocean," a mountain with springs, streams, and ponds where Kannon sits in the west on a diamond boulder on a plateau, surrounded by enlightened beings. Although Fudaraku/Potalaka is described as being in or on the ocean, the mountain is never called an island in the *Shin Kegon Sutra*. The mountain seems to exist in the ocean of wisdom that can be crossed thanks to the guidance of Kannon (ten Grotenhuis, 160-61).

An increasing amount of water imagery seems to be one of the transformations relating to Kannon's Pure Land as it was appropriated in East Asia. In China, Fudarakusen was localized as an island seventy miles offshore the coastal city of Ningbo. This island, called Putuoluojia or Putuoshan in Chinese, is strategically placed on the sea route that linked north and south China and also on the route that linked China and Japan. After the 8th century, Japanese navigators generally used this route when they sailed to China, stopping at Okinawa before arriving at Ningbo and Yuezhou. The sailors, merchants, and monk-pilgrims who traveled back and forth from Japan to China may have brought back tales about this island believed to be Kannon's Pure Land. Putuoshan, considered a Daoist heaven before the 7th century, became identified as Potalaka in the 10th century. Pilgrims are known to have committed religious suicide at Putuoshan either because they wished to end their earthly miseries and achieve a quick birth into the Pure Land of Kannon (Ch. Guanyin) or because they had experienced an ecstatic vision of Guanyin and wished to join the Bodhisattva immediately (Yü, 197-98).

NACHI TODAY

Nachi has experienced a revival in the late 20th century that is the result of a growing link between pilgrimage and tourism. In fact, a pilgrim's experience and a tourist's experience can be similar, especially in light of Turner's description of pilgrimage. Both pilgrims and tourists leave

their usual social settings. Many tourists, particularly those who are seeking to understand their history or culture or religion, may, like the truth-seeking pilgrim, experience "displacements" that change their understanding of the world. Tourists as well as pilgrims may have experiences that lead to new knowledge or creative growth. Both tourists and pilgrims then need to process their experiences when they return home.

Near the Fudarakusen temple, an old wooden marker and a new granite post alert pilgrims that they are on the Old Kumano Road. The revival of the Old Kumano (pilgrimage) road seems to be related to the "movement to revive rural areas" (*muraokoshi*), which has been promoted in Japan since the 1960s (del Alisal, 81). This movement is linked to worldwide, back-to-nature activities like organic farming and communal agrarian living. The search for an authentic past often underlies these movements. The new granite post at Nachi also calls the route the "way of the mandala." This designation may reflect a heightened interest in mandalas among some Japanese, perhaps related to the so-called esoteric boom of the 1980s. This esoteric boom in Japan was partly inspired by Kûkai's 1,150th death anniversary in 1985.

In 1992 a granite stele was erected at Fudarakusenji, listing the names of the twenty-five priests who, tradition holds, set sail from Nachi shore between the 9th and the 18th centuries bound for Potalaka. The boat of an enlightenment seeker, copied from a Nachi pilgrimage mandala, appears at the beginning of the stele (Fig. 14). An inscription at the end of the stele records that it was erected "to comfort the spirits of those who journeyed across the sea and also to pray for the revival or restoration of Kumano, which is a manifestation of the other world in this world." The temple displays wooden boards decorated with designs of peonies, which some believe are fragments of an enlightenment-seeker's boat that washed up on shore after the boat was wrecked at sea. The mythologizing of the earnest believers who could not wait for a natural death to make the journey to Kannon's Pure Land has certainly contributed to the contemporary "Kumano boom." A reluctant religious suicide is the protagonist of "Passage to Fudaraku," a famous story by the Japanese author Yasushi Inoue (1907-91), available in English in the collection *Lou-lan and Other Stories* (Inoue, 139-60).

Pilgrims to Nachi today will often bring home cotton hand and head towels called *tenugui* as personal souvenirs

Fig. 14
Stele Commemorating Enlightenment Seekers, Fudarakusenji, Nachi. Dated 1992.
Photograph Elizabeth ten Grotenhuis

or gifts for others. The towels can be worn on the head in different ways (Fig. 15) and often bear representations such as Nachi Falls and Seigantoji. A vertically oriented *tenugui* features Nachi Falls (Fig. 16). Other ephemera from the pilgrimage to Nachi are amulets (Fig. 17) which cost the equivalent of a few dollars. One amulet from Fudarakusenji promises "improvement of one's fortune" (*kaiun*). An enlightenment-seeker's boat is seen at the top of this amulet, which is made from a small piece of wood placed inside a cloth pouch. The inscription *kaiun* appears on the reverse. Other auspicious objects from Fudarakusenji include representations of sacred lotus petals with a design of an enlightenment seeker sailing out to sea accompanied by well wishers as well as the Eleven-Headed, Thousand-Armed Kannon associated with Nachi Falls. A common image appears on the reverse of each of the petals. Two amulets that are sold at Amida-ji on Mount Myôhô show entities associated with dates. The image of Dainichi is associated with the year of the monkey (one of the twelve zodiacal animals), meant to protect persons born in the years 1932, 1944, 1956, 1968, 1980, 1992, and 2004. Amida is associated with the year of the dog, meant to protect those born in the years 1934, 1946, 1958, 1970, 1982, 1994, and 2006.

In 1997, as mentioned earlier, officials representing Wakayama prefecture and officials of the Spanish Galician Community signed an agreement to link the Road to Santiago and the Kumano Pilgrimage Route. Since then, Japanese Buddhist monks have visited Santiago de Compostela along with youth groups, ecological association members, and hiking club members from Wakayama who have traveled under prefectural auspices. Each year more and more Japanese walk the whole way to Santiago following the French Road from Roncesvalles and Somport in the Pyrenees. In 2003 about 150 Japanese walked more than sixty miles on the pilgrimage. The Spanish response to this sister-pilgrimage agreement has yet to reach the enthusiasm of the Japanese (del Alisal, 81-82). We may hope that in the future increasing numbers of European and Japanese pilgrims will benefit from exploring not only their own pilgrimage routes but also the routes of other cultures.

See further reading on page 340

Fig. 15

Towel (*tenugui*) Showing ways to wear the towel on the head. Late 20th century.

Sylvan Barnet and William Burto.

Photograph Michel Raguin

Fig. 16

Vertical Towel Showing Nachi Falls. Late 20th century.

Sylvan Barnet and William Burto

Photograph Michel Raguin

Fig. 17

Group of Amulets from Fudarakusenji and Amidaji, Nachi. Late 20th century

Top Row: two amulets from Amida-ji on Mount Myôhô, on the left Dainichi, protector of the year of the monkey and on the right, Amida, protector of the year of the dog.

Middle Row: (Right) Fudarakusenji amulet of Eleven-Headed, Thousand-Armed Kannon associated with Nachi Falls. (Left) Fudarakusenji lotus petal amulet showing enlightenment seeker setting sail. The color copy image in the center appears on the reverse of each of the petals.

Bottom Row: Fudarakusenji amulet promising "improvement of one's fortune" (*kaiun*)

Collection of the author

Photograph Michel Raguin

CHRISTIANITY

Details of Fig. 24

Christian Pilgrimage in the Middle Ages and the Renaissance

Virginia C. Raguin

Christians have embraced pilgrimage as an essential search for stability in the face of the ephemera of life. The practice can be seen in relationship to the religion's central tenet, the incarnation of Christ. Within a triune God, consisting of the Father, Son, and Holy Spirit, the second person, the Son, is both God and Man through his birth from Mary (Fig. 1). Consequently, both the search for the physical trace of God on earth and the desire to depict the person of Jesus have galvanized Christian piety from its origins. At the beginning of the 8th century CE, John of Damascus eloquently articulated the principle:

> *Of old, God the incorporeal and uncircumscribed was never depicted. Now, however, when God is seen clothed in flesh, and conversing with men, I make an image of the God whom I see. I do not worship matter, I worship the God of matter, who became matter for my sake, and deigned to inhabit matter, who worked out my salvation through matter* (*Internet Medieval Sourcebook*).

Christians therefore believe that Christ possesses two natures, divine and human, and that his human nature died and rose from the dead, a tangible promise of the resurrection of the dead for all his followers. As Peter Brown states:

> *In believing in the resurrection of the dead, Jews and Christians could envision that one day the barriers of the universe would be broken.... The joining of Heaven and Earth was made plain even by the manner in which contemporaries designed and described the shrines of the saints. Filled with great candelabra, their dense clusters of lights mirrored in shimmering mosaic and caught in the gilded roof, late Roman* memoriae *brought the still light of the Milky Way to within a few feet of the grave* (Brown, 2, 4).

It is this tangible, human history of Christ that weighs so heavily in the development of Christian traditions such as veneration of the tomb and motivation of pilgrimage. Since the earliest evidence of the cult, adherents expressed a desire to be close to the sites of its origin. The first object of pilgrimage was the Holy Land, the place where Christ lived his life. The anonymous pilgrim of Bordeaux wrote around 333 CE, arriving in the Holy Land presumably while the construction of the basilica of the Holy Sepulcher was still in process.

These early pilgrims were desirous of returning with a tangible souvenir of the pilgrimage. Relics for the pilgrim might be a stone from the Holy Land, water from a well, or even a piece of cloth or a statue that touched Christ's tomb.

Felix Fabri was a Dominican brother from Ulm, Germany who visited the Holy Land between 1480 and 1484. His extensive commentary covers practical and topographic observations, accounts of his own actions, even critiques of what he considered dubious relics and unscrupulous vendors. He also speaks of what is apparently one of the oldest and most honored of pilgrimage practices, picking up dirt or stones from the places visited, and also buying materials that are touched to these holy places.

> *I rose up early, before sunrise, and having said matins, I stole out of the convent alone and rambled off to the holy places on Mount Sion, in the Valley of Jehoshaphat, and on the Mount of Olives. In each of these places I picked up pebbles, marked them, and put them into a bag which I carried with me for that purpose. Moreover, I gathered up some thorns which grow in the hedges on the side of the Mount of Olives and Mount Sion, and I bound twigs of them together and wove them into a crown of thorns in the way of the thorns wherewith I believe that the Lord Jesus was crowned. All that day I labored at gathering stones and cutting off branches of thorns… and brought them home with me to Ulm. Let no one think it useless or childish of me to bring pebbles to our country with me from the holy places, for I read that the holy men of old did this [Naaman:2 Kgs. 5:17]…. By no means, therefore, and in no wise, do pieces of stone brought from that illustrious land deserve to be despised and cast away, but to be gathered up with great devotion and placed among the chief relics of churches. And not only the earth itself and pebbles and bits of stone, but also beads and rosaries, rings and symbols in rosaries, which have touched the holy places are in some sort hallowed and made thereby more venerable and precious…. Neither is it we Western Christians alone who do this thing, but the Eastern Christians from the furthermost parts of the East collect these pebbles in the Holy Land and carry them as it were to the gates of Paradise as most respected relics….*
>
> *On the same day, also, I bought three costly cloths for our sacristy wherewith to cover the chalice when it is being carried out by the subdeacon, and when he holds the paten aloft: one of these cloths is white, another blue, and the third yellow. I carried these cloths to all the holy places, and often spread them out upon the Lord's sepulcher, upon the rock of the cross, upon the sepulcher of the blessed Virgin, on the Lord's manger, and elsewhere, to the end that by touching these holy places they might themselves become holier, and therefore of greater price.*

Felix Fabri. 1971. *The Book of the Wanderings of Felix Fabri*. Aubry Stewart, trans. 2 vols. Palestine Pilgrims Text Society 7-10. Reprint. New York: AMS Press, vols 9-10, 214-17

Fig. 1

Trinity: God the Father holding the Crucified Son with the Dove of the Holy Spirit between Them

York, England, St. John's Ousebridge End, c.1498

Donation of Sir Richard York, Lord Mayor of York

North Transept, York Minster

Photograph Virginia C. Raguin

Fig. 2
Reliquary chasse
English, Canterbury, 1207-1213
Copper shaped, engraved, chased and gilded, 7 x 10 x 4½ in. (17.8 x 25.4 x 11.4 cm)
The Metropolitan Museum of Art, The Cloisters Collection, 1980 (1980.417)

Fig. 3
Replica of a Nail of Christ's Passion from Santa Croce in Gerusalemme, Rome
Attestation certificate signed 1882
Wooden box with glass lid, 9 x 12 x 2½ in. (22.9 x 30.5 x 6.4 cm)
The Liturgy and Life Collection at the John J. Burns Library at Boston College
Photograph Michel Raguin

A 6th-century painted box now in the Vatican contains bits of soil and stones as souvenirs of places in the Holy Land. The interior of the lid depicts the Nativity, Crucifixion, Christ's Baptism in the Jordan, and other scenes, serving as a meditational summary of the pilgrim's experience (Elsner, 746). The faithful did not believe that the actual presence of the holy person remained in such relics (bones, clothes worn, or elements of martyrdom, such as the stones used to kill the first martyr, St. Stephen), but that these things would act as conduits to grace. These mementos were invariably encased in the most elaborate housing available to the owner, for example the copper gilt reliquary from Canterbury, dated 1207-1213 (Fig. 2), now in the Metropolitan Museum of Art.

Reverence therefore extended not only to Christ, but to the tangible remains of heroic Christians, the confessors and martyrs, especially for the founding of new churches. This desire encouraged the partition of bodies to allow the sacred "aura" to be shared within a growing community. Churches were founded with relics as their essential talismans, and stone altars with cavities inscribed with their list of relics, a practice that later became routine, date from 320. For the founding of Canterbury in the 5th century, according to Bede (673-735), the pope provided Augustine with "all the things needful for the worship and service of the church, namely, sacred vessels, altar linen, church ornaments, priestly and clerical vestments, relics of the holy Apostles and martyrs, and also many books" (Hist. Eccl., I, xxix). In another example, the French city of Rouen celebrated the arrival of relics from Rome in 396. Victricius spoke for the Christian community by pleading: "Give me these temples of saints.... If a light touch of the hem of the savior's garment could cure (reference to Christ healing the woman with the issue of blood when she touched his robe, described in Lk 8:43-48), then there is no doubt that these dwelling places of martyrdom (the relics) carried in our arms, will cure us" (Hillgarth, 23). Even the authorized replication of relics, as exemplified by the relic of the Nail of the Santa Croce in Gerusalemme (Fig. 3) (see essay *Rome's Santa Croce in Gerusalemme and Relics of the Passion of Christ*), continued through the centuries.

Fig. 4
York Passion Play (Play 35), enacted July 2006, York Minster church yard
Soldiers nail Christ to the Cross
Photograph Virginia C. Raguin

Fig. 5
York Passion Play (Play 35), enacted July 2006, York Minster church yard
Christ dies on the Cross
Photograph Virginia C. Raguin

THE CHRISTIAN LITURGY AND EMPATHY

The Christian liturgy each year presented a cycle of feasts that commemorated the redemption of the human race through Christ's Death and Resurrection. The year began with Advent, four weeks of preparation before Christ's Nativity; then the spring season of Lent, which leads to the commemoration of Christ's Passion and his Resurrection; and finally the descent of the Holy Spirit and the establishment of the Church at Pentecost. Feasts commemorating specific saints were interspersed along this calendar year. Associated with the priestly liturgy, however, were more public and participatory rituals, such as the cycle of Passion Plays performed from at least the 15th century in York, England, enacted not by the clergy, but by the trade organizations of the city. Forty-eight pageants depicting sacred history from the Creation to the Last Judgment were dragged through the streets on wagons and enacted in public squares. The action was dramatic; for example, the four soldiers at the Crucifixion (Play 35) complain, joke, insult (Fig. 4), struggle with ropes pulling Christ's hands and feet straight, and argue over dividing Christ's cloak – here, the senior officer claims it for his own. Thus, Christians were encouraged to pray by concentrating on these events and empathizing with the actors of this redemptive drama. Christ was central for his accepted suffering, but also the Virgin Mary who saw her son tormented (Fig. 5). Spectators were consistently enjoined to experience metaphorically the life of Christ; displacing themselves to experience their lives in the actual site on pilgrimage was simply the logical extension.

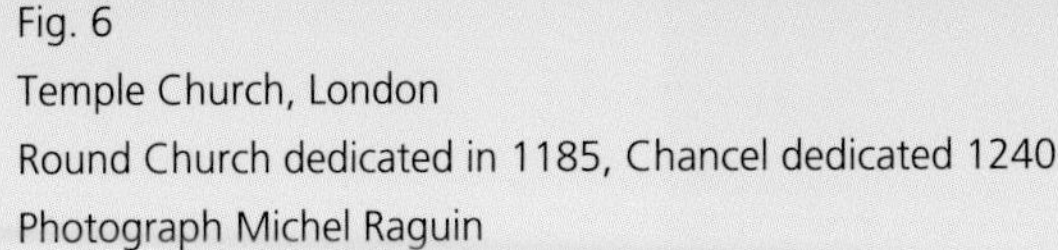

Fig. 6
Temple Church, London
Round Church dedicated in 1185, Chancel dedicated 1240
Photograph Michel Raguin

Fig. 7
Temple Church, London. Interior of Round Church.
1185, with interior embellishments 1240
Photograph Michel Raguin

Just as Christians were encouraged to imagine themselves at the side of Christ in their prayers, so too constructions that replicated – or at least evoked – the sacred sites of the Holy Land were popular. Architectural evocations of the sepulcher are noted at seventy European sites, thirty-one of which retain significant remains. In the 1120s a fraternity of the Holy Sepulcher is noted in Cambridge, and a round church, built around 1130, shows massive internal piers embodying the full force of Norman Romanesque. At this time the Latins occupied the Holy Land and were engaged in reconstructing the remnants of the Constantinian Church of the Holy Sepulcher, which had suffered extensive damages in 1009. This new building followed the Romanesque style then current in the West. The Knights Templar, the monastic military order founded in 1118 with the purpose of protecting pilgrims to Jerusalem, built a "Holy Sepulcher" as their London citadel (Fig. 6). It was dedicated in 1185 by the patriarch of Jerusalem, two years before Salah al-Din, the sultan of Egypt and Syria, was to reconquer Jerusalem. The round building does not copy the precise form of the structure in Jerusalem but it does evoke a lavish and dignified space through its vaulted ceiling, Purbeck marble piers, and sophisticated decorative carving (Fig. 7). At times when travel to the Holy Land was dangerous because of political hostilities, Roman sites which had significant relics became substitute destinations. Chief among them were Santa Croce in Gerusalemme with its relics of the Passion and Santa Maria Maggiore with its relics of the Infancy of Christ (see following essays).

Fig. 8

St. James as pilgrim, wearing hat with pilgrim's badges, and purse at his waist. He wears a traveler's cloak and carries a staff.

Switzerland, Monastery of Wettingen (CloisterW11a). Panel offered by Hans Hünegger and Regina von Sur, 1522

Photograph Virginia C. Raguin

THE UNCHANGING: "WHAT IS, ALWAYS WAS"

Later, Christians projected their sense of the pilgrimage onto Christ's followers through narratives of Christ's life that echoed contemporary behavior. Nicholas Love (d. 1424), a monk at Mount Grace, a Carthusian monastery in Yorkshire, wrote *The Mirror of the Blessed Life of Jesus Christ* addressed to the average person of the early 15th century. The vernacular text was based on the highly influential *Meditationes vitae Christi*, a Franciscan work of about 1374. In it the reader/listener is encouraged to spend the week retracing the life of Christ from birth to death and resurrection. In it we find numerous references to later-medieval practices. The Virgin Mary, for example, is described as actually venerating the cross on which her son died: "she knelede done & honourede the cross & seide, here made my son his ende, & here is his precious blode" (she knelt down and honored the cross and said, here my son came to his end and here is his precious blood) (Love, 186). Christians were encouraged to have physical contact with holy objects, such as the cross. As introduced in the essay *Origins and History of Pilgrimage for Christians, Muslims, and Buddhists* in this collection, sanctity could be transmitted by touch or at least physical proximity. Christians would pass by, touch, embrace, or kiss a relic, or have a relic imposed on their bodies.

Imagery supported this behavior. Throughout the Middle Ages and the Renaissance, historical images were presented in contemporary setting and dress. For example, St. James was invariably shown as a medieval pilgrim dressed in a long cloak, with staff, purse, and broad-brimmed hat with the scallop shell, the sign of the pilgrimage to Santiago (Fig. 8). Even the Virgin and Christ Child could be shown as pilgrims (Fig. 9). In another moment of retrospective appropriation, episodes in Christ's life, particularly episodes of travel, were conflated with contemporary practice. Viewers could empathize with the vicissitudes faced by Mary and Joseph as they fled Bethlehem for Egypt to escape from the wrath of Herod, who had ordered boys massacred when he learned from the Magi that a great king had been born (Mt 2). Urs Graf the Elder, an early 16th-century Swiss printmaker, shows travel and the exotic through Christ's arrival in Jerusalem just before his death (Mt 21; Mk 11; Lk 19; Jn 12). In the *Entry into Jerusalem* Christ is on a donkey with a cluster of men behind him and a mass of young boys on the right (Fig. 10). The city of Jerusalem is labeled *Hierusalem* and dominates the upper right. A walled medieval city, it contains a round structure to the far right. To the viewer it may seem a reference to the Church of the Holy Sepulcher – or to generic imagery used for ancient cities, such as Rome.

Fig. 9

The Virgin and Infant Christ as Pilgrims [the handle on the back of the statue suggests that it was carried in procession and extended to bless by touch]

Spain (Galicia), Compostela, 19th-20th centuries

Wood with polychrome, 11¾ x 6 in. (29.8 x 15.2 cm)

Museo das Peregrinacións, Santiago de Compostela; Ministerio de Cultura. Nº Inv.:236

Photograph Museo das Peregrinacións

Fig. 10

Entry into Jerusalem, 1506-09

Urs Graf the Elder, Swiss 1485-1527/28

Woodcut 8¾ x 6¼ in. (22.2 x 15.9 cm)

Art Institute of Chicago, Gift of Mr. and Mrs. Potter Palmer Jr., 1937.78

Photograph Art Institute of Chicago

One of the episodes in Christ's life most consistently associated with pilgrimage was the Supper at Emmaus (Lk 24:13–36). Indeed, in the performance of the Road to Emmaus in Play 40 of the York Mystery Plays, the characters are named Pilgrim 1 and Pilgrim 2. The day after Christ's death and resurrection, two of his followers went to a town called Emmaus, a day's walk from Jerusalem. While they talked, Jesus drew near them. Deeply troubled by their loss, they did not recognize him. As they conversed, Christ expounded on the meaning of the Scriptures and the necessity for the suffering of the Messiah. They then stopped at an inn and during supper when "he took bread, blessed, broke, and gave it to them… their eyes were opened and they knew him." The association of walking long distances, conversing about holy things, and arriving at a destination connect this experience to pilgrimage. Momentous events focused the pilgrim's purpose and hope. Each pilgrim longs to experience the encounter with the holy and feel the revered person speaking to the soul, as experienced at Emmaus. Thus it is not surprising that the Supper at Emmaus was frequently depicted with the apostles as contemporary pilgrims. Veronese painted in the mid-1570s a Supper at Emmaus showing a disciple wearing several pilgrim's badges (Museum Boijmans Van Beuningen, Rotterdam). One of the most memorable examples is Caravaggio's painting of 1601, now in the National Gallery, London, showing the astonished apostle to the right wearing a scallop shell on his vest. Earlier, a small print by Urs Graf actually shows Christ as the pilgrim, seated in the midst of his disciples and wearing the broad-brimmed hat with scallop emblem.

PILGRIMAGE AND MONASTICISM

Although Christian monasticism concerns the enclosure of the individual and pilgrimage the movement from place to place, the institutions became historically intertwined. Monasticism began as a practice of hermits located in areas of the eastern Mediterranean in the late 3rd to early 4th centuries. St. Antony (d. 356) and other men and women withdrew into the deserts to practice fasting, sexual abstinence, and intense prayer. As they began to attract followers, they developed modified systems conducive of a communal life. Monastic communities soon entered into the lives of cities, both in Eastern and Western Europe, ultimately becoming a significant economic, social, and intellectual force. By the time of the emperor Justinian in the 6th century, there were more than seventy monasteries in the city of Constantinople. In the West, St. Benedict (d. 547) withdrew to the wilderness in Southern Italy, founding twelve monasteries, the most important being Montecassino. The *Rule of St. Benedict*, compiled in the first half of the 6th century, set out a plan for communal and individual prayer, duties of the abbot, injunctions against private ownership, and rules for celibacy. By the 9th century, Benedictine monasticism had developed a typical architectural system, promoted by Louis the Pious, the son of Charlemagne. He encouraged the regularization of monastic life according to the Benedictine Rule; from this time we possess a manuscript known as the Plan of St. Gall, showing a schematic rendering of an ideal monastic establishment. The plan includes a church with adjoining structures for sleeping, eating, meeting, and storage located around an open court called a cloister. Additional structures such as a mill, gardens, forge, barns, and living quarters for agricultural workers suggested that the monastery was meant to function as an independent institution within a rural economy.

Since they produced no children, the monks (male or female) were able to consolidate wealth and to achieve a marked independence from both local ecclesiastical and secular authority. The monasteries were viewed as the place most given over to prayer – and prayer in this society was a vital currency of spiritual exchange. The reclusive life afforded freedom for such pursuits, and those outside the monasteries petitioned the monks for inclusion in their prayers. From early times many of the monastic sites were built around a spiritual leader. St. Benedict's relics were actually removed from the original site of Montecassino during a period of political unrest in the later 7th century and were transported to the monastery of Fleury-sur-Loire in the vicinity of Orléans. Renamed Saint-Benoît-sur-Loire, the monastery was one of the most influential of the Middle Ages. During the 12th century a massive vaulted church with a deep porch was constructed (Fig. 11). The north portal,

Fig. 12
Relics of St. Benedict taken from his tomb in Monte Cassino and placed in a reliquary
North porch, Saint-Benoît-sur-Loire, mid-13th century
Photograph Michel Raguin

Fig. 11
Saint-Benoît-sur-Loire, France
View of entrance porch, 12th century
Photograph Michel Raguin

built in the 13th century, shows Christ enthroned, and on the lintel below, the story of the relics. French monks open up the tomb of St. Benedict and remove the relics (Fig. 12); on their way north the relics heal the sick and restore the lame; at Fleury they are welcomed by the brethren with incense (Fig. 13). The thuribles that monks swung on chains evoke architectural forms and, as times progressed, the forms evolved with the architectural styles (Fig. 14).

Although the cloistered areas of monasteries were forbidden to all except the residents, often the churches were structured to allow access for outsiders to venerate important relics. Benedict's relics, and the list of miracles attributed to his intercession, were chronicled by the monks in the *Miracula S. Benedicti* and attracted pilgrims to the site. Such relics were invariably housed in splendid containers (Fig. 2). Like the thuribles, the reliquary forms evolved with the times. A church-shaped reliquary of the 15th century from Braunschweig, Germany, shows the pointed roof and thin towers characteristic of the later Gothic period (Fig. 15). Reliquaries frequently adopted liturgical forms that had became popular for the display of the Eucharist, that of the

Fig. 13
Relics of St. Benedict cure a sick woman and are welcomed by the monks of Saint-Benoît-sur-Loire
North porch, Saint-Benoît-sur-Loire, mid-13th century
Photograph Michel Raguin

monstrance into which the host was placed for adoration by the faithful. A Braunschweig monstrance of about the same era contains a relic of St. Christina and uses crystal as well metal (Fig. 16). Sight, as often observed in scholarly literature, was prioritized and transparent materials such as crystal were favored elements of such displays.

Santiago de Compostela is probably the quintessential example of the venerated tomb (see essays: *St. James: The Eternal Pilgrim* and *Medieval Christian Pilgrims' Guides and Pilgrims' Texts*). It, however, is not a monastic church but a cathedral, and from the first was set in the midst of a populated site. Indeed, the discovery of the body of St. James is attributed to Theudemirus (d. 847), Bishop of Ira Flavia. The subsequent church built over the tomb was set within the hierarchy of the Galician church. By the 12th century, however, a network of monastic foundations promoted the pilgrimage on several routes through France and northern Spain to Gallicia. These routes were called the Way of St. James (Camino de Santiago). The itinerary, written after 1137 by an anonymous Frenchman, names natural landmarks, local customs, and specific buildings with their venerated

Fig. 14
Censer
Hallmarked with the initials MO and tower of Genoa
Italian, Genoa, early 17th century
Cast silver, 9¾ in. (24.8 cm)
Loyola University Museum of Art, Martin D'Arcy Collection, Gift of Mrs. Donald F. G. Arthur Stromberg, 1976.07
Photograph LUMA

saints. Along this route flowed artistic, economic, and cultural exchanges. The great 12th-century churches, such as Vézelay to the north and Moissac in the south, evidenced the same forms of great vaulted spaces, ponderous weight of masonry, and awe-inspiring sense of permanence; this saint will be honored – and efficacious – forever.

As the monasteries interacted more and more with the secular world, particularly as sites of pilgrimage, their decorative programs reflected these purposes. The windows of Canterbury Cathedral's Trinity Chapel, to the east of the choir, depict the miracles St. Thomas Becket (1119-1170). Becket, archbishop of Canterbury, had been murdered by emissaries of Henry II in a dispute over clerical privilege (Fig. 17). The outrage was exacerbated by the fact that he was struck while he was in engaged in prayer in the cathedral, and his bloody tunic came to be venerated at Santa Maria Maggiore in Rome (see essay *The Relics of the Infancy of Christ at Rome's Santa Maria Maggiore,* Fig. 5). Becket was canonized two years after his death, and miracles were soon recorded at his tomb. The windows (Fig. 18), installed from 1185 to 1207 and 1213/15 to 1220, promulgated his cult, a tradition that formed the basis for Chaucer's *Canterbury Tales*, in which late 14th-century pilgrims journey "the holy blisful martir for to seke/ That hem hath holpen whan that they weere seeke." The shrine of Thomas Becket by Elias of Dereham dominated the center of the Trinity Chapel. The resplendent colors of the twelve surrounding windows recounting Becket's miracles reiterated the glow of the precious stones and richly worked metals of the shrine (Fig. 19). In an extraordinary diversity of armature designs, the windows recount the different miracles from all classes of society. Scene after scene shows the martyred archbishop who intervenes to rescue one man from drowning and resurrect another, and to effect a wide manner of cures of madness, suffocation, hemorrhaging, or mutilation, for people as diverse as a nun from Cologne, the king of France, and a naughty child from a neighboring town. Caviness demonstrated that the twelve windows represent a conflation of two major prose texts of Becket's miracles compiled by two monks of the cathedral, Benedict and William. The miracles are often grouped by type, such as resurrections to teach the validity of the belief in the Resurrection, rescue from secular courts, or healing of the sick in mind and body. The knight Eilward of Westoning, for example, is unjustly punished with blinding and castration but healed by Becket (Fig. 20). The windows made claims for the power of God through his saints as superior to that of lay medicine. Thus, Abbot Hugh of Jervaulx is cured when a monk pushes aside a layman physician and approaches the sick bed (Fig. 21).

Fig. 15
Church-Shaped Reliquary
Germany, Braunschweig, 15th century
Gilt copper and horn, 11 in. (27.9 cm)
Art Institute of Chicago; Gift of Kate S. Buckingham 1938.1956
Photograph Art Institute of Chicago

Fig. 16
Monstrance with Relic of St. Christina
Germany, Braunschweig, 1450-1500
Silver, crystal, and enamel, 8¾ x 3½ in. (22.2 x 8.9 cm)
Art Institute of Chicago; Gift of Mrs. Chauncey McCormack 1962.90
Photograph Art Institute of Chicago

linge· ynde he sprach tzo Salome
synre sustere. Ich weiss dat dye ioe-
den sych verurouwen sulken vã mi
nen doit ·mer ych sall hain veill be
schreiers ynd eyn edel begreuenysse
wolstu doẽ dat ich dyr sage Als ich
doit byn.soe lais sy alle doeden die
ich gheuangen hain · op dat mych
alle dat ioedesche lant beweyne we
der yren wyllen. Herodes hadde
in ghewonete dat he na al syn
re spysen eyn appel schelde yn
de ass yn Ind doe he dat metz
in synre hant hadde soe hoeste
he sere ynd he sach vmb sych of
yn yemant hynderen moechte
ynd he stach syn hant vyss sich
seluen tzo doeden·mer syn ne-
ue behylt syn hant ynd hinder
de yn· Inde tzo hans begonte
men zo weinẽ yn des konincks
salle dat he doit were Doe dat
antipater hoerde doe vervrou-
wede he sych.ynd he gheloueden
synẽ verwarerẽ veel· woldẽ sy
yn laissen ghaen· Ind do dat

Dye legend van sent thomas van kantel-berghe·:·

Fig. 17

St. Thomas Becket assassinated by the Knights of Henry II

Jacobus Voraginus: *Dat duytschen Passionaile*, 1495

Hand painted woodcut illustrations

Rare Books Department, Boston Public Library, Boston, Massachusetts BPL.Q.404.87. fol. 57.

Photograph Boston Public Library

Fig. 18

Window border (associated with St. Thomas Becket)

England, Canterbury Cathedral, c. 1200

Pot metal and uncolored glass with vitreous paint, 9¼ x 30⅞ in. (23.5 x 78.4 cm)

Loyola University Museum of Art, Martin D'Arcy Collection; Gift of Mrs. Gertrude Hunt in memory of her husband John and to commemorate Fr. Martin D'Arcy S.J., 1976.22

Photograph LUMA

Fig. 19

St. Thomas Becket emerging from his shrine to heal a petitioner

Canterbury Cathedral Trinity Chapel, n:III (1), 1213-15/20

Photograph Virginia C. Raguin

Fig. 20

Eilward of Westoning unjustly punished

Canterbury Cathedral, Trinity Chapel, n:III (16), 1213-15/20

Photograph Virginia C. Raguin

Fig. 21

Hugh, Abbot of the Monastery of Jervaulx cured

Canterbury Cathedral, Trinity Chapel, n:III (21), 1213-15/20

Photograph Virginia C. Raguin

The windows are an arresting display, a seemingly endless reiteration of the power of the martyr to intercede for his petitioners. The sheer brilliance of the multiple patterns – angular petals radiating from squares, circles divided in quadrants, canted squares and half circles, fan-shaped successions, quatrefoils within circles, alterations of circles and diamonds – reinforces the multiplicity of cures. Just as preachers developed sermons for specific purposes for an audience of laity, it is probable that the monks who led the pilgrims around Trinity Chapel explained the individual miracles. Pilgrim literature in the later Middle Ages, such as Margery Kempe's account of her visit to the Holy Sepulcher in 1414 (*The Book of Margery Kempe*, Ch. 28-29), describe the Franciscans leading pilgrims through the church and pointing out the sites: "Then the friars lifted up a cross and led the pilgrims about from one place to another where Our Lord had suffered his pain and his Passion, every man and woman holding a wax candle in her hand. And the friars always, as they went about, told them what Our Lord suffered in every place" (lines 2198-2202). Innumerable images from medieval times show such processions led by a cross, usually held before the leader (see essay *Relics Defined: Discoveries on Site, Invention, Translation, and* Furta Sacra, Fig. 3). Such crosses were made of varying materials according to the wealth of the commissioner. A cross in the Loyola University Museum of Art is in copper and bronze with a gold and silver overlay (Fig. 22). A cross of iron and bronze from Compostela carries the pilgrimage sign of the scallop shell at the sides and at the top (Fig. 23).

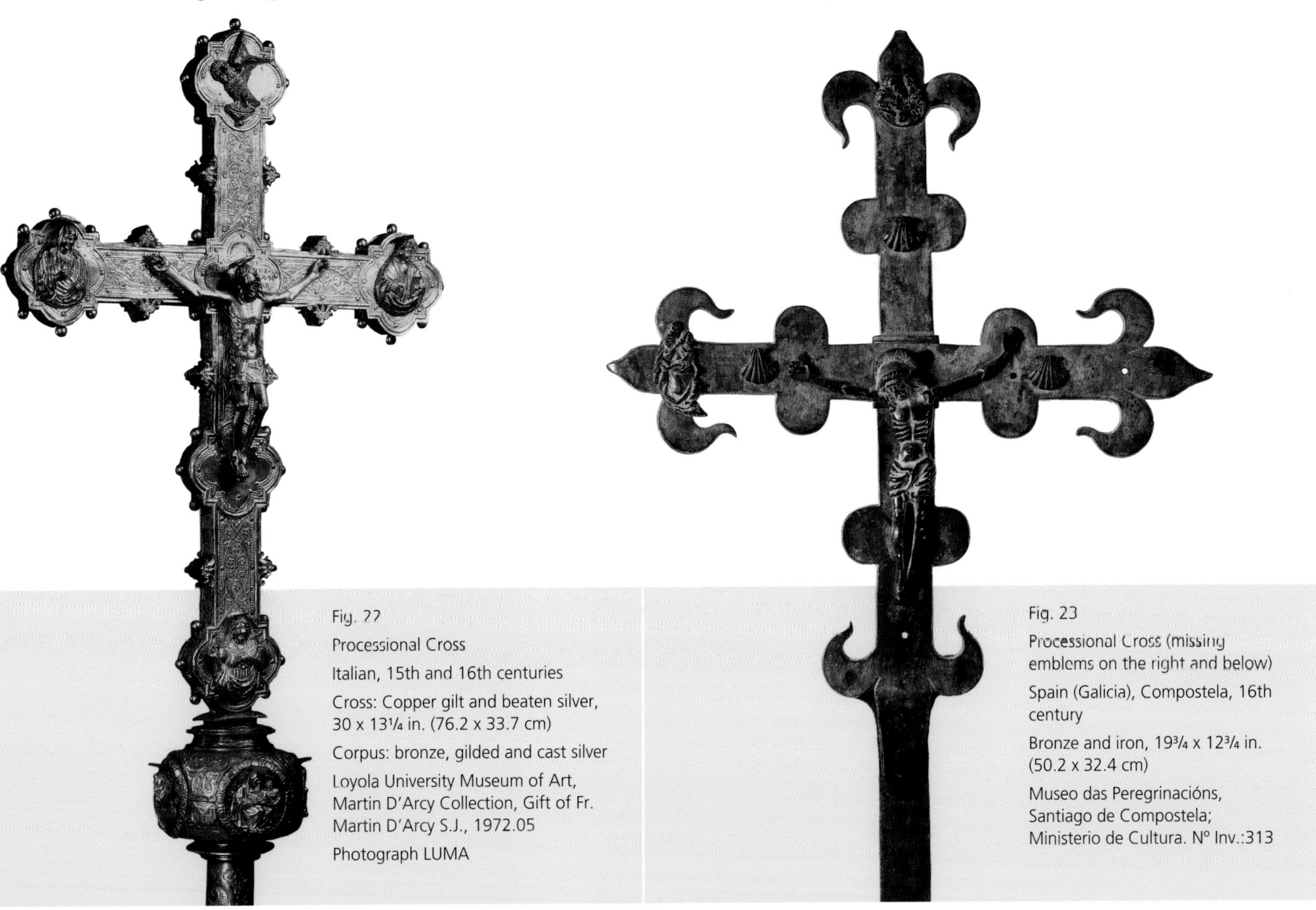

Fig. 22
Processional Cross
Italian, 15th and 16th centuries
Cross: Copper gilt and beaten silver, 30 x 13¼ in. (76.2 x 33.7 cm)
Corpus: bronze, gilded and cast silver
Loyola University Museum of Art, Martin D'Arcy Collection, Gift of Fr. Martin D'Arcy S.J., 1972.05
Photograph LUMA

Fig. 23
Processional Cross (missing emblems on the right and below)
Spain (Galicia), Compostela, 16th century
Bronze and iron, 19¾ x 12¾ in. (50.2 x 32.4 cm)
Museo das Peregrinacións, Santiago de Compostela; Ministerio de Cultura. Nº Inv.:313

PILGRIMAGE, CRUSADES, AND THE CONCEPT OF PURGATORY

Pious practice in early Christianity is impossible to understand without the concept of what later became known as "purgatory" and the development of institutionally controlled indulgences. The Church taught that only persons of exceptional virtue – saints – would have gained enough merit during their lives that, on leaving this one, they would be immediately welcomed into paradise. Most people were condemned to a period of attendance and suffering in a location called purgatory. This time, however, could be shortened by gaining special merit while alive or benefiting from the prayers and good works of others after one's death. Pious actions and good works included the seven Corporal Works of Mercy, discussed below. Other good works included the giving of alms for the construction of a church, the fulfillment of a pilgrimage, and the saying of prescribed prayers during a sequence of times or at visits to shrines, especially during the feast day of the saint. The Church developed a reward called an indulgence, forgiveness for the "temporal punishment" after death that was due for various types of transgressions or sins.

The indulgence's power was based on the belief in the superabundance of merits established by Christ that could be dispensed by his representative, the pope, to the faithful. Such concepts stemmed from biblical sources, specifically the position of Peter: "And I will give you the keys of the kingdom of heaven. And whatsoever thou shall bind on earth shall be bound in heaven, and whatsoever thou shall loose on earth shall be loosed also in heaven" (Mt 16:19). This practice of indulgences was impacted by the development of crusades to liberate the Holy Land from Muslim rule. Indeed the crusades, most important from the late 11th through the 13th centuries, are sometimes referred to as armed pilgrimages. In 1095, during the First Crusade, Pope Urban II established a "plenary," or complete, indulgence for those taking up the cross. The crusader confessed his sins and if he died while on crusade he received remission of all temporal punishment, and thus effectively received a promise of immediate entry into heaven.

Indulgences became increasingly current in the 12th century and developed into a standard aspect of piety, not just for pilgrimages. In the 14th century indulgences became linked to special years when the faithful were encouraged to visit Roman holy places. This began in 1300 with the declaration by Boniface VIII of a plenary indulgence for those visiting Rome during the "Jubilee Year." By the 15th century most prominent places of pilgrimages were part of an elaborate system of visits at specific times, with enumerated days. The term quarantine appears in medieval manuals of devotion. Derived from *quadragenae*, a 40-day fast, the indulgence would be equal to merit gained by a person undergoing a period of penitential fasting, as during the season of Lent. The community of saints could transfer such merits gained to others, and thus aid in the salvation of a friend or relative. The clergy could also pray for others, a practice that was particularly cherished in rituals for the dead. Such beliefs developed into Masses commissioned for the souls of the dead, elaborate tomb monuments, and the foundation of chantries, special chapels to commemorate the dead and focus prayer rituals. Christ's blessing was believed to come with special intensity at these moments of the Mass, as depicted in a 15th-century window showing a priest celebrating the Eucharist (Fig. 24). Within a world where ritual and display defined status, religion saw the embellishment of elements of ritual use as essential. Chalices used for Masses, such as a work from Siena of the 14th century, incorporated gold gilt over copper and exquisitely formed enamels (Fig. 25).

Just as the Holy Land and Christ's life were the primary focus of Christian thought and pilgrimage, indulgences associated with relics of Christ held the highest position. In 1239 Louis IX of France received from Emperor Baldwin II of Constantinople the relic of the Crown of Thorns. This renowned gesture was a response to French assistance against Muslim invaders. Louis responded by building the Sainte-Chapelle attached to his residence on the Ile-de-La-Cité in Paris. The entire program of sculpture and stained glass was designed to reflect the relic displayed on an elevated podium behind the altar. In Gloucestershire, England, a vial of Christ's blood became a focal point of indulgenced visits. The Cistercian abbey of Hailes was

Fig. 24

Miraculous Mass of St. Gregory.

Gregory Robert Colynson, whose sepulchral brass is located in the aisle of the church, left a will dated 1450 asking for devotions for the repose of his soul. A priest was funded to sing daily prayers honoring St. Gregory for three years after Colynson's death. Colynson may very well have also funded this window showing his patron saint elevating the host at Mass.

York, All Saints, North Street, window sVI, 1450s

Photograph Virginia C. Raguin

Fig. 25

Chalice

Giacomo Guerrino

Italian, Siena, c. 1375

Copper and gilt base and silver cup with basse-taille enamels, 9⅝ x 6⅛ in. (24.4 x 15.6 cm)

Loyola University Museum of Art, Martin D'Arcy Collection, Gift of Mr. and Mrs. Donald F. Rowe Sr. 1969-18

Photograph LUMA

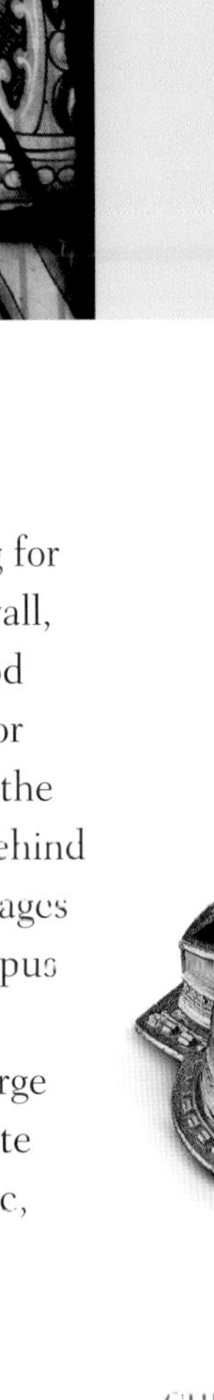

founded in 1246 by Richard of Cornwall in thanksgiving for deliverance from shipwreck. In 1269 Edmund of Cornwall, a nephew of Henry III, acquired a relic of the Holy Blood for the abbey. The Cistercian foundation suffered a major fire at the time, and in rebuilding the eastern section of the church, the monks placed the relic in a special shrine behind the high altar. Indulgences similar to those of all pilgrimages were given, augmented if the shrine were visited on Corpus Christi, the feast day commemorating the presence of Christ's body in the Eucharist. Though never housing large numbers of monks, the abbey had extensive and elaborate buildings, financed by pilgrims visiting its renowned relic, "the Holy Blood of Hailes."

CHARITY AND GOOD WORKS

Pilgrimage was linked to medieval spiritual values and the injunction to perform acts of charity. A window showing the Corporal Works of Mercy, built around 1410 at All Saints North Street, York, begins by showing people giving food to the hungry and drink to the thirsty (Fig. 26). Giving shelter to the homeless is then shown as welcoming pilgrims, easily a scene that could illustrate Chaucer's *Canterbury Tales*. The image of the host recalls Chaucer's description of the Merchant from the Prologue: "with forked beard and… motley gown, … upon his head a Flemish beaver hat."

Such images reflect the concern for educating the laity with such manuals as *The Lay Folks' Catechism*, issued in both Latin and English by William Thoresby, archbishop of York in 1357. The text, in use until the Reformation, stated that the seven works of mercy will be "rehearsed" by God from each Christian soul on the day of doom (the Last Judgment).

Of whilk the first is to fede tham that er hungry.
That other, for to gif tham drynk that er thirsty.
The third, for to clethe tham that er clatheless
The ferthe is to herber tham that er houseless.
The fifte, for visite tham that ligges in sekenesse.
The sext, is to help tham that in prisoner.
The sevent, to bery dede man that has mister.

Of which the first is to feed those that are hungry.
The next, to give drink to those who are thirsty.

Fig. 26
Three of the Seven Corporal Works of Mercy
Food to the hungry, drink to the thirsty, shelter to the homeless
York, All Saints, North Street
Stained glass, c. 1410
Photograph Virginia C. Raguin

The third, to clothe those who are without clothes.
The fourth is the shelter those who are homeless.
The fifth is to visit those who lay in sickness.
The sixth is to help those in prison.
The seventh is to bury the dead who are churched.

With the advent of printmaking and its ability to reach a broad public, such symbolic allusions often became more explicit. The German printmaker identified by his initials as Master I. B. devised a series of the Corporal Works of Mercy around 1525-30 showing Christ himself as the recipient of the charity. In *Feeding the Hungry* Christ is bareheaded with the cruciform light silhouetted against the dark curtain (Fig. 27). A man comes from the right bearing a plate: to the far right another man pours liquid into a beaker from a flagon. Similarly in *Clothing the Naked* Christ is seated wearing only a tunic (Fig. 28). On the right, a man comes forward with shoes, closely followed by a woman with a robe. In *Giving Shelter to the Homeless* Christ appears as pilgrim, dressed with broad-brimmed hat, staff, and leather pouch (Fig. 29). A woman is standing at the bottom of the steps and gesturing as if to welcome him into the house. Just as representations of St. James became synonymous with pilgrimage depictions, now Christ himself is shown affirming the value of pilgrimage, at a time when these time-honored activities were under attack by the Protestant Reform.

Fig. 27
Corporal Works of Mercy: Feeding the Hungry
Master I. B (B 58), German, d. 1525/30
Engraving, 2⅙ in. (5.5 cm)
Art Institute of Chicago, Gift of Mr. and Mrs. Potter Palmer, 1919.2303
Photograph Art Institute of Chicago

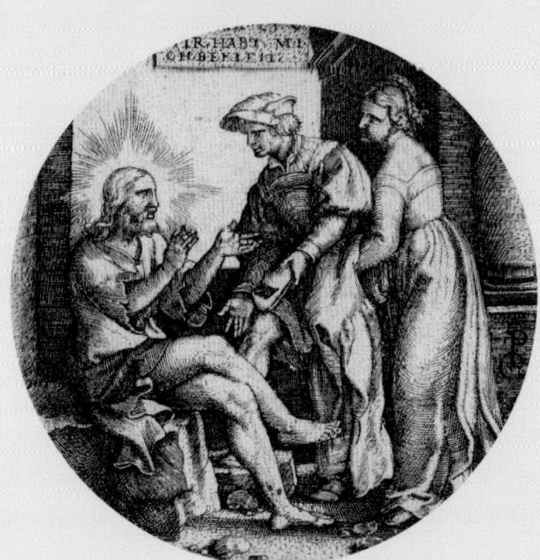

Fig. 28
Corporal Works of Mercy: Clothing the Naked
Master I. B (B 59), German, d. 1525/30
Engraving, 2⅙ in. (5.5 cm)
Art Institute of Chicago, Gift of Mr. and Mrs. Potter Palmer, 1919.2304
Photograph Art Institute of Chicago

Fig. 29
Corporal Works of Mercy: Giving Shelter to the Homeless – Lodging Pilgrims
Master I. B (B 62), German, d. 1525/30
Engraving, 2¼ in. (5.7 cm)
Art Institute of Chicago, Gift of Mr. and Mrs. Potter Palmer, 1919.2305
Photograph Art Institute of Chicago

PILGRIMAGE CRITIQUED

Christianity was not without its challenges to pilgrimages, even before the 16th century and the criticism of Luther and Calvin. Just as pilgrimage was a concept deeply imbedded in Christian practice, so were its abuses. In 1425 Thomas à Kempis commented in his widely read book *Imitation of Christ*:

> *Many people travel far to honor the relics of the saints, marveling at their wonderful deeds and at the building of magnificent shrines. They gaze upon and kiss the sacred relics encased in silk and gold.... Often in looking at such things, men are moved by curiosity, by the novelty of the unseen, and they bear away little fruit for the amendment of their lives, especially when they go from place to place lightly and without true contrition* (Book 4 Chapter 1).

As the Reformation progressed in Northern Europe, the exploitation of relics and even their falsification were noted. The humanist Desiderius Erasmus of Rotterdam (d. 1536), while remaining loyal to Rome, wrote with trenchant wit about the excesses of devotions. His satirical dialogue criticizing the exploitation of relics, *The Pilgrimage of Pure Devotion*, was quickly translated from Latin into English. Menedemus (so-called after a Greek philosopher) questions Ogygyus (the faithful believer). Ogygyus appears before Menedemus literally bristling with lead badges that were the common purchases at shrines (see essay *A Souvenir on Your Hat: Medieval Christian Pilgrims' Badges*) and with the scallop shells that identify the visit to Santiago de Compostela (Fig. 30).

> *"But I pray you what araye is this that you be in, me thynke that you be clothyd with cokle schelles, and be lade on euery syde with bruches of lead and tynne." Ogygyus responds, "I haue bene on pylgremage at saynt Iames in Compostella, & at my retourne I dyd more relygyously vysyte our lady of Walsyngã in England, a very holy pylgremage..."*

Fig. 30
Pilgrim's badge: scallop shell of St. James
French, 15th century
Lead, 13/16 x 9/16 in. (2.1 x 1.4 cm)
Metropolitan Museum of Art, Cloisters Collection, 1997.240.38
Image © The Metropolitan Museum of Art/ Art Resource, NY

Fig. 31
St. John Lateran, Rome
Relics Altar Baldachino
Giovani di Stephano, sculpture; Barna di Siena, frescos, 1367
Photograph Virginia C. Raguin

(Walsyngã is Walsingham in Norfolk, revered for its replica of the house in Nazareth where the angel Gabriel appeared to the Virgin Mary.)

In his best known work, *In Praise of Folly*, Erasmus further criticizes pilgrimages and miracles that attract the interest of the merely curious. He puts his words into the mouth of Folly, who speaks in praise of herself. She then names a series of individuals as her devoted followers:

> *But there is no doubt but that that kind of men are wholly ours who love to hear or tell feigned miracles and strange lies and are never weary of any tale, though ever so long, so it be of ghosts, spirits, goblins, devils, or the like; which the further they are from truth, the more readily they are believed and the more do they tickle their itching ears. And these serve not only to pass away time but bring profit, especially to mass priests and pardoners.* (Pardoners are individuals hearing confessions and granting indulgences.)

CODIFICATION OF REWARDS

Pilgrimage literature in the later Middle Ages, as contrasted to the 12th-century Guide to Santiago de Compostela, became increasingly focused on specified rewards. As Chaucer presented so vividly in *The Canterbury Tales*, when April comes with its good weather, its "showres soote," it was simply part of 14th-century life to set off for "foreign lands" or even closer to home for visits to shrines. The literature advertising the benefits of such travel made itemized lists of the spiritual currency. John Capgrave's guide to Rome, dated slightly later than Margery Kempe's visit in 1415, contained a long list. At St. Peter's alone the pilgrim could find:

> *Bodies of eight of the apostles, one-half of the bodies of both St. Peter and St. Paul (the other halves of their bodies were buried at St. Paul's Outside the Walls), the bodies of SS. Simon and Jude, the body of St. John Crysostum, the bodies of the martyrs St. Processus and Martinian, the body of the virgin St. Petronilla all lie at St. Peter's. The church also holds the head and arm of St. Andrew, the head of St. Sebastian, and the head of St. Luke the Evangelist.*

> *Whenever the face of our Lord Jesus Christ* (see essay *Saint Peter's in Rome and the Relic of Veronica's Veil*) *is shown there are 3000 years of indulgences, that is to say, those who live near Rome have 6000 years of indulgences, and those who come over the mountains and hills have 9000 of indulgences, and as many quarantines, and the remission of a third part of all sins.*

> *St. Peter's gives 48 years of indulgences daily, 48 quarantines, and the remission of one-third of all sins.*

> *Each side altar gives 28 years of indulgences. Among the side altars, there are seven of special rank: altar of the Blessed Virgin Mary, St. Veronica, St. Andrew, Pope St. Leo, St. Gregory, SS. Simon and Jude. On the feasts of these altars or the feast of St. Peter, Christmas, Easter, All Saint's Day, and all double feasts, the indulgences are doubled.*

The property surrounding St. John Lateran basilica was given to the church by the emperor Constantine the Great about 340. An already extant structure was made into a church that became the head of ecclesiastical worship in Rome and the seat of the bishop of Rome, the pope, and his residence. Even when the residence of the pope moved to the Vatican upon his return from Avignon in 1377, St. John Lateran remained his official seat.

In 1470, William Brewyn listed that St. John Lateran had a special indulgence attached to its altar, even suggesting its superiority to the Holy Land itself (Fig. 31). He argues that every day:

> *there are 48 years of indulgences, 48 quarantines and a remission of the third part of all sins.... Pope Gregory (I), who consecrated the church granted such great indulgences that no one can count them – they are known to God only.... Pope Boniface VIII confirmed (these), declaring that if men knew how great were the indulgences of the church of St. John Lateran, they would not cross over to the Sepulcher of the Lord in Jerusalem, nor to St. James in Compostela.*

THE REFORMATION

In the growing dissention concerning papal policies in the early 16th century, there were no issues more blatant than the accumulation of revenue at shrines, and the distribution of indulgences for charitable acts, such as the giving of money to support papal building campaigns. Martin Luther, an Augustinian monk and professor of theology at the University of Wittenberg, composed a text, later called the Ninety-Five Theses, condemning such practices. The Theses were delivered to the Archbishop of Mainz and Magdeburg, and also posted on the door of the Castle Church in Wittenberg. They were soon translated into German and received wide distribution through the new technology of the printing press. Luther's movement developed a core theology that among other things rejected the intersession of saints and justification by good works, and thus the authority of the Roman Church to define indulgences or even to state special graces for acts such as visits to the Holy Land. Over the next century, more than half of Germany and Switzerland, and the countries of Holland, Scotland, Norway, Denmark, and Sweden, broke their ties with Rome, and with the practice of pilgrimage.

England's Reformation was theologically nuanced but from the earliest years of Henry VIII's separation from Rome, the external manifestation of English "otherness" was the repudiation of devotional images and pilgrimage. Henry focused in 1538 on the veneration of the 12th-century Thomas Becket, especially that of pilgrimage to Canterbury and indulgence. The Royal Injunctions cautioned that "feigned images" that are "abused with pilgrimages or offerings of anything made thereunto" must be taken down and "henceforth no candles, tapers, or images of wax *(ex votos)* be set afore any image or picture" (Fig. 32).

CATHOLIC RESPONSE AND BEYOND

Rejected by Protestants, pilgrimage and relics became even more honored in the Catholic response through the regulations that followed the Council of Trent (1545-63). As the Reformation swept across northern Germany, the relics of many saints were destroyed. Others were sold to Catholic buyers. Cardinal Albrecht von Brandenburg, archbishop of Mainz, was able to acquire a vast treasury of relics during the 1520s and 1530s; however, political upheavals forced even this powerful cleric into dispersing his collection and melting down some of his finest reliquaries. The buying and selling of relics would continue well into the 17th century. Wilhelm V (r. 1579-97) and Maximilian I (r. 1597-1651), dukes of Bavaria, sought relics for the Jesuit church of St. Michael's and the Frauenkirche, the main parish church, in Munich. Wilhelm was particularly active in acquiring relics for the new Jesuit church, where they were displayed embedded yet always visible in the walls of his private oratory and, more publicly, in the numerous newly commissioned busts and reliquaries that adorned the altars. Munich held the relics of St. Benno, bishop of Meissen (r. 1066-1106) in the Frauenkirche and those of Cosmas and Damian, the patron saints of physicians, in St. Michael's.

Devotion to the saints for their aid in daily life continued unabated in Italy, France, Spain, and in the minds of Catholic immigrants to the New World. Margaret (Fig. 33), for example, who had emerged unscathed from the

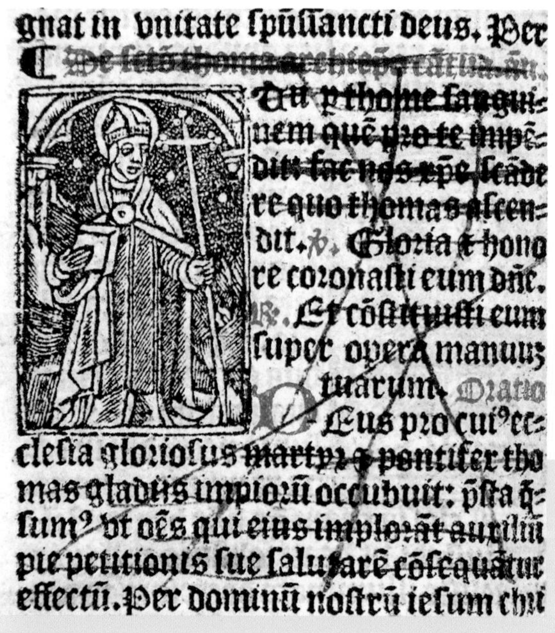

gnat in vnitate spũssancti deus. Per
[illegible]
Tu per thome sanguinem quẽ pro te impẽdit fac nos xpe scãdere quo thomas ascendit. ℣. Gloria et honore coronasti eum dñe. ℟. Et cõstituisti eum super opera manuũ tuarum. Oratio.
Deus pro cui⁹ ecclesia gloriosus martyr et pontifer thomas gladiis impiorũ occubuit: pstã quesum⁹ vt oẽs qui eius implorãt auxiliũ pie petitionis sue salutarẽ cõsequãtur effectũ. Per dominũ nostrũ iesum chri

Fig. 32
English suffrage to Thomas Becket crossed out after 1538 when Henry VIII abolished his cult.
Book of Hours printed in Paris by François Regnault, 1526
Stonyhurst College, Lancashire, S.3.6, fol.26v.

Fig. 33
St. Margaret
England, 1340-60
Pot metal and uncolored glass with vitreous paint
19 x 8¾ in. (48.3 x 22.2 cm)
Loyola University Museum of Art, Martin D'Arcy Collection; Gift of the Friends of the Martin D'Arcy Gallery, 1977-10

belly of a dragon, was revered as aiding women in childbirth. A set of small 18th-century silver statues, now in the treasury of Notre Dame Cathedral, includes the images of St. Barbara, St. Sebastian, and St. Agnes (Fig. 34). St. Barbara wears on her chest an imbedded glass-covered oval surrounded by a radiant nimbus within which a viewer reads the name of the saint and sees a relic set against gold-colored fabric. Barbara is invoked for protection against lightening and, as such, is seen as the patroness of those who work with firearms. On the base of the statue, the Latin inscription states that the image contains "fragments of the most holy bones of St. Barbara, Virgin and Martyr, with authentication, 1735." Perhaps more elegant in their graceful three-dimensionality than most reliquary containers, the statues are nonetheless typical of the small glass-encased reliquaries common since the 18th century. In numerous 19th-century Catholic churches in the United States, altars displayed relics, and certainly relics were deposited in the altar stones according to Church requirements. The Liturgy and Life Collection at the

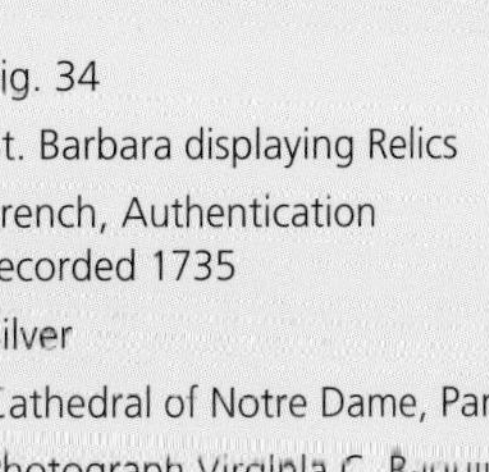

Fig. 34
St. Barbara displaying Relics
French, Authentication recorded 1735
Silver
Cathedral of Notre Dame, Paris
Photograph Virginia C. Raguin

John J. Burns Library at Boston College houses many objects such as reliquary monstrances, blessed medals, and other works associated with the cult of relics.

The experience of the pilgrimage to the Holy Land also continued. Counter-Reformation sentiment encouraged the construction of replica sites of Calvary. Kalwaria Zebrzydowska, located about thirty miles southwest of Cracow, is a vast religious park, now designated a UNESCO World Heritage Site (Fig. 35). Created in 1602 by Mikołaj Zebrzydowski, Voivoda (Region Head) of Cracow, and his wife, the site combines natural landscape and built construction to allow visitors to follow the episodes in the Passion of Christ. The Church of the Crucifixion was modeled after the Basilica of the Holy Sepulcher of Jerusalem. On a much smaller scale, replicas, such as that of the Holy Nail (see essay *Rome's Santa Croce in Gerusalemme and Relics of the Passion of Christ*), also testify to the power of relics to bring a desired immediacy to the believer. Here sacrality is communicated by touch as well as resemblance. The authenticating text attached to the replica declares that it "had been brought into contact with the sacred nail," a process similar to that described by Felix Fabri in 1484.

In many cases, reaction to calamity reveals deep-rooted beliefs, as demonstrated by the use of relics during episodes of the plague in late-16th-century Italy. Devotion to relics and intercessory saints was vital aspect of daily practice. The stricken prayed to the Virgin and St. Sebastian, an Early Christian martyr long revered as helpful in illness since he was shot with arrows (as in arrows of illness) by Roman executioners and healed through the ministrations of St. Irene. St. Charles Borromeo was an archbishop of Milan who played an important role in spiritual reform after the Council of Trent. He was particularly devoted to work in the city's lazzaretti, hospitals for victims of the plague that stuck Milan in 1576-77. He led processions to petition for the lifting of the plague

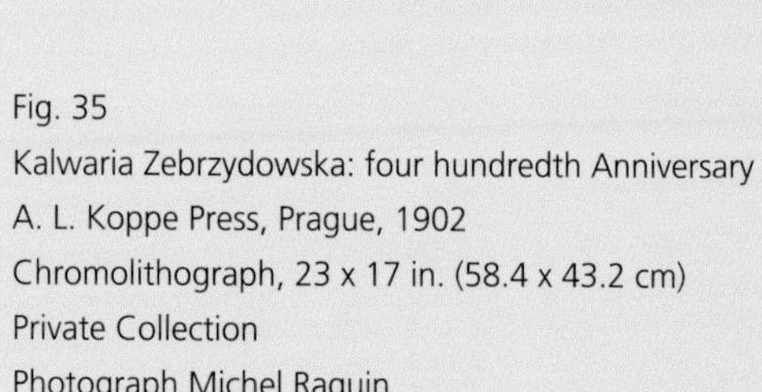

Fig. 35
Kalwaria Zebrzydowska: four hundredth Anniversary
A. L. Koppe Press, Prague, 1902
Chromolithograph, 23 x 17 in. (58.4 x 43.2 cm)
Private Collection
Photograph Michel Raguin

modeled after those of St. Gregory, who instituted penitential processions in 6th-century Rome. Milan's relic of the Holy Nail took pride of place, lifted up by the archbishop as a throng of penitents followed behind him.

As time moved on, differences between Catholics and Protestants became less extreme. The popularity of the Camino to Santiago now attracts Protestants and Catholics and those of many faiths, as well as agnostics, drawn equally by the dedication to a saintly intercessor and the personal challenge of the journey and solidarity among fellow travelers. Later concepts of pilgrimage became more romantic, transcending doctrine or miracle to focus on the journey itself as a path to self-realization. The pilgrim by the 18th century could be seen as a solitary figure, an individual on a quest, imbedded in the moment of a life played out against the challenges of nature. The solitude becomes a respite from the trivia of everyday life and the superficiality of human society.

A print after Canaletto's *Pilgrim in Prayer* can be equally appealing as a religious or a secular object (Fig. 36). At the side of a river, indicated by two men in a small boat, a pilgrim stops before a simple shrine. The pilgrim leans on a staff and a broad-brimmed hat is slung across his back. The edifice is simply a niche a little larger than a man's height, surmounted by a cross. It is empty and one side of the roof is missing. The path presumably taken by the pilgrim leads up a steep hill on the left, and to the far left is the beginning of a city with a half-ruined entrance arch. Here pilgrimage becomes a solitary endeavor, an exercise not only through space but through time. The spectator looks not so much at an image of devotion, but at one of nostalgia for a lost past, a time of belief and purpose.

See further reading on page 340

Fig. 36
Landscape with Pilgrim in Prayer, 1734-44
Caneletto, Italian, 1697-1768
Etching, 5½ x 8¼ in. (14 x 21 cm)
Art Institute of Chicago, The Joseph Brooks Fair Fund, 1955.1014
Photograph Art Institute of Chicago

Details of Fig. 3

The Relics of the Infancy of Christ at Rome's Santa Maria Maggiore

Virginia C. Raguin

Santa Maria Maggiore (St. Mary Major), one of the greatest of the Early Christian basilicas of Rome, was built between 432 and 440, a century after St. Peter's. The exterior of the church was completely reworked in the 17th century, but the interior survives relatively unchanged (Fig. 1). Numbering among the seven principal churches of the city, Santa Maria Maggiore was always a great site of pilgrimage. For the major Feast Days of the Virgin, the Annunciation (March 25), Assumption (August 15), and her Nativity (September 8), Santa Maria Maggiore was the site of Rome's Stational Liturgy. This was the place where the pope celebrated Mass on that day, a tradition operative since the era of Gregory the Great (590-604). Santa Maria Maggiore also held a particular importance as Rome developed pilgrimage paths that followed the stages of Christ's life in terms equivalent to what a pilgrim in Holy Land could experience (Nichols, 133-34). The church ultimately filled the place of Bethlehem for the Roman pilgrim, a tradition that developed after the capture of Jerusalem by Muslims in 638, when many Christians of the city moved to Rome, bringing relics with them. The relics of the Nativity, the wood and hay of the manger and cloth in which the Infant Christ was laid, were transferred at this time, as first mentioned in the church during the reign of Pope Theodore I (642-49), who himself came from Jerusalem. They are now enshrined in a Baroque reliquary in a crypt marked by an elaborate baldachino (Fig. 2).

Scenes of the Infancy of Christ appear in the splendid mosaics of the triumphal arch of 432-440. On the north side, the Adoration of the Magi presents the Infant Jesus on a bejeweled throne, almost as if the 5th-century mosaic

Fig. 1
Santa Maria Maggiore (St. Mary Major)
Nave looking towards reliquary shrine
Rome, 432-40
Photograph Michel Raguin

could predict the arrival of the Relic of the Manger some two hundred years later (Fig. 3). In 1291 Pope Nicholas IV sponsored the addition of a three-dimensional Nativity crèche. Although common in Christmas celebrations of the present, a crèche representing the Holy Family with the Shepherds and Three Kings was an innovation sponsored by the Franciscan Order, to which Pope Nicholas belonged. St. Francis of Assisi, the founder, is recorded as having erected a crèche in the church of Greccio in 1223. Arnolfo de Cambio sculpted figures of half-life-size to include two prophets, the three Magi, Joseph, the ox and the ass, and the Virgin Mary reclining (now lost and replaced with a seated Virgin and Child) (Fig. 4). Thus, from the 14th century onward, the hidden relic of the wood of the manger became a visible reality to the Roman pilgrims.

The English list of the *Stacions of Rome* of 1370 (Furnivall, 16-17) gives sixty verses to the description of the church and includes the Nativity relics, beginning "At seinte Marie the maiour/ ther is a chirche of gret honour." The manuscript's list of relics begins with the high altar where the body of St. Matthew is buried. The description of St. Jerome's tomb is lengthy: "the body of Saint Jerome, the holy doctor, he was once from the city of Damas and was brought to this place, he was placed before the chapel called Presepe [boards from the Manger of the Nativity] and upon his grave lies a stone with a cross engraved on it and a great iron girdle about the stone. We are told that there are many relics of Our Lady and her Son, including the cloth that Christ was put into when he was born and the hay on which Christ lay. There is also the arm of St. Thomas Becket, part of his brain, and a rochet [tunic] sprinkled with his blood." Today Becket's tunic is seen in a transparent reliquary displayed in the adjacent museum (Fig. 5). The *Stacions* then describes an image of Our Lady that Luke is said to have painted, but one done by angel's hands was put in its place. Then follows a list of indulgences given by the popes: one thousand years for each Holy Day and even more, forgiveness of sorrows and eight hundred years more pardon. At every feast of Our Lady there are one hundred years of pardon, and from the Assumption of the Virgin to her Birthday (August 15 to September 8, both Stational

Fig. 2
Reliquary of the Crib of the Infant Jesus
18th century
Rome, Santa Maria Maggiore
Photograph Michel Raguin

Fig. 3
Mosaics of the Annunciation, Adoration of the Magi, and Massacre of the Innocents
440s
Rome, Santa Maria Maggiore, Chancel Arch, north
Photograph Michel Raguin

Liturgies at Santa Maria Maggiore), fourteen thousand years' pardon.

William Brewyn's account in 1470 (Brewyn, 9) specifies "the mantle of the Blessed Virgin Mary in which her Son reposed in the manger; the cradle of Christ." He also focused on the indulgences available at the site: "On the ninth day of the month of May there is remission of all sins, which was given by Pope Pius the Second. Here, too, on all feasts of the Blessed Virgin Mary a thousand years of indulgences are bestowed; and from the feast of the Assumption of Mary [August 15] the Virgin to her Nativity [September 8] a thousand years of indulgences."

In 1540, John Capgrave's *Guidebook* listed forty-eight years of indulgences, forty-eight quarantines, and a third part remission of all sins. "Pope Pius II declared a plenary remission to the altar for May 9 and one thousand years of indulgences for attending any of Mary's feast days at St. Mary Major, and from the feast of the Assumption of Mary the Virgin [August 15] to her Nativity [September 8] a thousand years of indulgences." Relics included, below the main altar, the body of St. Matthew the Apostle. Capgrave also lists St. Jerome, St. Romula, and St. Redempta. Among other relics, this church possessed the mantle of the Virgin Mary with which she wrapped the infant Christ in the manger, the cradle of Christ, the stole of St. Jerome, and the arm of St. Thomas of Canterbury.

See further reading on page 341

Fig. 4
Two Magi from the Crèche Figures surrounding the Relic of the Crib
Arnolfo de Cambio, 1291
Rome, Santa Maria Maggiore
Photograph Michel Raguin

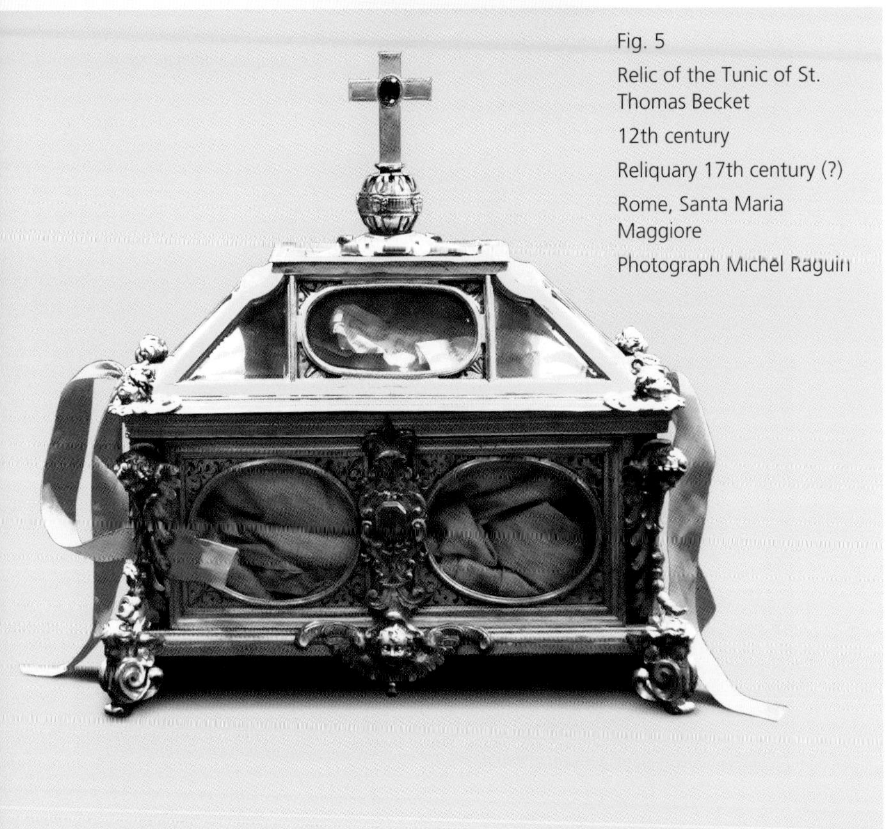

Fig. 5
Relic of the Tunic of St. Thomas Becket
12th century
Reliquary 17th century (?)
Rome, Santa Maria Maggiore
Photograph Michel Raguin

Details of Fig. 1

Rome's Santa Croce in Gerusalemme and Relics of the Passion of Christ

Virginia C. Raguin

In Rome, Santa Croce in Gerusalemme (Church of the Holy Cross in Jerusalem) played a vital role in devotional rituals associated with the Passion of Christ. As its name implies, it promulgates the veneration of the True Cross, which was believed to be discovered in Jerusalem during the reign of Constantine and enshrined in the Church of the Holy Sepulcher. The building has a solid archeological date, as it was located in the imperial residence called the Sessorian Palace occupied by the Emperor Constantine and his mother Helena from about 311 to 337. During their residence a chapel was built in the palace, and tradition has it that a relic of the True Cross and a nail that was used to pierce Christ's feet and hands were deposited there by Helena.

The present building of Santa Croce was remodeled in 1144 and again between 1743 and 1744 by Benedict XIV. Its early decoration is notable for medieval frescoes, inlay cosmati floor, and an impressive painting cycle with *The Legend of the True Cross* in the apse. The subject includes Helena's discovery of the three crosses, miracle of the resurrection of the dead, adoration of the Cross, and the return of the True Cross to Jerusalem by Heraclius, discussed below (Fig. 1). The fresco is the work of Antoniazzo Romano (c. 1430-c. 1510), the leading painter of the Roman school. Santa Croce also possesses a renowned Byzantine reliquary with a 14th-century mosaic image of the suffering Christ as Man of Sorrows. The image with its indulgence, focusing on the theme of the suffering Messiah, was widely copied. Brewyn describes it as "a picture of the Savior, which is called the picture of divine compassion (pietatis)" (Brewyn, 57).

Medieval writers believed that Helena had divided the wood of True Cross, leaving the largest portion (see essay *Egeria's Description of the Liturgical Year in Jerusalem: Excerpt for the Good Friday Veneration of the Cross*) in the Church of the Holy Sepulcher in Jerusalem, but distributing small sections to Rome and Constantinople.

Fig. 1
Legend of the True Cross (Helena verifies the True Cross by the miracle of a man brought back from the dead)
Apse Fresco, 1470s (?)
Rome, Santa Croce
Antoniazzo Romano
Photograph Michel Raguin

In 614 the Persian emperor Chosroes carried off the wood and other relics when he captured Jerusalem. The Byzantine emperor Heraclius defeated the Persians in a campaign between 622 and 628, and returned the relic to Jerusalem, as was ceremonially acknowledged March 21, 630. With the expansion of Arab power after the death of Muhammad in 632, however, Jerusalem was lost to the Byzantine Empire and in 635 Heraclius transferred the True Cross Relic to Constantinople. Christians travelling to the Holy Land were keenly aware of the absence of the relic, as expressed by the voyage of Friar Felix between 1480 and 1483. He writes that pilgrims were shown the grotto where Helena had found "three crosses, the nails, the crown of thorns, the tablet with its inscription placed on the cross, the point of the lance that pierces the heart of Christ, the staff with the sponge, and all the instruments that had been used during the crucifixion of Christ and the two thieves," a list that coincides with the known relics then in the possession of various Western European pilgrimage sites (II.183). The visitors could only contemplate the empty space. To render the place more venerable, Felix explains, those in charge had replaced the absent wood with a cross into which a tiny sliver of the True Cross has been inserted (II.174).

The presumably oldest relics at Santa Croce are those of the wood of the True Cross and Nail. They were originally displayed in a section of the building called the Chapel of St. Helena, but were later moved to an upper floor. Brewyn in the 1460s-70s already notes a division of relics: "The wood of the most holy Cross, together with one of the nails with which Christ was crucified on the cross, … are laid very reverently in the Sacrist's Chapel which is near the pulpit.… And it is shown five times in the year, that is to say, on Good Friday, on the feast of the Invention (Helena's Discovery) and Exaltation (Heraclius's Return of the Relic), on the day of the Station (Papal liturgy), on the dedication of the same church of the Holy Cross, and on the day of the consecration of the Jerusalem Chapel." (Romes Stational Liturgy of papal visitations for the fourth Sunday of Lent took place in Santa Croce.)

Over the years other relics were acquired to augment the focus on the death and burial of the Savior. The 1370 *Stations of Rome* lists, as well as the True Cross and Nail, the Titulus of Pilate, the wooden tablet posted above Christ's cross with the words "Jesus of Nazareth, King of the Jews," (Fig. 2) the sponge with gall and vinegar that was offered to Christ on the cross, and the cross bar of the cross of the Good Thief, who received mercy. In the later 15th century Brewyn gives the inventory of the Jerusalem Chapel, which

> *the blessed Helena, mother of the Emperor Constantine, built in what aforetime was her bed chamber.… And the notable relics, which are recorded below, were laid up in the altar of the aforesaid chapel by the hands of blessed [Pope] Sylvester, at the request of the aforesaid Helen, which relics, the blessed Helen brought from Jerusalem, at the request of the aforesaid Pope. First, the cord with which Christ was bound on the Cross, Two sapphires, one of which is filled with the precious blood of Christ and the other the milk of the glorious Virgin Mary, the Mother of Christ. Also a large piece of Christ's garment; a large piece of the veil of Mary.… Also XI thorns of the Lord's crown… "* (Brewyn, 54-55).

As pilgrimage became more difficult due to the Muslim control of the Holy Land, the sites of Rome began to develop a parallel function as places to which a pilgrim might travel to effectively relive the life and Passion of Christ. Santa Croce in Gerusalemme substituted for a visit to the basilica of the Holy

Fig. 2
Relic of the Nail and relics of the Titulus from the Cross of Christ's Crucifixion
Chapel of the Relics
Rome, Santa Croce
Photograph Virginia C. Raguin

Sepulcher; Santa Maria Maggiore's possession since the 7th century of relics of Christ's infancy would enable it to take the place of Bethlehem (see essay *The Relics of the Infancy of Christ at Rome's Santa Maria Maggiore*)

The church has been administered by the Cistercian Order since 1561 and the relics are now displayed in a chapel designed in 1930 by Florestano Di Fausto (Fig. 3). A replica of the Santa Croce nail was acquired before 1882 by an American patron, as attested by the certificate in wooden box with glass lid. The work is now in the Liturgy and Life Collection at the John J. Burns Library at Boston College (Fig. 4).

> *Universis et singulis praesentes literas [sic] inspecturis fidem facimus atque attestamur, hunc Clavum ferreum serica vitta rubri coloris parvo nostro sigillo munita colligatum, admotum fuisse sacro Clavo qui apud Nos Cistercienses adservatur in Sacello interiori sacrarum Reliquiarum Basil--- urbanae S. Crucis ab Hierusalem, quique unus ex illis est, quibus D. N. J. C. Cruxi affixus fuit; eumdemque adeo affabre elaboratum esse, ut simillimus videatur.*
>
> *Dat. Romae in nostro Monasterio S. Crucis Hierosolymitanae Die 10 (?) Mensis ---- (?) Anno 1882 [signature, faint] Abbas*
>
> *We pledge and attest to all and to individuals who will inspect this letter that this iron nail, bound with a red silk string marked with our small seal, had been brought into contact with the sacred nail which is preserved among us Cistercians in the interior little sacred shrine of the holy remains of Saint Basil – a nail from the elegantly polished Holy Cross from Jerusalem which is also one of those to which the Cross of Our Lord, Jesus Christ is affixed and this very same has been skillfully crafted in such an elaborate way that it seems very similar.*
>
> *Given at Rome in our Monastery of the Holy Cross of Jerusalem*
> *The 10th day of the month? In the year 1882 [signature,]*

The replication of the relic itself, with an attestation to the image's fidelity, was a common practice in the 19th century. Very often such an object was acquired on a visit to a pilgrimage site. Although the authenticity of thirty or more extant "holy nails" has been questioned (*Catholic Encyclopedia*, 6, 672), the nail preserved in Helena's own palace would presumably claim precedence. It is most likely that someone had visited Santa Croce in Gerusalemme and acquired the box with its nail and testimonial. To the Catholic faithful in America unable to take that journey, sight of the nail would have had similar value as for Roman worshippers, aiding them to make present the suffering of Christ whose death redeemed humanity.

See further reading on page 341

Fig. 3
Chapel of the Relics
Florestano Di Fausto, 1930
Rome, Santa Croce
Photograph Michel Raguin

Fig. 4
Replica of a Nail of Christ's Passion from Santa Croce in Gerusalemme, Rome
Attestation certificate signed 1882
Wooden box with glass lid, 9 x 12 x 2½ in. (22.9 x 30.5 x 6.4 cm)
The Liturgy and Life Collection at the John J. Burns Library at Boston College
Photograph Michel Raguin

Details of Fig. 6

Saint Peter's in Rome and the Relic of Veronica's Veil

Virginia C. Raguin

Begun about 319-22 by the emperor Constantine, St. Peter's was one of the largest buildings in the world and the most important pilgrim shrine in Europe. The building was constructed over a Roman cemetery that was believed to contain the grave of Peter, preeminent among Christ's Apostles and venerated in the Middle Ages as the first pope. The great Roman church had as its complement the church of the Holy Sepulcher in Jerusalem, constructed very much on the same pattern featuring a basilican plan of long nave, side aisles, and a transept to accommodate the flow of the faithful visiting the churches. Margery Kempe (*The Book of Margery Kempe*, c. 1440), reflecting on her pilgrimage to Rome in 1416, used St. Peter's as a metaphor of safety: Christ promises her that she and her companions "will go as safe as if they were in St. Peters Church" (Ch. 42).

The present building dates from the complete reconstruction begun by Pope Julius II in 1506. Old St. Peter's was leveled and new plans, altered several times during construction, were drawn up in the Renaissance style. Ultimately a centrally planned church (designed by Bramante and Michelangelo) was extended into a Latin cross to occupy roughly the same space as the original basilica. The addition of Bernini's great colonnade in the mid-17th century further enhanced the site by monumentalizing the square itself.

Pilgrims were attracted by the great wealth of relics and accompanying indulgences. The veil of St. Veronica, believed to have been imprinted with the image of Christ when he wiped his face just before his death, was one of the most venerated. Albrecht Dürer's widely admired woodcut Passion of 1495 depicts the event (Fig. 1). The popularity of the relic developed in the Latin West after the conquest

Fig. 1
Christ Carrying the Cross
Large Passion, 1495 (B 10 H 119)
Albrecht Dürer
Print Department, Boston Public Library, Boston
Photograph Boston Public Library

Fig. 2

Sudarium of Veronica with the Apostles Peter and Paul

Small Passion, 1510 (B 38 H 147)

Albrecht Dürer

Print Department, Boston Public Library, Boston

Photograph Boston Public Library

of Constantinople and plunder of its relics in 1204 during the Fourth Crusade. Constantinople had possessed an image of Christ's face believed of miraculous manufacture, but it became lost. The relic in Rome of Veronica's cloth thus became the exclusive means of coming "face to face" with Christ. In 1208 pope Innocent III decreed that the veil would be carried in procession from St. Peter's to the hospital of Santo Spirito on the Feast of the Miracle of the Wedding in Cana, granting indulgences for gifts of alms made to the hospital. Innocent explained that the choice of the Feast was related to the gaze of the viewer on the face of Christ facilitating a spiritual wedding between the worshipper and the Divine.

The elevated view of the Holy Face ultimately would elide with the elevation of the host as performed during the Mass and at other specific rituals. In 1215, The Fourth Lateran Council would make dogma the concept of Transubstantiation. This doctrine proclaimed that despite the visually unchanged appearance of the bread and wine of the Mass, through God's grace operating through the words of the priest, Christ's mystical body was present in the sacrament. The veneration of the Eucharist, the transformed bread of the Mass, came to dominate popular piety from the 13th century onward. Medieval theories of vision, as suggested by Innocent's association of the viewing with a marital union, impacted both these acts of devotion to the Eucharist and the Holy Face. To see the Eucharist was actually to receive it; to gaze upon the Holy Face was to receive the imprint of Christ on the soul. Innocent promulgated an indulgence for those who devotedly repeated a prayer to the Holy Face; it was widely believed that the prayer had been composed by the pope himself.

At this time appears the story of the holy woman, whose name *Veronica* parallels the relic's own, the *Vera Icon* (True Image). Although the Gospel writers speak of the holy women who accompanied Christ's mother Mary during the events of the Passion, there is no mention of the veil or the woman's name. Tradition, however, can work with limited material to elaborate a believed truth. A bust of Christ in the *Chronica majora*, executed in England by Matthew Paris shortly after 1245, is accompanied by the explanation of the relic in Rome and the story that it was received by a holy woman who accompanied Christ on his road to Calvary. The story and the image of the Veronica became widespread in the following centuries. A hymn, *Salve sancta facies*, widely circulated in prayer books, is dated to 1316-34: "Save (us) holy face of our Redeemer, whose glow reveals the sight of divine splendor." By such a dissemination of images, pilgrimage was both democratized and sacralized. If denied the opportunity of pilgrimage to Rome and vision of the actual Veronica, the faithful could experienced it through its many replications, at first in painted image and later in print, such as Dürer's 1510 devotional trio of Peter and Paul flanking Veronica (Fig. 2). At the same time, the importance of the site and its relic became a universal reference in popular understanding of approved devotional practices. Meditation on the suffering of Christ was aided by devotional images, for example the image of Christ surrounded by the *Arma Cristi*, emblems of the various moment of his Passion, which included the pillar on which he was scourged, the crown of thorns, the three nails with hammer used to attach them and the pliers used to remove them, the dice used by the soldiers to claim Christ's cloak, and Veronica's veil. Often these Passion emblems were carried by angels, either in triumph or commemorative sorrow (Fig. 3).

As in the Holy Sepulcher, the pilgrim in St. Peter's would be led through an itinerary, ultimately to the Chapel of the Holy Face. As illustrated in a number of early woodcuts, the relic was viewed on a marble and porphyry parapet. Addressing St. Peter's seven altars of special "grace and dignity," the *Stations of Rome* of 1370 begins with the one containing the "Vernicle" (Furnivall, 2-3). The rhymed couplets explain the several levels of grace given to those who have made different efforts: "Three thousand years, as I heard tell, for men that in the City dwell.... And thou that passed over the sea, twelve thousand years are granted to thee." John Capgrave (Capgrave, 63-64), an Augustinian Friar from King's Lynn, England, wrote at length of his pilgrimage to Rome about 1450 and devoted considerable space to a description of the Vernicle. He noted the aged look of the image because of the extreme suffering of Christ. Also in the 15th century, William Brewyn described the indulgences available when the relic was shown (Brewyn, 8).

Fig. 3

Angel carrying the Veil of Veronica with the Image of Christ

French, c. 1500

Oak, 34¼ x 12 in. (87 x 30.5 cm)

The Metropolitan Museum of Art, Gift of J. Pierpont Morgan, 1916 (16.31.195)

Fig. 4

Relics Balcony

St. Peter's Basilica, Rome

Gianlorenzo Bernini, 1633-1641

Photograph Virginia C. Raguin

Also whensoever the face of our Lord Jesus Christ is shown there are three thousand years of indulgences, that is to say, those who live near Rome have six thousand years of indulgences, and those who come over the mountains and hills have nine thousand years of indulgences, and as many quarantines, and the remission of a third part of all sins.

The same reference to pilgrims coming from afar is made by Dante in *Paradise*, the last of the three books of the *Divine Comedy*: "As he who comes perchance from Croatia to look on our Veronica, and whose old hunger is not sated, but says in thought so long as it is shown, 'My Lord Jesus Christ, true God, was then your semblance like to this?'" (Canto 31:103).

The face of the Savior figured as an important catalyst for the reconstruction of St Peter's in the 16th century when the crossing under Michelangelo's dome became the central viewing area for relics. Between 1633 and 1641, after completing the great bronze baldacchino, Bernini hollowed out the four piers of the dome to construct balconies to display the basilica's major relics. For each he utilized two spiral columns taken from the original Constantinian church (Fig. 4). The saints whose relics are honored, also associated with the Passion, appear as four colossal statues: Helena, who discovered the True Cross; Longinus, the centurion who proclaimed his faith at the moment he pierced Christ's side with the lance; the Apostle Andrew, also crucified, and whose head was given to Pius II in 1462, and returned to the Greek Orthodox Church at Patras in 1964 by Paul VI; and Veronica (Fig. 5). The dramatic image of Veronica was sculpted by one of Bernini's competitors, Francesco Mochi. The inscription above the statue's niche documents the presence of the "Savior's image on the Veil (Sudarium) of Veronica," whose setting was embellished by Urban VIII (r. 1623-1644), born Maffeo Barberini. Directly above is the papal coat of arms with the three bees of the Barberini family. The veil is still a significant object of pilgrimage and is ceremonially presented to the faithful on the fifth Sunday of Lent (Palm Sunday), when the tradition of the Stational Liturgy brings the pope to celebrate at St. Peter's (Fig. 6).

See further reading on page 341

Fig. 5
Statue of St. Veronica
St. Peter's Rome
Francesco Mochi, 1633-1641
Photograph Virginia C. Raguin

Fig. 6
Display of the Veronica Relic, 2006
Relics Balcony
St. Peter's Basilica, Rome
Photograph Nicole Lawrence

Details of Fig. 5

Relics Defined: Discoveries on Site, Invention, Translation, and *Furta Sacra*

David M. Perry

Sometime after 1222, a monk in the monastery dedicated to St. George, in Venice, told the story of the translation of the body of St. Paul, the "New" martyr, from Constantinople to Venice (Fig. 1). The monk emphasized the benefits that he hoped would now accrue to his institution and city, referring to the relic as a "precious gem" that might "adorn not only the monastery, but all of Venice. For, just as innumerable men and women come from all parts to visit the blessed Mark, so too it will become the glorious custom to see the blessed Paul" (Monk of St. George, 144). This passage exemplifies the rationale behind the medieval quest for relics; relics brought pilgrims, pilgrims brought donations and prestige, prestige could lead to even more donations.

No medieval pilgrimage site could compete with Rome, Jerusalem, Constantinople, or Santiago de Compostela, but lesser locales could elevate their status by discovering, stealing, buying, or being given new relics. Where a saint (via relics) was newly present, hopeful petitioners might well find themselves blessed by miracles. But possession of a relic was not enough to reap the rewards of pilgrimage. In order to encourage visitors, one had to alert potential travelers that one possessed a sacred item, convince them that the relic was genuine, and, above all else, prove that the saint was happy with his or her new home. To achieve these ends, monastic and clerical authors created new types of hagiographical narratives in order to promote or reinforce the veneration of acquired relics.

One can divide the *acta* of a saint into three parts – the life, death, and the post-mortem miracles (*vita, passio,* and *miracula post mortem*). All three parts of the *acta* held a particular type of importance to the medieval Christian. Saints often demonstrated their piety by working miracles during their lives, and, crossing the boundary between earth and heaven in their moment of death, created their most important relics by dying. Saints distinguished themselves from other pious humans, however, by remaining active on earth after death, and the *miracula post mortem* played a crucial role in the promulgation of saints' cults. These remnants of the dead became focal points for critical intersections between a community and God. In promulgating a new relic cult, therefore, authors turned to this third phase of a saint's *acta* in an attempt to link miracle to place.

Due to the clandestine and persecuted nature of early Christianity, many relic cults began with the furtive gathering of the body of the recently martyred. Roman judges sometimes complained that the joy of a local Christian community at acquiring the body seemed to mitigate the deterrent effect of the execution of a particularly recalcitrant Christian. Burning the body did not help, as followers of martyrs were perfectly happy to accept ashes as relics. It was to commemorate the gathering of the relics of the recently slain, whether ash or bone, that the earliest forms of hagiographical narratives were written.

INVENTIO

As devotional practice normalized, Christian communities began to search for relics of saints whose bodies had not been cherished at the moment of their demise. But how to know that the corpse one found was truly the body of a saint? More importantly, how to convince others that one's claims concerning the relic of a martyr were genuine? Released from persecution, Christian apologists evidenced a deep need to make public arguments about the veracity of their relics. These authors developed narrative accounts of the discovery of hidden relics – the genre of *inventio*. Within the narrative structure of *inventio*, one could assure the reader that the discoverer was properly pious, that the new site in which the saint would be laid to rest was worthy of such an honor, and, most of all, that authenticity was proven by miracles taking place at the moment of discovery and after the final interment. A famous example of this genre is the *inventio* of the True Cross by St. Helena (Fig. 2). The crosses of the two thieves were found in the same location but only the life-giving cross of Christ was able to resuscitate the dead (see essay *Rome's Santa Croce in Gerusalemme and Relics of the Passion of Christ*). A century later, St. Stephen's body was found in the Holy Land, revealed by a dream. When the tomb was unearthed along with those of three companions, a sweet smell wafted from Stephen's tomb alone, and the sick were healed by his relics.

Because *inventio*, as a genre, focused particularly on the meaning that a community would draw from the presence of its new-found relics, it served as a vehicle not only for discovery narratives of known saints but also for the construction of forgeries. *Inventio* leads to invention. In discovering a relic, one could add hitherto unknown details to another *vita* in order to claim a local connection, or even invent saints out of whole cloth. For example, during the Late Antique period, many urban Northern Italian churches used *inventio* to manufacture connections to St. Peter. Ravenna developed the legend of St. Apollinaris; residents claimed had he had been a disciple of St. Peter and that his relics were discovered in their city. Milan's cathedral claimed a connection via St. Nazarius (whose mother was baptized by Peter, according to Milanese tradition) and St. Barnabas. Aquileia invented two saints, Hermagoras and Fortunatus, who were disciples of St. Mark, himself the spiritual "son" of St. Peter and composer of the Petrine Gospel. In the process of forging the lives of Hermagoras and Fortunatus, Aquileian hagiographers added a mission to Aquileia into the otherwise well-known *vita* of St. Mark. Mark, they claimed, founded their church before heading to Alexandria to be martyred. Italian churches, in their battle for precedence, all had to yield primacy to Rome. But through promotion of local relic legends, the churches of Northern Italy battled each other for second place.

TRANSLATIO

Stories of *inventio* tend to be static – people discover lost relics in their own backyards. But over time, Christians began to move known relics from site to site, and thus the genre of *translatio* developed. *Translatio* narratives not only needed to include joy of a new population's "discovery" of the relic, common to *inventio*, but also needed to authenticate the relic by describing the journey. It is in the journey that one can trace the provenance from old site to new, and miracles during travel explicitly demonstrate the saint's pleasure at the voyage. *Translatio* probably originated out of a combination of *inventio* and secular Roman accounts of ceremonial arrivals, such as the entrance of an emperor into one's city. The story of the translation of the relics of St. Stephen from their discovery in the Holy Land, in 415, to Jerusalem, and then to Constantinople, where the saint shows his preferred place of burial by stopping the cart, appears in a window of the cathedral of Bourges (Fig. 3). Such moments of *adventus*, when converted to a saint's relics, featured all the ceremony and pomp of the secular event, but also the spiritual meaning that the community found in *inventio*. Stained glass in the cathedral of Chartres shows the bishop of Constantinople coming out of the city gates to welcome the procession of relics (Fig. 4). Properly authorized, public translations of

Fig. 1
Mosaic of St. Paul the Martyr
San Marco, Venice, 13th century
Photograph David Perry

Fig. 2
Helena discovers the True Cross in Jerusalem
Engraving from *Ecclesiae Anglicanae Trophaea*, 1584, pl. 8
Stonyhurst College, Lancashire

relics were occasions of celebration. Communities would annually commemorate the arrival with new liturgies composed for the occasion; production of *translatio* narratives were often part of the commemoration. Each phase of the journey received special ritual attention: the removal of the saint from his or her crypt, the travel itself, and then the new installation.

Translatio narratives might be produced regardless of the means by which one acquired a relic. Powerful people gave relics as gifts to curry favor or reward allies. The Byzantine emperors, for example, were particularly fond of taking tiny slivers of important relics, encasing them in gorgeously decorated reliquaries, and offering them to diplomats and important pilgrims. Bishops might move relics in their diocese from one religious house to another, depending on the chains of alliance and favoritism in which they operated. Even those buying relics, a practice widespread at many points during the Middle Ages, though hardly canonical, needed to prove that they had bought something authentic. Concern over the authenticity of translated relics was severe enough that some recipients would bury *authenticae* – documents proving the identity of the sacred items – with the new relics (although few of such interred receipts seem to have survived).

Fig. 3
Relics of St. Stephen "translated" by the widow Juliana from Jerusalem to Constantinople. Below: Demons attack the cart with the relics but are repulsed; Left: at sea, a storm threatens but an angel appears to sink the demon's ships. Right: The Byzantine emperor interviews Juliana, demanding that the relics be brought to Constantinople. Above: Reaching a place called Constantianus, the mules refuse to move. One speaks, stating that the saint has selected this place as his tomb.
Cathedral of Bourges, stained glass, bay 15, c. 1210-15
Photograph Michel Raguin

FURTA SACRA

But not all translated relics were gifts or were bought from a willing seller. People also stole relics, and a darker sub-genre of *translatio* records such actions. St. Benedict's body, as discussed in the previous chapter, was stolen by French monks from the abbey of Montecassino and brought to Fleury-sur-Loire. Martin of Tours, whose charitable gift of his mantle to a beggar has transfixed the ages, died at nearby Candes and his followers retrieved his body. A stained glass window in the cathedral of Tours (Fig. 5) happily displays the thieves removing the corpse through a window and transporting it by boat on the Loire. The stories of such deeds follow many of the text structures of public translations but also account for sins committed in the process of translation. In such contexts, the written and visual narratives serve as documents of both exoneration and authentication. Just as in *translatio* accounts, an author must explain how the relic moved from its original place to the new location. In cases of theft, the narrative must describe the act of theft or leave the new church wondering if it has acquired a forgery. Miracles not only help prove the authenticity of the relic, as with the genres discussed above, but also suggest that the saint forgives the thief. *Translatio* narratives call these actions pious thievery or sacred theft – *furta sacra* – frequently suggesting that they were motivated by the previous owner's neglect of the relics.

The power behind *furta sacra* as a genre stems from its acknowledgement of sin. It uses the forgiveness of

Fig. 4
Procession of Clergy to welcome the Relics of Stephen
Cathedral of Chartres, stained glass, bay 13 (20), c. 1200-1210
Photograph © Stuart Whatling

Fig. 5
Martin, the patron saint of Tours, died at Candes. His followers contrived to steal the body. The image shows them passing it out a window for transportation on the Loire river to the city of Tours where a great pilgrimage church was built.
Cathedral of Tours, stained glass, bay 8, c. 1300
Photograph Michel Raguin

transgression to demonstrate the saint's preference for the new location. Without admission of transgression, one cannot achieve the second part of the equation. Furthermore, the publication of a *furta sacra* narrative took the theft from the realm of the furtive into public light. By celebrating the arrival in public ritual and recording the theft in narrative, the proud owners of a stolen relic made their case for manifest absolution. Both written record and ritual make the same argument: if God had not wanted the relics stolen, miracles would have hindered, not helped. Because God wanted the relics stolen, as evidenced by the miracle, none can object. Facile, perhaps, but theologically sound.

Inventio, *translatio*, *furta sacra*, and *authenticae* (the buried manuscripts) – the existence of all four genres points to the power of relics in the Middle Ages and the importance of controlling not just the physical object, but also the meaning of the relic. Only then could one reap the rewards of saintly patronage, augmented prestige, and increased pilgrimage.

See further reading on page 341

Egeria's Description of the Liturgical Year in Jerusalem: Excerpt for the Good Friday Veneration of the Cross

Egeria was a woman (whether religious or wealthy layperson has been debated) who made a pilgrimage to the Holy Land, presumably from Galicia in the Iberian Peninsula, between 381 and 384. She wrote a long letter to companions at home. Only part of the letter has survived, copied in the 11th century at the Benedictine Abbey of Montecassino in what has become known as the Codex Aretinus. The manuscript was discovered in 1884 in the monastic library of Arezzo. Egeria's account describes sites, history, and in particular, devotional rituals experienced at the churches and shrines in the Holy Land. It is tempting to think that she was a nun because of the absence of any specific motivation, other than prayer, mentioned in her pilgrimage. She also shows a particular interest in liturgical practice and in lifestyles of the holy men and women she meets.

Intense activities took place during the entire Holy Week often involving processions, displacement to various sites, and night vigils. During the devotions of Good Friday, the commemoration of Christ's death on the Cross, the veneration of the Cross took place from the sixth to the ninth hour (from 12 noon to 3 PM). From Egeria's description, it is clear that the ceremony took place in the Church of the Holy Sepulcher in a chapel behind the site of the Crucifixion. It involved a large cross that could be seen from afar as well as the relic of the wood of the True Cross of a size demanding that a man use two hands. Thus we can affirm that by the late 4th century belief in the discovery of the True Cross and in

Stained glass window of Angel holding a gem-studded cross Rome, Santa Croce, vestibule of chapel of the relics built in 1930

Photograph Michel Raguin

ceremonies involving relics was firmly established. Elsewhere in Egeria's text she speaks of the feast of the dedication of the Holy Sepulcher, "celebrated with the highest honor, because the Cross of the Lord was found on this same day" (Ch. XLVIII).

The sacred viewing so intensely a part of Buddhist pilgrimage appears in Egeria's account. She notes that the bishop encouraged the people, "comforting them for that they have toiled all night and are about to toil during that same day, [bidding] them not be weary [for soon they will] be able to behold the holy wood of the Cross, each one of us believing that it will be profitable to his salvation."

Translation based on the text by Louis Duchesme, *Christian Worship* (London, 1923). See hypertext developed by Michael Fraser of the University of Durham, 1994. http://users.ox.ac.uk/~mikef/durham/egetra.html, accessed August 18, 2009

VENERATION OF THE CROSS (CH. XXXVII)

Then a chair is placed for the bishop in Golgotha behind the Cross, which is now standing; the bishop duly takes his seat in the chair, and a table covered with a linen cloth is placed before him; the deacons stand round the table, and a silver-gilt casket is brought in which is the holy wood of the Cross. The casket is opened and (the wood) is taken out, and both the wood of the Cross and the title are placed upon the table.

2. Now, when it has been put upon the table, the bishop, as he sits, holds the extremities of the sacred wood firmly in his hands, while the deacons who stand around guard it. It is guarded thus because the custom is that the people, both faithful and catechumens, come one by one and, bowing down at the table, kiss the sacred wood and pass through. And because, I know not when, someone is said to have bitten off and stolen a portion of the sacred wood, it is thus guarded by the deacons who stand around, lest anyone approaching should venture to do so again.

3. And as all the people pass by one by one, all bowing themselves, they touch the Cross and the title, first with their foreheads and then with their eyes; then they kiss the Cross and pass through, but none lays his hand upon it to touch it. When they have kissed the Cross and have passed through, a deacon stands holding the ring of Solomon and the horn from which the kings were anointed; they kiss the horn also and gaze at the ring... all the people are passing through up to the sixth hour, entering by one door and going out by another; for this is done in the same place where, on the preceding day, that is, on the fifth weekday, the oblation was offered

STATION BEFORE THE CROSS. THE THREE HOURS.

4. And when the sixth hour has come, they go before the Cross, whether it be in rain or in heat, the place being open to the air, as it were, a court of great size and of some beauty between the Cross and the Anastasis; here all the people assemble in such great numbers that there is no thoroughfare.

5. The chair is placed for the bishop before the Cross, and from the sixth to the ninth hour nothing else is done, but the reading of lessons, which are read thus: first from the psalms wherever the Passion is spoken of, then from the Apostle, either from the epistles of the Apostles or from their Acts, wherever they have spoken of the Lord's Passion; then the passages from the Gospels, where He suffered, are read. Then the readings from the prophets where they foretold that the Lord should suffer, then from the Gospels where He mentions His Passion.

6. Thus from the sixth to the ninth hours the lessons are so read and the hymns said, that it may be shown to all the people that whatsoever the prophets foretold of the Lord's Passion is proved from the Gospels and from the writings of the Apostles to have been fulfilled. And so through all those three hours the people are taught that nothing was done which had not been foretold, and that nothing was foretold which was not wholly fulfilled. Prayers also suitable to the day are interspersed throughout.

7. The emotion shown and the mourning by all the people at every lesson and prayer is wonderful; for there is none, either great or small, who, on that day during those three hours, does not lament more than can be conceived, that the Lord had suffered those things for us. Afterwards, at the beginning of the ninth hour, there is read that passage from the Gospel according to John where He gave up the ghost. This read, prayer and the dismissal follow.

EGERIA'S DESCRIPTION OF THE LITURGICAL YEAR IN JERUSALEM: EXCERPT FOR THE GOOD FRIDAY VENERATION OF THE CROSS

The Holy Land Experienced Vicariously in Lowlands Devotional Practices

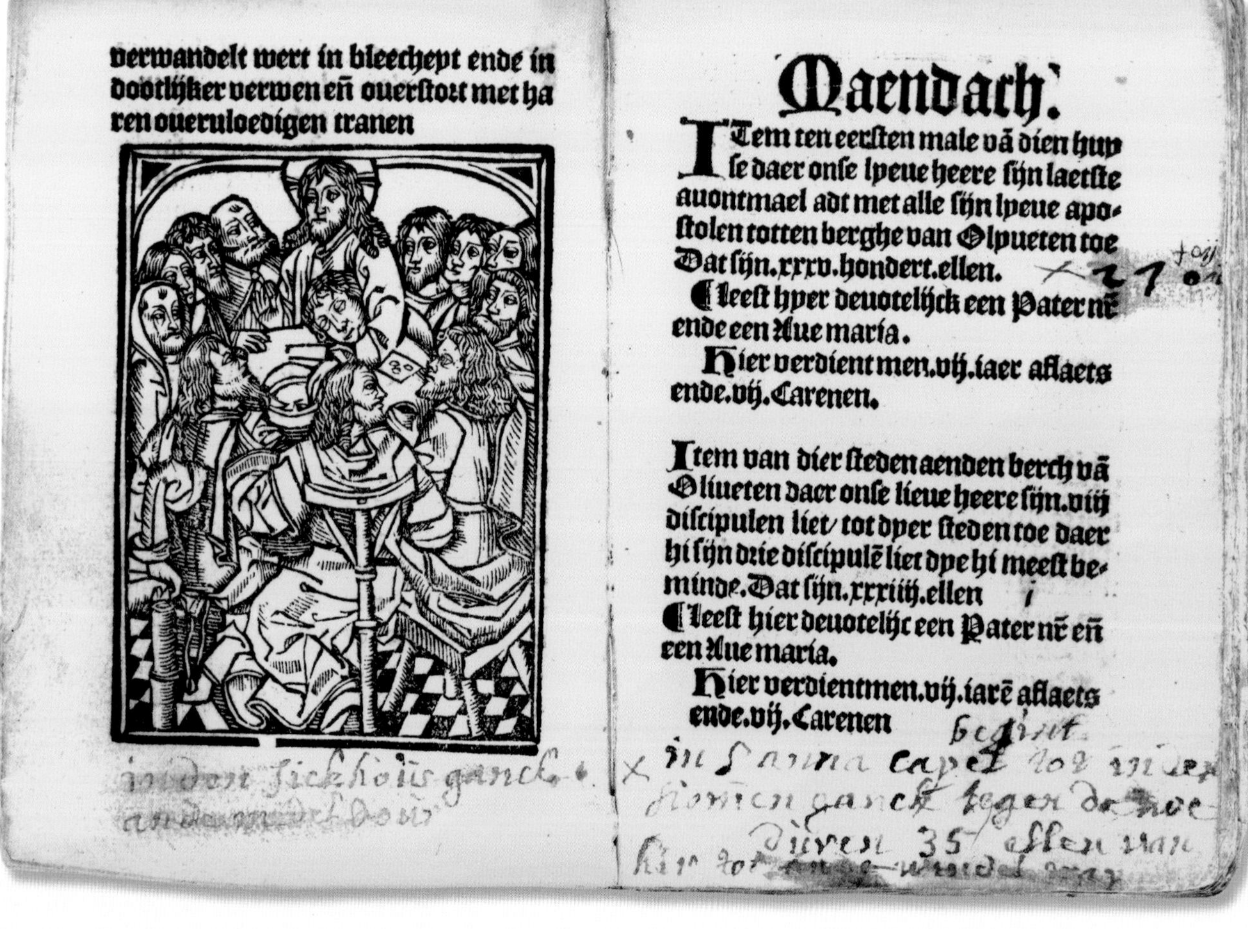

verwandelt wert in bleechept ende in doótlijker verwen eñ ouerstort met haren ouerulóedigen tranen

Maendach.

Item ten eersten male vā dien huyse daer onse lpeue heere sijn laetste auontmael adt met alle sijn lpeue apostolen totten berghe van Olpueten toe Dat sijn.xxxv.hondert.ellen.

Leest hper deuotelijck een Pater nr̄ ende een Aue maria.

Hier verdient men.vij.iaer aflaets ende.vij.Carenen.

Item van dier steden aenden berch vā Olijueten daer onse lieue heere sijn.viij discipulen liet/ tot dper steden toe daer hi sijn drie discipulē liet dpe hi meest beminde.Dat sijn.xxxiiij.ellen

Leest hier deuotelijc een Pater nr̄ eñ een Aue maria.

Hier verdientmen.vij.iarē aflaets ende.vij.Carenen

Fig. 1
Heer Bethlem's Guide
Published by Vorsterman, Antwerp, 1518
Koninklijke Bibliotheek, The Hague, Ms 231 G 22, fol. 4v-5r
Photograph Koninklijke Bibliotheek, The Hague

Cloistered Women's Strategies for Taking Mental Pilgrimages in Northern Europe

Kathryn M. Rudy

Being under lock and key, cloistered nuns forfeited their chance to go to the Holy Land. Instead, they invented, developed, and revised existing strategies for visiting Jerusalem and the other holy places. Jerusalem was especially important in late medieval piety, since devotion increasingly had to do with affective piety, mostly centered on the Passion of Christ. One of the most powerful, if not obvious ways to walk in Christ's footsteps was to go to Jerusalem and retrace the path that Christ had taken on his final walk to Calvary with his cross on his back.

An example of a virtual pilgrimage comes from the convent of Augustinian canonesses in Maaseik, a town located on the Meuse River in the Belgian province of Limburg, and birthplace of the painters Jan and Hubert van Eyck. The Van Eycks produced some of the most memorable altarpieces and devotional images of the 15th century, including the monumental Ghent altarpiece showing the adoration of Christ as the Lamb of God in the Heavenly Jerusalem, surrounded by pilgrims of all types, clergy, monks, hermits, soldiers, martyrs, and virgins. During the time of this important development of art and piety in the Lowlands, the canonesses copied hundreds of manuscripts, including several manuscripts containing a long prayer beginning, "These are the indulgences of the Holy City of Jerusalem and of the Mountain of Calvary" (*Dit is den aflaet der heiliger stat Iherusalem ende des berchs van Calvarien*). This text, which originated at this cloister or within its milieu, takes readers through twelve stations of Christ's Passion, pausing at each so the reader can meditate and obtain indulgences. The text also notes the distances between these sites in Jerusalem so that the reader can imagine walking from one to the next with some degree of topographic fidelity. Moreover, as the nuns copied the text, they transmogrified it from a detached third-person narrative to a second-person conversation with Christ. The act of copying served as one aspect of the devotional training; changing and personalizing it made the writer/reader a participant and witness.

This genre of affective literature continued in a group of printed books that drew on the Maaseik nuns' mental pilgrimage prayers. Printers attributed the text to a nonexistent priest named Heer Bethlem, who provides spurious eyewitness verification of the stations and places in the Holy Land, including the "distances" between the important places, such as Caiaphas's house, Pilate's house, the place where Pilate declared "*Ecce homo*," and so forth. The booklets, whose popularity is affirmed by seventeen print runs in three cities in the Low Countries, include wood-cut images depicting these sites or events on nearly every page. In one copy (published in 1518 by Vorsterman in Antwerp, and now located in The Hague), an early user has

written marginal notes that reveal her identity as a cloistered nun who used the booklet in a physical and active way: she selected buildings and specific sites in her cloister and redesignated them as the sites of Christ's Passion described in the book, then walked through the cloister, pausing at each place. For example, she falls on her knees at "the last stainedglass window in the corridor of the spinning house" *(tegen het leste gelas inden spinhous ganck valt hier...)* in order to meditate on Christ's encounter before the high priest Annas. She shows her devotion to Christ during his betrayal by Judas by praying in the "*werm hous*," where she declares her co-suffering for Christ's "wretched imprisonment" and notes that his suffering will not be lost on her *(Knielt ant werm hous en alle dijn heilige lyden an mij niet verloren en blijven vor dijn allendige gevangenis...)*; one cannot help but wonder if cloistered nuns demonstrated more devotion to the imprisoned Christ because they were also under lock and key. Additionally, numerous handwritten notes alongside the printed distances in the text indicate that she peregrinated around the entire cloister grounds for a fixed number of revolutions in order to pace off the same number of steps that Christ traveled as he moved from one travail to the next.

Other texts and images indicate that just before the Protestant Reformation, nuns throughout German- and Dutch-speaking Europe reidentified their cloistered settings as Jerusalem in order to perform imagined pilgrimages. A manuscript prayer book with prayers and devotions in Middle Dutch, that belonged to a nun in Brabant, contains a prayer to the "nine sufferings of Christ" (Ghent, University Library, Ms. 1734). Rubrics, which provide instructions for the reader, precede each of the sufferings. They indicate that the reader should imagine walking with Christ from one suffering to the next along the *via crucis* while she is going about her daily routine. During her walk from Mass, for example, she is to imagine walking to Pilate's house. When she walks to her midday meal, she is to imagine accompanying Christ from Pilate's house back to Herod's. She is to imagine other events on her way back from lunch, on her way to and from dinner in the refectory *(ter reventer)*, and during her trips to and from the evening reading *(avonds...als ge ter lex gaet and als gij uuter lexsen gaet)*. The nun could perform the entire sequence mentally during her quotidian walks through the convent.

The Poor Clares in the Bickenkloster in Villingen, a cloister in the Black Forest, constructed the most elaborate of these practices after the abbess Ursula Haider (1413-1498) obtained permission to hang more than two hundred placards listing indulgenced holy sites around Jerusalem, Bethlehem, and Rome, along with the indulgence value for visiting each. These painted signs appeared all over the cloister and afforded the nuns the opportunity to visit them whenever they desired to do so.

See further reading on page 342

Fig. 2
The Last Supper and the Agony in the Graden
Dining Hall of the convent Santa Monica inter Angelos near Spoleto, c. 1300
Fresco, 92¹¹⁄₁₆ x 100⁷⁄₈ in. (235.4 x 256.2 cm)
Worcester Art Museum, Museum purchase, 1924.24
Photograph Worcester Art Museum
Both male and female monastics identified the actions of their daily lives with those of Christ. Thus imagery of Christ sharing the final meal with his apostles was a common choice for dining halls (refectories), reinforcing the precept that the convent was indeed a surrogate for the Holy Land.

Anselm Adornes' Jerusalem Pilgrimage and the Jeruzalemkapel of Bruges

Mitzi Kirkland-Ives

The Adornes family, Genoan merchants and bankers residing in Bruges since the late 13th century, had a history of special devotion to the city of Jerusalem. According to tradition, Oppicino Adornes had visited the Holy Land before arriving in Flanders in 1269 (Gaillard, 1; Geirnaert, 19). His descendants, the brothers Pieter II and Jakob Adornes, are also believed to have made the journey to Jerusalem in the early 15th century, where Jakob was inducted as a Knight of the Holy Sepulcher. Pieter II's son Anselm Adornes, and Anselm's eldest son, Jan, continued this family tradition by traveling together to Jerusalem and further in 1470 and 1471. With three sequential generations of pilgrims (and possibly a 13th-century pilgrim forefather), the Adornes family was notable in its collective devotion to the sites of the Holy Land, as evidenced not only by its pilgrimage activities but by the extraordinary family chapel – the *Jeruzalemkapel* or Jerusalem Chapel – erected as part of the complex of buildings that served as the family's residence in Bruges.

Anselm Adornes' 1470 journey to the Holy Land is related in an account recorded by Anselm's eldest son, Jan, and in a second, Flemish-language report known from a 1490s transcription and likely extracted from notes taken by Jan de Ghausy, Anselm's chamberlain. The highlight of the journey was, as Jan Adornes' account describes, "a large church which is called the Holy Sepulcher, holiest of them all, and it is built at the holiest place in the world, and contains many sacred places of the Passion of the Lord." The visit to the Holy Sepulcher would generally be repeated on three separate nights during a pilgrim's stay (a recollection of Christ's three days in the tomb), with the pilgrim entering on one night and exiting at noon the following day. After the first visit on the Feast of the Exaltation of the Cross, Anselm Adornes' group returned for a second visit and was exceptionally able to stay in the church continuously for a full two nights and a day, as Jan de Ghausy describes, "shut in without exiting, visiting the Holy Places (of which there were many) as each pleased; this did not happen with many pilgrims." Jan Adornes adds, "each performed his devotions on behalf of himself, his prince, and for his relations."

The narrative commemorated at the Church of the Holy Sepulcher was not limited to the Entombment and Resurrection, but encompassed the entire Passion story, recalled during a formal procession organized by the Franciscans that led the pilgrims from station to station and from relic to relic within the church. The visit began on the north side of the church in the chapel of the Apparition to Our Lady; here the friars organized and prepared the pilgrims for a procession that traveled a circuit through the ambulatory to a number of radiating chapels commemorating

Fig. 1
Jeruzalemkapel, exterior
Bruges, mid-1470s to 1523
Photograph Mitzi Kirkland-Ives

Fig. 2
Jeruzalemkapel, interior
Three crosses with display of relics and Passion imagery
Photograph Mitzi Kirkland-Ives

a series of Passion episodes, and descended a set of steps into the Chapel of Helena, featuring the grotto in which she discovered the True Cross, the crown of thorns, the lance, and nails. From this point the pilgrims continued to a chapel that featured a fragment of a column from Caiaphas' house, and continuing on this ambulatory circuit – now toward the west – reached a set of steps leading up the hill of Calvary. The procession ended with the pilgrims' approach to the Holy Grave itself, a structure standing in the center of the Anastasis Rotunda.

Like their ancestors, Anselm and his son Jan were not content to recreate their Jerusalem experience through their written record or in their memories. Upon his return from the Holy Land, Anselm undertook a renovation and elaboration of the Jeruzalemkapel – the family's private chapel erected in Bruges by Anselm's forefathers (Fig. 1). The still-extant structure, built between the mid-1470s, after Anselm's return from his pilgrimage, and 1523, when further renovations were made, was not the first architectural project at this location that memorialized the Adornes family's special devotion to the Holy Land. There was at the beginning of the 15th century a convent for the elderly on the site, which by 1440 was popularly referred to as *Jerusalem*. The earliest report of a Jeruzalemkapel can be found in a 1427 papal bull responding to a petition by the pilgrims Pieter II and Jacob Adornes, in which they had noted that their forefathers had erected a "Chapel in the honor and memory of the salvific Passion of our Lord Jesus Christ and of his Holy Sepulcher known popularly under the name of Jerusalem." The renovated chapel was consecrated, fittingly, on Palm Sunday of 1429 by the Archbishop of Tournai.

The Jeruzalemkapel today features a tall centralized tower topped by a copper onion dome, conspicuously oriental and exotic among the steep gables of the medieval Flemish city center. Inside, visitors are confronted by three stone crosses set above a sculpted sandstone hill strewn with the traditional *arma christi* and related elements – details such as Judas' purse; the column to which Christ was bound; whips with which Christ was scourged; and the ladders, hammer, and nails – serving as mnemonic devices to assist in a reconstruction of the narrative of Christ's last tormented hours (Fig. 2). A selection of relics brought back from the Holy Land are also enshrined in the five niches carved into this tableau at the "base" of the hill, just above the altar, while between these niches four small scenes from the Passion are also depicted. These episodes – the Imprisonment of Christ,

Fig. 3
Jeruzalemkapel, interior
Effigy of Christ entombed
Photograph Mitzi Kirkland-Ives

the Carrying of the Cross, the *Ecce Homo*, and Christ on the Cold Stone – offer for viewers a more overtly narrative form of imagery than the more abstracted *arma christi* imagery above. Devotees can enter into a complex narrative engagement with the wealth of objects available as prompts for meditation.

From this location visitors can progress even further in their devotions, passing through either of two small doorways tucked underneath the stairways leading to the upper choir, like tomb entrances carved into this extended hillside, to enter the low vaulted crypt behind the nave wall under the choir. Through an even smaller doorway set into the east wall of the crypt, so low that one is forced to crouch or kneel to enter, one enters an unusually small, still-more-cramped space, perhaps two meters wide, literally tomb like. Here a "sepulcher" set against the south wall in the form of a rectangular, white marble sarcophagus is fronted with an iron grill that permits viewing of a stone effigy of the body of Christ within (Fig. 3). A single circular oculus at the peak of the vault opens to the sky.

While the formal and metric correspondences between the Church of the Holy Sepulcher in Jerusalem and the Jeruzalemkapel of Bruges are only approximate in modern terms, on a conceptual level the two experiences would have been understood as closely analogous. Approaching the church from outside, visitors are able to begin to transport themselves to an ersatz Jerusalem, to imagine themselves as pilgrims visiting the Holy Sepulcher, having in a sense metonymically followed in Christ's footsteps and imaginatively recreated the various episodes of Christ's Passion, much as did the pilgrim navigating the ambulatory of the Holy Sepulcher church in Jerusalem with the aid of the Franciscan procession.

The Jeruzalemkapel remained central in Bruges residents' relationship with the Holy Land through the 16th century. Around 1520 a Jerusalem Brotherhood was formed in Bruges (whose members included, among other notables, the painter Jan Provost); the brotherhood reached an accord with the Jerusalem Foundation for the yearly use of the chapel, and enjoyed the benefits common to such institutions in cities elsewhere, such as Utrecht and Leiden, including an annual mealtime gathering and the prerogative to carry palm fronds within the Palm Sunday procession. In 1522 the group received permission to further expand its Palm Sunday processional trajectory, during which the early modern city was temporarily reidentified as Jerusalem. The centering of such a procession on Jerusalem in Bruges would have added to this sense of identification of place: again, in this yearly mimetic exercise the chapel becomes Jerusalem. At roughly the same time as the addition of the sepulcher, a black marble tombstone marked with a Jerusalem cross and a stylized depiction of Golgotha was set into the floor at the north end of the crypt. This memorial marks a final prerogative of the Brotherhood of the Holy Sepulcher: a site within the chapel where members were allowed to be buried. At home in Bruges these 16th-century pilgrims, by a practice of equivalence, achieved every pilgrim's dream of being buried in Jerusalem.

Details of Fig. 3

A Souvenir on Your Hat: Medieval Christian Pilgrims' Badges

Jennifer Lee

Pilgrims generally wore special clothing to symbolize their mission both for practical and spiritual purposes. The proper dress of a late medieval pilgrim would have consisted of a loose frock or long smock, over which was thrown a separate hood with a cape. A low-crowned, broad-brimmed hat was common, often identified in writing as a "pilgrim's hat" (see essay *Medieval Christian Pilgrims' Guides and Pilgrims' Text*). A pouch or wallet was usually attached to a walking staff or belt. Similarly, pilgrims wore a sign to designate the site to which they were traveling. These badges also protected the pilgrims from assault and enabled them to pass through even hostile ranks.

In Western Europe, the pilgrimage souvenir trade became formalized in the 12th century. The most common token for pilgrims to acquire was a purchased badge to be worn usually on the hat or bag, or pinned to an outer garment. In this way the badge did double duty first as a personal keepsake for the pilgrim to recall his or her journey and secondly to announce to the world that the wearer was a pilgrim who had visited a particular shrine.

The first European pilgrims' badges were the scallop shells associated with the shrine of St. James at Compostela in Galicia in northwestern Spain. The shells came from the sea some twenty miles away from the pilgrimage church, but were sold in the square outside the cathedral. After 1137, an anonymous French cleric wrote the famous traveler's guide known as *The Pilgrim's Guide*, and noted the tradition of selling the shells to pilgrims. The author refers to the practice in an offhand way, implying that it was already well known to everyone at the time. Scallop shells have been found in firmly dated tombs on the pilgrimage route in Spain from the 10th century and throughout the Middle Ages.

By the middle decades of the 12th century, we find the manufacture of metal pilgrims' badges. The earliest sites of such badges were those dedicated to the Virgin Mary at Le Puy and Rocamadour in southern France (Spencer 1998, 233-34, Bruna, 95-97). Made of tin and lead, cast in molds, and nearly flat, many of these badges adopted the almond shape that was frequently used for seals on documents. At their center was an image of the Virgin and around the edge a brief inscription of the holy site. Some had tiny loops at the corners for stitching them onto one's clothes. Others were so thin that a needle could be poked right through for sewing them onto the hat. These were inexpensive ornaments that almost any pilgrim could afford; their importance came not from their material value but from their meaning.

Pilgrims' badges soon became standard items for sale at shrines throughout Europe. Each location produced a distinctive badge that referred to the relics or images the pilgrims came to venerate. In most cases, the clergy who cared for the shrine probably also oversaw the making of the molds, which could be leased out to local artisans who cast the badges and sold them at market stalls in the town or outside the pilgrimage church.

Most badges can be traced to their shrines of origin; they often depict saints with their emblems and some localizing element from the shrine. Some, however, present a challenge to historians, although presumably they would have been more readily identifiable to most people in the Middle Ages. The stories of many saints refer to the instruments of their martyrdoms. Thus, badges from Geraardsbergen in Belgium showed St. Adrian holding an anvil (he was dismembered on an anvil) and those of St. Erasmus included a windlass (he was disemboweled and his intestines wound on a windlass). Others referred to miraculous events surrounding a place, such as those from Walsingham in England (Fig. 1). The Walsingham shrine contained a small house that was believed to have been built in 1061 by a noblewoman named Richeldis under the Virgin's direction. English pilgrims, unable to go to Jerusalem, were thus given access to a replica of the house where the Virgin received Gabriel's message that she would give birth to the Messiah. From the pilgrimage to Rome, the crossed keys of St. Peterwere popular, as were images of the Holy Face on St. Veronica's veil (see essay *Saint Peter's in Rome and the Relic of Veronica's Veil*). So many badges represented famous statues of the Virgin Mary that today historians have trouble telling which badges came from which site. The scallop shells from Santiago de Compostela remained popular badges, and eventually came to signify not only the pilgrimage to St. James' shrine but the whole concept of pilgrimage in general. They were often worn in combination with badges from other shrines.

One of the most popular medieval pilgrimages was to Canterbury and the shrine of Thomas Becket. As archbishop, Becket resisted the efforts of King Henry II to extend his authority over the clergy, and in 1170 four knights loyal to the king struck him down while he was at prayer in a side chapel of the cathedral. The incident was an immense shock to contemporaries; the news traveled across all of Europe and

Fig. 1
Lead alloy pilgrim badge from Walsingham
English, 14th century
© Museum of London

Fig. 2
Pilgrim's ampulla from Canterbury
English, early 13th century
Musée national du Moyen Age-Thermes de Cluny, Paris, France.
Photograph Réunion des Musées Nationaux/Art Resource, NY

Fig. 3
Pewter pilgrim badge of the head of St. Thomas Becket
English, 14th century
© Museum of London

Becket was swiftly elevated to sainthood. The translation of Becket's relics into the new choir, on July 7, 1220, was a state occasion and became a commemorated feast day throughout England. The focal point of the choir was Becket's shrine, designed by Elias of Dereham sometime between 1205 and 1216. Faced with gold and decorated with jewels, it stood on an elevated base in the middle of the Trinity Chapel, at the east end of the church, as depicted in one of the stained glass windows and also in pilgrim badges.

Because of its popularity over more than three hundred years, Canterbury also had an unusually wide variety of pilgrim's badges. The earliest were small vessels, called *ampullae*, that pilgrims wore around their necks as pendants (Spencer 1998, 38) (Fig. 2). These *ampullae* contained Canterbury water, a mixture of water that the pilgrims believed was tinged with infinitesimally minute amounts of the blood shed by Thomas Becket when he was violently murdered. Fragrant herbs and oils may also have been added to the mixture. These *ampullae* served as portable reliquaries that allowed pilgrims to literally take some of the saint's physical remains away with them. The Canterbury water was also famous for its healing qualities. The pilgrim could swallow it as a medicine or save the dose for a later emergency. The *ampullae* had images in low relief on their surfaces. Usually they portrayed Thomas Becket in his bishop's vestments. A few showed the murder perpetrated by four knights. Some included inscriptions that referred to the healing properties of the Canterbury water and the power of the saint.

By around the year 1300, Canterbury pilgrims could buy badges as well as *ampullae*. Badges were cheaper and easier to cast than *ampullae*, so they soon outnumbered the *ampullae* many times over. The badges were just images, with no Canterbury water, but they could be easily worn pinned to the hat, so they had the advantage of being easily visible. The most popular badges were images of Thomas Becket's reliquary bust. This silver and gold statue of the saint's head and shoulders enclosed the top of his skull, severed during the murder. It was destroyed in the 16th century when the pilgrimage site was forcibly shut down by the ministers of King Henry VIII, but for more than two hundred years it was displayed in the Corona Chapel at the east end of Canterbury Cathedral (Lee, 59-61) (Fig. 3). The reliquary bust badges range widely in quality. The finest are about three inches high and show the crisply molded bust inside an elaborate gothic frame. At the other end of the spectrum the badges are smaller and sketchier, with almost childishly simple features and often sloppy molding. Despite the variations in quality, the message they conveyed would have been the same (Figs. 4-7).

Some pilgrims probably treasured their badges for the rest of their lives. There are suggestions that some people kept them as mementos or as talismans against hardship, even hanging them in the house or barn to protect the inhabitants or burying them in the fields to protect the crops. Other pilgrims may have discarded them on the way home or soon after getting back. Except for a very few badges that were stitched into the pages of private prayer books, those in today's museum collections have been discovered by archaeologists. Whether they were dropped by mistake, tossed into rivers like coins in a wishing well, or thrown out with the garbage, pilgrims' badges eventually made their way into the ground. Because of the chemical properties of the metal, they survived best in wet conditions. Thousands have been found in the mud at the bottoms of rivers in Great Britain and continental Europe. Excavations of medieval village sites in wet, low-lying regions of the Netherlands continue to turn up pilgrims' badges by the thousands. The Museum Boymans-Van Beuningen in the city of Cothen in the Netherlands holds the largest collection and database (Kicken). Other sizeable collections can be found in museums in New York and Canterbury, and in museums with published catalogs in London (Spencer 1998), Salisbury (Spencer 1990), and Paris (Bruna 1996). Today there are more surviving pilgrims' badges than any other type of image-artifact from the Middle Ages. Amateur excavators play a role in the discoveries too. Individuals with metal detectors are often the ones who find medieval pilgrims' badges. In London, where the tidal banks of the River Thames are popular with metal detectorists, badges are taken first to the Museum of London for photographing, documenting, and sometimes purchasing for the permanent collection. If not bought by the museum, they can be sold to collectors. Volunteers with metal detectors have also helped on formal archaeological projects by searching through large amounts of soil that had been hurriedly removed from excavation sites in advance of urban building projects. This popular participation

Fig. 4
Ampula of Becket
English, late 13th or 14th century
Tin, 2⅛ x 1¹³⁄₁₆ in. (5.4 x 4.6 cm)
The Metropolitan Museum of Art, Gift of William and Toni Conte, 2002 (2002.306.1)
Image © The Metropolitan Museum of Art/Art Resource, NY

Fig. 5
Pilgrim's Badge, Becket's gloves; made in Bury St. Edmunds, England
English, 15th century
Tin/pewter, 1³⁄₁₆ x 1¼ in. (3 x 3.2 cm)
The Metropolitan Museum of Art, Gift of William and Toni Conte, 2002 (2002.306.20)
Image © The Metropolitan Museum of Art/Art Resource, NY

in the recovery of medieval pilgrims' badges is fitting for a type of image that was also used by the general population during the Middle Ages.

Because of the haphazard survival of pilgrims' badges and the archaeological nature of their recovery, the overwhelming majority of extant badges are made of tin and lead. However, written records indicate that badges of higher quality metals were available to wealthy pilgrims. For instance, when King René of Anjou visited a shrine of Sainte-Cathérine de Fierbois in 1451, he purchased large gold badges for himself and his immediate family, smaller gold badges for his chamberlains, two dozen large silver badges for the ladies and gentlemen of his household, and four dozen small silver badges for his household officers (Lightbown, 195-96). Until recently, none of these more expensive badges had been discovered. Now, a few silver and silver-gilt examples have been found in excavations as well as stitched into the pages of expensive manuscripts. Most such badges of precious metals, however, were probably recycled centuries ago.

The popularity of pilgrims' badges seems to have peaked between 1350 and 1450. In addition to the many examples recovered archaeologically, there are also paintings from this period that depict pilgrims wearing badges. The traditional costume of broad-brimmed hat, bag, and walking stick may have been sufficient to designate someone as a pilgrim, but a badge or a cluster of badges indicated precisely where the pilgrim had traveled, which saints protected him on the road, and how many shrines he had visited. Today, modern pilgrims who are retracing the medieval pilgrims' routes, whether as historical reenactments or as personal devotional journeys, can buy and wear badges copied from medieval examples. Their low price, combined with their flexibility to serve as both private keepsakes and public declarations of pilgrim status, ensures their continued appeal.

See further reading on page 342

Fig. 6
Pilgrim's Badge, bust of crowned Becket
English, 15th century
Tin-lead alloy, 1 5/16 x 15/16 in. (3.3 x 2.4 cm)
The Metropolitan Museum of Art, Gift of William and Toni Conte, 2002 (2002.306.18)
Image © The Metropolitan Museum of Art/Art Resource, NY

Fig. 7
Pilgrim's Badge, St. Thomas Becket
English, Canterbury, 15th century
Tin-lead alloy, diam. 15/16 in. (2.4 cm)
The Metropolitan Museum of Art, The Cloisters Collection, 1986 (1986.77.4)
Image © The Metropolitan Museum of Art/Art Resource, NY

Details of Fig. 2

"Pilgrimage on a Page": Pilgrims' Badges in Late Medieval Manuscripts

Megan H. Foster-Campbell

Although pilgrims commonly wore their souvenir badges on their clothing, such a hat, bag, or cloak, some badges were actually sewn into private prayer books. Surviving evidence suggests that the fastening of pilgrim badges in manuscripts was practiced as early as the mid-15th century and lasted well into the mid-16th century. While the lower and middle classes affixed badges to their clothing as an outward sign of their pilgrim status, members of the nobility were more likely to use lavish prayer books – usually Books of Hours – to hold their souvenirs. The practice was popular in the Southern Netherlands and northern France, with examples stretching into the Northern Netherlands and even as far as south-central France. Many of the identifiable badges in manuscripts are from shrines mainly in the Low Countries and in north, northeastern, and central France, as well as Burgundy.

The presence of pilgrims' badges in prayer books demonstrates that multiple forms of private devotion were increasingly significant in the religious lives of late medieval laity. These people were seeking not only a private spiritual experience by reading a book of prayers, but also a personal response within the larger, public space of pilgrimage. Insertion of badges in prayer books combines these aspects of an individual's private religious experiences: one object, the book, was used daily, and the other, the badge, was a memento of an extraordinary occurrence. Placed together, they became more intimate and personal, to be viewed primarily by the book's owner.

Pilgrims' badges in prayer books also could serve other purposes. They could function mnemonically, as devices of pilgrimage that evoked a devotional memory. They acted as a constant reminder of the pilgrimage experience whenever the book was opened, allowing the reader to relive her or his own concrete pilgrimage journey. In effect, they allowed the owner to go on a mental pilgrimage. They could also be apotropaic; that is, seen as capable of warding off evil. While some pilgrims pinned badges to their clothing in hopes of a safe return from a holy site, the sewing of badges into a manuscript suggests the book's spiritual and material worth and its need of the protection and blessing of apotropaic objects.

Pilgrims' badges were sewn into different areas in every manuscript; therefore, the precise location of badges in manuscripts may indicate their primary function within the book and the book's relationship with these souvenirs. Sometimes a collection of badges was affixed to a blank page, usually in front or back of the manuscript. In such instances, the manuscript seems to function primarily as a sort of scrapbook for souvenirs. Book owners could also disperse their collection of badges throughout the manuscript, relating them to its contents. In these cases, the souvenirs appear to have been added to the book for specific devotional reasons, perhaps to create direct resonances with the surrounding texts or illuminations.

The latter is the case for a manuscript now in Oxford, England (Bodleian Library MS Douce 51), a Book of Hours originating in France around 1490. Originally, at least six thin metal badges were placed in the margins throughout the manuscript, usually next to an illuminated miniature; of these, five still survive, dispersed over four separate leaves. The prayers that the owner supplemented with badges are all related to the Virgin Mary. Perhaps not by coincidence, several of the badges inserted also depict the Virgin.

After the 12th century, and the greater lay participation in the Church, the image of the Virgin and Child shifted from one emphasizing the theological concept of the Incarnation, the World made Flesh, to that of an accessible intermediary capable of empathizing with the human condition. Thus the artists, and their patrons, gravitated to images emphasizing loving relationship between mother and son (Fig. 1). In sculpture, painting, or stained glass, the Virgin appears more like a contemporary person, richly dressed, but recognizable. A pilgrimage badge on the verso (back) of folio 45 is adjacent to a full-page illumination of a gentle Virgin and Child surrounded by kneeling angels (Fig. 2). Partially covering the yellow panel border in the upper left corner is a square badge

Fig. 1

The Virgin Mary holding the Christ Child

French, 14th century

Limestone with traces of polychromy, 26 x 9 5/16 in. (66 x 23.7 cm)

The Metropolitan Museum of Art, Mr. and Mrs. Isaac D. Fletcher Collection, Bequest of Isaac D. Fletcher, 1917 (17.120.1)

Image © The Metropolitan Museum of Art/ Art Resource, NY

with a heart-shaped frame containing a scallop shell, the image most associated in the West with pilgrimage. On the shell is a representation of the Virgin Mary, with the Infant Christ in her left arm, in a small enclosed arch.

Unfortunately, the pilgrimage site for the badge cannot be identified; images of the Virgin and Child were popular pilgrimage motifs for many sites. However, the subject clearly relates to the adjacent miniature and text. The image on the page opens the set of prayers used for the Votive Mass of the Virgin, appropriately showing the Virgin and Child. Equally striking are the similarities in shapes and patterns between the badge and the illumination. In the miniature, the tips of the sloping wings of the angel in the background reach to the sides of the archway; combined with the rounded forms of the two arches, the wings' edges form the shape of a heart. This form is similar to the heart-shaped frame of the metal badge, suggesting that the owner very possibly directed the illuminator to compose the image to reflect the badge.

Dozens of manuscripts that contain (or once contained) pilgrims' badges still survive in library archives. In fact, the practice likely prompted later manuscript illuminators to paint representations of pilgrims' badges in book margins, as represented in The *Hours of Louis Quarré* (Oxford, Bodleian Library MS Douce 311, fol. 21v).

See further reading on page 342

Fig. 2
Opening of the Votive Mass of the Virgin, with attached pilgrim badge
France, c. 1490
Oxford, Bodleian Library MS Douce 51, fol. 45v
Photograph courtesy Bodleian Library

Details of Fig. 10

Medieval Christian Pilgrims' Guides and Pilgrims' Texts

Paula Gerson

Pilgrimages have been exhorted in texts from biblical times. In Deuteronomy 16, the tribes of Israel are ordered to appear three times a year at the Lord's chosen place. This, by the era of David, was Jerusalem, a site which has remained a crucible for religions and for pilgrimage ever since. In fact, the earliest guides written by pilgrims or for pilgrims are guides to Jerusalem and the Holy Land.

In the Christian world, there were three great pilgrimages: those to the Holy Land, to Rome, and to Santiago de Compostela. All three centers required travel to far-distant places, and are thus distinguished from local pilgrimages, which sometimes could even be accomplished in a single day. The earliest texts for Jerusalem date to the 4th century and continue throughout the Middle Ages, with the greatest number written during the period of the Latin Kingdom (1099-1187) when Christians ruled that segment of the Middle East. Extant texts for Rome date from the late 6th and early 7th centuries. One major pilgrim's guide to Santiago de Compostela was written in the 12th century, with a few others being from the 14th and 15th centuries.

From our 21st-century perspective, we would expect a guide to explain how to get to a site and what to see and do once there, and to give a firsthand, vivid report about the experience. In fact, such a comprehensive manual does not appear until the 12th-century *Pilgrim's Guide to Santiago de Compostela*, although earlier texts have at least one of these components. Guides varied with the intentions of their authors. Some were meant to assist subsequent pilgrims visiting the same sites, while others were far more personal memoires of individual experiences. Still others were records brought or sent home for those who could not travel, and served as literary evocations of the holy places.

It is also difficult to know whether a guide book was actually used, and if so by whom and in what manner. In the Middle Ages, most guidebooks were written in Latin (although one cited below was written in Russian), and would have been understood by clerics and other members of the educated classes. Very possibly information in Latin guides was reformulated and read in local languages to pilgrims before they left on their travels. In a predominantly oral society, word-of-mouth exchange of information was vital. Information, reliable or not, was certainly communicated by local guides at the holy sites. Today, in hospices along the routes to Santiago de Compostela, we see such practices, presumably echoing those of centuries earlier (Fig. 1). Each of the three major pilgrimage centers was visited for different reasons, and this is also reflected in the types of guides. Pilgrims to the Holy Land went to see for themselves the sites mentioned in the Old and New Testaments, and to

visit those places important in the life and Passion of Christ, especially following in his footsteps on his last days. Pilgrims to Rome had other objectives. Some came to venerate the tombs of Saints Peter and Paul, and to visit the many cemeteries, tombs, and relics of other martyrs and saints. Others were on "business," as Rome was the ecclesiastical center of the Church in the West. Newly appointed bishops came to accept the pallium (badge of office) from the pope. Many came on penitential pilgrimage. The pilgrimage to Santiago de Compostela was accomplished with one main objective – a visit to the tomb of the apostle St. James Major in northwest Spain. While pilgrimage to the Holy Land and Rome can be traced back to the period between the 2nd and 4th centuries, the tomb of James was not discovered until the 9th century. The first recorded pilgrim to Santiago de Compostela was the French bishop Godescalc of Le Puy, who traveled during the winter of 950-951. For much of Europe, travel to the tomb of Christ's Apostle was easier and less costly than was travel to either Rome or the Holy Land.

Fig. 1
Pilgrims on the Santiago Camino, El Cebreiro, Spain, waiting for entrance into the hostel.
June, 2008
Photograph Virginia C. Raguin

THE EARLY GUIDES

A text records a pilgrim traveling from Bordeaux to the Holy Land in 333, within the first generation of Christian religious support by the Roman Empire (http://www.christusrex.org/www1/ofm/pilgr/00PilgrHome.html). The format of his text follows that of Roman *itineraria* such as the Antonine Itinerary, which lists the distances between towns and settlements along the roads of the Roman Empire, and includes stations where horses may be changed as well as places to stop for the night. Most of the Bordeaux Pilgrim's text consists of the itinerary of the overland route between Bordeaux and Jerusalem and the return trip with one leg by sea (between Valona and Otranto). It is only when the pilgrim arrives on the coast of Palestine that he begins to mention biblical sites, although with scant description of the sites themselves. Old Testament sites predominate before his arrival in Jerusalem; it is only when he is in the city itself that New Testament sites are more frequently visited. The Bordeaux pilgrim also made two excursions from Jerusalem, one to Jericho and the Dead Sea and the other to Bethlehem and Hebron. He mentions no sites or monuments on his return trip to Europe, only the details of the route he took.

Evidence of cultic practice comes to us from the text of Egeria written between 381 and 384. Egeria seems to have been a nun, or a religious, possibly from Galicia in Spain, and she addresses her text to her "sisters" with whom she hopes to be reunited when her travels are over (Wilkinson, *Egeria*, 3-8, 122-123; Davidson and Dunn-Wood, 109). We do not have Egeria's complete text, but only the middle part. This includes a visit to Mount Sinai, a trip from Jerusalem to Mt. Nebo, one to Carneas, and the journey from Jerusalem to Constantinople by way of Antioch, with a side trip to Edessa. The text also includes a very long section on the liturgy as practiced in Jerusalem, which Egeria compares to practices back home. She must have been wealthy and with good connections, as she is assisted by bishops along the way and seems to be traveling with a number of monks and clerics. Most of her overnight stays are in monastic settlements, and for part of the trip from Mount Sinai back to Jerusalem her group is assigned a military escort for their protection by the Roman authorities.

Egeria is energetic and enthusiastic and is enthralled

Fig. 2
Jerusalem from Afar
David Roberts, *The Holy Land:* London, F. G. Moon, 1842-1849
John J. Burns Library at Boston College

Fig. 3
The Holy Sepulcher; women surrounding the Stone of Unction, where Christ was anointed before burial.
David Roberts, *The Holy Land:* London, F. G. Moon, 1842-1849
John J. Burns Library at Boston College

by her visits to Old Testament sites, which outnumber those of the New Testament. She wants to see everything and questions monks and ecclesiastics about the places she visits, frequently leaving offerings and often receiving "blessings," which appear to be fruit or small amounts of food. Egeria describes what she has seen so that it is comprehensible to her sisters back home, whether landscapes or liturgy, maintaining a discrete objectivity (Fig. 2). Although she describes services in the Holy Sepulcher in which many people are weeping, she does not say that she, too, wept (Wilkinson, *Egeria*, 138).

We do have a description of strong emotions elicited on pilgrimage in St. Jerome's obituary of Paula (Letter 108) written in 404. Paula and her daughter Eustochium were wealthy Roman aristocrats who were friends and students of Jerome in Rome. Having traveled to the east separately, they meet in Antioch around 386 and begin their pilgrimage toward Jerusalem, guided part of the way by local ecclesiastics and part of the way by Jews (Wilkinson, *Jerusalem Pilgrims*, 1-2, 47 n.2). While Jerome does not tell the reader what he himself felt at the holy places they visited, he does tell in detail what Paula experienced. Written some eighteen years after the event, Jerome's obituary recording Paula's reaction at shrines is extraordinarily vivid. At the Holy Sepulcher:

> *... she... started to go round visiting all the places with such burning enthusiasm that there was no taking her away from one unless she was hurrying on to another. She fell down and worshipped before the Cross as if she could see the Lord hanging on it. On entering the Tomb of the Resurrection she kissed the stone which the angel removed from the sepulchre door, then like a thirsty man who has waited long, and at last comes to water, she faithfully kissed the very shelf on which the Lord's body had lain. Her tears and lamentations there are known to all Jerusalem – or rather to the Lord himself to whom she was praying* (*Wilkinson,* Jerusalem Pilgrims, *49*) (Fig. 3).

The Bordeaux Pilgrim traveled just after Constantine's mother Helena discovered the sacred places in Jerusalem

(325-329) and before the extensive construction campaigns in and around the city, so it is not surprising to find that he mentions more Old Testament sites than those of the New Testament. However, even at the end of the 4th century, Egeria, Jerome, and Paula also show intense interest in Old Testament sites once they are outside the city of Jerusalem itself.

By the 6th century this situation has changed dramatically, as evidenced by the very engaging text of the Piacenza Pilgrim written around 570. From the moment he arrives on the coast of Syria his primary interest is directed to places mentioned in the New Testament. At Cana, he tells us that he "actually reclined on the couch [on which Christ sat]. On it (undeserving though I am) I wrote the names of my parents…" (Wilkinson, *Jerusalem Pilgrims*, 79). He visits the tombs of Christian saints found between his port of arrival and Jerusalem, and he is drawn to sites where miracles occurred. He also frequently mentions making offerings at shrines and "gaining a blessing." We learn a great deal about religious observance from his text, which records relic veneration. The Piacenza Pilgrim lists many of the relics at the basilica of Holy Sion [now known as *the Coenaculum* or the Cenacle], noting, "I saw a human head enclosed in a reliquary of gold adorned with gems, which they say is that of St. Theodora the martyr. Many drink out of it to gain a blessing and so did I" (Wilkinson, *Jerusalem Pilgrims*, 84). He himself experiences a miracle at the end of his pilgrimage when he has fallen ill in Jerusalem and cannot leave with the rest of his companions. "But with my own eyes I clearly saw a vision of Blessed Euphemia and Blessed Anthony, and when they came to me they cured me" (Wilkinson, *Jerusalem Pilgrims*, 89).

ITINERARIES

Much more common from the early period are the rather dry itineraries, based on the format of the Bordeaux Pilgrim's guide. Two handbooks from the early 6th century in particular seem to have been written to help visitors and pilgrims find their way around; these are the *Breviarius* and Theodosius' *Topography of the Holy Land* (Wilkinson, *Jerusalem Pilgrims*, 4-5, 59-71). The *Breviarius* leads the pilgrim around the various holy sites within Jerusalem, beginning at the Basilica of Constantine and moving on to Golgotha and then to the Holy Sepulcher. From there, the pilgrim is directed to Mt. Sion, the Tomb of Mary, and then the Valley of Jehoshaphat. Theodosius' text offers a number of itineraries devoted to Jerusalem and its environs, with very brief mentions of places in Egypt, Cappadocia, and Asia Minor. His text is, for the most part, similar to our GPS navigation systems, but for those walking. The pilgrim is told that it is fifteen miles from the Gate of the Tower in Jerusalem to Mount Buzana "where David fought Goliath" (Wilkinson, *Jerusalem Pilgrims*, 65), and gives distances for many destinations near Jerusalem. For the circuits within Jerusalem, the number of miles is replaced by the number of paces between major sites. Thus, "From the Tomb of the Lord it is 15 paces to the Place of the Skull"

Fig. 4

Puerta de las Platerias (south transept)

c. 1105

Cathedral of Santiago de Compostela "In the south portal of the Apostle's basilica are two entrances, as we have said, and four doors." *The Pilgrim's Guide*

Photograph Michel Raguin

Fig. 6

Puerta de las Platerias (south transept)

c. 1105

Cathedral of Santiago de Compostela "Nor should it be forgotten the woman who stands next to the Lord's Temptation holding between her hands the stinking head of her lover, cut off by her rightful husband, which she is forced by her husband to kiss twice a day. Oh what ingenious and admirable justice for an adulterous wife; it should be recounted to everyone!" *The Pilgrim's Guide*

Photograph Michel Raguin

(Wilkinson, *Jerusalem Pilgrims*, 66). Both texts, while useful in establishing where pilgrims went and what they saw, are impersonal and tell little about the experiences of a pilgrim. However, they do confirm the shift from interest in Old Testament sites to interest in those of the New.

Itineraries such as those for the Holy Land are also among the earliest guides we have for the city of Rome. Pilgrims to Rome were drawn to the tombs of Saints Peter and Paul and the many other martyrs buried there. One of the earliest lists that has come down to us is that compiled in the late 6th century by Queen Theodolinda's chaplain, John. This Lombard queen had been amassing a treasury of relics, and John appears to have been sent to Rome to collect others. He has left us a partial list of the tombs he visited, starting at St. Peter's and traveling clockwise around the city and continuing to the cemeteries and catacombs outside the walls. At each shrine he collected oil from lamps in small vessels (or flasks) called ampullae, which he labeled with the name of each shrine and brought back to his queen (Birch, 13). The relics and reliquaries were later donated by Theodolinda to the basilica of St. John in Monza, where many objects remain today.

Fig. 5
Puerta de las Platerias (south transept)
c. 1105
Cathedral of Santiago de Compostela "Between the two entrances, in truth above the pillar, are two other ferocious lions, one of whom holds its rump to the rump of the other." *The Pilgrim's Guide*
Photograph Michel Raguin

The route that John followed in visiting shrines may reflect an earlier guide or a customary path to follow through the city. There are two guides from the 7th century, one of which, *De locis sanctis martyrum*, describes the same route as that taken by John starting at St. Peter's. A second guide from the 7th century, the *Notitia ecclesiarum urbis Romae*, follows the same circuit but counterclockwise, ending at St. Peter's (Birch, 12-13). It is precisely during the 7th century that access to the Holy Land becomes difficult due to the Moslem conquest of 638, and this may account for the greater number of guides appearing for Rome (see essay *The Relics of the Infancy of Christ at Rome's Santa Maria Maggiore*). More extensive is the Einsiedeln Itinerary from the 9th century. It includes eleven walking tours through Rome, noting what can be seen on the right of the walker and what on the left. The lists include both Christian and older Roman monuments like baths.

THE 12TH CENTURY

Guides and texts written in the 12th century reflect the major changes occurring in intellectual culture and writing in general in the West. This is the period of the birth of the universities, a time when scholars more fully analyze works of the past and present their own ideas with greater frequency and freedom.

Santiago de Compostela

One of the earliest examples of this new approach is found in the Pilgrim's Guide to Santiago de Compostela, written after 1137 and incorrectly attributed to Aimery Picaud. Although the name of the author is unknown, he was clearly French and he claims to have written his guide so that those traveling can anticipate the expense of the pilgrimage. The guide is one part of a five-part compilation dedicated to the cult of St. James Major. Whereas guides to the Holy Land and

Fig. 7
Statue of Marcus Aurelius (replica)
Rome, 166 CE
Bronze with traces of gilt
During the Middle Ages believed to be an image of Constantine, the first Christian Emperor, and thus brought from outside the Lateran Palace to the Campidoglio in 1537 on the order of Pope Paul III
Photograph Virginia C. Raguin

Fig. 8
Pantheon, later known as Santa Maria Rotonda
118-125 CE
Photograph Michel Raguin

Rome tend to follow models, there was no previous guide for Compostela, so the author invented his own format.

This guide comes closest to a modern-day tourist guide in the comprehensiveness of the information contained. It begins with an itinerary of four routes through France and one through Spain, and the stages of the routes. The author follows this with a chapter on good and bad drinking water along the route, and then a chapter on the characteristics of the people and the lands the pilgrim is likely to meet along the way, in which we learn, "The Gascons talk much trivia, are verbose, mocking, libidinous, drunkards, prodigious eaters, badly dressed in rags and bereft of wealth; however, they are given to combat but are remarkable for their hospitality to the poor." Pilgrims are cautioned to beware of ferrymen in the foothills of the Pyrenees who overload their boats, tip them over in the river and then steal the possessions of drowned pilgrims. They are warned where to watch out for thieves, and to be wary of the Navarrese, who "practice unchaste fornication with animals" (Shaver-Crandell, Gerson, and Stones, 68-74). The next chapter is devoted to the saints' shrines along the routes through France and Spain. For each shrine mentioned we learn a good bit about the saint whose relics are found there and the Feast Day for that saint. This section is followed by a description of the town of Santiago de Compostela, and a long description of the architecture and sculpture of its cathedral, including its altars and church furnishings. The guide concludes with the number of canons, how the offerings at the altars are divided, and how pilgrims should be treated as they travel. The description of the sculpture on the cathedral's façades is the very first in the West after the Roman period (Figs. 4-6).

Rome

The *Marvels of Rome (Mirabilia Urbis Romae)* by Benedict, a canon of St. Peter's, generally dated c. 1143, is indicative of this new approach to writing and to guidebooks. The guide is divided into three parts. Part I, "The Foundation of Rome," contains the history of Rome going back to the time of Noah who, with his sons, established the first city. This is followed by an enumeration of the walls, gates, arches, hills, baths, palaces, theatres, bridges, columns, cemeteries, and places of martyrdom in Rome. Part II is titled "Famous Places and Images in Rome." Benedict retells legends related to these monuments that include the statues of the Dioscuri and of Constantine's Horse (the Marcus Aurelius statue, Fig. 7), the Pantheon (Fig. 8), and the Colosseum (Fig. 9), among

Fig. 9
Colosseum
Rome, 70-76 CE
Photograph Michel Raguin

Fig. 10
Mosaic of Christ with Saints Peter, Valerian, and Cecilia
Rome, Santa Cecilia in Trastevere, 9th century
Photograph Michel Raguin

others. Many of the legends are rather far-fetched pseudo-history (for instance, the Colosseum was a temple to the sun), but the author makes every effort to connect Christian Rome to its ancient past. Part III is titled "A Perambulation of the City"; it takes the pilgrim through the sites of Rome region by region. This tour begins at the Vatican and ends in Trastevere (Fig. 10), and as the author moves through the city he indicates churches currently there as well as what (he believes) had been there in pagan times.

There are no liturgical services mentioned in the guide, nor any relics, although there is a description of the three churches built by Constantine, including St. Peter's and the sarcophagus of Peter. Benedict concludes his text with the following:

> *These and more temples and palaces of emperors, consuls, senators and prefects were inside this Roman city in the time of the heathen, as we have read in old chronicles, have seen with our own eyes, and have heard the ancient men tell of. In writing we have tried as well as we could to bring back to the human memory how great was their beauty in gold, silver, brass ivory and precious stones* (Nichols, 46).

His desire to record the historical past of his city foreshadows the interest in the antique and is another indication of why the 12th century is considered a period of renaissance. Based on the number of copies of Benedict's text, it appealed to readers of the next few centuries.

The Holy Land

In 1099 the Crusaders captured Jerusalem, making access to the Holy Land easier than it had been since the Moslem conquest in 637. Pilgrims flocked to the Latin Kingdom of Jerusalem and wrote guides and reports of their journeys. In fact, there are as many texts from the 12th century as there are for the preceding eight centuries combined.

The earliest in this group is the guide of Daniel the Abbot, a Russian writing from 1106-08, whose first-person voice is very clear (Wilkinson, Hill, and Ryan, 120-71). Daniel's text starts in Constantinople. The author informs his reader that a pilgrim needs to have a good guide and interpreter in order to see all of the Holy Land, and he does see more of the country and its monasteries than many pilgrims before him. Throughout his text he transmits considerable information on the sites and monuments he visits, including measurements that he himself has made.

Very savvy, he early on ingratiates himself to Baldwin I, king of Jerusalem (brother of Godfrey of Bouillon, who had been the first ruler of the Crusader State). Baldwin's protection seems to have allowed him special travel arrangements as well as more private access to some sites. At the Holy Sepulcher he gave a small gift to the keeper of the key to Christ's Tomb, and in return was rewarded with a piece of the rock as relic. However, he is warned not to let anyone in town know about it. Daniel also explains specific rites; for example, he describes the descent of the Holy Fire at the Holy Sepulcher during the Holy Saturday services, a ritual that later became extremely important for Orthodox Christians visiting the church.

John of Würzburg wrote a guide almost as comprehensive as Daniel's around 1170 (Wilkinson, Hill, and Ryan, 244-73). He writes to a certain Dietrich so that Dietrich will be able to find the holy places easily if he makes a pilgrimage to the Holy Land. John does not seem to have visited more than Jerusalem and Nazareth himself, but he is compulsively complete in his descriptions of monuments, including paintings, in these cities. He also copies all inscriptions he finds "whether in prose or verse," and he notes at least one inscription which gives wrong information. John is critical of things told to him for which he sees scant evidence. For example, at a church dedicated to Mary Magdalene he questions the truth of a picture shown him and a relic said to be the Magdalene's hair. His is certainly a scholar's approach, and for places he does not visit he uses good source material to fill in lacunae.

LATE MEDIEVAL GUIDES

Pilgrimage to the Holy Land never fully recovered after the fall of Jerusalem in 1187. Increasing warfare against the remaining states of the Latin Kingdom made travel more difficult until the fall of Acre in 1291, after which it was exceedingly difficult. Activity seems to increase in the 14th century, and there are texts by three travelers, although they seem more like tourists than pilgrims. This may be due to the fact that pilgrims were carefully supervised by the Moslem authorities and their freedom of movement was controlled. Since travel to the Holy Land was restricted, more pilgrims traveled to Rome, but they seem to have been primarily concerned with gaining indulgences. After the first jubilee of 1300, many of the "guides" for Rome are merely lists of churches and the indulgences gained by visiting. Pilgrimage continued to Santiago de Compostela, but the texts add little new to our knowledge.

Without doubt, the most interesting text from this period is the *Book of Margery Kempe* (http://www.holycross.edu/departments/visarts/projects/kempe/). Margery Kempe was an English mystic who traveled to Jerusalem and Rome between 1413 and 1415. Eight chapters of her book (Chapters 26-43) are devoted to her pilgrimage. Her experiences, described in the third person, are intense, especially her hours in the Church of the Holy Sepulcher (Figs. 11-12):

> *And this creature wept and sobbed as plenteously as though she had seen Our Lord with her bodily eyes suffering his Passion at that time. Before her in her soul she saw him in truth by contemplation, and that caused her to have compassion. And when they came up on to the Mount of Calvary, she fell down because she could not stand or kneel, but writhed and wrestled with her body, spreading her arms out wide, and cried with a loud voice as though her heart would have burst apart, for in the city of her soul she saw truly and freshly how Our Lord was crucified. Chapter 28*

Empathy remains a perennial goal for the pilgrim, sought after in Rome, Santiago, and the Holy Land, and at countless local shrines. Kempe's religious fervor brings us back to the intense emotion ascribed to Paula on her visits to the Holy Sepulcher almost one thousand years earlier. The seeker desires closeness to the holy person, and to experience in a way that collapses the distance between them. Thus the restrictions of distance, gender, class, even time are surmounted. The abode of the dead welcomes the living, and the pilgrim's experience cements a bond of intimacy between the worshipper and saint.

See further reading on page 342

Fig. 11
Entrance Façade of the Church of the Holy Sepulcher
David Roberts, *The Holy Land*, London, F. G. Moon, 1842-1849
John J. Burns Library at Boston College

Fig. 12
The Church of the Holy Sepulcher; Tomb of Christ
David Roberts, *The Holy Land*, London, F. G. Moon, 1842-1849
John J. Burns Library at Boston College

Details of Fig. 3

St. James: The Eternal Pilgrim

Virginia C. Raguin

James is one of Christ's Apostles, often mentioned in the Gospels. James and John were brothers, the two sons of Zebedee. James, John, and Peter were the three Apostles with Christ at the moment of his Transfiguration (Mt 7:1-9) and at his Agony in the Garden of Gethsemani (Mt 26-37). After Christ's death, the legend describes James Major as evangelizing Spain, and then returning to Jerusalem. There he was executed by the order of Herod Agrippa: "and he killed James, the brother of John with the sword" (Acts 12:1-2). James was thus the first of the Apostles to die a martyr's death. As is often the case in saintly biographies (see essay *Relics Defined: Discoveries on Site, Invention, Translation, and* Furta Sacra), the story continues with divine intervention. His followers carried his body to the coast and put it in a boat without a rudder. Because of James's great affection for the Iberian Peninsula, angels guided the boat through the straights of Gibraltar to the coast of northern Spain. There his body was buried, and the exact location of the tomb was forgotten for eight hundred years. In the meantime, Muslims entered Spain and by the 9th century achieved control of all of the Iberian Peninsula except for the small northern strip of land of the Asturias. St. James' remains were subsequently discovered and Alfonso el Casto (791-842), ruler of Léon, ordered the relics transferred to Santiago. The discovery of the body of St. James became a rallying point for Christian incursion into Muslim-held territories (see essay *St. James as Pilgrim or Moorslayer in the* Poem of the Cid). The presence of one of Christ's closest Apostles soon attracted pilgrims seeking personal salvation from far beyond Spain (see essay *Medieval Christian Pilgrims' Guides and Pilgrims' Texts*). Soon Santiago rivaled Rome and Jerusalem as a pilgrimage goal.

See further reading on page 343

Fig. 1
Map of 12th-century Pilgrimage routes through France and Spain. Courtesy Paula Gerson

Fig. 2
Santiago is a UNESCO World Heritage Site for its position as a pilgrimage and cultural site for all of Europe. It is also the capital of the autonomous community of Galicia. The medieval cathedral is now encased in a 17th- to 18th-century architectural overlay. The west facade displays a Churrigueresque style designed by Fernando Casasy Nóvoa between 1738 and 1750. Statues of St. James in pilgrim's garb multiply across the towers, but in the two niches on the central section of the towers appear James' parents, Zebedee to the left and Salome to the right. On the feast of St. James a false portal is added for fireworks to remember the burning of the cathedral by Almansour.
Photograph Paula Gerson

Fig. 3
Famous in legend and song is the Portal of Glory, carved between 1168 and 1188 by Master Mateo. The profusion of statuary is characterized by immense plasticity in form and vigorous individualization. On the central door, flanking the image of the seated James, are his fellow Apostles, Peter being instantly recognizable by his keys and John the Evangelist by his open book and youthful, beardless face. Today the portal is accessible after one passes though the new construction of the facade.
Photograph Michel Raguin

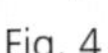

Fig. 4

The cathedral's interior remains much the same as it was in the 12th century. This characteristic structure has been referred to as a "pilgrimage church" because the long nave on the west accommodates the people, and side aisles surrounding the church enable access to side altars and ultimately the tomb of the saint in the east.

Photograph Michel Raguin

Fig. 5

A harmonious intersection of piers, arcades, galleries, and vaulted spaces characterizes the sophisticated architecture of the time. Across the nave and transepts are barrel vaults, an unbroken half-circle bordered by a molding between the bays; the flanking aisles show groin vaults producing a sequence of four-part units. The galleries of the upper level are provided with double arcades to accommodate visual access for additional onlookers.

Photograph Michel Raguin

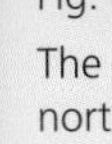

Fig. 6

The church's transept, the area going north to south, is as wide as the nave, permitting a large number of worshippers and sight access to the ceremonies at the center of the church. The Feast Day of St. James, July 25, is celebrated with fervor. Processions, festivals, and songs are shared events with other patronal feasts. Distinctive to Compostela, however, is the cathedral's great hanging censor called the Botafumeiro, created in 1851 based on a late medieval model. On St. James' Day, it is lowered from the vaults and incense is burned. The censor is then swung from one end of the transept to the other in a gigantic arc intersecting with the massive proportions of the building.

Photograph Michel Raguin

Fig. 7

Clouds of incense billow from the Botafumeiro. The swings of the censor can reach a dizzying speed.

Photograph Paula Gerson

Fig. 8

The seated figure of St. James (St. James of the Embrace) was certainly in place for the consecration of 1211. Later, in the renovations to the tomb between 1657 and the 1680s, the statue was reworked to receive an elaborate pilgrim's robe carved to evoke brocade. At this time the towering tabernacle was constructed and the statue placed at the top of a series of steps. Present-day pilgrims climb the steps in single file and are still able to kiss the statue.

Photograph Michel Raguin

Fig. 9

Bust of St. James as Pilgrim

Spanish, 17th century

Wood with polychrome,
9 x 7 in. (22.9 x 17.8 cm)

Museo das Peregrinacións, Xunta de Galicia. No Inv.: D-836.

Photograph Museo das Peregrinacións

Santiago is shown as sharing the life of the pilgrim by appearing in the wide-brimmed pilgrim's hat with a prominent scallop shell badge

Fig. 10

St. James

Spain, 16th century

Wood with traces of polychrome,
24½ x 8¼ in. (62.2 x 21 cm)

Museo das Peregrinacións, Santiago de Compostela; Ministerio de Cultura. Nº Inv.:262

Photograph Museo das Peregrinacións

Wearing pilgrim attire, long cloak, hat with scallop shell, and holding a staff, James also holds a book. The attitude highlights the importance of the Sacred Scriptures, accessible almost exclusively in the Latin translation called the Vulgate. Preachers communicated sermons in the vernacular, promulgating an understanding of the Life of Christ and the major stories of both the Old and New Testaments. Thus St. James is portrayed not only as a pilgrim but as a source of authority confirming the teaching prerogatives of the clergy.

Fig. 11

St. James with book and pilgrim's staff

Spanish, Castile, 16th century

Linen and cotton embroidered with silk and gold thread,
6¾ x 8¾ in. (17.1 x 22.2 cm)

Museo das Peregrinacións, Xunta de Galicia. Nº Inv.: D-109.

Photograph Museo das Peregrinacións

Vestments and covering for altars were costly items used for celebrations for the most sacred rites of the Christian Church. The level of elaboration followed the importance of the feast. Images of Santiago were frequently integrated into Spanish liturgical celebration, exemplified by a fragment of a border either for a priest's robe or for an altar cloth.

Fig. 12

Tiles, in Spanish *azulejos*, were frequently embellished with the image of the St. James scallop shell. Spain, very likely because of its long experience under Muslim rule developed the art of glazed clay endemic in Islamic cultures located in regions such as Egypt, Persia, and Turkey. These tiles of slightly varying form, each about 9¾ x 5 in. (24.8 x 12.7 cm), were produced in the 15th or 16th centuries in Seville. They were certainly a part of large-scale production of architectural revetment similar to the function of 13th-century tiles from Iran that show a fragment of inscription from the Quran and an animal combat (see essay *The Pilgrim, the Image, and the Word in Islam*).

Museo das Peregrinacións, Xunta de Galicia. N° Inv.: D-786 and D787.

Photograph Museo das Peregrinacións

Fig. 14

Glazed tile also became a viable medium for the production of souvenirs. Pilgrims frequently bought or commissioned items to facilitate the memory of a pilgrimage. Such objects could represent a pilgrimage site for those who had not been able to visit, or simply reinforce devotional attitudes toward the revered individual. The tradition continues, exemplified by a ceramic plaque depicting St. James with pilgrim staff beneath a niche ornamented with scallop shells from the Buño Studio, 5½ x 4 in. (14 x 10.2 cm), dated to the second half of the 20th century.

Museo das Peregrinacións, Santiago de Compostela; Ministerio de Cultura. No Inv.:33

Photograph Museo das Peregrinacións

Fig. 13

Seville's production of high-quality tile work is further demonstrated by a series of three tiles of emerald green and gold. The glazes were applied at the same time, resulting in some seepage between the background and motif of the shell. The intense but fluctuating density of the green evokes the shifting colors of the sea that carried St. James.

Museo das Peregrinacións, Santiago de Compostela; Ministerio de Cultura. N° Inv.:103

Photograph Museo das Peregrinacións

Fig. 15

Santiago's influence permeated Europe. In Rome's Santa Prassede, a tomb slab from the late 13th century demonstrates the pilgrimage to Santiago as an archetype for pilgrimage in general. Giovanni de Montpoli lists his profession as apothecary: his dress is a fur overcoat to repel rain and retain warmth. He carries a staff, and wears a wallet slung over his shoulder. His broad-brimmed hat holds a scallop shell, the symbol of St. James's shrine in Compostela.

Photograph Michel Raguin

Fig. 16

Santiago's popularity continued unabated through the Renaissance. Switzerland, as did other countries, encouraged confraternities called "Jacobsbrüdershaften" to promote pilgrimage to Santiago. Freiburg, a major point for pilgrimage from southern Germany, the Tyrol, and central Switzerland, lists such an association since about 1475. Evidence of such activities is seen in the stained glass of cloister glazing. In the Monastery of Wettingen (West XIa), St. James dressed as a pilgrim appears in the heraldic panel of Hans Hünegger and Regina von Sur, of 1522.

Photograph Virginia C. Raguin

Fig. 17

Santiago's scallop shell as generic pilgrim emblem continued. The church of Sainte-Clotilde in Paris, a precursor of the Neo-Gothic, shows ambulatory glazing designed by Nicolas-Auguste Hesse and fabricated by Laurent and Gsell. Elevated to sainthood in 1297 during the reign of his grandson Philip le Bel, Louis IX is the only French monarch to be canonized. Louis engaged in two crusades – on the last, in 1270, he died of illness in Tunis. In the stained glass of 1855, Louis embarks for the Crusade. Although the royal saint apparently never visited the shrine of Santiago, he is shown with scallop shells on his cloak and accepting the pilgrim's staff. Clearly, to the mid-19th century, pilgrimage was identified with the emblem of St. James.

Photograph Virginia C. Raguin

Details of Fig. 3

St. James as Pilgrim or Moorslayer in the *Poem of the Cid*

Alexander J. McNair

"In the name of the Creator and the Apostle St. James,
Hit them to your heart's content, knights, hit them with all you've got,
For I am El Cid, Ruy Diaz of Vivar!"

(*Poem of the Cid*, lines 1138-1140)

The epic *Poem of the Cid* has the distinction of being the earliest surviving work of considerable length composed in the Spanish vernacular. The only extant manuscript of the *Poem* from the Middle Ages is a mid-13th- or early 14th-century copy of a lost "original" whose date is dutifully recorded by the scribe as May 1245 of the Spanish Era (1207 CE). The historical Cid, Rodrigo (or Ruy) Díaz de Vivar, had died more than a century earlier (1099) in Valencia on the Mediterranean coast of Spain, which the Castilian expatriate had conquered and ruled independently since 1094. But within a few years of his death this Christian mercenary of history – often in the service of Muslims fighting against Christian rivals in eastern Spain – was rapidly being transformed by oral tradition into a mythic hero of the *Reconquista* (the Christian "Reconquest" of territory lost to Islamic expansion nearly four centuries before). By the end of the 12th century a series of defeats against the North African Almohads, who had recently brought a more austere version of Islam to the Iberian Peninsula, encouraged Christian Spain to look back on a hero who had managed to hold his own during a similar wave of fundamentalism in the previous century.

The *Poem of the Cid* is also in many ways a product of the *Camino de Santiago*, probably taking its final written form around the year 1200 in Burgos, near the pilgrimage route where it was probably still being recited for the entertainment of pilgrims on their way to and from the shrine of St. James. Coincidently, Santiago (St. James) was undergoing a radical transformation in the Iberian imagination around that same time. The saint was, of course, depicted with pilgrim staff in the iconography of the Middle Ages (Fig. 1), but he was also developing a martial alter ego: Santiago Matamoros, or St. James Moorslayer. By the mid-12th century Christian soldiers were invoking his name in battle; a military order was founded in his name in 1170, and by the middle of the 13th century chronicles and clerical poems were attesting to his armed intervention in Christian military victories dating back to the legendary battle of Clavijo (844). From humble traveler

Fig. 1
St. James (Santiago) holding scroll and pilgrim staff
Portico of Glory, Master Mateo, c. 1166-1188
Cathedral of Santiago de Compostela
Photograph Michel Raguin

Fig. 2
St. James the Moorslayer (Santiago Matamoros)
Tympanum of St. James at the Battle of Clavijo, 1238-1260
Cathedral of Santiago de Compostela
Photograph Michel Raguin

to sword-wielding knight (Hajj to jihad, to press a Muslim analogy), Santiago's transformation solidified Christian Iberia's relationship with pilgrims from north of the Pyrenees and the zeal for crusade that often came with them.

Today we may be tempted to think of Santiago Matamoros as a timeless figure in the Spanish imagination, linked almost to the very beginning of Muslim-Christian relations on the Iberian Peninsula. So much of Spanish, specifically Castilian, identity since the 13th century has been wrapped up in this militant figure. From the 14th though the 16th centuries, as the Spanish – with Castilians at the core – completed their *reconquista* of the peninsula and transformed themselves into a world empire, they defined themselves as a chosen people, heirs to the legacy of St. James Moorslayer (Castro, 449-66; Sánchez-Albornoz, 265-85; O'Callaghan, 104; Lowney, 110-12, 255). The faith of Spaniards, which was often militant, found confirmation in the belief that St. James had intervened on their behalf; the sword and cross would take them to the ends of the earth in the age of exploration, and names such as Santiago and Matamoros dot the Americas today as witness to the importance of the Moorslayer to Spanish identity. Nevertheless, it is clear that St. James as Moorslayer is a later phenomenon in reaction to a specific historical moment (i.e., the coming of the fundamentalist Almohads to Islamic Spain in the mid- to late 12th century); the sense of the Spanish Reconquest as a crusade or holy war was absent

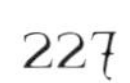

from the highly nuanced diplomacy of Alfonso VI (and of his exiled subject Rodrigo Díaz, El Cid) in the late 11th century (MacKay, 19-20; Bishko, 419-20; Fletcher 1984, 294-99; O'Callaghan, 2003). Indeed, while some sense of crusade existed among Spaniards of the 12th century, a case can be made that it was tenuous at best until about the year 1209, when the Christian monarchs of León, Castile, Navarre, and Aragón finally came to peaceful terms with one another in order to present a unified front against the Almohad threat (O'Callaghan, 239-45). So to which attribute of St. James does the *Poem of the Cid* refer when he is invoked: pilgrim or moorslayer?

Santiago peregrino and *Santiago matamoros* are, of course, not mutually exclusive – the line between crusade and pilgrimage must have seemed a rather thin one in the Middle Ages (Moore, Raulston). But, when the poet invokes St. James in Spain's first vernacular epic, does he have in mind the legendary slayer who rode in from the heavens on a white steed, slaughtering Muslim foes at Clavijo more than 350 years before? Probably not – a look at the portrayal of St. James in the art and Latin literature of Spain before the *Poem of the Cid* makes it difficult for us to convict him as a Muslim-killer before the 1230s. The exchange of battle cries recorded in line 731 of the poem – "Moors cry 'Muhammad!' and Christians, 'St. James!'" – is consistent with the battle cries mentioned around 1160 in the Latin chronicle of Alfonso VII (*Chronica Adefonsi Imperatoris*). That chronicle documents the following during a campaign in the 1130s or 1140s: "Once the battle had begun, the Saracens cried out and appealed to Mohammed with bronze trumpets, drums and voices. For their part, the Christians cried out with all their hearts to Lord God, the Blessed Mary and Saint James so that they would take pity on them and forget the sins of their kings, their own and those of their relatives" (Barton and Fletcher, 215). Most commentators note that the presence of St. James in the invocations and battle cries of the *Poem of the Cid* would have been inspired by the legends of Santiago's armed intervention against Muslims in the 9th-10th centuries (e.g., Menéndez Pidal 1908-11, 841; Smith, 285; Michael, 130n; Such and Hodgkinson, 85). However, on closer inspection it appears more likely that the battle cry inspired the legend than the other way around.

The call to St. James (and the Virgin Mary) in the *Chronica Adefonsi Imperatoris* is for forgiveness, perhaps divine protection, as in the miracle literature of the 12th century in Latin and later in the 13th century in Spanish. Miracles relating to St. James are recounted in the *Liber Sancti Jacobi* (1140-1170) and are similar to the *Milagros de Nuestra Señora* composed in vernacular verse by Gonzalo de Berceo (c. 1250): apparitions, assistance, intercession for those who show a special devotion to St. James (or the Virgin in the case of Berceo's verses); but the sword is conspicuous in its absence: none of the legends tell the Matamoros episode of Clavijo or any other battle. A legend of St. James

appearing on horseback, bathed in white light, to announce Christian victory in the siege of Coimbra, is told in the *Historia Silense*, a chronicle dated to the first two decades of the 12th century. According to this legend, King Fernando I conquered Coimbra with the "material sword" while "James, the knight of Christ, ceased not to implore his Master to bring about the king's victory" (Barton and Fletcher, 50). This is the first mention in the historical record of St. James as a knight, but his role is clearly only intercessory (Barton and Fletcher, 50-51; Fletcher 1984, 296-97; Salvador Miguel). A vague reference to Santiago's "miraculous apparition" at the battle of Clavijo can be found in a forged diploma of the late 12th century (Domínguez-García) – but only in the 1230s would St. James bloody a sword for the first time in a reference to battle with Muslims (in the Latin chronicles of Lucas de Tuy and Jiménez de Rada). A stone relief sculpture in the Cathedral of Santiago, the "Tympanum of Clavijo," from 1238-1260, is the earliest visible artifact of St. James with sword upraised (Moore, 317, 322-27) (Fig. 2).

By the mid-13th century the transformation of St. James was complete; the early Medieval destroyer of vice, whose "pious intercession" was needed "to kindle in us the fervor of chastity and love and other virtues" according to a sermon from the *Liber Sancti Jacobi* (Coffey, Davidson, and Dunn, 55), had become the destroyer of infidels. In the popular imagination of late Medieval Spain, the humble pilgrim who had achieved martyrdom on the edge of Herod's sword was dispatching his foes with a blood-stained sword of his own. That image was propagated as the centuries passed, typified by a figure of Santiago mounted on a gleaming white horse in an 18th-century Spanish painting (Fig. 3). A box produced for the 1926 Holy Year of Santiago de Compostela shows the saint leading an army of crusaders at the Battle of Clavijo (Fig. 4). The tradition continued into the New World, enjoying a long life, as evidenced by the image of the Moorslayer executed in the 1700s, now in the retable behind the main altar in the church of Cristo Rey in Santa Fe, New Mexico (Fig. 5).

See further reading on page 343

Fig. 3
St. James the Moorslayer (Santiago Matamoros)
Spanish, 18th century
Oil on copper, 17¾ x 15¼ in. (45.1 x 38.7 cm)
Museo das Peregrinacións, Xunta de Galicia. Nº Inv.: D-701
Photograph Museo das Peregrinacións

Fig. 4

Commemorative Casket for the Santiago Holy Year of 1925: St James at the Battle of Clavijo and (opposite side) Translation of the Relics of St. James.

Spain, Studio of los Hernandez, 1926

Copper with enamel over a wood base
$6^{3}/_{4} \times 9^{3}/_{4} \times 4^{13}/_{25}$ in. (17.1 x 24.8 x 11.5 cm)

Museo das Peregrinacións, Santiago de Compostela; Ministerio de Cultura. Nº Inv.:222

Photograph Museo das Peregrinacións

Fig. 5

St. James the Moorslayer (Santiago Matamoros)

High Altar retablo, detail, 18th century

Formerly, Our Lady of Light Chapel, now Cristo Rey, Santa Fe, New Mexico

Photograph Virginia C. Raguin

Details of Fig. 7

Paths through the Desert: Hispanic Pilgrimage Experiences in Mexico City and Chimayó

Edward Holgate

LA BASÍLICA DE NUESTRA SEÑORA DE GUADALUPE / THE BASILICA OF OUR LADY OF GUADALUPE, MÉXICO, DISTRITO FEDERAL

Overview

México is a land of miracles. Apparitions of the Virgin Mary, the Lord Christ, and various saints dot the republic, marking moments of intercession on behalf of the local population and laying out the sacred geography of Mexican history. No fewer than ten major pilgrimage sites exist, with numerous localized traditions as well, many dating back centuries and carrying historic ecclesiastical approbation. Marian sites greatly outnumber any other, perhaps signaling the importance of the Virgin Mother in the life of Christ and the high regard in which *la madre* is held in Mexican culture. A few of the pilgrimage centers have seen their cults reach far beyond the Mexican border to wherever the narrative of the miraculous event and the search for God find fertile ground.

Primary among these holy places is the Basilica of Our Lady of Guadalupe in Mexico City. Known throughout Latin America as the center of devotion to the Virgin Mary, it attracts nearly twenty million people annually, a number that rivals the statistics for the Vatican, the most frequented shrine in the Christian world (Fig. 1). Not all of these visitors are pilgrims, although the vast majority of them are. The pilgrims fall into three major categories. There are those that visit out of religious institutional obligation, as in celebration of a First Communion; those that visit to fulfill a *promesa* or promise to the Virgin for favors received; and finally, those that come, fitting the narrowest of pilgrimage definitions, as a wholly voluntary act to seek the divine through transformative contact with a sacred site.

Fig. 1
Pilgrims from San José del Tunal, 2004
Basilica of Our Lady of Guadalupe, Mexico City
Photograph Queen of the Americas Guild

Fig. 2
Pilgrims in procession, 2004
Basilica of Our Lady of Guadalupe, Mexico City
Photograph Queen of the Americas Guild

Whatever the myriad motivations for the visit to Guadalupe, pilgrims have characteristics in common. The pilgrim is making a break from everyday life. Not unlike *The Canterbury Tales* with its collection of diverse seekers of experience, contemporary accounts at Guadalupe record visitors seeking something beyond quotidian experience. They are often seeking a sense of community that has been lost in modern life even as they pursue a personal goal in their journey. Known for her miraculous powers to cure the sick, Our Lady is especially invoked during times of illness; yet petitioners also seek Guadalupe's aid for other matters great and small. Finally, and uniquely, in the Mexican psyche Guadalupe's religious significance cannot be separated from national identity. Thus, a pilgrim, in reaching the Villa de Guadalupe, is not only fulfilling a religious intention but is also reinforcing his or her Mexicanidad. "In México we are not all Catholics, but yes we are all Guadalupanos" (Quiroz Malca, 118).

They come by busloads, on the metro, streetcar, *combi* vans, via private car, or on foot. The most devout climb the countless steps up the Hill of Tepeyac, at the end of the Villa de Guadalupe where the Basilica is located, on their knees. Pilgrims also come on bicycles; some confraternities have long made this a custom (Fig. 2). In the late spring and early summer, when First Communions are typically celebrated throughout the Republic, legions of pilgrim celebrants and their sponsors arrive at the Basilica, timing their arrival so that the girls arrive days before the boys.

During the week preceding the feast of Our Lady of Guadalupe (December 12), the Basilica swells with millions of pilgrims. Aztec dancers compete with souvenir vendors selling every imaginable object adorned with the shrine's central image. Guadalupe iconography can be seen on pilgrimage medals, holy cards, prints, statues, key chains, T-shirts, and the tattooed musclemen parading around the Villa. A pilgrim can have his own picture taken as San Juan Diego, the peasant to whom Our Lady appeared, by standing behind a life-sized wooden cutout parodying one of the famous Guadalupe images. Canaries, held in rickety wooden cages, emerge at the behest of their owner (and a few pesos) to tell you your fortune. Balloons, candies, slices of jicama or cucumber with lime and chile, Coca-Cola, and Chiclets beckon from food stalls. Candles, too, are sought by every visitor, as are *milagos*, small votive offerings for healing and protection that are made of base metal and shaped like body parts. Finally, every pilgrim must have

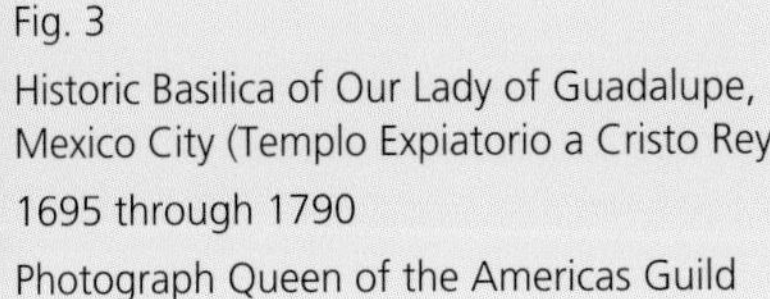

Fig. 3
Historic Basilica of Our Lady of Guadalupe, Mexico City (Templo Expiatorio a Cristo Rey)
1695 through 1790
Photograph Queen of the Americas Guild

one print of the famous cloak that bears the holy image of the Virgin.

History

In 1531, according to religious accounts, an Indian convert named Juan Diego Cuatlatoatzin was walking on the Hill of Tepeyac in what is now Mexico City when he heard beautiful, sweet singing and a celestial voice call to him. He followed the voice to the top of the hill and saw a maiden whose "perfect grandeur exceeded all imagination: Her dress shone like the sun" (Zarebska, 102). She told Juan Diego that she desired a shrine to be erected at the site to "show Him [God], exalt Him… to give Him to the people with all my personal love, my compassionate gaze, with my help, my salvation" (Zarebska, 103). Juan Diego brought her request to the bishop of México, Don Fray Juan de Zumárraga, who dismissed his account, demanding proof from the peasant convert. The next day, when Juan Diego was on Tepeyac, the Virgin called out to him. "What is wrong my youngest son? Where are you going? Where are you headed?" Juan Diego, afraid, insisted that he be allowed to continue to find a priest to hear his uncle's confession, for he was gravely ill. The Virgin replied, "Am I, your Mother, not here? Are you not under my shadow and my protection? Am I not the source of your happiness? You may be certain that he is now well" (Zarebska, 111). Then she asked why Juan Diego had not answered her request. He replied that the bishop wanted proof. She led Juan Diego to the top of the hill. There, in the dead of winter in the evening light, he saw all variety of flowers including Castilian roses blooming; their fragrance overwhelmed him. Believing this to be the proof the bishop sought, Juan Diego gathered the flowers in his *tilma* (cloak) and took them to the bishop's palace. When Juan Diego opened his cloak at his audience with Zumárraga, the flowers tumbled to the ground and on his cloak was emblazoned the miraculous image of the Virgin. Bishop Zumárraga fell to his knees and kissed the cloak.

In 1561, thirty years after the apparitions and a mere forty years after the conquest of México by the Spanish, the first church was built at the Tepeyac site. Following custom, the Spanish chose as a location a preconquest sacred site, one associated with the Aztec mother goddess Tonantzin. The popularity of Guadalupe and accounts of her miraculous intercession multiplied; religious and city leaders encouraged her patronage. By 1601, through alms-giving, a new church had been built. In 1696 a larger basilica was designed in the

Baroque style, enclosing three naves. It was completed in 1790 (Fig. 3).

Although Guadalupe's popularity was immense in Mexico City, in the early centuries after the arrival of the Spanish she was not without rivals. Historian Stafford Poole cites Our Lady of the Rosary and Our Lady of Remedies among other claimants to México's spiritual crown, especially in protecting the city from major calamities such as floods and fires. All this changed in 1810 with the Cry of Independence known as *El Grito de Dolores*. Father Miguel Hidalgo, along with a band of Independistas, raised a banner with an image of Our Lady of Guadalupe in the fight for independence from the Spanish. Mexican national identity and religious fervor were forever fused. The Independistas' rallying cry was "Long live Our Lady of Guadalupe and death to the Spaniards." Spanish loyalists had united under the flag of Los Remedios – Our Lady of Remedies – which forever doomed her cause (Zarebska, 174). The success of the Independistas' campaign left no doubt as to the question of spiritual hegemony over the capital city and all of México. Guadalupe reigns supreme.

Pope Benedict XIV, in his Bull *Non est equidem* of May 25, 1754, named Our Lady of Guadalupe as Patroness of México. He quoted Psalm 147: "Non fecit taliter omni nationi / To no other nation has such a wonder been done." In 1895 Guadalupe was elevated to Queen of México; in 1910, Heavenly Patron of Latin America; and finally, in 1945, she became Empress of the Americas. In 2002, on his last visit to Mexico, Pope John Paul II canonized San Juan Diego Cuahtlatoatzin before a crowd of twelve million. The tearful goodbye song "Golondrinas," a Mexican classic, was sung to the departing pontiff as the country wept with emotion for both its ancient patron and its newest saint.

The Baroque Basilica, now a museum, houses an important collection of art made by the pilgrims themselves, predominantly from the 19th and early 20th centuries. From floor to the ceiling in the entranceway, *ex votos*, small paintings on tin named from the Latin "after the vow," attest to the miracles attributed to the Virgin's intercessions. Lovingly painted in a naive style, each depicts the specific event as well an image of the Virgin of Guadalupe, usually shown in an upper corner, with an explanatory text at the bottom. The public display of these *ex votos* is an important part of the pilgrim ritual of giving thanks for favors received.

> *Inside the vast Modernist basilica built in 1977 to accommodate the ever-increasing throngs of pilgrims, Mass schedules are posted, noting hourly Masses during festival season. To the right of the main altar, a steady stream of visitors disappears behind a large, imposing wall. After a couple of inquiries, one learns that this nameless line has formed to view the famous* tilma *that bears the miraculous image of the Virgen de Guadalupe. The line moves apace and one soon learns why. Behind the partition, opposite the sacred image, which is hung high on the wall, four rows of moving walkways keep the masses bustling past the image. Frequent visitors to the Basilica have dubbed this "the dance of the* tilma*" for the balance, speed, and coordination it takes to view the holy image while keeping one's balance. Contemplation is impossible. The sense of faith of the community of believers, however, is palpable, as is the kinetic energy of the religious and historic artifact that draws them.*

Personal Accounts

Valente Corona went on pilgrimage to Our Lady of Guadalupe as a child to receive his First Communion. From the pueblo of San José Iturbide, Guanajuato, Corona and his brother made their way to the city of Querétaro, Querétaro, where they joined a large group of similar male celebrants headed for México. As each child had to pick a sponsor on the spot, Corona chose a man he knew from church who he supposed had a good smile and an easy laugh. The sponsors primarily looked after the physical needs of the children and led them on the five-day walk to the Basilica.

Corona, now forty, recalls the tortuous hours and endless walking, but he mostly despised the food. "I had never had such fatty food, so ill-prepared. I was used to my mom's cooking. It came as quite a shock to me, after a whole day of walking, that we would have to eat that food. It was all part of the journey, hardship and all, I suppose. But the singing along the way was lovely, you really felt something!" Provisions for the trip were transported in long-bed trucks that converted into bunk-bed sleepers for the boys. On the day before reaching the Basilica, in an enormous open field, pilgrims from all over the north of the republic converged and a celebratory mass was given and each boy received his First Communion in the open air. The next day they entered the city and visited the Basilica of Our Lady of Guadalupe for the first time in their lives. All of these events (in May) were timed to occur a week or so before the First Communion girls arrived at the Basilica. "I still think they do it that way to emphasize purity."

Jorge Arévalo remembers pilgrimages to the Basilica with his mother and sister Lupe, one especially when his sister was ill. His mother had a great devotion to the Virgin and prayed to her for sustenance and guidance. "We would go to the Virgen, being from Mexico [City], for any and everything. Life in México is hard, just ask anyone." Later, when he was a seminarian in Veracruz, his knowledge and devotion to all things spiritual intensified. Arévalo grew pensive as he returned to his earlier thought. "I suppose as a Mexican man you have two choices: alcohol or devotion to the Virgen. I'm glad I finally chose the latter."

For María del Carmen Álvarez, visiting the Virgencita was a custom that began with her mother when she was a little girl. Annually they would make the pilgrimage from San Miguel de Allende, Guanajuato, to México during the time of the fiesta of the Virgin in December. "For us Mexicans, the hill of Tepeyac was a sacred site venerated even before the Virgen appeared to Juan Diego." From all parts of the Republic pilgrims descended upon the Basilica on the 12th of December to pay homage to the Virgin and draw upon the collective sense of faith so present among the fellow pilgrims.

Pilgrimages were always arranged in groups by church. One never saw an individual pilgrim, Álvarez declared. Traveling together created a greater sense of unity and faith among the group. "As we walked we'd recite prayers and sing to the Virgin. One of our favorite hymns was: 'Adiós, Reina del Cielo / Hello, Queen of the Heavens.'" She sings the chorus:

Adiós, Reina del Cielo,
Madre del Salvador.
dulce prenda adorada,
de mi sincero amor.

Hello, Queen of the Heavens,
Mother of the Savior,
sweet adored darling,
of my sincere love.

One pilgrimage was of especial importance to Álvarez because her son had been stabbed and was on the verge of dying. After she made many prayers and petitions to the Virgin to save her son, he survived and regained his health. Álvarez then made a pilgrimage to Guadalupe to *pagar la manda* – to pay back the promise. Filled with tears of thanksgiving and love, Álvarez speaks of joining other pilgrims on her journey to the Basilica, completing the cycle of intention, promise, and thank offering.

Delfina Juárez of Chalma, México, similarly gave thanks to the Virgin of Guadalupe for favors granted. Having prayed to find a suitable husband, at last she was married and shortly thereafter she made a pilgrimage to the Basilica. There, alongside the countless letters of thanks, hospital bracelets, *milagros*, and photographs, she placed her wedding bouquet. "Everything depends on the faith the person has for the Virgin. If she speaks of matters of the heart, from the heart, the Virgin hears. If such a person has devotion and faith, she can understand the answer."

Pilgrimages in the Latin American world are marked by the highly personalized relationship that the faithful have for their saints. The divine is not an abstract concept, something intangible; rather it is a wellspring of love, support, and guidance. For the devoted, spiritual matters are an integral part of daily life with the *santos* (saints) as vital members of the family, who, along with the dead, serve as intercessors to Christ. Guided by a rich visual vocabulary, the stories of the major pilgrim sites, such as Our Lady of Guadalupe, are part of every Mexican's religious and cultural education. Pilgrims, thus, participate in an intimate way in creating a story of cultural and cosmic significance.

EL SANTUARIO DE CHIMAYÓ / THE SANCTUARY OF CHIMAYÓ CHIMAYÓ, NEW MEXICO

Overview

High in the windswept plateau of northern New Mexico, travelers brave the elements on their way to the oldest and most important pilgrimage site in the United States. Chimayó is nestled in a fertile valley of fruit orchards, sheep and horse pastures, and small farms that have marked the coming of the Spanish to this part of the world. But it is not the physical respite from the surrounding desert for which tens of thousands of pilgrims descend upon this town, particularly during Holy Week, with their numbers reaching a climax on Good Friday. Rather it is the spiritual awakening, fulfillment *of promesas* or promises, and the healing earth that draw them (Fig. 4).

History

The name *Chimayó* derives from the Tewa *Tsimmayo*, which literally means *place where the big stone stands*, but suggests also a pool, and a larger site of healing spirits (Howarth and Lamadrid, 15-16). The Tewa Indians had been coming to this site as early as 1100 for its healing and sacred properties, so it is no wonder that the first Spanish settlers, spreading north from Santa Fe and reaching the Chimayó valley around 1696, continued this association. The displacement of the native peoples was not without conflict, and thus the town was built around a fortified main plaza, much of which remains today (Treib, 164). Like the many great sacred sites of Europe built upon "pagan" ritual centers, the Santuario at Chimayó rests upon land long held sacred.

According to Hispano tradition, the founding of the Sanctuary of Chimayó centers upon the historical figure of Bernardo Abeyta. A merchant and landowner, he experienced many miracles at Chimayó, not the least of which was the apparition of Our Lord of Esquipulas, the black Christ from Guatemala. As a leading merchant, Abeyta is known to have traveled along the *Camino Real* or Royal Road that linked Mexico City to Santa Fe, and he was undoubtedly familiar with the commercial advantages of a town with a holy shrine. It is unlikely that he reached Guatemala in his travels; nevertheless, the practices at Esquipulas were known in the Chimayó area by 1805 (Howarth and Lamadrid, 18). Thus, in 1813, Abeyta, as the representative of nineteen families, petitioned the vicar general of the diocese for permission to build a chapel in honor of the Lord.

Like the surrounding buildings, the Santuario was built in a fortified style, and constructed from wood beams and adobe clay (Fig. 5). The main altar screen, or *reredo*, is the work of the *santero* Antonio Molleno, with other major contributions by José Aragón and Miguel Aragón. Together they created vivid *bultos*, or wooden statues, and paintings of beloved Franciscan subjects, such as the Holy Trinity, Our

Fig. 4
Gathering of Pilgrims
Santuario de Chimayó, New Mexico
Good Friday, 2005
Photograph Edward Holgate

Fig. 5
Courtyard before Church, 2006
1826-1850
Santuario de Chimayó, New Mexico
Photograph Virginia C. Raguin

Fig. 6

Main Altar (Reredos) with Crucifix of Our Lord of Esquipulas, 2006

Antonio Molleno, with José Aragón and Miguel Aragón, 1826-1850

Santuario de Chimayó, New Mexico

Photograph Virginia C. Raguin

Lady of Sorrows, and St. Francis himself, to surround the crucifix of Our Lord of Esquipulas (Fig. 6). Most of the work was completed between 1826 and 1850.

One of the most distinct aspects of the Santuario de Chimayó is the sacred *pozito* or dried well from which the faithful draw *tierra bendita* or blessed earth. Housed in an adjacent room off the nave, the well was enclosed purposefully within the sacred space of the church, sanctifying the Tewa custom of using the sandy earth at Chimayó as an external and internal curative. From the earliest days, Spanish settlers, too, recounted miraculous events and healings at the spring. Moreover, the Chimayó example parallels the Esquipulas ritual of geophagy, the practice in which earth with healing properties is ingested by the faithful. At Esquipulas, fine white clay is formed into tablets impressed with holy images (Howarth and Lamadrid, 19). The blessed earth of Chimayó is the tangible goal for most pilgrims today and is said to alleviate cancer, depression, paralysis, arthritis, and pain in general. Often called the Lourdes of the Desert, the New Mexican sanctuary offers pilgrims spiritual solace while providing a beloved ritual upon which to anchor their prayers (Fig. 7).

Officially, pilgrimages began at Chimayó in 1945 when large numbers of New Mexican soldiers were taken prisoners of war by the Japanese in WWII as part of the infamous Bataan Death March. The Church responded in part by instituting a pilgrimage to Chimayó to address the pastoral needs of the families of the POWs.

In addition to the famed Good Friday pilgrimage, three other pilgrimages have been added to the official calendar at Chimayó. The Mother's Day pilgrimage, held on the Saturday before Mother's Day, is sponsored by the Guadalupanas. Men as well as women walk on one of six routes. The Vocations Pilgrimage honors those in all vocations, especially those in the priesthood and religious life. Finally, there is the annual Youth Pilgrimage Against Drugs, from the San Juan Indian pueblo to the Santuario, when police officers, judges, and various treatment providers join together to offer solutions to the problem of drugs among the youth of northern New Mexico.

Pilgrims not only take from Chimayó, but leave countless offerings as well. In the cramped, candlelit prayer room where the sacred well is located, a small chapel to the Santo Niño de Atocha has been erected. (Arising from a rival devotion following the death of Abeyta, credited with the founding of the Santuario, the Child Jesus of Atocha soon eclipsed the Lord of Esquipulas in popularity.) In this miniature chapel next to the well (where some say the Santo Niño de Atocha originated), a large statue of the saint holds sway surrounded by a panoply of plaster statues and framed prints of Christ, the Virgin Mary, and major saints. Further examination reveals various written petitions pinned to his clothing, and also offerings of jewelry, *milagritos*, and baby shoes (Figs. 8-9), following the custom of bringing a replacement for the Child Jesus because he wears them out so quickly in his nightly errands of goodwill on behalf of children, travelers, the poor, captives, and others held against their will. Crutches, canes, and braces line the wall and floor, attesting to the Santo Niño's miraculous curative

Fig. 7
Santuario de Chimayó, 2006
Cult rooms of the Blessed Earth
Display of images and *ex votos* left by pilgrims
Photograph Virginia C. Raguin

Fig. 8
Santo Niño de Atocha, 2006
Santuario de Chimayó
19th century
Photograph Virginia C. Raguin

Fig. 9
Shoes left as *ex votos* for the Santo Niño de Atocha, 2006
Santuario de Chimayó
19th century
Photograph Virginia C. Raguin

interventions, the blessed earth perhaps being the vehicle through which such healing transformations have occurred.

Personal Accounts: Chimayó Today

On Good Friday a steady stream of cars lines the High Road to Taos. From Nambé to Chimayó, vehicles park along the roadside, indicating the point where the occupants have commenced the walking portion of their pilgrimage. It's ten miles from Nambé to Chimayó, and twenty-eight miles from Santa Fe, from which some sturdy pilgrims have been walking since dawn. License plates from Texas; California; Chihuahua, México; and Ontario, Canada are sprinkled amongst the New Mexico ones.

Along the route, way stations, both public and private endeavors, provide needed sustenance to weary pilgrims. The towns of Nambé and Chimayó have medical and emergency facilities at the ready. Fruit vendors from Albuquerque and Santa Fe have set up large stands offering free water, oranges, lemons, and tomatoes. Other water stations offer free bibles. One industrious individual is giving away a truckload of requisite pilgrim's staffs made from bamboo stalks.

Felipe Mirabal of Albuquerque, New Mexico, tells of his Aunt Erminia Mirabal's journey in 1946 to pray for her husband's safe return. At this time the Santuario was filled with photographs of GIs and a special mass was said by Edwin V. Byrne, archbishop of Santa Fe. Following the successful release of the GIs, fame of the Santuario grew, as did favorable reports of the miraculous healing earth. Nine years later, Mirabal's parents made the four-hundred-mile round-trip trek from Carrizozo, New Mexico, to Chimayó, to ask the Santo Niño for a second child (him). Depositing a pair of baby shoes with their initial request, and candles and clothing when their request was answered, they took a single shoe as a reliquary of the miracle of their child's birth.

Mirabal recalls his family's descriptions of pilgrimages of the 40s and 50s. "Lodging and food were not concerns for my

Fig. 10
Ex votos from pilgrims left on tree, 2006
Santuario de Chimayó
Photograph Virginia C. Raguin

Fig. 11
Wooden crosses with varied inscriptions carried for the Good Friday march and left against the fence.
Photograph Edward Holgate

Fig. 12
Commemorative Cross inscribed: Andres Romero/ Made a Promise To The Santo Nino in 1943/ That He Would Visit the Santurio (sic) Every Year/ For the Rest Of His Life and Completed The Promise/ Till 1995 When He Passed Away (2006)
Photograph Virginia C. Raguin

family then. My aunt [on that first pilgrimage] stayed in the home of some *chimayosos* who offered her a cot and a fried egg in the morning." Mirabal emphasizes the leveling nature of walking – not only in quieting the mind, but in ensuring that everyone arrived at the shrine in the same manner: "God's way." "The long trips are very tiring as there is no place to rest and not a stick of shade anywhere. I remember an old man inviting us into his house to drink water in a glass and not from the hose as we had asked to do. Aid to the pilgrim is one of the spiritual works of charity."

Joaquin of Bernalillo, New Mexico, comes every year if possible. A tattooed biker with a marshmallow heart, he comes for the sense of community and for a special love of the Santo Niño. The family of Francine Vigil had tee shirts made and came as a devotion to honor their mother/sister. A large Hispanic family, they embrace easily, and tears of sadness are replaced by tears of joy and renewal.

An endless line of pilgrims snakes from the entrance of the shrine for hundreds of yards. At times it seems motionless. A slight breeze brings a whiff of roasted corn or hamburgers and a family nearly breaks rank. Behind the Santuario, at the outdoor amphitheatre, a large display of the Stations of the Cross has been augmented with *ex votos* from pilgrims (Fig. 10). Upon close inspection, one can see that simple crosses, hundreds of them, made from sticks or palm fronds (from Palm Sunday) have been tied into the fence (Figs. 11-12).

Teacher Jerome Cardenas of Rio Rancho, New Mexico, stopped by Chimayó on the way to Taos to see his family for Easter. An uncle in Las Vegas, New Mexico, passed away in August and "it seemed only right to light a candle for him and for my tía [aunt] who's *pelando postas* – meaning times are real tough for her right now." Cardenas also left a bouquet of daffodils for the Santo Niño. "I teach about the saints and the *santos* to my students in Albuquerque, so it's great to see so many of them here. This is a part of their living culture, their *gente* [people]. Maybe the Santuario and the healing dirt are the active agents, but truly it's the people's faith that brings them together. And I don't just mean religious faith. Faith in one another and in community."

At the end of the day, sun-scorched and exhausted pilgrims hitch rides from the many pickup trucks heading back to cars parked in Nambé, Dixon, Taos, and Española. Sitting in the back of one of these trucks, I visited with a young mother from Santa Fe who came regularly with her son. Four years ago, the entire family came to pray for her mother who was suffering from cancer. (Mother is better now, thank you.) Her new boyfriend, Michael, an Iraqi vet, was making his first pilgrimage to Chimayó this year. Michael kept admonishing her to hold on to the side of the truck as we bounced up the highway. *He* held tight to the under rail with both hands. I wondered what he was thinking about, what he had prayed for at the Santuario, this man who had seen war on the other side of the globe. My fellow pilgrim.

CONCLUSIONS

The Sanctuary at Chimayó and the Basilica of Our Lady of Guadalupe provide a rich framework within which to understand the pilgrimage experiences of the Hispanic world. The Guadalupe site – at the heart of first contact with Europeans – represents an apex of Baroque artistry and colonial history and is a Marian site unmatched in the Christian pantheon. By contrast, Chimayó represents the hardscrabble outpost of Spanish colonization where even the earth itself has sacred meaning. Within the pilgrimage experience, the ways in which religious and cultural characteristics interplay to form a collective identity are uniquely Hispanic. Moreover, the highly personalized relationships that the Hispanic faithful have with the divine link these two sites in inextricable ways. The spiritual and communal transformations that occur at the sites, however, belong to a broader community of faith.

See further reading on page 344

ISLAM

Details of Fig. 7

Mecca and the Hajj

F. E. Peters

Every Muslim assumes a fivefold religious obligation. The first is a matter of faith, to pronounce and adhere to the conviction expressed in the Muslim two-line creed, which begins with the generic statement of monotheism, "There is no god but the God," and ends with the specifically Muslim affirmation, "… and Muhammad is the Envoy of God." There follow four prescribed ritual acts: formal liturgical prayer five times daily; the payment of a annual alms; dawn-to-dusk fasting during the lunar month of Ramadan; and, finally, the performance, at least once in a lifetime, of the Hajj or pilgrimage to Mecca if physically and financially able.

The Hajj was a long-standing pre-Islamic ritual in the environs of Mecca; how long we cannot say, though its rites seem redolent of primitive Semitic practices. The same word, *hag*, is used in Hebrew to describe the three great site-tied festivals of Passover, Shabuoth or Weeks, and Sukkoth or Tabernacles, when all Israelites who could were constrained to "go up" to Jerusalem and offer sacrifice there. Something similar was occurring among the Arabs in the neighborhood of Mecca long before Islam. The Bible itself is silent on such matters but the post-Biblical Jewish tradition (*midrash*) filled in many vivid details on the life of Abraham, and though there is no mention of Abraham in the pre-Islamic Arab tradition, Jews in Arabia, some of them later converts to Islam, may well have told stories of Abraham and even of his coming to Mecca.

All we know for certain about the origins of the Hajj is that it long antedated Muhammad's lifetime, as did the *umra*, a more local Meccan festival celebrated by the townspeople in and around the Ka'ba. Though Muslims are loathe to imagine the Prophet in any connection with paganism, we have no real reason to think that Muhammad did not participate in the Hajj before his call to prophecy in 610 CE, nor indeed even after that date, at least until his famous "migration" (*hijra*) to Medina in 622. Though prevented by the Quraysh tribe in 628 CE, Muhammad made an agreed-upon *umra* at Mecca in 629. Mecca fell in 630 and Muhammad made the *umra* again later that year. Muslims were then free to make the Hajj and they did so in 631, but Muhammad was not among them. He made his one and only Muslim Hajj in 632, the famous "Pilgrimage of Farewell," and it was on that occasion that by word and example, what Muslims call his *sunna*, the Prophet made whatever modifications were deemed necessary to purify this ritual that in Muslim eyes had originally been instituted by Abraham himself.

To understand the Hajj we must try to understand 7th-century Mecca, an extremely difficult task since we have, apart from the Quran, no contemporary sources on the place and, in addition, later Muslim writers had no great interest in the pagan era – they called it "the days of ignorance" – that preceded Islam. What we do know is that it was a tiny settlement squeezed into an inhospitable canyon in the highlands rising westward from the Red Sea to the central Arabian steppe plateau. The place was obviously settled because it had water, a spring that must at some point have become sacralized, since by at least a century before Muhammad there was a sacred zone, a *haram* in Arabic, around it and, in the midst of the open Haram, a crudely built shrine called "The Cube" *(al-ka'ba)* that was thought to house the presence of an aniconic deity called simply "The God" *(al-ilah or allah)*.

By Muhammad's day, as Muslims now contend, the Haram was crowded with idols and shrines. The Meccans had contrived to turn it into a pantheon, and even more consequently, had succeeded in persuading the normally hostile and skittish Bedouin to come in off the steppe and, under the protection of a "truce of God," to worship and trade in Mecca for a spell each year. The paramount Arab tribe of Mecca had taken advantage of the arrangement to build a local trading network tribe. It was good business for the Meccans, and it was also good for young Muhammad, who had married into some small share of Meccan commerce. Thus Mecca was a shrine town whose business was religion and whose religion was chiefly business.

Fig. 1
Quran: Paper Mâché cover with lacquer painting of profuse flowers
19th century, Iran [possible same commission as below: lavish family book with the dates of birth of family members inscribed on the flyleaf from 1837]
Ink, opaque watercolor, lapis lazuli, and gold on paper, 8½ x 11 in. (21.6 x 27.9 cm)
Private Collection
Photograph Michel Raguin

Ibn al-Kalbi (737-819 CE), an Arab historian, gives an explanation for pagan customs, similar to the gathering of pilgrimage mementos that developed due to reverence of the Ka'ba. He argues that the Arabs, even when dispersed and practicing a corrupted religion, still remembered the purified religious practice of Abraham and devotions associated with the Ka'ba.

> *When Ishmael, the son of Abraham, settled in Mecca, he begot many children. [Their descendants] multiplied so much that they crowded the city and supplanted its original inhabitants, the Amalekites. Later on Mecca became overcrowded with them, and dissent and strife arose among them, causing them to fight among themselves and consequently be dispersed throughout the land where they roamed seeking a livelihood.*
>
> *The reason that led them to the worship of images and stones was the following. No one left Mecca without carrying away with him a stone from the stones of the Sacred House as a token of reverence to it, and as a sign of deep affection to Mecca. Wherever he settled he would erect that stone and circumambulate it in the same manner he used to circumambulate the Ka'ba (before his departure from Mecca), seeking thereby its blessing and affirming his deep affection for the Holy House. In fact, the Arabs still venerate the Ka'ba and Mecca and journey to them in order to perform the pilgrimage and the visitation, conforming thereby to the time-honored custom which they inherited from Abraham and Ishmael.*
>
> *In time this led them to the worship of whatever took their fancy, and caused them to forget their former worship. They exchanged the religion of Abraham and Ishmael for another. Consequently they took to the worship of images, becoming like the nations before them....*
>
> *Whenever a traveler stopped at a place or station [in order to rest or spend the night] he would select for himself four good stones, pick out the finest among them and adopt it as his god, and use the remaining three as supports for his cooking pot. On his departure he would leave them behind, and would do the same on his other stops.*
>
> *The Arabs were wont to offer sacrifices before all these idols, baetyls [stones from ancient ruins], and stones. Nevertheless they were aware of the excellence and superiority of the Ka'bah, to which they went on pilgrimage and visitation. What they did on their travels was a perpetuation of what they did at the Ka'bah, because of their devotion to it.*

The Book of Idols by Hisham Ibn-al-Kalbi. **Nabih Amin Faris, trans. Princeton: Princeton University Press, 1952, 4; 28-29**

Peters, F.E. *The Hajj.* 1994. Princeton: Princeton University Press, 21.

We do not know a great deal about either the business or the religion, though much has been imagined about both. What does emerge from the later accounts is that there was one set of very local religious practices called the *umra* – precise sense uncertain – that centered on the Ka'ba, which featured the ritual of circumambulation (which also has its Jewish parallels around the Temple in Jerusalem) around the Ka'ba. And there was another set of practices called the Hajj, which unfolded in various places outside the town.

According to the traditional chronology, in the year 610 CE, when he was about forty, that same Muhammad, an otherwise unremarkable citizen of the provincial Mecca, had a vision which he experienced as a call from God to relay to his townsmen a message from on high. For twenty-two years he publicly proclaimed that message in what he called the Quran, "The Recitation" (Figs. 1-3). What God required was "submission" (*islam*), that is, submission to a relentless and unremitting monotheism: there was in fact no god but The God, the same deity worshiped by the Meccans and whose Holy House stood in their midst. All the others whose many

Fig. 2

Quran: Paper Mâché cover with lacquer painting of profuse flowers

19th century, Iran. [Small miniature book used for travelling, decoration mainly confined to opening Surah]

Ink, opaque watercolor, lapis lazuli, and gold on paper, 4 x 6 in. (10.2 x 15.2 cm)

Private Collection

Photograph Michel Raguin

idols defiled the Haram were false gods: delusions, fantasies, and empty names.

This was troubling news for the great majority of Meccans who wanted no part in "The Submission" that was Islam, since it meant the end not only of their prosperity but of their livelihood as well. They got rid of their troublesome prophet, who found asylum in the oasis of Medina, but it was only a temporary respite. In the end, Muhammad returned in triumph: the Meccans became "submitters" (*muslimun*) and the Haram was cleansed of its idols. Though not of all its rituals: the *umra* remained, and so too did the Hajj.

It is clear from the Quran that Muhammad had accepted in principle both the *umra* and the Hajj of the Mecca of his day as legitimate forms of worship of the one true God. Out of them either he or someone soon after him "constructed" the Muslim Hajj by combining the two rituals, though without completely obliterating the distinction between them, and arranging them in a sequence. The Quran achieved this absorption of what might seem to be a complex of pagan rituals by providing the Muslims with an

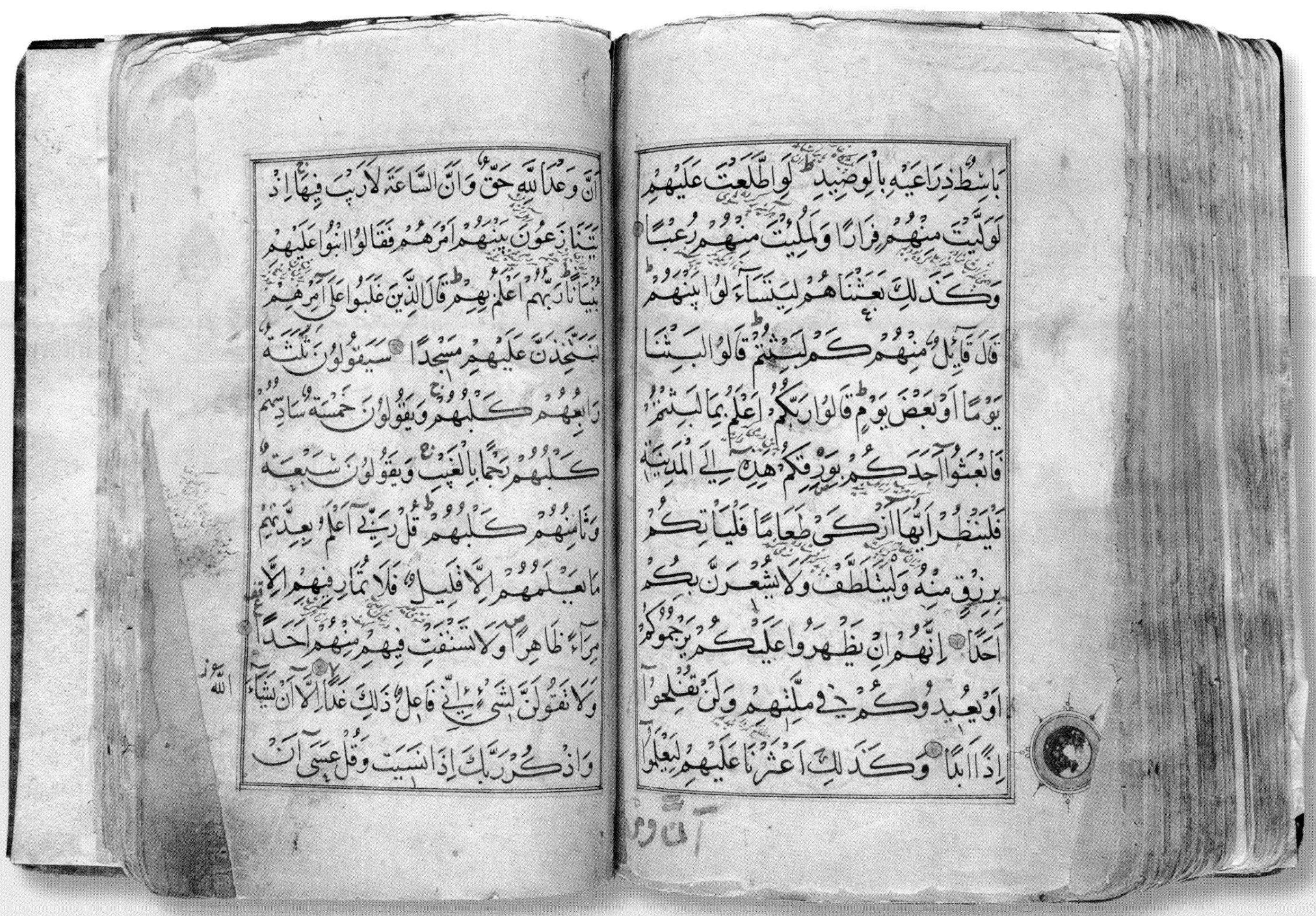

Fig. 3
Quran: Sporadic Persian translations in red of Arabic text; sporadic notes in red on vocalization as pronunciation aid; some embellishment possibly added at a later date; marks of heavy usage
19th century or earlier, Iran (?)
Ink opaque watercolor, and gold on paper, 5 x 9 in. (12.7 x 22.9 cm)
Private Collection
Photograph Michel Raguin

explanation of why the Hajj was now a religious obligation for them. In performing the Hajj, it was explained, the Muslim was reenacting, at Abraham's own command, a series of acts that unfolded during the days when Abraham, Ishmael, and the latter's mother Hagar all dwelled in Mecca.

The pre-Islamic Hajj was not, at any time we can observe it, a single, unified ritual act in the manner of a drama, but was rather a concatenation of barely connected activities spread over a number of days. Or so it appears to us, since whatever etiological myths the Arabs once possessed to explain these now baffling rituals are entirely lost. Perhaps they had already disappeared by Muhammad's own day. But the Quran now provided the believers with their own properly Muslim explanations. The Hajj rituals were now understood in reference to Abraham and his sojourn in Mecca. Here at Arafat Abraham stood and prayed before God. Here at Mina he was bidden to sacrifice his son and was then given an animal in substitution. Here too Abraham was tempted by Satan, and so the three "Satans" in the form of pillars are stoned. And more.

Over the course of the centuries these rituals had been transformed by the paganism that had engulfed Mecca, and it was now the duty of the Prophet to purify and restore the "religion of Abraham" and its original rituals, like the Hajj. How much was actually changed? We are ill-informed on the pre-Islamic Hajj, but some judgments are possible. First, the commercial fairs associated with the earlier pilgrimage either were abolished or disappeared soon after Islam. Second, some of the more manifest trappings of paganism were removed. Certain prayers or arrivals and departures that fell at sunrise or sunset, for example, and so suggested sun or planetary worship, were moved slightly off those points in an effort to break the earlier pagan associations. Sacrifices that had been commonplace in and around Mecca were abolished; only the one at a place called Mina survived. But for all that, remarkably little seems to have been changed in what was, to all appearances, a very old and very primitive series of rituals (Fig. 4).

There does not appear to have been any resistance to the incorporation of this pre-Islamic ritual into Islam as the new faith; indeed, it may have come as welcome news to the Meccans who were still concerned – quite needlessly, as it turned out – that the new faith would undermine their business and perhaps destroy their town. And the ritual remains unchanged since Muhammad save for its logistics and its setting. A journey that once took a month by caravan from the nearest large cities and a year or more from the far outposts of the Islamic world is now accomplished by air in a matter of hours; and where first hundreds, then thousands of Muslims made the perilous journey to Mecca, now the pilgrims number in the millions, who must be transported, registered, housed, fed, guided, and protected from themselves and others for as long as they are in the Holy City. That responsibility belongs to the sovereigns of the place, who have long gloried in the title of "Servants of the Two Noble Sanctuaries," that is, of Mecca and Medina. Since 1926 the title has belonged to the House of Sa'ud, and by now it is an extraordinarily expensive honor and an exceedingly worrisome responsibility: Mecca, overcrowded and over excited during the Hajj, while it is the focus of attention of the entire Islamic world, is also an enormous public health hazard – the world's first cholera epidemic broke out there in the 1860s – and the potential ignition point of a social or political catastrophe.

For all but the local Arabian Muslims, the Hajj usually begins long before the event. The pilgrims must not only be certified as genuine Muslims – and provided with Saudi Hajj visas – before they leave, but are also increasingly "packaged" by an elaborate, rapidly developing and lucrative set of agencies that have grown up for that purpose. In non-Muslim states these are generally independent commercial enterprises, but in Muslim-majority countries like Turkey, Indonesia, and Pakistan, they are government-run or government-controlled entities that operate as half banker or credit union and half travel agency for the prospective pilgrim: they arrange for everything from certification to transportation, lodging, food, credit, entertainment, bilingual guides and, one may anticipate, some modest health insurance.[1]

MECCA

Ka'ba and Al-Haram Mosque. Pilgrims circle the Ka'ba seven times at the beginning and the end of the Hajj.

MUZDALIFA

Pilgrims stay the night in a vast tent city.

MINA

On return, pilgrims stone three pillars that symbolize Satan's temptation of Abraham.

ARAFAT

Pilgrims stand and pray on the plain of Arafat.

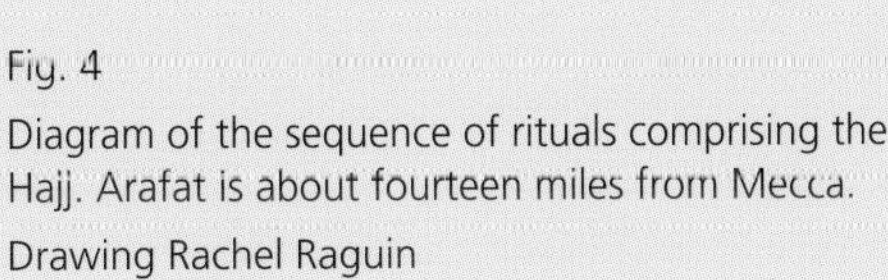

Fig. 4

Diagram of the sequence of rituals comprising the Hajj. Arafat is about fourteen miles from Mecca.

Drawing Rachel Raguin

Fig. 5
Female pilgrims in white on the plains of Arafat, 1974
Photograph S. M. Amin/*Saudi Aramco World*/SAWDIA

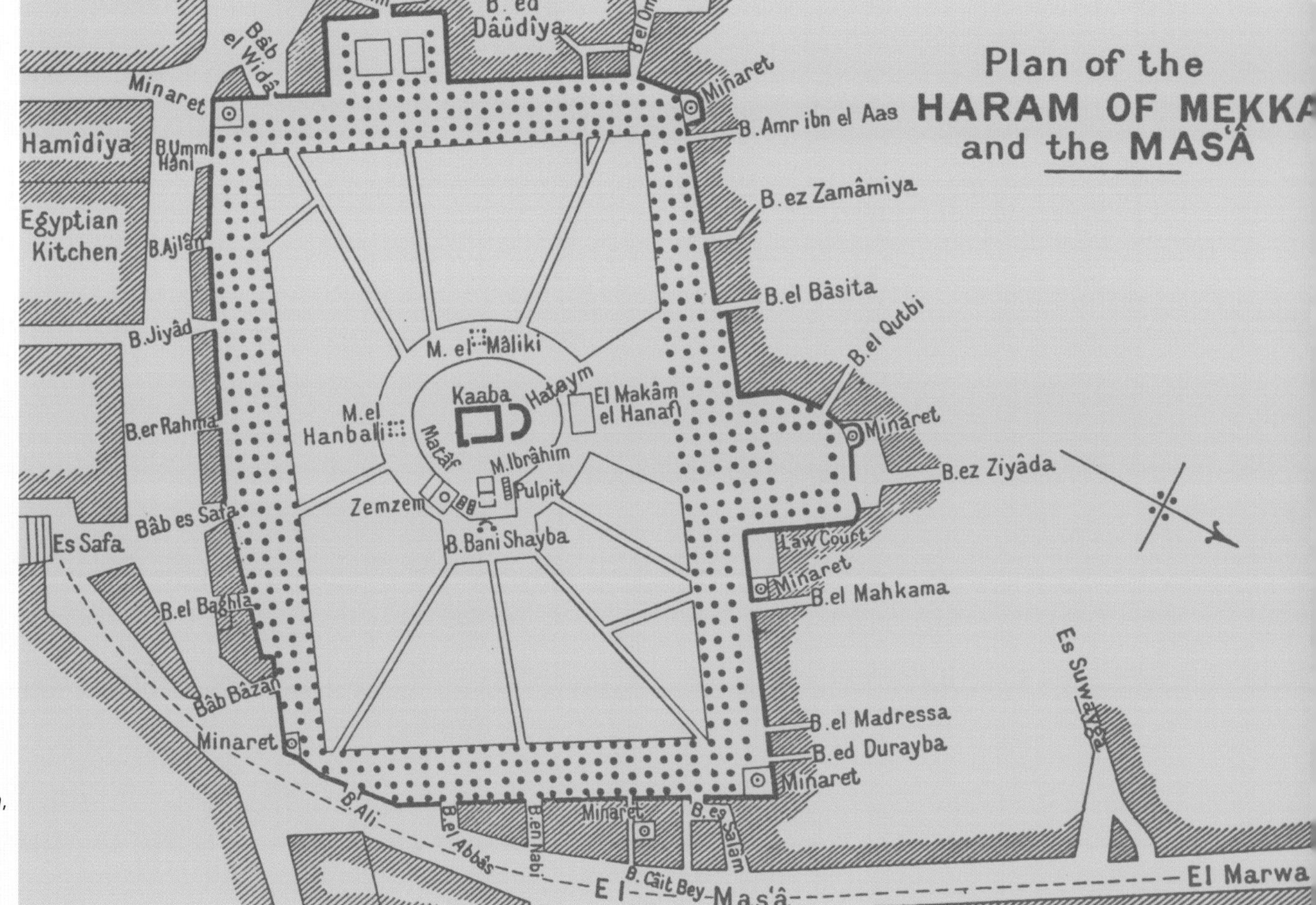

Fig. 6
Plan of the Haram of Mecca
Eldon Rutter, *The Holy Cities of Arabia*, London, New York: G. P. Putnam's Sons, 1928.

Fig. 7

Haram at Mecca, folio from a manuscript of the Javahir al-ghara'ib Tarjomat Bahr Al-Aja'ib (Gems Of Marvels: A Translation of the Sea of Wonders) of Cennabi

1582

Opaque watercolor and gold on paper, $11\frac{1}{4}$ x $7\frac{5}{16}$ in. (28.6 x 18.6 cm)

Harvard Art Museum, Arthur M. Sackler Museum, The Edwin Binney, 3rd Collection of Turkish Art at the Harvard Art Museum, 1985.219.1

Photograph Allan Macintyre © President and Fellows of Harvard College

In addition to the Haram or sanctuary area in the middle of town, Mecca is surrounded by a larger taboo area that is marked by points or "stations" along the main roads leading into the Holy City. This too seems to be pre-Islamic, and then as now the pilgrim, before he or she reaches one of those points, must enter a sacralized state, *ihram*, "to become haramized." This is done by undergoing a complete ablution and by donning a special garment made up of two simple white sheets, one tied around the waist and reaching the knees and the other draped over the left shoulder and tied somewhere beneath the right arm; head and insteps must remain uncovered. This for the men; no particular dress is prescribed for the women, though most are fully covered, head to toe, in white (Fig. 5). The Ihram garment alone is worn throughout the pilgrimage, and no further grooming is permitted. Nor are sexual relations: any indulgence in the latter renders the Hajj void.

Upon entering Mecca (Figs. 6-7), the pilgrim proceeds as soon as possible to the performance of the sevenfold, counterclockwise circumambulation of the Ka'ba, the first three at a somewhat quickened pace (Fig. 8). Many pilgrims attempt to kiss or touch the Black Stone that is embedded in the eastern corner of the Ka'ba as they pass it, though the pilgrimage throng often makes this impossible (Fig. 9). The circuits of the Ka'ba completed, the pilgrim goes to the place called Safa, on the southeast side of the Haram, and completes seven "runnings" between that and another place, called Marwa, a distance altogether of somewhat less than two miles. Today both hills, and the way between, are enclosed in an air-conditioned colonnade. The circuits of the Ka'ba originally formed part of the Meccan *umra*, but the "running" between Safa and Marwa was connected to it by Muhammad himself, as we can still read in Quran 2:153.

There is a certain flexibility in the performance of those Meccan rituals – some prefer to do them very late at night when the weather is cooler and the crowds thinner – but precisely on the eighth of the month of Dhu

Fig. 8
Ka'ba enveloped by the Kiswa, 1974
Photograph S. M. Amin/*Saudi Aramco World*/ SAWDIA

Ibn Battuta (1304-1369), who travelled widely throughout the Islamic world, records prayers at mosques in imitation of the standing at Arafat

> *It is the custom of the people of Damascus and all the other cities of that region to go out [of the covered art of the mosques] after the mid-afternoon payer on the day of "Arafa" and to stand in the courtyard of the mosques such as the sanctuary of Jerusalem [the Al Aqsa mosque], the Umayyad congregational mosque [at Damascus], etc. Their imams stand with them bare-headed, their bodies humbly bowed in prayer, with lowly voice and downcast eyes, entreating the blessing of God. Observing thus the hour which the homagers of God most High and pilgrims to His House [The Ka'ba] stand at Arafat, they continue in humble reverence and prayer and earnest supplication imploring the favor of God Most High through the Pilgrims to His House, until the sun sets, when they hurriedly disperse, in imitation of the rush of the pilgrims, weeping that it has been denied them to join in that illustrious station at Arafat, and praying God Most High that He may bring them thither and not withhold from them the blessing of His acceptance of that which they have done [on this day].*

Gibb, Sir Hamilton, ed. 1958. *The Travels of Ibn Battuta*, vol. 1. [The Hakluyt Society] London: Cambridge University Press, 152-53.

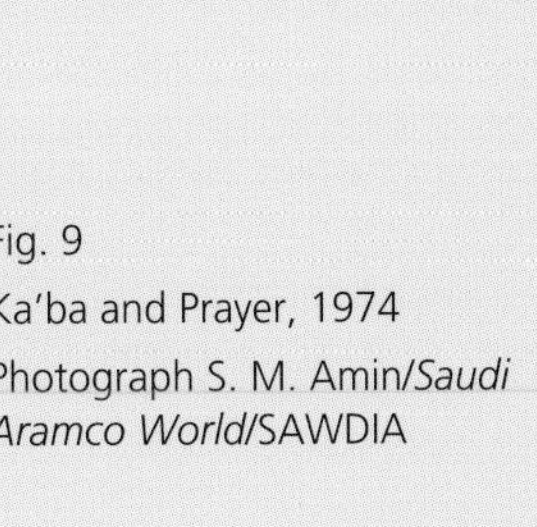

Fig. 9
Ka'ba and Prayer, 1974
Photograph S. M. Amin/*Saudi Aramco World*/SAWDIA

Fig. 10
The tent tops of Mina spread out across the plain, 2008
Photograph Courtesy Ministry of Hajj, Kingdom of Saudi Arabia

Fig. 11
Tents at Mina, 1974
Photograph
S. M. Amin/*Saudi Aramco World*/SAWDIA

al-Hijja, the Hajj proper begins. The pilgrims proceed to Mina, a village five miles east of Mecca, where most spend the night in what becomes, for that solitary evening, one of the largest cities in the Middle East (Figs. 10-11). Some may proceed directly to the plain of Arafat, fourteen miles from the Haram. The next day, the ninth, is the heart of the Hajj. The pilgrims now assemble and stand, in what is now their many hundreds of thousands, on the plain of Arafat that surrounds the tiny hill called the Mount of Mercy. At times sermons have been delivered during this interval, but they have nothing to do with the ritual, the point of which is precisely the "standing before God," from noon to sunset (Fig. 12). Just before sunset there occurs the "dispersal," a sometimes pell-mell rush to Muzdalifa, a place halfway back toward Mina. The night is spent here, and the next morning, the tenth, there is another "dispersal" as the pilgrims hasten to Mina, where occurs the ritual of the "Stoning of Satan," the casting of seven pebbles at a stone pillar (Fig. 13).

With the Stoning of Satan, the Hajj has reached its official term, but there remain a number of rites which are part of the pilgrims' desacralization. As already noted, the pilgrim must sacrifice an animal – this is the *îd al-adhâ* or "Feast of Sacrifice" celebrated concurrently with the Meccan event by the entire Muslim world, though some Muslim legal experts permit ten days of fasting as an acceptable substitute for this blood sacrifice. The men's heads are then shaved (although there are now exceptions), and the women's locks lightly clipped, to signal the end of the *ihram* state – the sexual prohibitions remain a short while longer. The pilgrims return to Mecca and perform another circumambulation of the Ka'ba. Some are sprinkled with water from the well of Zamzam, and then all bathe. The next three days, the eleventh, twelfth, and thirteenth of the month, complete the desacralization. The pilgrims return to Mina, now completely freed of all taboos. On each of the three days the pilgrims again stone the great pillar there, as well as two smaller ones. The Hajj is then complete, and though it is in no sense part of the Hajj, many pilgrims proceed to Medina to pay their respects at the Prophet's tomb there before returning home. Contemporary pilgrims very often precede the Hajj with a visit to Medina.

To the outsider, even one who can recognize and acknowledge the Abrahamic bloodlines and family resemblances of Jews, Christians, and Muslims, the Hajj, with its crowds, its intensity, and the near edge of fatal panic, might seem like an exotic ritual that threatens to explode in unforeseen and possibly fatal consequences. For the Muslim, however, it has often proven to be a powerful life-altering and community-confirming experience, a solitary epiphany that comes in the midst of millions of other Muslims.

There is little wonder, then, that the Hajj has produced a large and engaging literature, and not only from Muslims like Nasir-I Khusraw, Ibn Jubayr, and Ibn Battuta, who incorporated detailed and perceptive accounts of their pilgrimages into their travel books (Nasir-I Khusraw wrote first of the Hajj of 1050, Ibn Jubayr on the Hajj of 1184, and Ibn Battuta of that in 1326). Europeans too have journeyed to Mecca, earlier in disguise, more recently as converts to Islam. The most famous Hajj-in-disguise narrative is undoubtedly that of the British explorer-adventurer Richard Burton, whose *Personal Narrative of a Pilgrimage to Mecca and al-Medina* describes his experience on the Hajj of 1853; another, among the growing number of accounts by converts, the *Autobiography of Malcolm X*, includes the highly personal story of how the Hajj of 1964 transformed an American radical.

Fig. 12
Pilgrims on the Plains of Arafat, 1974
Photograph S. M. Amin/ *Saudi Aramco World*/ SAWDIA

As outlined in the introduction essay, these transformations are not restricted to the Meccan experience, but occur at other times in Muslim practice. During these journeys, called pious visits *(ziyara)*, the Muslim may visit Mecca at other times of the year but also, as we have seen, the Prophet's tomb at Medina, the Dome of the Rock and other sites around the Haram al-Sharif on the Temple Mount in Jerusalem, and Islam's hundreds of other tomb shrines,

Fig. 13
Pilgrims throwing stones at the pillars that symbolize Satan and his temptation of Abraham, 2002
Photograph Samia El-Moslimany/*Saudi Aramco World*/SAWDIA

like those at Karbela and Najaf in Iraq and Mashhad in Iran. The transformation may be aided by of the individual nature of the experience. The Hajj itself is profoundly performative: the *hajji* is in Mecca not merely to be present in the Holy City or to observe the liturgy of others, but to perform himself, though in the company of other Muslims, an elaborate set of liturgical rites in which he is the sole and unique actor. Though he may be assisted through the intricacies of the complex and unfamiliar ritual – Mecca has had from the beginning a guild of professional guides who shepherd the pilgrims through everything from lodging to liturgy to leaving – his guides are only prompters; there are no intermediaries, no priests or clergy who mediate his actions to God. Like Abraham himself on that same terrain, he stands solitary before his God.

1 These Hajj logistics are brilliantly described by Robert Bianchi in his *Guests of God: Pilgrimage and Politics in the Islamic World* (New York: Oxford 2004).

Primary Sources on Pilgrimage to Jerusalem and Mecca

Details of Fig. 4

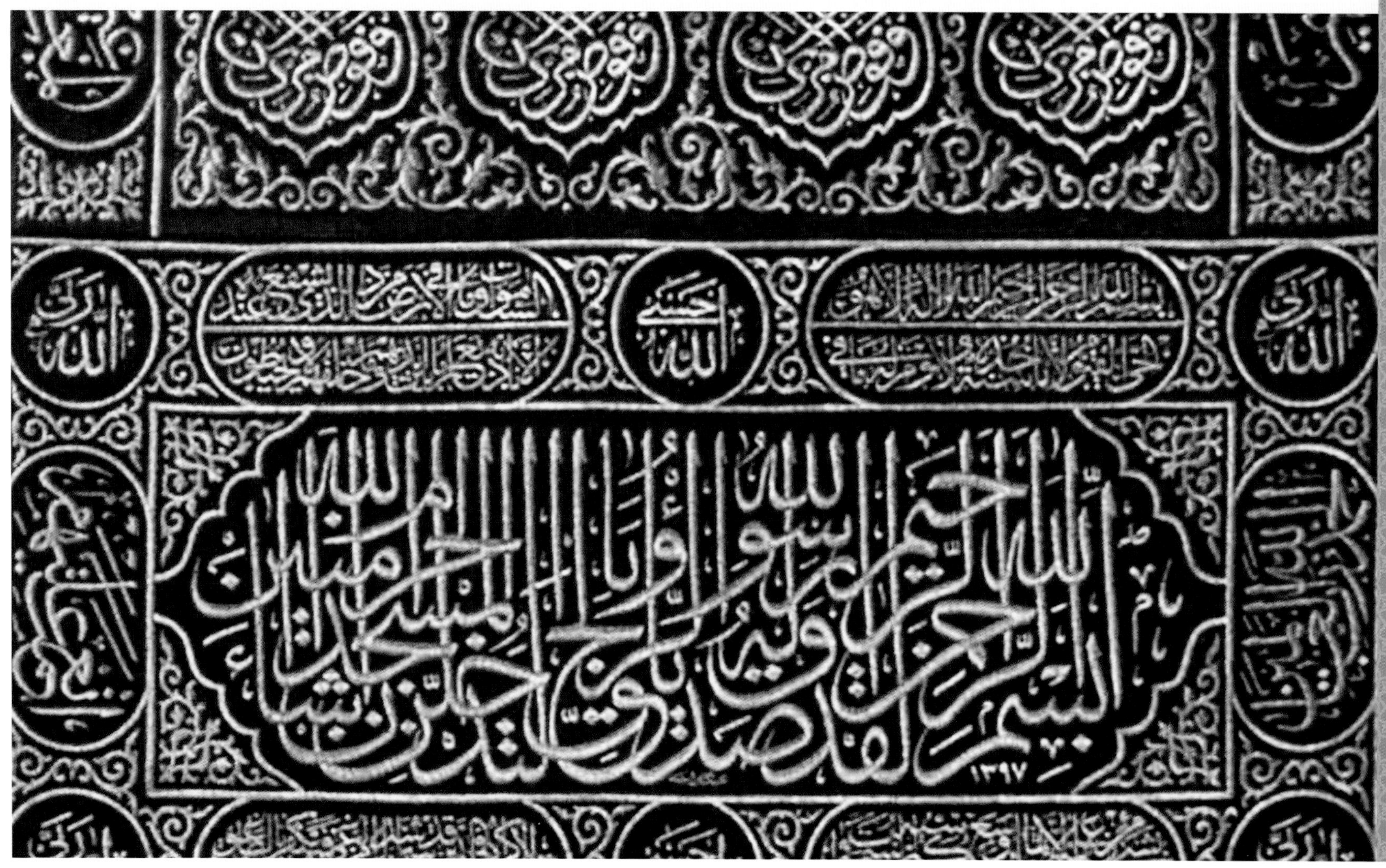

The Kiswa: The Curtain of the Ka'ba

Virginia C. Raguin

Ibn Batuta (1304-1369 CE) was a legal scholar, born in Morocco, who traveled extensively across Northern Africa, The Middle East, India, and China. In 1325, at the age of twenty-one, he embarked on his first Hajj to Mecca. His journey took him through Cairo and Damascus. He passed through Medina, giving reverence at the tomb of the Prophet Mohammed, before arriving at Mecca. He then headed east, where he was occupied for almost twenty-four years. Upon returning, he visited Mecca again. Once at home, he was encouraged by the Sultan of Morocco to write an account of his journeys. These accounts give invaluable insights into customs, peoples, and monuments as they existed across the Islamic world of the 14th century.

MECCA AND THE KA'BA

> *We presented ourselves forthwith at the Sanctuary of God Most High within her, the place of abode of His Friend Ibrāhīm and scene of mission of His Chosen One, Muhammed (God Bless and give him peace). We entered the illustrious Holy House, wherin 'he who enters is secure,' [Quran 3:97] by the gate of the Banū Shaiba and saw before our eyes the illustrious Ka'ba (God increase it in veneration), like a bride who is displayed upon the bridal-chair of majesty, and walks with proud step in the mantles of beauty, surrounded by the companies which had come to pay homage to the God of Mercy, and being conducted to the Garden of Eternal Bliss. We made around it the [seven-fold] circuit of arrival and kissed the holy Stone; we performed a prayer of two bowings at the Māquam Ibrāhīm [site of stone used by Abraham to build the Ka'ba] and clung to the curtains of the Ka'ba at the Multazam [curved wall] between the door and the black stone, where prayer is answered; we drank of the water of Zamzam [the well where Hagar is believed to have found water for herself and her son Ismail in the desert]... then having run between al-Safa and al-Marwa, we took up our lodging there in a house near the gate of Ibrahim* (188).

> *The interior of the illustrious Ka'ba is paved with marble inlaid with arabesques and its walls have similar facing. It has three tall pillars, exceedingly high and made of teak; between each pillar and the next is a distance of four paces, and they stand [lengthwise] in the middle of the space inside the illustrious Ka'ba, the central one being opposite to the midpoint of the side between the [Yamanite] and Syrian angles. The hangings of the illustrious Ka'ba are of black silk, with inscriptions in white; they gleam upon its walls with light and brilliance and clothe it entirely from the top to the ground* (195).

THE KISWA

On the day of the sacrifice the [new] curtain of the illustrious Ka'ba is conveyed from the [headquarters of the] Egyptian caravan to the Holy House and laid on its roof (Figs. 1-4). *Then, on the third day after the Day of Sacrifice, the Shaibis set about draping it over the illustrious Ka'ba. It is a jet-black covering of silk lined with linen and at the top end of it is an embroidered band on which is written in white [lettering]: God hath established the Ka'ba, the Sacred House, to be a Station and so on to the end of the verse. [The full verse reads: Allah made the Ka'ba, the Sacred House, an asylum of security for men, as also the Sacred Months, the animals for offerings, and the garlands that mark them: That ye may know that Allah hath knowledge of what is in the heavens and on earth and that Allah is well acquainted with all things (Yusufali).]*

On all sides of it are embroidered bands having the verses of the Quran inscribed upon them in white, with a glistening radiance which glows out against the black background of the curtain. When it has been adjusted its ends are looped up, as a protection against men's hands. Al-Malik al Nasir is [the ruler; the ninth Mamluk Sultan of Egypt (r. 1293-1341)] who has the charge of providing the curtain of the Ka'ba, he also sends the emoluments of the qadi, preacher, imams [leaders of prayer in the mosque], muezzins [who lead the call to five-times daily prayer from the minarets of the mosque], mosque servitors and overseers, and all the requirements of the illustrious Sanctuary in candles and oil every year (247) .

Gibb, Sir Hamilton, ed. 1958. *The Travels of Ibn Battuta*, vol. 1. [The Hakluyt Society] London: Cambridge University Press.

Fig. 1
Embroidering the Kiswa in 1974. For many years the Kiswa was the responsibility of the Sultan of Cairo, as described by Ibn Battuta who spoke to the responsibilities of Al-Malik al Nasir (r. 1293-1341)] in caring for the Ka'ba. After the conquest of Cairo by the Ottoman Sultan, in 1517 the Kiswa was always embroidered in Cairo. This ended in 1927, when an establishment was founded in Mecca where today over two hundred Saudi weavers and craftsmen produce the grand covering of black-died silk.
Photograph S. M. Amin/*Saudi Aramco World*/SAWDIA

Fig. 2
Calligrapher designing script for embroiderers, 1985. Given the importance of the sacred script of the Quran and the traditional absence of figural imagery in religions settings, calligraphy is a highly respected art in the Islamic word.
Photograph Katrina Thomas/*Saudi Aramco World*/SAWDIA

Fig. 3

Kiswa Embroidered Panels, 1974. The Kiswa's forty-seven rectangular pieces measure overall 2,650 square meters (28,524 square feet). A border, ninety-five centimeters wide (three feet), is embroidered in gold-plated silver wire with verses from the Quran and Islamic religious formulae.

Photograph S. M. Amin/*Saudi Aramco World*/SAWDIA

Fig. 4

A portion of the Kiswa's door curtain, the Sitara, was given to the United Nations in the name of "the servitor of the two noble sanctuaries" (Mecca and Medina), King Fahd ibn 'Abd al-'Aziz Al Sa'ud. It was presented on January 1, 1983.

Delegates' Lounge, United Nations, New York

Photograph Katrina Thomas/*Saudi Aramco World*/SAWDIA

Nicolas de Nicolay: A French View of the Hajj in the 16th Century

Virginia C. Raguin

Nicolas de Nicolay was a French cartographer, military strategist, diplomat, and author during the reign of Henry II. From 1551 to 1552 he accompanied a French delegation to Istanbul on a mission to Sultan Suleyman the Magnificent, the Ottoman ruler. The purpose was to convince the Sultan to join an alliance with France against the forces of the Emperor Charles V in Italy. Occupied with the production of maps and troubled by the religious wars and persecution of Protestant Huguenots in France, Nicolay waited fifteen years to publish his detailed and lively description of his travels: *Four Books of Voyages and Peregrinations in the East*. He gives a comprehensive overview of the different lands, peoples, religions, and customs in the Ottoman Empire, carefully eschewing judgments, and apparently communicating a deep interest in the diversity of his subjects. Like all people we have noted on pilgrimage, Nicolay articulates a deep purpose for his displacement, his observations, and his reasons for reflection and communication after his return. Although not strictly on a religious quest, Nicolay reports on many aspects of religion and life of the time, stressing the relevance to contemporary French politics of the time.

> *"Nicolay unfolds a panoramic representation of the Ottoman Empire which, like a giant screen, allows for a complex reflection on the French monarchy. By offering to his readers alternative models of political order, cultural diversity, and religious practices, which for the most part are safely contained in the Orient, an imaginary, distant space of profound alterity, Nicolay indirectly advocates a political agenda that favors loyalty to the monarchy, religious moderation and tolerance, and unity based on a collective history and a sense of national belonging"* (p.19).
>
> *Keller, Marcus. 2008. "Nicolas de Nicolay's Navigations and the Domestic Politics of Travel Writing."* L'Esprit Créateur *48/1: 18-31*

Nicolay, Nicholas, 1568. *Les Quatre livres des navigations et peregrinations orientales de Nicolas Nicolay*. Lyons: G.Roville.

Copy used for reference: 2nd edition issued by Guillaume Silvius, Antwerp, 1576. Translations by Raguin.

PILGRIMS TO MECCA, THAT THE TURKS CALL HAGISARS (HAJJIS) (Fig. 1)

Once they have come from their own localities, a great caravan is assembled first in cities, in Damascus, or Cairo. For they do not willingly leave until they are at least thirty to forty thousand in a company with a good number of

Fig. 1

Pilgrims to Mecca

Nicolay, Nicholas de, sieur d'Arfeuille, 1517-1583.

Le navigationi et viaggi nella Tvrchia, di Nicolo de Nicolai del Delfinato signor d'Arfevilla.

Nouamente tradotto de francese in uolgare, da Francesco Flori de Lilla…

Antwerp, Guillaume Silvius, 1576

Photograph Boston Public Library

Fig. 2

The Sacquaz Water Carriers: Pilgrims in Mecca

Nicolay, Nicholas de, sieur d'Arfeuille, 1517-1583.

Le navigationi et viaggi nella Tvrchia, di Nicolo de Nicolai del Delfinato signor d'Arfevilla.

Nouamente tradotto de francese in uolgare, da Francesco Flori de Lilla…

Antwerp, Guillaume Silvius, 1576

Photograph Boston Public Library

Janissaries [an elite militia], delegated to security, guidance, defense, and safety of the caravan to prevent it from being pillaged by the Arabs who day and night track them in the desert in order to surprise and rob the pilgrim travelers.... Once they have crossed the desert, the pilgrims arrive at Medina... where they go into the temple and rest their gaze on the tomb of Muhammad.... The next day they take up their journey to Mecca, which is three small days of travel from Medina. They first go into the Temple to pray; afterwards they circle seven times around a square tower inside the Temple [Ka'ba], at each circuit kissing a corner. From there they go to a well of salt water they call Birzenzen [Zamzam]... saying these words: "May all this be to the honor of God most merciful; may God pardon me of my sins." [He then notes bathing, and the ritual honoring of Abraham's sacrifice]... offering several sheep, which are slaughtered and sacrificed and distributed to the poor in the honor of God. After having accomplished all these ceremonies, they leave to go to Jerusalem which they call Cuzumobarech and they visit the sacred mount where was once the Temple of Solomon which they hold in great reverence. This is because they do not consider their pilgrimage good, or agreeable to God if after this they do not continue to the Promised Land. When they leave the temple of Solomon, each begins the path home or elsewhere, as it would seem. And so they go in troupes, carrying great banners with a crescent at the top through the cities and villages singing the praises of Mohammed and asking for charity in the name of God. And what is given to them they eat together sitting in the middle of the public square (199-201).

THE SACQUAZ WATER CARRIERS: PILGRIMS IN MECCA (Figs. 2-3)

They daily go through streets, squares, and assembly places in the cities, towns, and villages of the said provinces with a leather sack full of water from a well or fountain hanging as a sling at their side under a beautiful cloth embroidered all around with plants – or even with nothing. In one of their hands they carry a cup of fine Corinthian ware gilt and damascened, through which with great charity they present the cup and give drink to anyone who wishes it. But also to make the water even more beautiful and more delectable to drink, they put in the cup several and different stones of Chalcedony, Jasper, and Lapis Lazuli, and carry in the same hand a mirror that they show before the face of those to which they give drink and exhort them inciting them with dramatic words to think on death. For carrying out this pious office they demand no payment or recompense. But, if justifiably, one gives then a piece of money they accept most willingly (204).

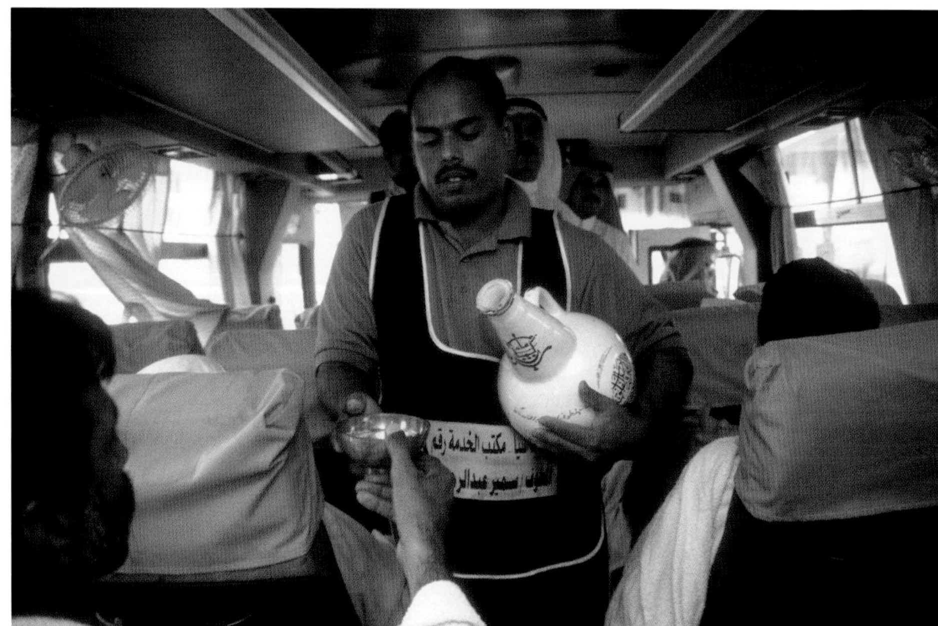

Fig. 3

On the ninety-five-minute bus ride from the airport to a hotel in Mecca, a pilgrim from Pakistan receives a bowl of Zamzam water from a distributor known as a zamzami, 2002

Photograph Samia El-Moslimany/*Saudi Aramco World*/ SAWDIA

Richard Burton: An Englishman at Mecca and Medina in 1853

Virginia C. Raguin

Richard Francis Burton (1821-1890) was a British explorer, translator, diplomat, and prolific author. He traveled widely in Asia and Africa and possessed a remarkable facility for languages. He may be best remembered for his unexpurgated translations of *The Kama Sutra* in 1883 and *A Thousand and One Nights* (also known as the *Arabian Nights*) in 1884. Employing his knowledge of Muslim practice from his eight-year residence in India, in 1853 he traveled in disguise as a Pashtun to Mecca and Medina, making the Hajj. In his recollections published in 1855, he devotes an entire chapter to the description of the "House of Allah" – the Ka'ba and its setting – and then follows with his own experience.

THE HARAM AND THE KA'BA

We entered by the Bab al-Ziyadah, or principal northern door, descended two long flights of steps, traversed the cloister, and stood in sight of the Bayt Allah.

.... There at last it lay, the bourn of my long and weary pilgrimage, realizing the plans and hopes of many and many a year; ... yet the view was strange, unique, and how few have looked upon the celebrated shrine! I may truly say that, of all the worshippers who clung weeping to the curtain, or who pressed their beating hearts to the stone, none felt for the moment a deeper emotion than did the Hajj from the far north. It was as if the poetical legends of the Arab spoke truth, and that the waving wings of angels, not the sweet breeze of morning, were agitating and swelling the black covering of the shrine. But, to confess humbling truth, theirs was the high feeling of religious enthusiasm, mine was the ecstasy of gratified pride.

Few Moslems contemplate for the first time the Kaabah, without fear and awe; .... Advancing, we entered through the Bab Benu Shaybah, the "Gate of the Sons of the Old Woman." There we raised our hands, repeated the Labbayk, the Takbir, and the Tahlil; after which we uttered certain supplications, and drew our hands down our faces. Then we proceeded to the Shafei's place of prayer – the open pavement between the Makam Ibrahim and the well Zem Zem – where we performed the usual two prostrations in honor of the mosque. This was followed by a cup of holy water and a present to the Sakkas, or carriers, who for the consideration distributed a large earthen vaseful in my name, to poor pilgrims (see essay *Nicolas de Nicolay: A French View of the Hajj in the 16th Century*). We then advanced toward the eastern angle of the Kaabah, in which is inserted the Black Stone, and standing about ten yards from it, repeated with upraised hands, "There is no god but Allah alone, Whose covenant is truth, and whose servant is victorious. There is no god but Allah, without sharer; his is the kingdom, to

Fig. 1
Mount Arafat during the Pilgrimage (Burton del.; Hanhart Lith.) 9 x 6 in. (22.9 x 15.2 cm)
Richard F. Burton. *Personal Narrative: Pilgrimage to Al-Madinah and Meccah. Vol. 3. Meccah*. London. Longman, Brown, Green and Longmans, 1856

him be praise, and he over all things is potent." After which we approached as close as we could to the stone. A crowd of pilgrims preventing our touching it that time, we raised our hands to our ears, in the first position of prayer, and then lowering them, exclaimed, "O Allah (I do this), in thy belief, and in verification of thy book, and in pursuance of thy Prophet's example – may Allah bless him and preserve! O Allah, I extend my hand to thee, and great is my desire to thee! O accept thou my supplication, and diminish my obstacles, and pity my humiliation, and graciously grant me thy pardon!" After which, as we were still unable to reach the stone, we raised our hands to our ears, the palms facing the stone, as if touching it, recited the various religious formulas, the Takbir, the Tahlil, and the Hamdilah, blessed the Prophet, and kissed the fingertips of the right hand.

Then commenced the ceremony of "Tawaf," or circumambulation.... I repeated after my Mutawwif or cicerone [Meccan guide], "In the name of Allah, and All is omnipotent! I purpose to circuit seven circuits unto almighty Allah, glorified and exalted!" [Burton then continues explaining the seven circuits, replete with different prayers as sections passed, kissing the stone, recollection prayers afterward, and exit.]

[The footnote adds] The Prophet used to weep when he touched the Black Stone, and said that it was the place for the pouring forth of tears. According to most authors, the second caliph also used to kiss it. For this reason most Moslems, except the Shafei school, must touch the stone with both hands and apply their lips to it, or touch it with the fingers, which should be kissed, or rub the palms upon it, and afterwards draw them down the face (199-213).

Fig. 2
Stoning the "Great Devil" at Mina (Burton del.; Hanhart Lith.) 9 x 6 in. (22.9 x 15.2 cm)
Richard F. Burton. *Personal Narrative: Pilgrimage to Al-Madinah and Meccah*. Vol. 3. *Meccah*. London. Longman, Brown, Green and Longmans, 1856

ARAFAT (Fig. 1)
Arafat is about six hours' march, or twelve miles, on the Taif road, due east of Meccah. We arrived there in a shorter time, but our weary camels, during the last third of the way, frequently threw themselves on the ground. Human beings suffered more. Between Muna [Mina] and Arafat I saw no less than five men fall down and die on the highway: exhausted and moribund, they had dragged themselves out to give up the ghost where it departs to instant beatitude. [The footnote adds: Those who die on a pilgrimage become martyrs.]....

Arafat, anciently called Jebel Ilal, the Mount of Wrestling in Prayer, and now Jebel el Rahmah, the "Mount of Mercy," is a mass of coarse granite split into large blocks, with a thin coat of withered thorns, about one mile in circumference and rising abruptly from the low gravelly plain.... Nothing can be more picturesque than the view it affords of the blue peaks behind, and the vast encampment scattered over the barren yellow plain below. On the north lay the regularly pitched camp of the guards that defend the unarmed pilgrims. To the eastward was the Sherif's encampment with the bright Mahmals [decorative litters for transport] and the gilt knobs of the grander pavilions; whilst on the southern and western sides, the tents of the vulgar crowd, the ground disposed in dowars, or circles, for penning cattle. After many calculations I estimate the number to be not less than 50,000 of all ages and sexes.

[The footnote adds] The Arabs have a superstition that the numbers at Arafat cannot be counted, and that if less than 60,000 mortals stand upon the hill to hear the sermon, the angels descend and complete the number. Even to this day my Arab friends declare that 150,000 spirits were present in human shape (252-59).

MINA (Fig. 2)

We were now to mount for "the throwing" – as a preliminary to which we washed "with seven waters" the seven pebbles brought from Muzdalifah and bound them in our Ihrams [pilgrim's clothes]. Our first destination was the entrance to the western end of the long line which composes the Muna village. We found a swarming crowd in the narrow road opposite the "jamrat el Akabah," or as it is vulgarly called, the Shaytan el Kabir – the "Great Devil." These names distinguish it from another pillar, the "Wusta," or the Muna, and a third at the eastern end, "El Yla," the "first place."

The Shaytan el Kabir is a dwarf buttress of rude masonry, about eight feet high by two and a half broad, placed against a rough wall of stones at the Meccan entrance to Muna. As the ceremony of "Ramy," or Lapidation, must be performed on the first day by all pilgrims between sunrise and sunset, and as the fiend was malicious enough to appear in the rugged pass, the crowd makes the place dangerous. On one side of the road which is not forty feet broad, stood a row of shops belonging principally to barbers. On the other side is the rugged wall of the pillar.... The narrow space was crowded with pilgrims all struggling like drowning men to approach as near as possible to the Devil; it would have been easy to run over the heads of the mass. Among them were horsemen with rearing chargers. Bedouins on wild camels, and grandees on mules and asses, with outrunners, were breaking the way by assault and battery....

We both sat down on a bench before a barber's booth, and schooled by adversity, waited with patience an opportunity. Finding an opening, we approached within about five cubits of the place, and holding each stone between the thumb and the forefinger of the right hand, cast it at the pillar, exclaiming, "In the name of Allah, and Allah is Almighty! (I do this) in hatred of the Fiend and to his shame." After which came the Tahlil and the "Sana" or praise to Allah. The seven stones being duly thrown, we retired, and entering a barber's booth, took our places upon one of the earthen benches around it. This was the time to remove the Ihram or pilgrim's garb, and to return to Ihlal, the normal state of El Islam. The barber shaved our heads, and, after trimming our beards and cutting our nails, made us repeat these words: "I purpose loosening my Ihram according to the practice of the Prophet, whom may Allah bless and preserve! Allah, make unto me every hair, a light, a purity, and a generous reward! In the name of Allah and Allah is Almighty!" (282-85).

Burton, Richard F. 1856. *Personal Narrative: Pilgrimage to Al-Madinah and Meccah*. Vol. 3. Meccah, London: Longman, Brown, Green and Longmans.

The Prophet's Tomb in Medina

Virginia C. Raguin

IBN BATTUTA (VISIT OF 1326)

On the third day they alight outside the sanctified city [of al-Madina] the holy and illustrious, Taiba, the city of the Apostle of God (God bless and give him peace, exalt and ennoble him!). On the morning of the same day after sunset we entered the holy sanctuary and reached at length the illustrious mosque. We halted at the gate of peace to pay our respects. And prayed at the noble Garden between the tomb [of the Apostle] and the noble palm-trunk that whimpered for the Apostle of God (God bless him and give him peace) which is now attached to the pillar standing between the tomb and the minbar, on the right as one faces the quibla. We paid the meed of salutation to the lord of men, first and last, the intercessor for sinners and transgressors, the apostle-prophet of the tribe if Hashim from the Vale of Mecca, Muhammed (God bless and give him peace, exalt, and ennoble him).

Gibb, Sir Hamilton, ed. 1958. *The Travels of Ibn Battuta*, vol. 1. [The Hakluyt Society] London: Cambridge University Press, 163-64.

ASHCHI DEDE (VISIT OF 1898)

With the chief guide in front and we behind, reciting the appropriate prayers, we approached the grille [surrounding the tomb] of the Prophet. There we prayed for a long while. Then, going a few paces farther, we likewise recited prayers before [the tomb of] Abu Bakr, may God be pleased with him. After that we went one or two steps farther and repeated special prayers before [the tomb of] Umar, may God be pleased with him. Going from there to the lower end of the Prophet's Garden, we prayed similarly where the angels of the Divine Presence stood. Then, at the foot, we paid our respects to our mother Fatima, may God be pleased with her. Then going a few steps farther, we recited prayers and the sura Ikhlas (Quran 112) [out] through the Door of Gabriel for the souls of the Companions of the Prophet, their wives and children buried in the perfumed earth of the Garden of Baqi'a, may God be pleased with all of them. After that, passing before the special platform for the Aghas of the Noble Sanctuary, facing toward Abbas, the uncle of the Prophet who is buried an hour away on Jabal Uhud, we again recited prayers and the Ikhlas. Then we again came before the presence of the Prophet, performed special prayers, withdrew one or two paces, faced the qibla, gave praise and thanks to God and rendered benedictions (Findley, 488-89).

[A few days later, Ashchi Dede had occasion to return to the tomb.]

On account of the approaching arrival of the Amin al-surra, they raised the inner curtains of the Prophet's tomb

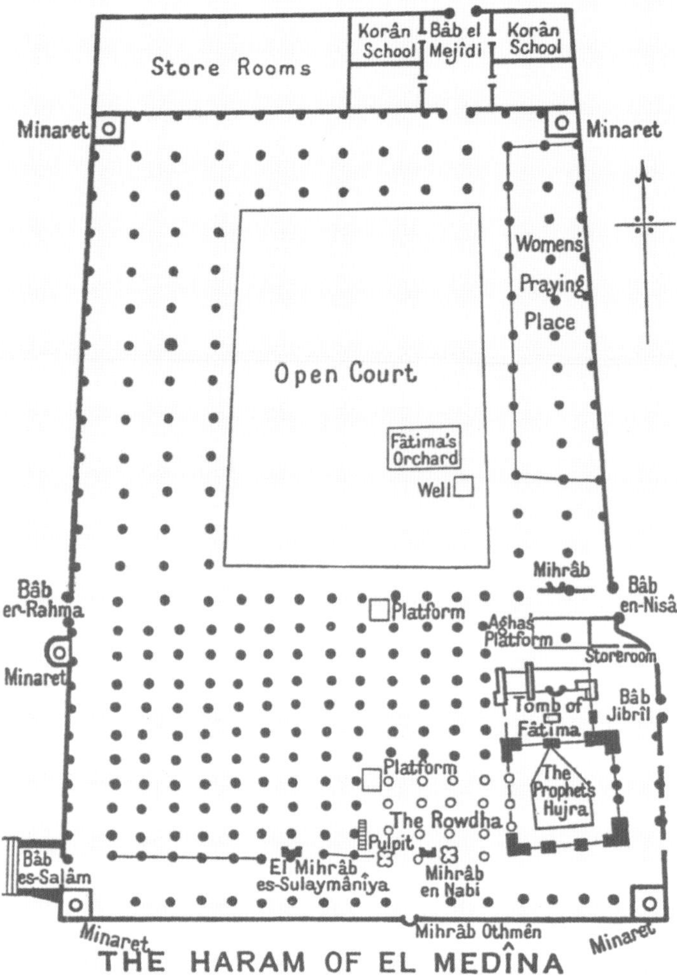

Fig. 1

Plan of the Haram of Medina

Eldon Rutter, *The Holy Cities of Arabia*, London, New York: G. P. Putnam's Sons, 1928.

Fig. 2

Illustration of the Prophet's Tomb at Medina from Majmu`ah (anthology) of Persian Texts

16th-17th centuries

Ottoman, Ottoman Empire 680-1342/1281-1924 CE

Opaque watercolor, ink and gold on paper, 9 x 6 in. (22.9 x 15.2 cm)

Harvard Art Museum, Arthur M. Sackler Museum, The Edwin Binney, 3rd Collection of Turkish Art at the Harvard Art Museum, 1985.265

Allan Macintyre © President and Fellows of Harvard College

Fig. 3
Medina Mosque, 1974
Photograph S. M. Amin/*Saudi Aramco World*/SAWDIA

Fig. 4
Medina; principle entrance to the mosque
Photograph Abdullah Y. Al-Dobais/*Saudi Aramco World*/SAWDIA

to sweep. Thus it became possible to observe the interior completely. Immediately summoning all my boldness and saying "If you please, O Messenger of God," I drew near to the grille. Kneeling down doglike [in humility], I looked upward through the window. The morning sun was just presenting its supplication through the tiny windows of the dome, the sides of the blessed tomb were veiled in satin, and the drapery was fastened with rings of iron to aloe-wood poles there. Thus there was an interval where the part above the poles, the upper part of the blessed tomb, could be seen. How that sacred place caught my eye! How it touched me! My soul attained the Beloved! My soul attained its Lord. My reason departed from my head and I arrived at the wilderness of possession. Giving way at my knees, I collapsed there like a lifeless dog. After a while, I recovered my wits, and my ardor quietened. Truly the spiritual light and the divine manifestations that I saw – praise be a hundred thousand times – remained imprinted on my poor heart (Findley, 491-92).

Findley, Carter Vaughn. 1989. "A Muslim's Pilgrim's Progress: Asci Dede Ibrahim Halil on the Hajj 1898." In C.E. Bosworth, et al. (eds.). *The Islamic World from Classical to Modern Times: Essays in Honor of Bernard Lewis*. Princeton: Darwin Press.

Peters, F.E. 1994. *The Hajj*. Princeton: Princeton University Press, 262-63

Fig. 5
Medina; interior of the mosque
Photograph Abdullah Y. Al-Dobais/*Saudi Aramco World*/SAWDIA

Fig. 6
Medina Mosque: facing tomb of the Prophet Mohammed
Photograph S. M. Amin/*Saudi Aramco World*/SAWDIA

Charity for Pilgrims on the Hajj and Elsewhere

Ibn Battuta visited Mecca in 1326 on what would then become a life of extended travel and exploration. Born in Tangier in 1303, he was raised in the family profession of the law and embarked alone to Mecca at the comparatively young age of twenty-two. After Mecca and Medina he traveled within Mesopotamia and Persia, and then returned to Mecca for a year. In 1347, after an extended stay in India and the Far East, he revisited Mecca as he made his way back to Fez, then the capital of Morocco, where he settled in 1353. Ibn Battuta was a practicing lawyer in Sunni courts, but he was apparently also attached to Sufi mysticism, recording moments when he visited Sufi mystics and shrines.

> *The departure from Mecca (God most high ennoble her). Included in this caravan were many water-carrying camels for the poorer pilgrims, who could obtain drinking water from them, and other camels to carry provisions [for issue] as alms and to carry medicine, potions, and sugar for those who should be attacked by illness. Whenever the caravan halted food was cooked in great brass cauldrons, called dasts, and supplied from them to the poorer pilgrims and those who had no provisions. With the caravan also was a number of [spare] camels for the carriage of those who were unable to walk. All of this is done to the benefactions and generosity of the Sultan Abu Said* (249-50).

> *The varieties of the endowments at Damascus and their expenditure are beyond computation, so numerous are they. There are endowments in aid of persons who cannot undertake the Pilgrimage [Hajj]; out of which are paid to those who go in their stead sums sufficient for their needs. There are endowments for supplying wedding outfits to girls, to those namely whose families are unable to provide them [with the customary paraphernalia]. There are endowments for the freeing of prisoners, and endowments for travelers, out of which they are given food, clothing, and the expenses of conveyance to their countries. There are endowments for the improving and paving of streets, because the lanes in Damascus all have a pavement on either side of which the foot passengers walk, while the riders use the roadway in between. Besides these there are endowments for other charitable purposes....*

> *The people of Damascus vie with one another in the building and endowment of mosques, religious houses, colleges, and sanctuaries.... Any who is a stranger there living on charity is always protected from [having to earn it at] the expense of his self-respect.* (148-50)

Gibb, Sir Hamilton, ed. 1958. *The Travels of Ibn Battuta*, vol. 1. [The Hakluyt Society] London: Cambridge University Press.

Hebron, a city south of Jerusalem, is visited by Jews and Christians as well as Muslims because of the reputed burial place of the Patriarchs Abraham and Jacob. Mujir al-Din is Jerusalem's chief Arab historian. Writing in 1496 CE, he describes the tombs of Abraham and his wife Sarah, and Jacob and his wife Lea. Those monuments were constructed, as he understands it, by the Umayyads, who reigned from 692-750 CE. The mosque adjacent is the center of a massive charity kitchen.

> *Outside the wall of Solomon, in the section that looks east is a mosque of extreme beauty. Between the wall of Solomon and the [Jawali Mosque] is a long vestibule with vaulted ceiling, adding to its magnificence an imposing majesty.... [The Mosque] was begun in the month of rabi in the year 718 (1318 CE) and finished in the month of the same name, in the year 720 (1320 CE), during the reign of El Malek en-Naser Muhammad, son of Qelaoun [El Malek en-Naser Mohammed was a remarkable leader who three times made the Hajj].*
>
> *At the southern side of the Jawali Mosque is the kitchen where they prepare the jashisha [a plate of ground and boiled wheat] for those who are on retreat and for travelers. At the door of the kitchen every day after the 'Asr or afternoon prayer the ceremonial drums [Tabl-Khânâh] are sounded to signal the distribution of the meal. This meal is one of the marvels of the world. Both the residents of the town and visitors take part. It consists of bread that is made [fresh] each day and given out on three occasions daily: in the morning and at midday the distribution is for the local residents; after the afternoon prayer the distribution is for both the residents and travelers. The daily quantity of bread distributed reaches to about 14,000 or even sometimes 15,000 small loaves. The endowments set up for this purpose have an almost incalculable income, and no one, rich or poor, is excluded from the meal.*
>
> *The origin of the custom of beating of the Tabl-Khânâh each day after the 'Asr, at the time of the distribution of the meal, goes back to our father Abraham. As the guests who had come to him were dispersed into lodgings, he beat a drum so that they would know that the food was ready...*
>
> *At the entry of the mosque [of the Patriarchs], where they sound the drums, are the buildings where the meal is prepared. They consist of ovens and mills. It is a large complex which encloses three ovens and six mills to grind the grain. Below are the granaries where the wheat and barley are stored. Looking at this place, whether above or below, one is seized with admiration: the wheat that goes in comes out only as bread. As for the eagerness displayed in the preparation of the meal by the great number of people occupied in grinding the grain, kneading the dough, turning it into bread, getting the wood for the fires and other paraphernalia, as well as making all the other necessary preparations, this too is another marvel almost without parallel among the powerful sovereigns of the earth, and yet one of the least miracles of this noble Prophet.*

Mujir al-Din, 1876. *Histoire de Jérusalem et d'Hébron depuis Abraham jusqu'à la fin du XVe siècle de J.-C.: Fragments de la Chronique de Moudjir-ed-dyn*. Henry Sauvaire, trans. Paris: Leroux, 19-20.

Peters, F.E. 1985. *Jerusalem: The Holy City in the Eyes of Chroniclers, Visitors, Pilgrims, and Prophets*. Princeton: Princeton University Press, 386.

The German Dominican friar Felix Fabri visited Hebron close to the same date, 1480 CE. He explains that this was a place where Abraham lived and built a sepulcher for himself and his children. The westerner spends considerable time praising the Islamic charity work.

> *The Jews built an oratory over the rock of the cave, and afterwards the Christians destroyed the oratory of the Jews and built a great church above it, wherein they appointed a bishop and canons. After the loss of the Holy Land, the Saracens made a mosque of the church, and have fenced it with lofty walls and towers, and at this day it stands in the midst of the city like a strong castle.... There are many priests in this mosque, both Soquis [Sufis] and Alhages [Al-Hajjis], so that no hour passes either by day or by night without there being singing beside the double cave, for they relieve one another by turns....*
>
> *After we had viewed the mosque and the double cave, we went down a little way and came to the door of the hospice for poor people, which is below the mosque. We were let in and saw its fine offices, and in the kitchen and bakery great preparations were being made for Saracen pilgrims, of whom a great number come every day to visit the double cave, the sepulcher of the Patriarchs. This hospital has annual revenues amounting to more than 24,000 ducats. Every day twelve hundred loaves of bread are baked in its ovens and are given to those who ask for them; neither is charity refused to any pilgrim, of whatever nation, faith, or sect he may be. He who asks for food receives a loaf of bread, some oil, and some thick soup which we call pudding.... Rich Saracens and Turks daily send alms thither for the support of pilgrims and to show honor to the Patriarchs; also rich people, when they are about to die, set up perpetual memorials of themselves at this place, and leave legacies to the hospice. At the hour when the dole is served out, they make a terrible noise with a drum.... In the serving out of the loaves of bread, they sent a basketful to our inn for our use, albeit we had never asked them for anything.*

Fabri, Felix. 1971. *The Book of the Wanderings of Felix Fabri*. Aubrey Stewart, trans. vols. 9-10. Palestine Pilgrims Text Society 1887-97; Reprint. New York: AMS Press, 416-18.

Peters, *Jerusalem*, 496-97.

Details of Fig. 8

Muslim Visits to Jerusalem and the Dome of the Rock

F. E. Peters and Virginia C. Raguin

The Dome of the Rock that sits atop the Haram al-Sharif (the Noble Sanctuary) is one of the great mysteries of Islam (Figs. 1-2). The Haram – that is the precinct defined by the platform of roughly the same size, if perhaps not height – was erected by King Herod for the site of the Jewish Temple. After destruction under the Romans, and neglect under the Christians, the area was again invested with special meaning with the Muslim conquest of Jerusalem. The building is not a mosque but a shrine, a very large and elaborate shrine. Indeed the Haram contains the Aqsa mosque on its periphery, in a juxtaposition that clearly speaks to the other purpose of the building in the center (Figs. 3-5).

Fig. 1

View of Jerusalem from Mount of Olives showing the Haram al Sharif (Noble Sanctuary), with the Al Aqsa mosque and the Dome of the Rock.

David Roberts, *The Holy Land: Syria, Idumea, Arabia, Egypt and Nubia. From* Drawings made on the Spot by David Roberts, with Historical Descriptions by the Rev George Croly, Lithographed by Louis Hage. London, F. G. Moon, 1842-1849.

Fig. 2

Dome of the Rock, Jerusalem

691-92; exterior reclad in glazed tile by Suleyman the Magnificent, 1546

Ermete Pierotti, *Jerusalem Explored: Being a Description of the Ancient and Modern City*, Thomas G. Bonney, trans. London: Bell and Daldy, 1864, pl. XXVI

15½ x 11 in. (39.4 x 27.9 cm)

Fig. 3
El-Aqsa Mosque, Al-Haram al-Sharif, Jerusalem
Rebuilt 1034-36
View from southwest
Ermete Pierotti, *Jerusalem Explored: Being a Description of the Ancient and Modern City*, Thomas G. Bonney, trans. London: Bell and Daldy, 1864, pl. XXI
15½ x 11 in. (39.4 x 27.9 cm)

Fig. 4
El-Aqsa Mosque, Al-Haram al-Sharif, Jerusalem
Rebuilt 1034-36
View from southwest
Photograph David Shankbone

Fig. 5
Façade El-Aqsa Mosque, Al-Haram al-Sharif, Jerusalem
12th century
Ermete Pierotti, *Jerusalem Explored: Being a Description of the Ancient and Modern City*, Thomas G. Bonney, trans. London: Bell and Daldy, 1864, pl. XIII
15½ x 11 in. (39.4 x 27.9 cm)

Nasir-I Khusraw was a Persian who traveled in his early years through northern India (visiting Jerusalem in 1047 CE). The position of the mosque is explained while Islamic control still extends over the Holy Land.

> *The mosque lies at the (south) east quarter of the city, whereby the eastern wall forms also the walls of the mosque (court). When you have passed out of the mosque, there lies before you a great level plain, called the Sahirah, which, it is said, will be the place of the Resurrection, where all mankind shall be gathered together. For this reason men from all parts of the world come hither to make their sojourn in the Holy City till death overtakes them, in order that when the day fixed by God – be he praised and exalted! – shall arrive they may thus be ready and present at the appointed place (24-25).*
>
> *The Friday mosque (which is the Aksa) lies on the east side of the city, and (as before noticed) one of the walls of the mosque (Area) is on the Wadi Janannum. When you examine the wall, which is on the Wadi, from the outside of the mosque, you may see that for the space of a hundred cubits it is built up of huge stones, set without mortar or cement. Inside the mosque (Area) it is level all along the summit of the wall. The Aksa mosque occupies the position it does because of the stone of the Sakhrah. This stone of the Sakhrah is that which God – be he exalted and glorified! – commanded Moses to be instituted as the Kiblah (or direction to be faced at prayer). After this command had come down, he himself lived but a brief time, for of a sudden his life was cut short. Then came the days of Solomon – upon him be peace! – who seeing that the rock (of the Sakhrah) was the Kiblah point, built a mosque round the rock, whereby the rock stood in the middle of the mosque, which became the oratory of the people. So it remained down to the days of our Prophet Muhammed, the Chosen One – upon him be blessings and peace! – who likewise first recognized this to be the Kiblah, turning toward it at his prayers; but God – be he exalted and glorified – afterward commanded him to institute as the Kiblah, the House of the Ka'abah (at Mekkah) (26-27).*

Nasir-I-Khusrau. 1971. *A Journey through Syria and Palestine*. Guy Le Strange, trans. Palestine Pilgrims Text Society, London, 1895; Reprint New York: AMS Press, vol. 4.

Unlike almost all of the other Muslim *qubbas*, or domed shrines, that we know of, the Dome of the Rock does not enshrine the remains of a saint but rather enshrines a rock, an otherwise unremarkable outcropping on the surface of the Temple Mount. It may very well have been somehow connected with the Jewish Temple there, or perhaps with the stone of Abraham's sacrifice, but why it was built remains a mystery.[1] One theory put forward by the Muslim sources and adopted by some Western historians is that the Caliph Abd al-Malik, who completed the building in 692 CE, had it in mind to divert the Hajj from Mecca, which was then in rebellion against his authority, to Jerusalem.[2] This is possible, though not very convincing, but it did not, in any event, succeed. Though there was a certain amount of friendly jostling for the primacy of holiness among Mecca, Medina, and Jerusalem,[3] it was chiefly a rhetorical exercise, and there is no evidence that any substantial numbers of Muslims took the issue of primacy seriously enough to act upon it: Mecca was and is the premier holy place in Islam and the only one in which pilgrims could fulfill a pilgrimage obligation.

MUSLIMS IN JERUSALEM

All of that is not to say that Muslims did not visit Jerusalem. It is simply that we do not know a great deal about them, as least as compared with others visiting the city. Jews and Christians have left detailed personal accounts of their spiritual journeys to Jerusalem, as Muslims have of their Hajj to Mecca. But for Muslim accounts of Jerusalem we have to turn primarily to geographers, historians, and, most notably for our purpose, travelers. For most of its history Islam has been a society in motion. Countless men and women set out on the road for either of two peculiarly Muslim motives: the search for knowledge, or the religious obligation to make the pilgrimage to Mecca. The generic name of the literary genre describing this activity is "The Book of Travel" or, more simply, "The Journey" *(rihla)*. This name originally described the roving search for religious knowledge. This generally took the form of visits to persons who had reports *(hadîth)* going back to the prophet Muhammad or his contemporaries. In time this type of knowledge was chiefly found institutionalized in the teaching chairs of the law schools that covered the face of the Islamic world from the 11th century onward.[4] At that point *rihla* had come to mean a description of a visit to places, famous law schools for example, often in Ibn Battuta, and eventually the term broadened out to include descriptions of all forms of travel, with the more specific *rihla hijaziyya*, a "Hajj Journey," reserved for a description of a trip to Mecca,[5] an enterprise that in the 14th century might take a couple of years, in the 19th a couple of weeks, and now a matter of days.

Many of those travelers at least passed by Jerusalem, as we shall see, en route to other places, but Jerusalem as such has also exercised its own attraction to Muslims, not on such a broad scale as the Meccan Hajj, certainly, but strongly enough to catch the attention of at least some reporters. Nasir-i Khusraw, for example, who was in the city in 1047, reported that thousands of people from all the ends of the earth went to Jerusalem, chiefly to be buried there. There is no surprise in that, given the eschatological associations connected with Jerusalem in all three faiths. What *is* surprising is his further information that people who were unable to make the Hajj performed the "standing" of Arafat and the sacrifice of Mina on the Haram al-Sharif, and at least one author condemned as

Fig. 6
Qanatir (arches) to southwest of the Haram al-Sharif, Jerusalem
Photograph Mark A. Wilson

Fig. 7
Bab Hitta, the gate on the northern edge of the Haram al-Sharif, Jerusalem
C. W. Wilson, ed. *Picturesque Palestine, Sinai and Egypt*, vol.1. New York: D. Appleton and Company, 1881, 21.
11½ x 9 in. (29.2 x 22.9 cm)

"innovation" the notion that four such annual celebrations was the equivalent to an actual Meccan Hajj.[6]

There are, however, few if any formal accounts of Muslim visits to Jerusalem as such. Many if not most Muslim visitors to Jerusalem in premodern times considered the journey a leg on their more explicit Hajj to Mecca, much as Jerusalem-bound Christians made side visits to Sinai or Damascus. But not all routes to Mecca pass by Jerusalem. Hajjis en route from Cairo, Baghdad, or Yemen, three of the great marshalling points for the Meccan caravans, bypassed Jerusalem by a wide margin, and it was only the Damascus caravan that occasionally permitted the pilgrims a side voyage to Jerusalem.[7] None of these stops are very well documented.

A JERUSALEM LITURGY?

Did the Muslims perform any liturgy at Jerusalem? None is prescribed by Islamic law, which does not much care about *ziyaras*. In fact, Muslim law, like Jewish law, has little sympathy for visits to tombs. But it appears, as Amikam Elad has demonstrated, that there was a kind of liturgy atop the *Haram al-Sharif*, and that it was, in the manner of the earliest Christian liturgies in Jerusalem, and the later Way of the Cross, stational; that is, the visitor proceeded from one holy place to another in a set order. One such stational liturgy, described in *The Merits of Jerusalem and Syria and Hebron* by the 11th-century author Ibn al-Murajja, begins within the Dome of the Rock, circles around the smaller domed shrines atop the Haram, then visits the gates of the Haram enclosure, goes to the Mount of Olives, and ends at David's oratory on the western side of the city[8] (Figs. 6-7).

And since such liturgies were informal, they were also prone to abuse. The chief evidence for these comes from a purist, al-Qashashi (d. 1660), who disapproved of almost everything he saw there. He noted that on "The Days of the Pilgrims," probably the days when the Mecca-bound Hajjis were in the city, there is a festival in the Haram al-Sharif, accompanied by a great deal of buying and selling and the most shameless mingling of sexes. More interestingly, at the occasion of the "Standing at Arafat" on the ninth of Dhu al-Hijja, there was a parallel ceremony in which a sermon was delivered from atop the Dome of the Rock, as if that itself were Mount Arafat. Qashashi was appalled.[9] There is doubtless more along this line, but it remains to be uncovered and studied.

THE BUILDING

The beauty of the building has transfixed viewers throughout history (Figs. 8-9). Indeed, in an oft-quoted text of 985 CE, the Muslim geographer Muhammad Ibn Ahmad al-Muqaddasi attests to its possible genesis as a response to the attractions of the great Christian buildings in Jerusalem.

> *Now one day I said, speaking to my father's brother, "O my uncle, truly it was not well of Caliph al-Walid to spend so much of the wealth of the Muslims on the mosque at Damascus. Had he expended the same on making roads or for caravanserais or in the restoration of fortresses, it would have been more fitting and more excellent of him." But my uncle said to me in answer, "O my little son, you have not understanding! Truly al-Walid was right and he was prompted to do a worthy work. For He beheld Syria to be a country that had long been occupied by the Christians, and he noted herein the beautiful churches still belonging to them, so enchantingly fair and so renowned for their splendor; even as are the Kumâmah [Holy Sepulcher] and the churches of Lydda and Edessa. So he sought to build for the Muslims a mosque that should prevent their admiring these and should be unique and a wonder to the world. And in like manner, is it not evident how Caliph Abd al-Malik, noting the greatness of the Dome of the Kumâmah and its magnificence, was moved lest it should dazzle the minds of Muslims and so erected, above the Rock, the Dome which is now seen there?*[10]

Later in his text he would continue to cite competition with previous buildings, noting that the Al Aqsa Mosque "is even more beautiful than that of Damascus for during the

Fig. 8
Dome of the Rock, Jerusalem
691-92; exterior reclad in glazed tile by Suleyman the Magnificent, 1546
Photograph Bill Lyons/*Saudi Aramco World*/SAWDIA

Fig. 9
Dome of the Rock with al-Aqsa Mosque, at twilight
Photograph David H. Wells/*Saudi Aramco World*/SAWDIA

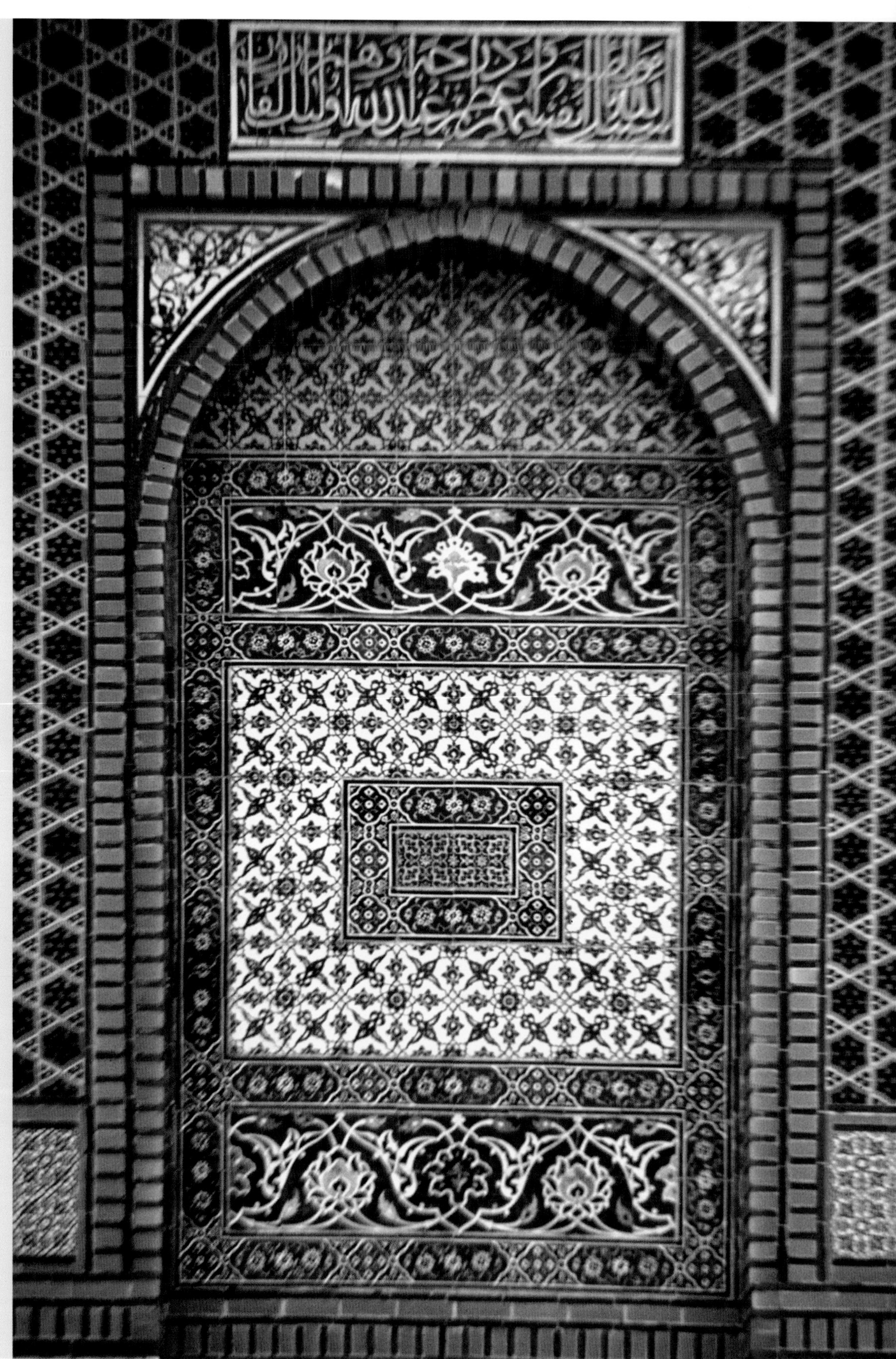

Fig. 10
Dome of the Rock, exterior
Detail of tiled arch – Suleyman the Magnificent, 1546
Photograph William Tracy/*Saudi Aramco World*/
SAWDIA

Fig. 11
Dome of the Rock, interior
691-92
Photograph David H. Wells/*Saudi Aramco World*/SAWDIA

building of it they had for a rival and as a comparison, the great church [Holy Sepulchre] belonging to the Christians at Jerusalem."[11]

As observed by Oleg Grabar, the Dome of the Rock is one of the most remarkable works of Islamic architecture, designed as "a *ciborium*, or reliquary above a sacred place on a model which was fairly common among Christian *martyria* throughout the Christian empire."[12] He suggests that its planning was long range, beginning even with Mu'awiyah (602-680), the founder of the great Umayyad Dynasty. It sits on the site of the Temple of Solomon as one of Abd al Malik's first major constructions in the newly conquered city. The building is an octagon, surrounding a high, cylindrical dome. Four porches supported on slender columns mark the four identical entrances into the shrine. Its form can be associated with churches such as the 4th-century Holy Sepulcher in Jerusalem and the 6th-century octagonal San Vitale in Ravenna, Italy. Lavish decorations included sheathing on the interior and exterior of mosaics and marble plaques. In the 16th century the great builder Suleyman the Magnificent reworked the exterior into its present array of dazzlingly intricate geometric and stylized floral motifs (Fig. 10). The interior, however, is well preserved and demonstrates the context of Mediterranean cultural exchanges of the 7th century. Reflecting traditions of style and technique from Late Antique and Early Christian art, the mosaics of the interior are almost certainly the product of Christian artists from Constantinople (Fig. 11).

However enigmatic the textual references have proven to the definition of a precise function as a shrine, its form and decoration suggest a layering of multivalent meanings. First, the site was intimately associated with the central place of Jewish worship. Whatever the original beliefs connected to the 10th-century BCE Temple of Solomon, or Herod's reconstruction in 19 BCE, by the early medieval period, Jewish tradition associated the rock with the Temple's Holy of Holies and the place of Abraham's sacrifice of Isaac. To the conquerors in the 7th century CE, Jerusalem as a whole embodied the power of Christian rulers, especially the Byzantine Empire, even if the sacred locus had been shifted from the Temple Mount to the martyrium of the

Holy Sepulcher. Grabar suggests that the significance of the Haram is associated with the desire of Caliph Umar to revive the importance of Jerusalem.[13] After all, Jerusalem had been the original Muslim qiblah, the place toward which Muslim's turned to pray. It was only in 623 CE, a year and a half after Muhammad's arrival in Medina, that the focus turned to Mecca.

The Umayyad inscriptions within the shrine further suggest the builders' awareness of the importance of the temple and the city. A long series of quotations from the Quran appear above the arches of the inner octagon. The first inscription praises God, the second praises the prophet, and then follow references to God's unity and independence. Most pointed is the inscription (4:169-71) that explicitly addresses the nature of Jesus as a prophet and calls to Christians to turn from the erroneous belief that God is a Trinity of persons:

> *People of the Book, go beyond the bounds of your religion, and say not as to God but the truth. The Messiah, Jesus son of Mary, was only the Messenger of God, and His Word that he transmitted to Mary, and a Spirit from Him. So believe in God and His Messengers, and say not "Three." Refrain; better is it for you. God is only one God. Glory to Him – that He should have a son! To Him belongs all that is in the heavens and the earth; God suffices for a guardian. The Messiah will not distain to be a servant of God. Neither the angels who are near stationed to Him. Who distains to serve Him, and waxes proud, He will assuredly muster them to Him, all of them.*[14]

Further inscriptions repeat that Jesus is the son of Mary, clearly exhorting Christians to come to the true faith as revealed through Muhammad, God's final prophet.

Given the history of the city as a crossroads of competing cultures, the compelling beauty of the building itself, enhanced by its placement, gleaming in marble against the brick and stone of Jerusalem, ineluctably drew associations. By time of the historian Al-Ya'qubi (d. 897), Muslims associated the rock with Muhammad's Night Journey *(isra)* and Ascension *(mi'raj)*. The iconic place now

Fig. 12
St. Stephen Walbrook, London, Interior showing dome
Christopher Wren, 1672
Photograph Michel Raguin

held by the Dome of the Rock in world culture is revealed in the rehabilitation of London's St. Stephen Walbrook (Fig. 12) after the bombing of World War II. Built in 1672 by Christopher Wren, it was the prototype for St. Paul's cathedral, and the first classically inspired dome to be erected in London in the Early Modern era. When faced with the need for repair, the congregation looked to a modern restatement of it mission. A centrally located altar was commissioned from the prominent sculptor Henry Moore, who produced an altar of travertine marble from quarries used by Michelangelo. The axis of the church is now located under the dome, and thus open to all sides. In placing the great stone in the center, the congregation was aware that it was evoking the Dome of the Rock (Fig. 13). The gesture was meant to recall the Abrahamic tradition and the patriarch's willingness to sacrifice Isaac as prefiguring of the sacrifice of Christ. The resultant space is mystical in its simplicity; the white mass of the altar reflects the pale hue of the columns. The rounded arched windows let in light that enhances the sculpted forms of both altar and dome.

Fig. 13
St. Stephen Walbrook, London, Interior
Altar of travertine marble by Henry Moore, 1987
Photograph Michel Raguin

1 Elad, Amikam. 1992. "Why Did Abd al-Malik Build the Dome of the Rock? A Re-Examination of the Muslim Sources." In *Bayt al-Maqdis. Abd al-Malik's Jerusalem*. Part One. Julian Raby and Jeremy Johns, eds. Oxford, New York: Oxford University Press, 33-58.

2 The pertinent texts are cited in Peters, F.E. 1994. *The Hajj*. Princeton: Princeton University Press, 197-99, 601, nn. 21-22; and Grabar, Oleg. 2005. "The Umayyad Dome of the Rock." In *Jerusalem*. Oleg Grabar, ed. Ashgate Variorum, 1-19.

3 Peters, *The Hajj*, 336-40.

4 Gellens, Sam. 1990. "The Search for Knowledge in Medieval Muslim Societies: a Comparative Approach." In *Muslim Travellers: Pilgrimage, Migration and the Religious Imagination*. Dale Eickelman and James Piscatori, eds. Berkeley: University of California Press, 53.

5 El Moudden, Abdurrahmane. DATE. "The Ambivalence of *rihla*: Community Integration and Self-Definition in Moroccan Travel Accounts, 1300-1800." In *Muslim Travellers*, 70, 73.

6 Abdel Aziz Duri. 1995. "Bait al-Maqdis in Islam." In *Studies in the History and Archaeology of Jordan*. Vol. I. Adnan Hadidi, ed. Amman: Department of Antiquities, Hashemite Kingdom of Jordan, 354. Duri cites similar reports from both earlier and later times. See for example Elad, Amikam. 1995. *Medieval Jerusalem and Islamic Worship: Holy Places, Ceremonies and Pilgrimages*. Leiden, New York: E.J. Brill, 51-77.

7 The main caravan route from Damascus to Medina passed well east of Jerusalem, through Ayn Zarqa, Balqa, and Qatrana in the Transjordan.

8 Elad, Amikam. 1995. *Medieval Jerusalem and Islamic Worship: Holy Places, Ceremonies and Pilgrimages*. Leiden, New York: E.J. Brill, 68-78; Peters, F.E. 1985. *Jerusalem: The Holy City in the Eyes of Chroniclers, Visitors, Pilgrims, and Prophets*. Princeton: Princeton University Press, 374-75.

9 Peters, *Jerusalem*, 496-97.

10 Ibid., 198; Le Strange, Guy, trans. 1971. *Al-Muqaddasi. Description of Syria, including Palestine*. Palestine Pilgrims Text Society Reprint vol. 3.: New York: AMS Press, 22-23.

11 Ibid., 41.

12 Grabar, "Umayyad Dome of the Rock," 20.

13 Ibid., 12.

14 *The Koran Interpreted, a Translation by A. J. Arberry*. New York: Simon & Schuster.

Seeing Jerusalem from afar for an Arab Traveler

Virgina C. Raguin

Fig. 1

Muhammad's Ascent to Heaven (Painting, Verso; Text, Recto), Folio from a Manuscript of the Khamsa (Layla and Majnun) by Nizami

The winged steed Buraq brings Mohammed from Mecca to Jerusalem where he prays with others, then remounts Buraq to ascend to the heavens where injunctions concerning the Muslim faith are revealed.

Early 16th century, Persian Safavid

Ink, opaque watercolor and gold on paper, 15 13/16 x 10 7/16 in. (40.2 x 26.5 cm)

Harvard Art Museum, Arthur M. Sackler Museum, The Norma Jean Calderwood Collection of Islamic Art, 2002.50.3

Photograph Katya Kallsen © President and Fellows of Harvard College

Mujir al-Din (1456-1522 CE) is widely accepted as the most reliable and comprehensive source on Jerusalem during the era when Muslims exercised full control of the site. He stressed its religious significance for Muslims as heirs of the monotheistic tradition and described its shrines and topography. His works makes it clear that the burial places of Joseph, Abraham, Isaac, Jacob, and their wives were revered in Muslim tradition. He responds to the sight of the al-Aqsa mosque (literally, the "Farthest Mosque"). Muslim tradition accepts the raised area where now is found the al-Aqsa mosque and the Dome of the Rock as the site of Muhammad's Night Journey: Quran: 17:1: Glory to (Allah) Who did take His servant for a Journey by night from the Sacred Mosque to the farthest Mosque, whose precincts We did bless, in order that We might show Him some of Our Signs: for He is the One Who heareth and seeth (all things) [Yusufali]. Commemoration of the Night Journey, celebrated as the *Lailat al Miraj*, is particularly meaningful for families and children and one of the most important events in the Islamic calendar. A 16th-century Persian painting (Fig. 1) shows Muhammad, Buraq, and Gabriel – to the left, acting as guide – soaring through a sky of deep and brilliant blue, lit by golden flames, and accompanied by winged heavenly beings.

MUJIR AL-DIN PRAISES JERUSALEM (Fig. 2)

The constructions of Jerusalem are of an extreme solidity, all of the districts are of cut stone and vaulted; not a single brick is used in the edifices, nor a piece of wood in the roofs. Voyagers affirm that there is not a city in the empire with constructions more firmly built or possessing so agreeable an allure as Jerusalem. It is the same with Hebron. Nonetheless, the constructions of the holy city have even greater strength and solidity; those of Naplous come close. The solidity of the buildings in these three cities is due to the fact that they are located in mountainous areas where stone is abundant and its extraction easy.

As for the view of Jerusalem from afar, filled with brilliance and beauty, it is a great, celebrated wonder. The most attractive view is that which one enjoys from the eastern side, from the Mount of Olives. It is likewise from the south. But from the west and the north you can see only a small part of the city because of the mountains that conceal it. The cities of Jerusalem and Hebron are in effect situated on steep and rocky mountains where the traveler advances with difficulty on a circuitous path. The mountains that surround these two cities extend for nearly three days' march, calculating with a pack animal, in width and breadth. Nonetheless, when God grants the pilgrim the favor of arriving at the solemn al-Aqsa shrine and the prayer station venerated by Abraham, he experiences an indescribable feeling of joy and well-being and forgets the pains and troubles he has endured. The poet Ibn Hujr improvised the following verses to precisely that point when he came on pilgrimage to Jerusalem:

"We came to Jerusalem with the hope of gaining pardon of our sins from a generous Master. For love of Him we have passed through Hell, but after Hell, there is nothing but Paradise."

Mujir al-Din,1876. *Histoire de Jérusalem et d'Hebron*. Fragments of the Chronicle of Mujir al-Din translated from the Arabic by Henri Sauvaire. Paris: Ernest Laroux, 183-84.

Peters, F. E. 1985. *Jerusalem: The Holy City in the Eyes of Chroniclers, Visitors, Pilgrims, and Prophets*. Princeton: Princeton University Press, 390.

Fig. 2
View of Jerusalem from the south showing the Haram al Sharif (Noble Sanctuary), with the Al Aqsa mosque and the Dome of the Rock.
David Roberts, *The Holy Land: Syria, Idumea, Arabia, Egypt and Nubia. From Drawings made on the Spot by David Roberts*, with Historical Descriptions by the Rev George Croly, Lithographed by Louis Hage. London, F. G. Moon, 1842-1849.

Details of Fig. 3

Observations on Pilgrimage and Art in the Islamic World

Oleg Grabar

Anyone working on or practicing Christianity (at least in its non-Protestant forms) or Buddhism is constantly surrounded by architectural monuments and objects – high works of art or products of popular artisanship – that reflect or depict liturgical or simply pietistic aspects of pilgrimages or visits, compulsory or not, to holy places, in order meet ritual obligations, enhance one's spiritual purity, or satisfy some personal need.

In theory at least, the same results can be assumed for the world of Islamic culture. A pilgrimage to Mecca, the Hajj, has a precisely orchestrated ritual attached to it. That ritual was established over many centuries, and resembled its present form by the 11th century. It involves a number of visually arresting features. These include the white ritual clothing (see essay *The Hajj Today – Connecting the Global Village*, Fig. 6) that is so different from everyday wear, and that illustrates the equality of all men and women in front of God; a huge textile, the kiswa, which covers the building and is replaced every year, today with black with gold writing (see essay *The Kiswa: The Curtain of the Ka'ba*, Figs. 1-4) but probably polychrome in earlier times; and the *mahmal*, a richly decorated and usually empty palanquin ceremonially carried to Mecca on a white camel and then brought back to Cairo, Istanbul, or Damascus, at least until 1952, when that ceremonial trip was abandoned largely for practical reasons, as camel caravans were no longer used to travel throughout Arabia.

I shall return to other features associated with the Hajj, but it is important to add that, beginning in the Middle Ages, pilgrimages developed at many other levels than the canonical yearly event in western Arabia. There were other pan-Islamic sites such as Medina, also in Arabia (see essay *The Prophet's Tomb at Medina*, Figs. 1-6), where the Prophet was buried and where, for a while at least, knowledge flourished about sacred things; and Jerusalem and Palestine, with a host of memorable places to visit and, at least in certain times, a proper atmosphere for learning and meditation. There were restricted Shi'ite sites in Iraq, Iran, and India that were sought by sectarian believers from all parts of the world. New sites are even being created today, like the sanctuaries commemorating several female descendants of Ali, which were built during the past decade in Damascus for Iranian pilgrims. These sanctuaries copy Iranian architectural and decorative forms in a profoundly non-Iranian setting. Pilgrims also came to the holy places built around the tombs of holy men in Egypt, Anatolia, Iran, Central Asia, and India, especially founders of mystical *sufi* sects or of religious societies and helpers in meeting the perils of life. And, finally, from West Africa to China or Malaysia, the Muslim world

Fig. 1
The Khoda khana (House of God), 1351, in the Friday Mosque of Shiraz, Iran.
Photograph Archnet

is covered with tombs of local saints. Their names are often forgotten but, for limited moments of time, the health and well-being of the population of surrounding villages depended on the intercession of these saints. Occasionally they are revived before falling again into oblivion. There is something at the same time moving and frightening about seeing the blood of secretly sacrificed animals on the fallen stones of a ruined mausoleum in a deserted area.

Sociologists and anthropologists have made maps of some areas with sanctuaries and have occasionally analyzed their impact on society, especially in the Shi'ite world. But can one define or identify an artistic production associated with these sanctuaries? Did they inspire unique works of art or artisanal sponsorship of buildings and objects?

No definitive answers can be given to these questions. But it is possible to outline three areas in which pilgrimage has affected the arts. These are the making of copies, the manufacture and distribution of souvenirs, and the more complex phenomenon of contributions to a common visual language. The remarks that follow are preliminary observations on each one of these activities, which must remain hypothetical and tentative in the absence of adequate research.

Literal copies of places of Muslim pilgrimage are rare, in contrast to those of Christianity or in Buddhism. The Ka'ba in Mecca remains a unique monument. The exceptions to this statement have local explanations which have usually not been uncovered. Thus, the courtyard of the *masjid-i atiq* ("the old mosque") in Shiraz in southern Iran contains a unique cubic monument comparable to the Ka'ba in Mecca. It is known as the *Khuda Khane*, "the House of God," or the *bayt al-mushab*, "House of the leaves (of the scripture)," and it is dated to 1351 (Fig. 1).The mode of construction of this building is unusual for southern Iran, and its function or symbolic meaning is unclear, although it is likely to have been erected to house precious manuscripts of the Quran. From a technical point of view it may be connected to a very original mode of construction found in Anatolia in the 14th century, and its location in the mosque fits it into the series of very original buildings erected at times in the courtyards of mosques all over the Islamic world.[1] I am also aware of a contemporary mosque in Dhakka, the capital of Bangladesh, which has the shape of the Ka'ba for reasons that are not known to me (Fig. 2). There may be other instances of this sort, especially at the remote frontiers of the Islamic world, where there was a psychological need to reinforce the awareness of the basic shapes of Muslim faith. On the whole, however, the Ka'ba remained unique in form and in the rituals which accompany it.

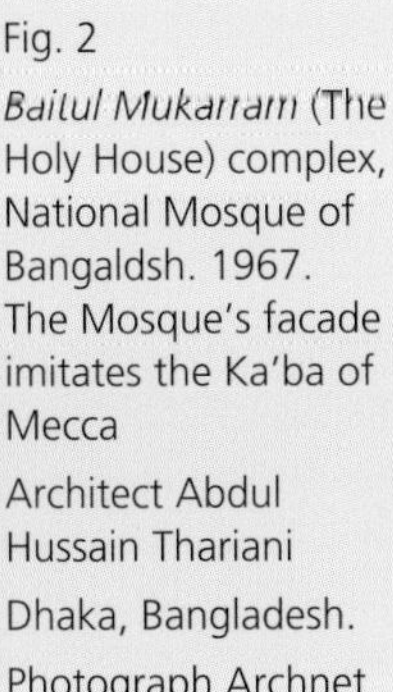

Fig. 2
Bailul Mukarram (The Holy House) complex, National Mosque of Bangaldsh. 1967. The Mosque's facade imitates the Ka'ba of Mecca

Architect Abdul Hussain Thariani

Dhaka, Bangladesh.

Photograph Archnet

Fig. 3
Hazrat-i Ma'suma Shrine Complex, 17th century, Qum, Iran.

Photograph Archnet

Matters are a bit more complicated when we turn to the Shi'ite centers for pilgrimage in Iraq, as in Karbela, Najaf, or Samarra; and in Iran, as in Qum (Fig. 3) and Meshed. With any number of local variants, these sanctuaries all exhibit the same vocabulary of forms: a domed room where some holy personage is buried, a large *iwan* (rectangular vaulted hall opening to the outside at one end) in front of the dome, an open court with a water basin, and various ways of housing practical purposes, often involved with teaching. Most of these sanctuaries were frequently redone and few of them existed, in their present shape, earlier than the 16th century. Their golden cupolas dominate the landscape of many cities and serve as beacons in the countryside. It is possible that they all reflect some ideal plan for a truly meaningful *ziyara*, "pious visit," and some research in literature associated with the lives of descendants of the Prophet Muhammad, especially his son-in-law Ali, may confirm the existence of an ideal architectural setting for holy places connected with the chain of Shi'ite *imams*. An intriguing possibility exists that the shapes of numerous bronze objects, especially inkwells and incense burners from the 20th century onward, which are covered with domes and imitate buildings, were inspired by holy sanctuaries used for pilgrimages. But other explanations for their form exist as well.[2]

The making of souvenirs from places of pilgrimage is as old as pilgrimage itself, and the contemporary Islamic world is littered with miniaturized sanctuaries adorned with all sorts of spoken, musical, or visual additions seeking to recall the holiness of a place. It is more difficult to establish how early such objects were made and how common they were in the past. The earliest souvenir-like item recalling Mecca known to me is a marble plaque fifteen by thirty-three centimeters in size. It was located in the Baghdad Museum and hopefully is still there. It came originally from Mosul in northern Iraq, where it had been fixed on the wall of a Shi'ite sanctuary. It was later transferred to a Sunni mosque. The plaque contains a schematic representation of the Ka'ba with a selection of other holy fixtures arranged around the Ka'ba proper. The inscription above and below the drawings praises the building of a mosque by a prince of the Uqaylid dynasty, which ruled Mosul from 991 to 1093, and adds that the mosque was near the tomb of an otherwise unknown woman. Inscription and representation of the holy site are carefully framed by a border enclosing a tall rectangle with a semicircular top.[3] In other words, this object, which could easily be moved, was carefully executed and meant to be exhibited; it was, in fact, used in more than one place. Was it a souvenir from the holy city acquired in some shop of mementos in Mecca itself?

Fig. 4
Tile depicting Mecca, Topkapi palace, 16th century, Ottoman, Istanbul.
Photograph Mika Natif

Was it, more likely, a local northern Iraqi attempt to evoke the holy sanctuary and, by its presence in a mosque or in a mausoleum, enhance the holiness of a space and demonstrate the piety of a patron who had been on a pilgrimage to Mecca? Or was it an *ex voto* made to satisfy some wish or need?

We have no way of answering these questions for this particular piece, but whatever its prime meaning when it was created, it illustrates the first steps in the formation of arts related to pilgrimage. The most visible later examples are the numerous faience tiles from Iznik, near Istanbul and other centers (Fig. 4), for the production of colorful Ottoman ceramics with representations of the Meccan sanctuary and occasionally of the one in Medina.[4] The size of these plaques varied. Their exact ritual function may have varied as well, although the primary one seems to have been to remind the faithful of the place toward which they prayed. The visual commemoration of the holy places – Mecca, Medina, and at times Jerusalem – appears also in pilgrimage certificates, often brought by pilgrims who substituted for important figures, such as Salah al-Din in the late 12th century[5] (see essay *The "Objectivity" of the Hajj*, Fig. 1). And then a whole literature developed describing the holy places and the various ways of getting to them, with illustrations showing every site.[6] Such illustrated books were common within the Ottoman Empire, especially after the 16th century, and were also common in remote areas like Indonesia and central Africa.[7] As with the Ottoman plaques, it is difficult to determine whether these examples were primarily connected to pilgrimage rather than to topographical descriptions in travel books, a category of knowledge which is quite different from the more spiritual or emotional impact of pilgrimages. A particularly striking example of such representations of places of pilgrimage, whose point may be either didactic or commemorative, occurs on a map showing Mecca and Medina and all places visited by pilgrims around the holy sites. The map is datable to the 17th or 18th century. It was made in China and used to hang in a mosque, although it is now in the Xian National Museum.[8] It adjusts the Muslim sanctuaries of Arabia to a very Chinese organization of space.

An immediate visual transformation created by the pilgrimage to Mecca exists in popular art, as the houses of pilgrims were, and still are, painted over, sometimes with very elaborate designs and representations, always in striking colors, just as the departure and return of a pilgrim are usually accompanied by joyful singing and dancing. An interesting and unusual early artistic version of this sort of commemoration is a pen case at the Hermitage Museum in St. Petersburg. It is dated 1148, and was made by an inhabitant of Herat in Afghanistan for the return of the latter's brother from the Hajj. Successful pilgrimages took years to be completed and no one could be sure that a Hajji would survive to return home.[9]

There are also images that have been associated with holy places or sacred events and that could have been connected to pilgrimages. Such is a luster-painted plate in the Kabul Museum. The present whereabouts of the plate are unknown to me, but it has been interpreted as the representation of an episode in the life of Husayn, the son of Ali and a major Shi'ite figure.[10] In the Musée de la Céramique in Sèvres, near Paris, there is a unique luster painted large ceramic plate of the 14th century, with the representation of the horseshoe of Ali's horse and a text of pious content associated with the foundation of a sanctuary for pilgrimages. A companion piece, now disappeared, showed a beautiful tent covered with a dome and preceded by a horse and a camel.[11] Such objects may well be examples of a genre that we have not learned to identify and explain properly.

The problem with all these examples is whether it is appropriate to consider them as works of art rather than as simple artifacts answering very practical and immediate needs. Although some of the examples I have provided can be considered as significant works of art, most of them belong to artisanal types and reflect the existence of a visual by-product of pilgrimage, the main pan-Islamic Hajj, or local and sectarian *ziyara*. But, except perhaps in Ottoman times, this by-product was a secondary streak in the creativity of Muslim culture. At least, I would argue, this is clear when we weigh the considerable importance of the Hajj and of local pilgrimages against the quantities of books, textiles, ceramics, glass, and metalwork that characterize traditional Islamic art. Further investigations into the actual operation of visual forms within traditional societies may lead to hitherto unsuspected associations between pious activities and forms. There may in fact be a level at which attitudes toward and reactions to pilgrimages did create visual presence in most Islamic settings, except perhaps within the ultra-orthodox Puritanism of present-day Arabia. Such may be the importance taken by the cult of the dead, which made cemeteries, tombs, and domes of mausoleums a ubiquitous feature in most Muslim settings. Perhaps even the golden or blue colors of the domes over tombs acquired a saintly meaning that recalled or fostered pilgrimages. We can recall the fact that the ritual white cloth in which one dressed for the pilgrimage often became a shroud, and thus all visual signs of death could be seen as reflections of the pilgrimage of life.

1 Wilber, Donald. 1972. *The Masjid-i atiq of Shiraz*. Shiraz: Asia Institute, Pahlavi University.

2 See Melikian-Chirvani, Assadullah S. 1986. "State Inkwells in Islamic Iran." *Journal of the Walters Art Gallery* 44: 70-94 for many examples of such objects, but with a very different explanation.

3 Strike, V. 1976. "A Ka'bah Picture in the Iraq Museum." *Sumer* 32: 195-201.

4 Ettinghausen, Richard. 1934. "Die bildliche Darstellungen der Ka'ba," *Zeitschrift der Deutschen Morgenlandischen Gesellschaft*, Bd. 87: 111-37; Erdmann, Kurt. 1959. "Ka'bah Fliesen," *Ars Orientalis* 3: 192-97.

5 Sourdel-Thomine, Janine. 1986. "Une image musulmane de Jérusalem." In *Jérusalem, Rome, Constantinople*. D. Poirion, ed. Paris: Presses de l'Université de Paris-Sorbonne.

6 Milstein, Rachel. 2001. "Kitab Shawq-nameh, an Illustrated Tour to Holy Arabia." *Jerusalem Studies in Arabic and Islam*, 25: 275-345.

7 Witkam, Jan Just. 2002. *De geschiedenis van de Dala'il al-Khayrat van al- azuli*. Leiden: Universiteitsbibliotheek.

8 Cowan, Jill S. 2001. "A pictorial Map in the Dongdasi." *Oriental Art* 47: 84-92.

9 Giuzalian, L.T. 1968. "The Bronze *qalamdan* from Heratt." *Ars Orientalis* 7: 95-119.

10 It is illustrated in Ettinghausen, Richard, Oleg Grabar, and Marilyn Jenkins-Madina, 2001. *Islamic Art and Architecture 650-1250*. New Haven: Yale University Press, fig. 271. The Shi'ite interpretation was proposed by Dr. Firuz Bagherzadeh.

11 Adle, Chahriyar. 1972. "Un disque de fondation en céramique, 711/1312." *Journal asiatique*, 260: 277-97; and Idem. 1982. "Un diptyque de fondation." in Chahriyar Adle, ed. *Art et Societé dans le Monde iranien*. Paris: Editions sur les Civilizations.

Details of Fig. 4

The "Objectivity" of the Hajj

Mika Natif

The preliminary goal of this essay is to examine works of art and objects that are linked to the pilgrimage to the holy sanctuary in Mecca. Such artifacts may range from Hajj certificates to inlaid metal work and from brocade banners to glazed ceramic tiles. The commonality or cohesion of such works of art is that they bear witness to the successful fulfillment of one of the Five Pillars of Islam – the performance of the Hajj pilgrimage.[1] I will explore the visuality of Hajj objects through their aesthetic language rather than in chronological order, and attempt to scrutinize them as a group and to establish whether their linkage to pilgrimage yields a shared common artistic expression.

During the process of the pilgrimage to Mecca, the faithful believer goes through a spiritual transformation of humbling himself, and thus bringing him/herself closer to the divine. The pilgrim leaves the everyday world behind, notably his everyday clothes, and instead wears a special white robe to perform prescribed rituals. Thus he undergoes a process of shedding his colorful, worldly behavior and replacing it, at least for a while, with the blank and undifferentiated holiness of the House of God.

Upon completing the Hajj, the believer, male or female, attains a certificate signed by the authorities in Mecca, attesting to the fulfillment of this pious act. Such documents, called Hajj certificates, have survived since the 11th century, and a large number of them were discovered in the Great Mosque of Damascus.[2] The certificates vary greatly in execution: some are calligraphed or consist of a woodblock print in black ink with no embellishment, while others are elaborately painted and colored. This difference undoubtedly reflects the social level and ability to pay of each Hajji, and both types of certificates were produced at the same time in Mecca (TKS scroll and the BL scroll).[3] Rachel Milstein argues that illustrated scrolls from the Ayyubid period show very similar Hajj testimonial texts, baring a few minute differences. Their depictions of the places of the Hajj may be linked to Late Antique pre-Islamic representations of Jewish and Christian holy sites and heavenly cities.[4] Therefore the Meccan illustrated scrolls created a visuality of the Hajj, one that commemorated the pilgrim's visits to the holy places and thus fixed into artistic form what was an interior, spiritual experience.

A scroll from the British Library (Add. 27566) presents a magnificent example of such transformation (Fig. 1). The document attests that in 836/1432-3 Maymunah, daughter of Muhammad ibn Abdallah al-Zardli, completed her Hajj pilgrimage, and that she visited both holy cities of Mecca and of Medina. Beginning with the *bismallah* and then divided into sections, the certificate shows a schematic depiction

Fig. 1
Hajj Certificate, made for Maymunah, daughter of Muhammad ibn Abdallah al-Zardli, 836/1432-3
British Library, London
Opaque watercolor, ink and gold on paper

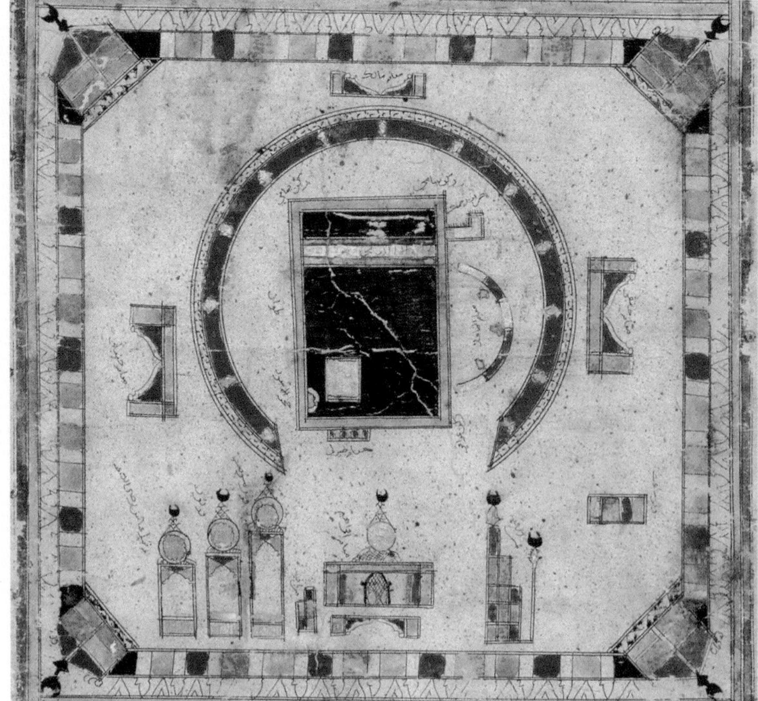

Fig. 2
Detail of the Ka'ba from the Hajj Certificate, made for Maymunah, daughter of Muhammad ibn Abdallah al-Zardli, 836/1432-3
British Library, London
Opaque watercolor, ink and gold on paper

Fig. 3
Detail of the Tomb of Muhammad in Medina from Hajj Certificate, made for Maymunah, daughter of Muhammad ibn Abdallah al-Zardli, 836/1432-3
British Library, London
Opaque watercolor, ink and gold on paper

of the holy places from several points of view, using a mixed perspective of frontal and bird's-eye views. Hence the sanctuary of the Ka'ba appears as a black square (covered by the *kiswa*) and, shown in profile, the hills of Marwa and Safa are represented as circles (Fig. 2). Moreover, the mosque on mount Arafat appears as a dome with the mosque of Abraham and the tomb of Adam below, and a water pool (four posts, two huge ceremonial candelabras), while the architecture is intertwined with Quranic verse from surat al-Fath (the Victory or Conquest; 48:1).[5] The tomb of the Prophet in Medina is a geometric arrangement of a rectangle and a triangle, and at the bottom of the scroll there is an imprint of the Prophet's sandal (Fig. 3). Other stations on the Hajj are also illustrated, and the places are labeled. Quranic verses linked with the duty of the Hajj are calligraphed between the different sections. The scroll is lavishly painted in bright colors of red, blue, green, and gold, and through the geometric and architectural forms it conveys a sense of glory, a commemoration of a magnificent event.

The overall composition of the British Library scroll follows a known model of illustrated Hajj certificates, dating as early as the 12th century.[6] As Milstein notes, these depictions do not include geographical information about the sites, but focus on the religious landscape of the Hajj, showing the "most important symbolic details."[7] While the style of the 13th-century Ayyubid Hajj scrolls is more schematic, the Mamluk (BL) paintings are even more abstract, utilizing the purity of geometry.

These types of representations can also be found in illustrated manuscripts dealing with the holy sites of the Hajj that were used as guidebooks for pilgrims. Milstein links the practice of abstraction in paintings of the holy place in Mecca, Medina, and Jerusalem with calligraphy, and she further points to parallels in the visual language used in the 13th-century Hajj scrolls and the 16th-century Ottoman guidebook manuscripts.[8] One such example is an illustration of the Ka'ba in Mecca from an Ottoman Pilgrimage Guide dated to the 16th-17th centuries. In this image (Fig. 4) we may notice the "Ottomanization" of the holy sanctuary through the addition of the thin tall minarets, which have been recognized as landmarks of Ottoman presence. Milstein confirms that according to historical sources, the Ottomans initially added six minarets to the Haram in Mecca and that the seventh minaret was commissioned by Sultan Suleyman in 973/1565-66.[9] We also notice the extensive use of blue tiling on the ground and on the walls in the illustration, which may be further linked to the Ottoman ceramic industries, and to the renovation of the pavement that was ordered by Suleyman the Magnificent (r. 1520-1566). Hence, even though these paintings are images of religious landscapes of the Hajj, the viewer is confronted with clear Ottoman statements of power and sovereignty over the holy sites. Therefore, no matter how schematic the depiction, how flat the perspective, and how abstract and geometric the view of the buildings, the dynastic affiliation is immediate, made through the specifics of the minarets and the blue tiles on the ground. Consequently we are no longer looking at the Ka'ba, but rather we are looking at the Ottoman presence in Mecca.

In this Ottoman painting the names of the gates around the sanctuary are indicated, as well as the Zamzam well, and other important places. While the overall perspective is of a bird's-eye view, each structure is shown either laying flat on the ground or in frontal view. Milstein explains that some of these features are connected to Ottoman cartography and map painting, such as the work by Matrakçi Nasuh.[10] She argues that the overlapping structures, the diagonal placement of monuments, and the strong colors of the buildings are related to Ottoman practice of cartographic illustrations, transformed here into colorful patterns.[11]

Shown from the east, the Ka'ba in Fig. 4 is depicted with its black cover (*kiswa*) including the large gold inscription cartouche and the closed door. The area immediately around the Ka'ba, which is used for the ritual of circumambulation, includes several edifices. That part is marked by a *riwaq* with hanging lamps, and paved floor with blue ceramic tiles. Immediately next to the Ka'ba (on the right) is the traditional burial place of Hajar and Isma'il (called the *hatim*), which is marked by a half circle. Several places are indicated in front of the Ka'ba: the stone where Abraham set his feet (maqam Ibrahim) in the center shown as a small pavilion, the Zamzam well on the left with its relatively large edifice, and a large-scale *minbar* (pulpit) on the right. At the bottom of the tiled area there is the old gate of Banu Shayba, to whom Muhammad gave the keys to the Ka'ba. Milstein identifies the two small pavilions below the gate of Shayba as "a treasury of olive oil or carpets, and a store for drinking water."[12] There are also three domed structures from which the imams performed their prayers. The Shafi imam had the most prestigious place behind maqam Ibrahim, while the hanbali imam had a small structure on the left; the maliki was located above the Ka'ba, and the hanafi had a large building on the right.[13] The entire area of the Haram in Mecca is enclosed by an arcade with suspended lamps, and by a wall with domes and gates. Standing out among them is *bab* Ibrahim (gate of Abraham), which is shown at the top of the page.

Similar to the composition of the Haram in Mecca as seen in illustrated Pilgrimage Guides and in Hajj scrolls, there are representations of the Ka'ba on tiles or stone, dating as early as 1104.[14] An early example of engraved marble (or granite) was entrusted first at the Maqam Ibrahim shrine in Mosul, where it was placed on the wall with no embellishment.[15] When comparing this 12th-century engraving of the Ka'ba to later images of the holy sanctuary, we may notice the addition of various monuments to the masjid al-Haram. In the Mosul relief, several structures are identifiable, such as the courtyard surrounded by riwaqs, the black stone, the door to the Ka'ba, and the *kiswa*. Then there is the Hajar Isma'il, the *minbar*, two small minarets, and the Gate of the Banu Shayba. The tombs of Hajar and Isma'il are surrounded by a semicircular wall, and the three domed structures on the left are probably the Maqam Ibrahim, the Zamzam well, and the arch of Banu Shayba.[16]

Ottoman tiles depicting the Ka'ba, such as the one from the mosque of Rüstem Pasha in Istanbul (Fig. 5), or the ones ordered by Sultan Mehmed II at the Topkapi Saray palace in Istanbul (see essay *Observations on Pilgrimage and Art in the Islamic World*, Fig. 4), also have a commemorative role. Like a tile in the Victoria & Albert Museum, produced in Turkey, c. 1650, these representations evoke the memory of the holy places, but they also testify to the prestige of the Ottoman sultans who controlled the major holy sites in the Muslim world (Mecca, Medina, and Jerusalem). Furthermore, the tiles commemorated the pilgrimage of the Hajj and attested to

Fig. 4
Haram at Mecca from Majmu`ah (anthology) of Persian Texts
1550-1600
Ottoman, Ottoman Empire 16th-17th centuries
Ink, opaque watercolor, and gold on paper, 8¾ x 5⅝ in. (22.2 x 14.3 cm)
Harvard Art Museum, Arthur M. Sackler Museum, The Edwin Binney, 3rd Collection of Turkish Art at the Harvard Art Museum, 1985.265.20
Allan Macintyre © President and Fellows of Harvard College

the completion of this spiritual duty. In this way, they fulfill a role similar to that of the certificates, but in clay and glaze rather than paper. Moreover, Aksoy and Milstein suggest that some of the Hajj scrolls were framed and hung for public view.[17] Likewise, Ka'ba tiles, such as one at the Walters Art Museum (from about 1600, Turkey) operated as public visual commemorative plaques for the completion of the rite of pilgrimage, and served as a visual memory and a reminder for the believer of his/her duty to perform the holy pilgrimage.

When we examine the aesthetic aspect of these representations of the Ka'ba, we may notice that the various edifices in the masjid al-Haram are shown in disproportional relationship to one another. Hence, the minbar is relatively large, and the minarets and gates are small. It seems that the artists were concerned with the significance of the buildings rather than with their actual proportionate appearance.[18] However, the artists chose certain characteristics by which we can immediately recognize the important buildings. Hence there are some exclusive features, such as the cubical form of the sanctuary with its *kiswa*, the rendition of the Ka'ba doors and their special covering, and the adjacent half-circle structure of Hajar Isma'il, that, grouped together, transformed a representation of the Ka'ba into an iconic form. Furthermore, in these iconic images the artists made extensive use of geometry, which does not seem to be purely an aesthetic decision.

The choice of geometric ornament has been recently explored by a number of scholars, such as Oleg Grabar, Yassar Tabbaa, and Gulru Necipoglu. The idea behind the usage of geometry was, according to Grabar, part of a process of elevating these images "into a work of higher or more expressive quality," since geometry had acquired a place of "prestige" in Islamic visual tradition, reflecting ideas of divine harmony and balance.[19] Other scholars, such as Seyyed Hossein Nasr, regard geometry as part of the language of *tawhid*, the Unity of the Divine.[20] The utilization of geometry in this specific Islamic artistic language "forces one to look and to decide what to think, what to feel, and even how to act."[21] At the same time, these aesthetic compositions may be thought of as "stimulating mediators," encouraging us to contemplate the divine.[22]

Fig. 5
Tile with Plan of the Ka'ba, c. 1561-63
Rüstem Pasha Mosque, Istanbul, Turkey
Photograph Mika Natif

Another object that is related to the Hajj is the *kiswa* – the covers of the Ka'ba. In all representations of the Ka'ba, the square building housing the black stone is covered by a special curtain (usually black) embellished with embroidery of Quranic verses. Being a prerogative of the Caliph, a new *kiswa* was manufactured and sent to the Ka'ba. Contributing to the covering of the Ka'ba was considered to be so important, according to Wensinck, that "during Umar's caliphate [r. 634-44] the building threatened to collapse on account of the many coverings hung on it."[23] However, since the end of the Caliphate in the 13th century, according to Wensinck, the covering had been commissioned and produced in Egypt. Since the modern period, the curtains have been replaced every year, while the old ones have been divided by the Banu Shayba, who then "distributed and sold them as relics"[24] (Fig. 6).

According to some legends, the new *kiswa* was transported to the Ka'ba in a special palanquin, called the *mahmal*, that was tied to the back of a camel. However, Lane dismisses this story and argues that even though the *mahmal* and the *kiswa* were sent at the same time to Mecca, the palanquin was not used to transport the new curtains to the Ka'ba (Fig. 7).[25]

Early historical narratives relate that the *mahmal* was used for the transportation of pilgrims to Mecca, and since the 13th century it has acquired political symbolism. As such, the *mahmal* proclaimed the political power of the ruler as the protector of the Holy Places, and symbolized the commencement of the journey to Mecca. The palanquin was tied to a camel and decorated with cloth hangings that propagated the name of the ruler, and thus served as an emblem of power.[26] The "political *mahmal*," according to Buhl and Jomier, was first used by Sultan Baybars (r. 1260-1277) in 1266 and is linked to his display of sovereignty and his oversight of the pilgrimage route with respect to the aftermath of the Mongol conquest of Baghdad in 1258.[27] In

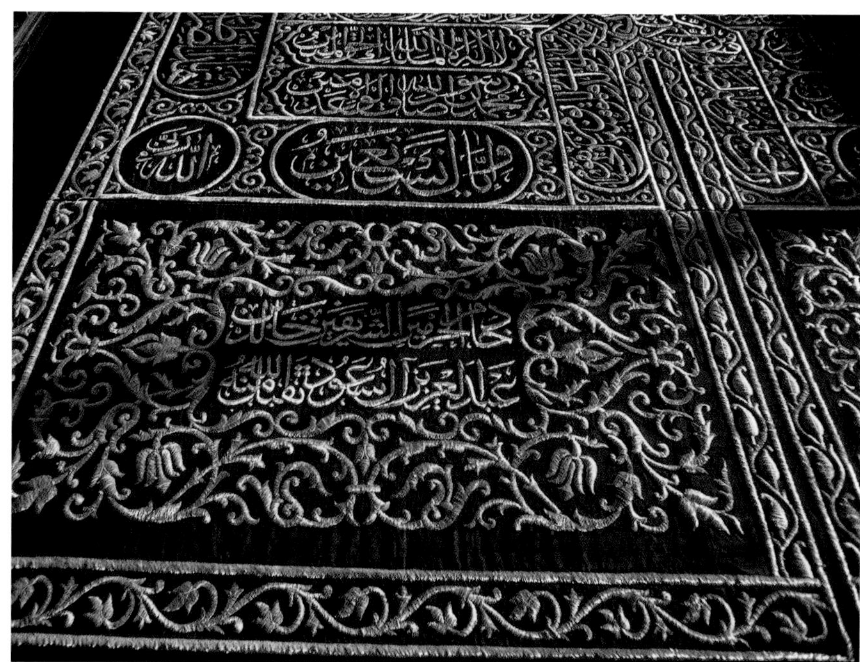

Fig. 6
Detail of the lower part of the Sitara, originally part of the Kiswa, 1985
Delegates' Lounge, United Nations, New York
Photograph Katrina Thomas/*Saudi Aramco World*/SAWDIA

Fig. 7
Old Photograph of the Mahmal going from Egypt to Mecca
Photograph public domain

two illustrated manuscripts of the *Maqamat* of al-Hariri, one in Paris dated 1237 the other in Leningrad and considered to be earlier, there is a visual testimony for the usage of a palanquin in the context of the sacred pilgrimage.[28] In this *maqamat* episode, the protagonist decides to join a caravan going to Mecca. Grabar states that "though the text does not specify that the event took place during the pilgrimage," the white cloths of the personages can be identified as the special Hajj dresses, and the depiction of the ornamented *mahmal* "surrounded by dancers, musicians, and flag bearers" further emphasizes the link to the Hajj.[29] These illustrations may be the earliest visual evidence that we currently have of the usage of the *mahmal* for the pilgrimage to Mecca, and should be compared to the descriptions of these processions in contemporary historical sources.

Since the political display of Sultan Baybar's *mahmal*, other contending *mahmals* were sent from the rival places of Yemen and Syria. During the gathering of the Hajj, the *mahmals* would be on display in Mecca and then at Arafat, affirming the authority and the presence of their senders/rules.[30] Such a scene of the Hajj was written and illustrated in a 16th-century poem by Lari called *Futuh al-Haramayn* (The Openings of the Two Sanctuaries), which describes the two holy cities of Mecca and Medina. Lari writes about the richness of the textiles of the two rival *mahmals*, one from Egypt and the other from Syria, and he also mentions a black one, which Milstein identifies as the Abbasid *mahmal* that no longer existed in the 16th century; she interprets its inclusion as a nostalgic gesture on the part of the author.[31] In these illustrations, the *mahmals* are shown as large cubical structures with a high steep roof, parked at the foot of mount Arafat. However, such depictions were devoid of figures that would have accompanied the *mahmals* with their colorful banners and spirit of festivity.

One such example of a pilgrim's banner from North Africa, dated 1094/1683, is now at the Harvard University Art Museum.[32] The banner consists of a large geometric inscription of the Surat al-Fath (the Victory or Conquest 48:1-3) from the Quran and a depiction of the double-bladed sword of Ali composed of the same verse of Surat al-Fath.[33] Just below the large inscription there is a mention of the places and the ceremonies of the Hajj, and the name of the 12th-century leader of the Qadiriyya order, Abd al-Qadir al-Jilani. Consequently, Renard suggests that this banner was carried on the Hajj by a pilgrim who was a member of the Qadiriyya.[34] Such custom was recorded by al-Wasiti, who, in his illustration to the *Maqammat* of al-Hariri from 1237, pictured the group of pilgrims with their Hajj banners and the camel with the *mahmal*, departing on their journey to Mecca (Fig. 8). Nicolas Nicolay described pilgrims to Mecca in 1568: "And so they go in troupes, carrying great banner with a crescent at the top through the cities and villages singing the praises of Mohammed and asking for charity in the name of God (see essay *Nicholas de Nicolay: A French View of the Hajj in the 16th Century*, Fig. 1).[35] This carrying of banners related to pilgrimage can be found in similar practices in Christianity, as described in a 1512 printed Book of Hours (see essay *Origins and History of Pilgrimage for Christians, Muslims, and Buddhists*, Fig. 1).

Fig. 8
Schematic drawing after the illustration of the *Maqammat* of al-Hariri from 1237, Thirty-first *maqama*. Paris, Bibliothèque Nationale, *arabe* 5847, fols. 94v, 95.

Another practice that may share some features with other religions and may be subjected to similar spiritual practices in Christianity and in Buddhism is the veneration of footprints. In the sanctuary of Mecca there is a place known as Maqam Ibrahim in which there is a stone that bears the footprints of Abraham. According to tradition, Abraham stood on that stone when he was building the Ka'ba with his son Isma'il, and miraculously his feet left their mark there. The Maqam Ibrahim can be seen in every representation of Mecca, just in front of the Ka'ba, and it is included in the circumambulatory rout of the Hajj performance.[36] His footprints join other famous marks, such as that of Christ, who was believed to have left his footprints on the rock of his Ascension[37] or of the Buddha whose footprints are frequently depicted as souvenir images (see essay *Pilgrimage Traditions in Nepal*, Fig. 28).

Not all objects that are linked to the Hajj speak in the same visual language, as we have seen so far. Two commemorative objects of very different sorts connect their owners to the Hajj. One is a bronze pen case (*qalamdan*) dated 542/1148, and the other, known as the "Bobrinski bucket," is dated 559/1163; both are at the Hermitage Museum. The pen box is ornamented with inlaid silver and bronze, and decorated with several medallions containing a bird shown in profile, vegetal motifs in a geometric composition, and inscriptions. Based on the quality of the work and the reading of the inscriptions, Giuzalian concludes that the *qalamdan* was made by an amateur and presented as a gift to someone close (from the merchant class) upon the completion of the Hajj.[38]

The Bobrinski bucket, on the other hand, is a sophisticated and fascinating object. Its shape follows the form of buckets that were used in bathhouses, but its bronze body is inlaid with red copper and silver. It is unlikely that this object would have been used for bathing, because of the fragility of the inlaid metals. Thus, the maker appropriated the form of a utilitarian bucket for what was actually a luxury object.[39] The bucket contains several inscriptions, one of which identifies the giver and the receiver of the object. Made in the city of Herat, Khurassan, in 1163, this piece was commissioned by al-Rahman ibn Abdallah al-Rashidi for his brother Khoja Rukn al-Din, after the latter returned from a pilgrimage to the holy city of Mecca.[40]

The body of the bucket is decorated with a series of registers containing figural scenes and inscriptions. The subject matter of the scenes ranges from animals running to enthroned figures, and from scenes of social entertainment, such as drinking, playing games, and music-making, to representations of horsemen who are fighting and hunting. Interestingly, the figural decoration does not reflect any activity or location related to the Hajj, but it portrays scenes of royal and nomadic pastimes: drinking, hunting, fighting, backgammon playing, and musical entertainment.

To conclude, we may suggest here that there is no one unified artistic language used for the artistic creation of objects of the Hajj. Some pieces have more of a secular iconography, attesting to the fashions and trends of a certain place and time, while others include large Quranic inscriptions and no figural representation. Several artworks may be directly linked to the symbolism of dynastic political power, when others adhere to the purity of geometry. However, through geometry the representation of the Ka'ba and the holy places in Mecca and Medina became icons of religion and power, encapsulated in the visual memory of the holy duty of the Hajj.

1 The Ka'ba has been depicted in a wide variety of illustrated manuscripts. Great literary heroes such as Majnun and Iskandar visited the holy sanctuary in Mecca and these episodes and similar ones have been widely painted. In this article I shall not discuss these pictures, since my goal is to deal with works of art and artifacts that are historically linked to the performance of the Hajj. For a discussion on urban centers and pilgrimage in the Muslim world see David J. Roxburgh's article "The Pilgrimage City," in S. Jayyusi and others, *The City in the Islamic World* (Leiden, 2008), vol. 2, 753-74.

2 See Sourdel, Dominique and Sourdel-Thomine, Janine. 2006. *Certificats de pèlerinage d'époque ayyoubide: contribution à l'histoire de l'idéologie de l'Islam au temps des croisades*. Paris: Académie des inscriptions et belles-lettres.

3 Sourdel and Sourdel-Thomine's publication has shown that the majority of the painted scrolls from the Damascus repository were made for female patrons.

4 See the fascinating article by Rachel Milstein, "The Evolution of a Visual Motif: the Temple and the Ka'ba," *Israel Oriental Studies* 19(1999): 23-48.

5 Surah al-Fath 48:1-3: "We have given you a splendent victory that God may save you from earlier and subsequent blames, and complete His favours on you, and guide you on the straight path, and help you with surpassing help." Translated by Ahmed Ali.

6 See Sourdel, Dominique and Sourdel-Thomine, Janine. 2006. *Certificats de pèlerinage d'époque ayyoubide: contribution à l'histoire de l'idéologie de l'Islam au temps des croisades*. Paris: Académie des inscriptions et belles-lettres; S. Aksoy and R. Milstein, 2000. "A Collection of Thirteenth Century Illustrated Hajj Certificates." In *M. Ungur Derman 65th Birthday Festschrift*. Irvin Çemil Schick, ed. Istanbul, (2000), 101-134; Milstein, Rachel. 2006. "Futuh-i Haramayn: sixteenth-century illustrations of the *Hajj* route." In *Mamluks and Ottomans: Studies in Honour of Michael Winter*. David J.Wasserstein and A. Ayalon, eds. London: Routledge, 169; Id., "The Temple and the Ka'ba."

7 Milstein, "Futuh-i Haramayn," 169.

8 Ibid., 170.

9 Ibid., 173.

10 Sarıcaoğlu, F. 2002. "Ottoman Cartography." In *The Turks 3: Ottomans*. H. Celal Güzel, C. Cem Oğuz, and O.Karatay, eds. Ankara: Yeni Türkiye, 831-40; Brentjes, S. 2005. "Mapmaking in Ottoman Istanbul between 1650 and 1750: A Domain of Painters, Calligraphers or Cartographers?" In *Frontiers of Ottoman Studies: State, Province, and the West*. C. Imber and K. Kiyotaki, eds. London: Tauris, 125-156.

11 Milstein, "Futuh-i Haramayn," 170.

12 Ibid., 172.

13 Ibid., 171. Milstein explains that the Ottomans adhered to the Hanafi school of law in Islam, and thus they enlarged the Hanafi edifice in the Haram.

14 See Strika, Vincenzo. 1976. "A Ka'bah Picture in the Iraq Museum." *Sumer Journal* 32:195-201. The dimensions of the slab are 15 x 33 cm. Id., 196.

15 Strika argues that this representation was linked to renovation works in the shrine. See inscription in *naskh* script on the slab.

16 Ibid., 200-201.

17 Aksoy and Milstein, "A Collection of Thirteenth Century Illustrated Hajj Certificates," 103.

18 See for example the Ka'ba tile from the Rustem Pasha mosque in Istanbul, fig. 3, or the one from the David Collection in Copenhagen.

19 Grabar, Oleg. 1992. *The Mediation of Ornament*. Princeton: Princeton University Press, 119.

20 S.H. Nasr, *Islamic Art and Spirituality* (Albany: State University of New York Press, 1987), 3-14. Grabar correctly objects to these interpretations, which have no historical basis. Grabar, *Mediation of Ornament*, 51.

21 Grabar, *Mediation of Ornament*, 154.

22 Ibid.

23 *Encyclopaedia of Islam*, 2nd ed. (Leiden: Brill, 1960–2004), s.v. "Ka'ba" (A.J. Wensinck and J. Jomier).

24 Ibid. The lock and key of the Ka'ba have also been regarded as precious relics from the sanctuary at Mecca. The earliest lock, according to Janine Sourdel-Thomine, is from the 9th century, and there are several keys that date back to the 12th century. These objects are usually engraved with Quranic verses and they carry the name of the Caliph. In the Chamber of Sacred Relics at the Topkapi Saray Palace in Istanbul there are several locks from the entrance to the Ka'ba as well as from the door of the walls around the sanctuary of the Haram (known as the Door of Forgiveness), which the Ottoman Sultan Murad III (r. 1574-1595) brought to Istanbul at the time of his renovation in Mecca.

25 The lucky camel that was chosen to carry the *mahmal* every year to Mecca and back was not used for any other work or task throughout the year. Edward W. Lane, *An Account of the Manners and Customs of the Modern Egyptians: The Definitive 1860 Edition*, vol. 2 (Cairo; New York: American University in Cairo Press, 2003), 162; *Encyclopaedia of Islam*, 2nd ed. (Leiden: Brill, 1960–2004), s.v. "Maḥmal" (Fr. Buhl and J. Jomier).

26 Buhl and Jomier describe two kinds of *mahmal* hangings. The official and more ceremonial one had the name and emblem of the Sultan embroidered on it, with Quranic verses.

27 This custom was abolished by the Wahhābīs in the first half of the 20th century. "Maḥmal" (Fr. Buhl and J. Jomier).

28 Thirty-first *maqamah*. Paris, Bibliothèque Nationale, *arabe* 5847, fols. 94v, 95; Leningrad Academy of Science, S.23, pp. 213, 223. O. Grabar, *The Illustrations of the Maqamat* (Chicago: University of Chicago Press, 1984), 10-11, 79-81.

29 Moreover, in the Leningrad manuscripts the figures are shown to be praying. Ibid., 80.

30 "Maḥmal" (Fr. Buhl and J. Jomier).

31 Milstein, "Futuh-i Haramayn," 179.

32 HUAM 1958.20. Published in *Images of Paradise in Islamic Art*, ed. By S Blair and J. Bloom (Hanover, N.H.: Hood Museum of Art, Dartmouth College, 1991), cat.# 8a, pp. 45, 74. John Renard further discusses this piece in his book *Windows on the House of Islam* (Berkeley, Calif.; London: University of California Press, 1998): 88. A later but similar banner is dated 1225/1810, probably from Ottoman Turkey. See the Metropolitan Museum of Art # 1976.312.

33 Renard, *Windows on the House of Islam*, 88. For the text of the surah see note 5.

34 Renard, *Windows on the House of Islam*, 88.

35 Nicolas Nicolay, *Les Navigations, peregrinations, et voyages* (Antwerp: Guillaume Silvius, 1576; first edition, Lyons 1568), 199.

36 Other famous footprint stones exist in the Muslim world. For example, Muhammad left his imprints at the Dome of the Rock in Jerusalem, in a mosque near Damascus, in Istanbul, in Egypt, and in Delhi. For further discussion on the phenomenon of Qadam Rasul or Qadam Sharif see the article by Perween Hasan, "The Footprint of the Prophet," in Muqarnas 10 (1993): 335-343, with some inaccuracies regarding the Dome of the Rock.

37 See an image of the Ascension with footprints left on a rock, in a Moralized Bible, Flanders c. 1465, The Hague, Koninklijke Bibliotheek, 76 E 7 fol. 219. The commonality of the subject is attested by the similar iconography in the Ascension depicted in the east window of the Church of Saints Peter and Paul, East Harling, c. 1463-80. The footprints of the Buddha are represented in a relief from the Stupa in Sanchi. For two different interpretations of this image see the articles by Susan Huntington "Early Buddhist Art and the Theory of Aniconism," *Art Journal* (Winter 1990):401-408; and V. Dehejia, "Aniconism and the Multivalence of Emblems," *Ars Orientalis* 21 (1991): 45-67. On other footprints in Buddhist tradition see the article by D. Klimburg-Salter, "Lama, Yidam, Protectors," *Orientations* 35/3 (2004): 48-53.

38 See the translated inscriptions. L. T. Giuzalian, "The Bronze Qalamdan (Pen-Case) 542/1148 from the Hermitage Collection," *Ars Orientalis* 7 (1968): 98, 102.

39 Richard Ettinghausen, "The Bobrinski "kettle": patron and style of an Islamic bronze," *Gazette des Beaux-Arts* 6 per., 24 (1943): 193-208.

40 The inscription on the handle of the bucket provides us with the date of the vessel, while the inscription on the rim gives us the names of the men who ordered the vessel, the owner, and the two artists. Ibid., 196-197.

Details of Fig. 3

The Pilgrim, the Image, and the Word in Islam

Amanda Luyster

Contrary to popular belief, Islam does not oppose figural representation. Transfixed by the episode of the Danish cartoons of September 2005, a western audience has witnessed a consistent polemic about the prohibition of imagery in Islamic tradition. The Quran, however, is silent on the use of images. Conflation of the formative years of Islam and Jewish tradition, a concept pursued by Muhammad himself, has encouraged comparison of Muslim practice to the Jewish commandment regarding the prohibition of graven images. Yet a multitude of images have been produced by Muslim artists and for Muslim audiences. Mecca's Haram and Ka'ba as well as Medina appear in multiple illustrations, and various texts contain illustrations of Muhammad's Night Journey, as shown in previous essays. The story of Yusef (Old Testament, Joseph) sold into slavery in Egypt has been frequently illustrated. Not only religious but also secular subjects have been finely painted in luxurious manuscripts.

Still, we see an emphasis on religious text rather than religious image in Islam. The Islamic focus on holy words rather than holy images should probably be related to the particular period of history in which Islam arose, the 7th century. Around this time, the difficulties of representing God were topics of ardent exchange. The Christian Byzantines went through periods of iconoclasm, or image-destruction, in the 8th and 9th centuries. Indeed, many religions, including Christianity and Judaism, have tended to avoid or shun religious images during certain periods of their history. In the Islamic tradition, the image of God's Word from the Quran is used to suggest the presence of God in a direct and evocative way. The Word is rendered with consummate artistry, in gesture and form. Its background is frequently embellished with elegant and twining ornaments, geometric or vegetal, to show all due honor to the Word of God.

In the Five Pillars of Islam, the Muslim is enjoined to pray five times a day in a way that emphasizes the ritual auditory reception of the holy text of the Quran. During the Hajj, ritual behavior increases and focus on the words of prayer intensifies. Human comforts (and beautiful images) are left behind; colorful clothing is put aside in favor of white garments. Personal luxuries are renounced. The whiteness, the simplicity of self and of soul, are all. Such weeding-out and casting-off of excess encourages intense introspection. Stones, sand, sun, and the Ka'aba – these purify the self, these connect the pilgrim with God.

After the conclusion of the Hajj, after rituals of barbering and dressing to return one to normal life, the images and objects of day-to-day existence return. Upon return from pilgrimage, objects might be commissioned in celebration – pen cases and basins (see essay *The*

"Objectivity" of the Hajj) are among the type of artworks which might be made to greet the returning pilgrim. A pen case, made of painted paper maché, depicts the natural world of lush, identifiable flowers, and resembles the contemporaneous books covers of several Qurans (Figs. 1-2).

After the conclusion of the pilgrimage, the pilgrim still wishes to think upon God, to focus his or her thoughts upon the holy. At that time a Muslim man or woman may look to some object – perhaps a book, or a prayer mat, or a painted tile – in order to take the daily mental pilgrimage from here, this world, to the next. Objects can provide the focus for this mental pilgrimage, the short journey out of oneself. But how best can objects, made up of earthly materials by earthly hands, inspire thoughts of God? For some Muslims, the purest and most powerful way to represent the absolute otherness of God is not through any "picture" at all, but through writing. Reciting, hearing, or reading the Word of God, then, rather than spiritual vision or physical ecstasy, is understood as the most direct way of coming closer to God. The visual emphasis in much Islamic art on the Word can be understood as resting upon this theological basis.

The potential of the Word to evoke the divine is further developed in a particular genre of "art object," the verbal portrait. The calligraphic portrait of Muhammad is known as a *hilye* (Fig. 3). Even in images of Muhammad from the Night Journey, the face of the Prophet is generally covered with a white veil. The *hilye* takes this same concern with the holy image, and adds to it the sacredness of the Word, and creates a "portrait" of the Prophet that is entirely non-figural. Such a "picture" could be hung on the wall of a private home or school as a beautiful reminder of the prophet, describing his features and having an edging of fine colors and gold. The round field at the top is known as the "belly" of the piece, and a rectangle at the bottom is known as the "skirt." The *hilye*, then, can be understood as a physical portrait of the Prophet, and a reference to his body, although it contains no figural image. Such *hilye* are still produced today, demonstrating the continuity of Islamic tradition (Fig. 4).

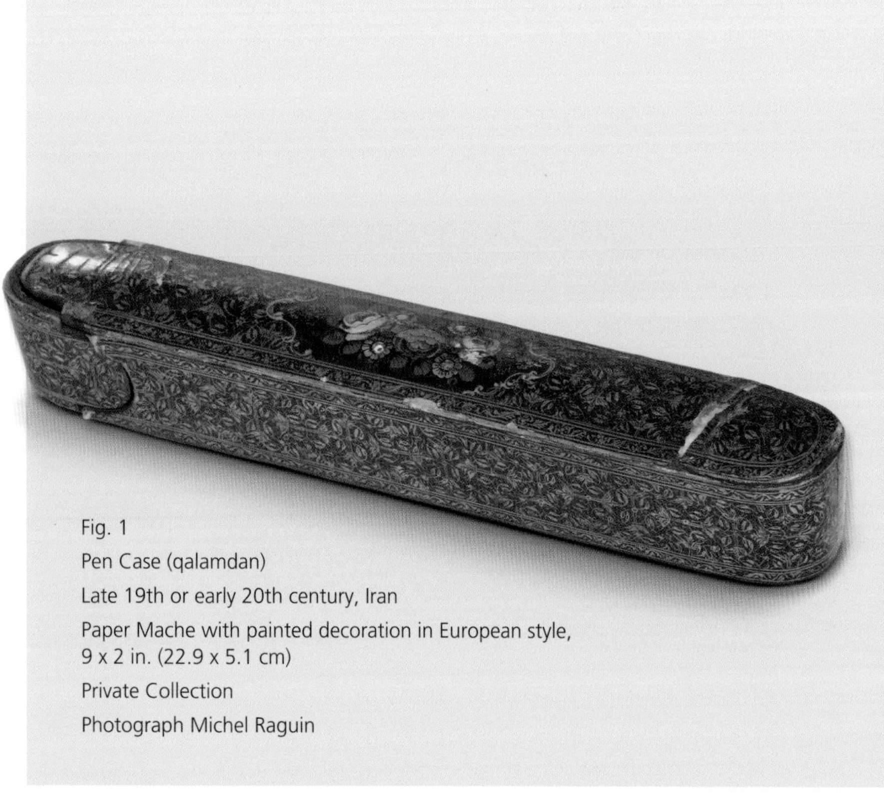

Fig. 1
Pen Case (qalamdan)
Late 19th or early 20th century, Iran
Paper Mache with painted decoration in European style, 9 x 2 in. (22.9 x 5.1 cm)
Private Collection
Photograph Michel Raguin

Fig. 2
Quran: Paper Mache cover with lacquer painting of profuse flowers
19th century, Iran
Ink, opaque watercolor, lapis lazuli, and gold on paper, 8½ x 11 in. (21.6 x 27.9 cm)
Private Collection
Photograph Michel Raguin

Fig. 3
Calligraphic Portrait of the Prophet Muhammad (*hilye*)
c. 1700-1712, Ottoman
Ink, color and gold on paper, 19½ x 11⅞ in. (49.5 x 30.2 cm)
Harvard Art Museum, Arthur M. Sackler Museum, The Edwin Binney, 3rd Collection of Turkish Art at the Harvard Art Museum, 1985.288
Photograph Imaging Department © President and Fellows of Harvard College

Fig. 4
Calligraphic Portrait of the Prophet Muhammad (*hilye*)
Mohammed Zacharia, 2001
Ink, color and gold on paper, 19½ x 11⅞ in. (49.5 x 30.2 cm)
Photograph Mohammed Zacharia

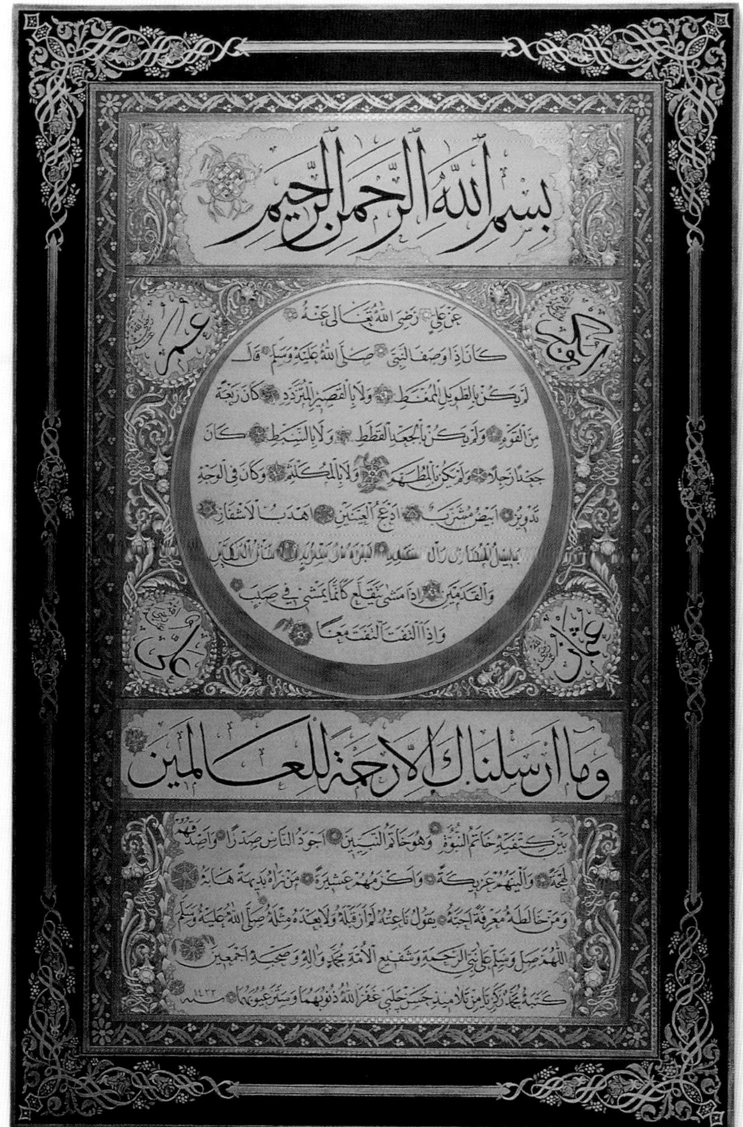

Calligraphy and ornament similarly evoke a "portrait" in a piece on the shrines of Arabia (Fig. 5). A tiny image of the shrines appears in the center, looking almost as if it is a window cut through the paper. The composition features a circle in the top half of the page, echoing the *hilye*, although the lower section is differently arranged. Despite the tiny painting of the shrines, the major focus is on their calligraphic description, suggesting again the power and holiness of the word as against the image. The illusion that the view through to the shrines has been simply cut through the paper suggests, perhaps, this deeper meaning – that it is only by means of the word that we, the viewers, can "see" the true appearance and importance of the shrines.

Although the importance of religious words in general, in describing the Prophet and describing the shrines, is unmistakable in the art objects above, the text of the Quran itself is the holiest text in Islam, as it is considered the Word of God. Many Qurans, like family Bibles, were treasured by their owners and became the repositories of family history, like this one, in which family births and deaths were recorded (Fig. 6).

Fig. 5
Vertical Wooden Panel: The Shrines of Arabia Calligraphy
19th century
Paint on framed wood panel, 22 5/16 x 9 15/16 x 9/16 in. (56.7 x 25.2 x 1.4 cm)
Harvard Art Museum, Arthur M. Sackler Museum, The Edwin Binney, 3rd Collection of Turkish Art at the Harvard Art Museum, 1985.342
Photograph Imaging Department © President and Fellows of Harvard College

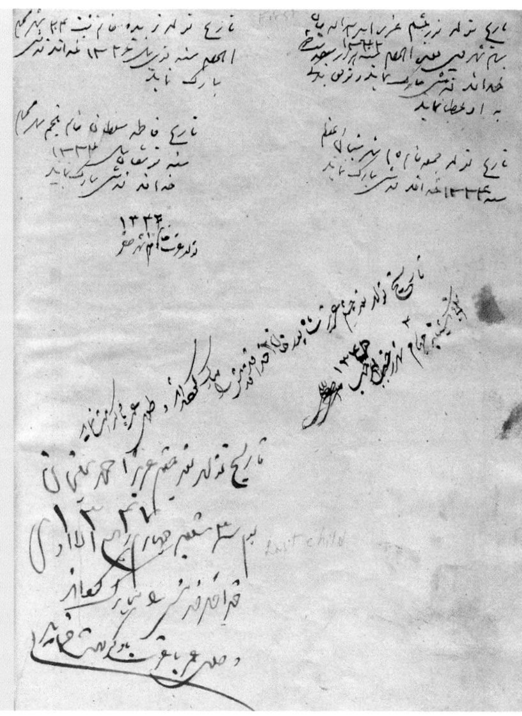

Fig. 6
Quran with dates of birth of family members from 1837 inscribed on the flyleaf
19th century, Iran
Ink, opaque watercolor, lapis lazuli, and gold on paper, 8½ x 11 in. (21.6 x 27.9 cm)
Private Collection
Photograph Michel Raguin (see also *Mecca and the Hajj*, Fig. 1)

The text of the Quran inspired many other related works, such as the story of Yusef. The narrative is an expansion of Surah 12, which tells the story of Yusuf or Joseph, the son of Jacob who is also known to Christians and Jews. While Muslims revere the Quran as the last word of God sent to man, they also honor the legitimacy of the earlier Torah (the first five books of the Old Testament), the Psalms, and the four Christian Gospels. They believe that Christians, Jews, and Muslims worship the God of Abraham, and for that reason they accord Christians and Jews the title "People of the Book" as a way of recognizing this shared heritage. Joseph, after being thrown down a well by his brothers and then sold into slavery, finds himself in the service of a great lord. Because of Joseph's amazing beauty, his lord's wife desires him, but he flees from her, and as he leaves, she tears the back of his shirt (Fig. 7). When she later accuses him of attempting the seduction, instead of the reverse, it is because his shirt is torn at the back, rather than at the front, that the truth comes out. Other illustrated versions of this story show the splendor of Joseph's surroundings, including music and dancing in front of fine wall paintings (Fig. 8).

Fig. 7

Story of Yusuf and Zulaykha (Potiphar's wife) (Retelling with amplification of Quran 12)

Zulaykha tries to seduce Yusuf

19th century, Iran

Ink, opaque watercolor and gold on paper, 8½ x 11 in. (21.6 x 27.9 cm)

Private Collection

Photograph Michel Raguin

Fig. 8

Khamsa (Quintet) Including stories of Yusuf and Zulaykha; Khusrau and Shirin; and Layla and Majnun

19th century, Iran, Isfahani Commercial Style

Ink, opaque watercolor and gold on paper, 7½ x 10 in. (19.1 x 25.4 cm)

Private Collection

Photograph Michel Raguin

Religious texts, whether from the Quran itself or prayers inspired by Quranic tradition, were considered so powerful that they were often seen to have the ability to avert evil, and hence were written on parchment or paper and stored in metal amulets. These amulets were worn, serving as a constant reminder of the centrality of the divine and its protection (Figs. 9-10). An eloquent expression, "In the Name of God, the Compassionate, the Merciful, O God! Thou art the First, there is naught before Thee, Thou art the Last, there is naught after Thee," envelops the wearer. Even shirts and body armor carrying Quranic texts are known to exist.

It is perhaps not surprising, then, to find that texts form parts of both religious and secular environments. Such texts appear on luster tiles, beautifully ornamented with metallic and deep blue glazes on a cream ground, that are highly prized in many Islamic areas. In an example from the 13th century, the text of the Quran is set against a background of foliage and birds, and very possibly could have decorated the wall of a mosque or shrine (Fig. 11). The images of birds are unusual in a fully sacred context. Similar Quranic tiles with birds, found in the shrine of '/Abd al-Samad at Natanz (1308), were defaced by later viewers who believed that such imagery of living beings had no place in a shrine (Blair and Bloom, 11). Later Islamic tradition has generally not favored the images of living beings in sacred spaces. The graceful, twining forms behind the birds suggest vines and foliage, and are therefore known as vegetal ornament. Such ornamentation suggests the luxuriant gardens of the Muslim paradise.

Another luster tile, of similar color palette, shows beasts in combat next to a single human figure (Fig. 12). This tile would have been most likely used in a palace or residential context. Wild animals and human figures might be viewed as

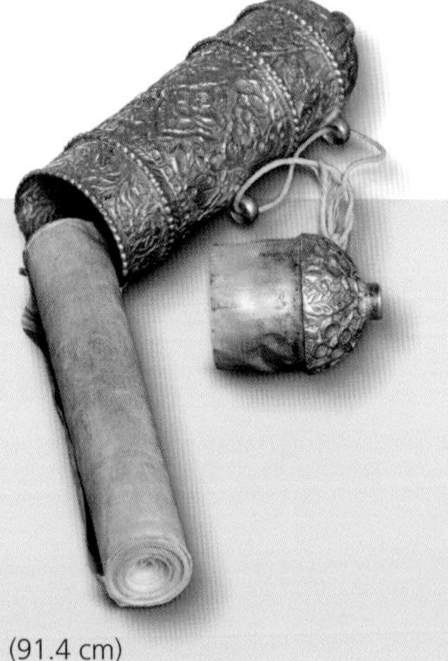

Fig. 9
Amulet
19th or 20th century, Iran
Silver, 6 x 2 in. (15.2 x 5.1 cm)
Containing a scroll with prayers: 36 in. (91.4 cm)
In the Name of God, the Compassionate, the Merciful
O God! Thou art the First, there is naught before Thee,
Thou art the Last, there is naught after Thee
Thou art the Manifest, there is naught above Thee
Thou art the Hidden, there is naught below Thee
Thou art God, the Mighty, the Wise (Medallion)
There is no god but Thee...
Followed by a litany of divine Names (O Tender One! O Generous One! etc...) and ends with the traditional invocation of blessings upon the Prophet.
The scroll has a date at the end: 1282 hijra/1869-70 C.E.
Ink, opaque watercolor and gold on paper: blue, red, and other touches of color all in vegetal motifs and geometric patterns
Private Collection
Photograph Michel Raguin

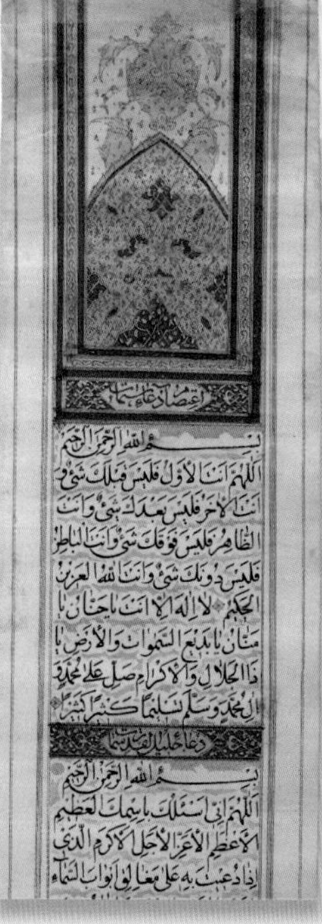

Fig. 10
Amulet
19th or 20th century, Iran
Detail of opening verses of a scroll of prayers
Private Collection
Photograph Michel Raguin

Fig. 11
Quranic tile
Kashan, Iran, 1200-1250
Glazed and painted ceramic; DIMS
Collection of the Newark Museum
Gift of Herman A.E. Jaehne and Paul C. Jaehne, 1937 37.242

illustrations to various adventure stories, or, alternately, might be understood by the viewer to have more a metaphorical, spiritual importance. A parallel in Christian culture would be the many images of the unicorn, in tapestry and other media, which was understood by many to be a metaphor for Christ. The gloriously profuse poems and stories in Islamic culture frequently make reference to Islam, and are to be understood in an Islamic context, just as (for instance) Christian medieval romance is to be understood in a Christian context, without the pretense that any and all meanings and features of these stories can be encapsulated by religion.

Contemporary Islamic art sometimes makes close reference to historical works of art, as is the case in a work by Wasma'a Chorbachi (Fig. 13). Like the Quranic luster tiles of some eight hundred years previous, ceramic tiles provide the ground for both holy words and twining decorative forms. On some of Chorbachi's tiles, the words of sacred prayer are starkly foregrounded, while on others, text shares the limelight with graceful ornament, and in others, the luxuriant growth of the vegetal forms seems to have nearly hidden the holy words. Yet in every tile, those sacred words remain present, whether at the surface or deeper. Such is the case, too, with the pilgrim. While one is on pilgrimage, sacred words and forms, asceticism and purity, are foregrounded sharply in the light of the blinding sun. Upon one's return from pilgrimage, the more colorful sights and sounds, the stories and concerns of everyday life, may grow back, kaleidoscoping in front of one's eyes. Yet always, for the pilgrim, the sacred world remains, in the foreground or the background, its features indelibly drawn – as image, and as Word.

See further reading on page 344

Fig. 12
Tile Adorned with Man Witnessing a Feline Attacking a Bull
Iran, 13th century
Glazed and painted ceramic: DIMS
Collection of the Newark Museum
Gift, 1949 Howard W. Hughes Collection 49.503

Fig. 13
The Mystery of Supplication, selection from 8 tiles
Wasmaa Chorbachi
1993
Stoneware with incised and pressed decoration, gloss glazed, each tile 14 in. (35.6 cm)
Harvard Art Museum, Arthur M. Sackler Museum,
Gift 2006.195.1-4 and 2008.130.1-4 in honor of Mary Anderson McWilliams
Photograph Imaging Department © President and Fellows of Harvard College

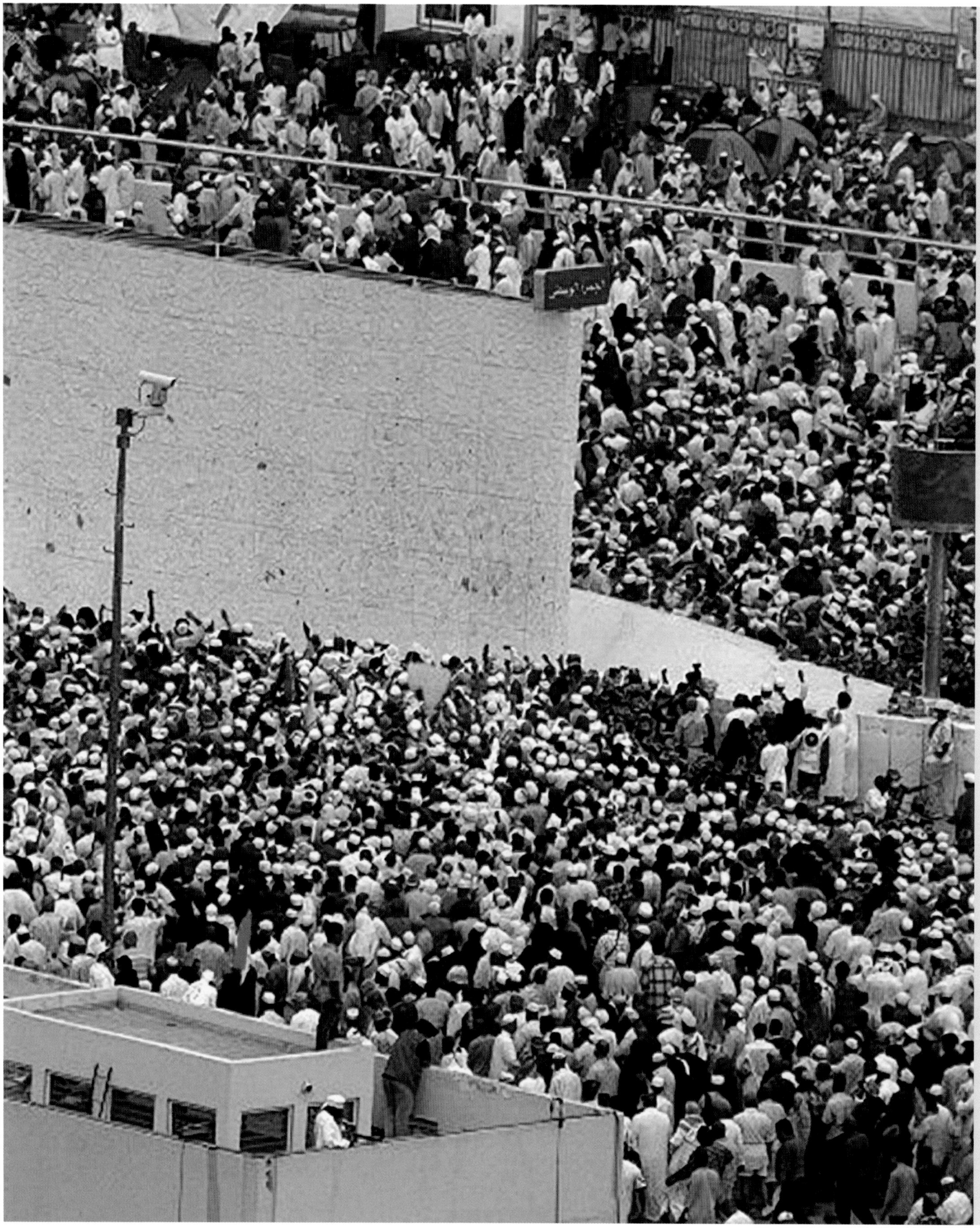

Details of Fig. 7

The Hajj Today – Connecting the Global Village

Anisa Mehdi

"Perform the pilgrimage and the visit to Mecca for Allah."

Quran 2:196 (Pickthall)

It is a straightforward and clear command. For more than fourteen centuries, Muslims from around the world have responded to this mandate, converging on the city of Mecca every year in pursuit of purification through a series of rituals. The rituals are also straightforward and clear – prayer, circling the Ka'ba, hurrying through the *sayee*, going to Arafat, throwing small stones at pillars, more walking and more praying – and they blossom into something absolutely spectacular in the 21st century, when millions of people from all over the planet endeavor to complete them simultaneously.

Time was it would take years to accomplish the visit to Mecca and the pilgrimage. Men and women traveled on horseback, by camel, in caravans across desert, by dhow across the Red Sea, and eventually by steamer from even farther seas, to arrive at the holy places on the western side of the Arabian Peninsula, a region known as the *Hijaz* (Fig. 1). Nowadays people arrive from their homelands in a matter of hours.

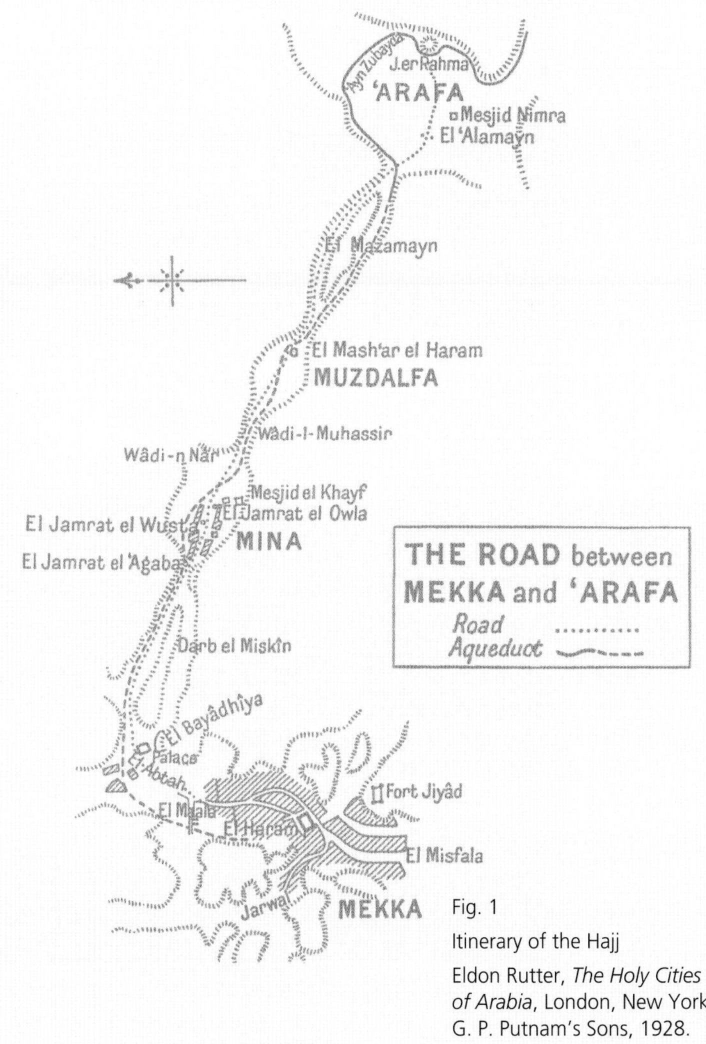

Fig. 1
Itinerary of the Hajj
Eldon Rutter, *The Holy Cities of Arabia*, London, New York: G. P. Putnam's Sons, 1928.

Long ago bandits scoured the routes to Mecca; disease and poor sanitation haunted travelers; no central government serviced those in need. Today health clinics and over-the-counter drugs are commonplace, helping combat the bacterial cocktails made by multinational multitudes. Rules and security guards abound, sometimes to the point of interfering with pilgrims' progress; your pocket may be picked, but your passport is safe.

For today's pilgrim, the threat of bandits and cholera is obsolete. Threatening the 21st-century pilgrim's experience may be impatience and arrogance. His body is tested on an ancient treadmill; she braces her soul against entitlement. The numbers and variety of people, the expanding facilities on a limited landscape, and the essential intention to perform prescribed rituals within a set period of time all bring into sharp relief the confluence of old and new, of tradition and modernity.

IN EARLIER DAYS

"And proclaim among men the Pilgrimage: they will come to you on foot and on every lean camel, coming from every remote path."

Quran 22:27 (Shakir)

In times gone by pilgrim caravans with four thousand camels laden with passengers and provisions would depart Damascus for Mecca. It took days to exit the city and weeks were spent en route (Fig. 2). Caravans snaked overland in lines as long as three miles. Security details rode alongside, alert for bandits and land pirates hungering for pilgrim supplies and cargo. Pilgrims brought not only food and water, but alms for the poor; flasks in which to collect water from the spring of Zamzam and to drink from at Arafat; latched boxes, inlaid with mother-of-pearl, in which to store trinkets and treasures; prayer rugs; and ritual clothing. From the West they docked at the port of Jeddah, from there traveling the final fifty miles or so farther east to the Holy City. Travelers coming from more easterly routes, like Baghdad and Central Asia, took refreshment at stations along "Zubayda's Way," which connected Mesopotamia to Mecca. Zubayda's Way was named after the philanthropist and visionary Queen Zubayda wife of Harun al-Rashid, Caliph of Baghdad in the early 9th century. Out of her coffers improvements to the roads were financed and maintained (Peters, 71).

By the mid-7th century pilgrims were coming from Damascus and Baghdad, Tunis and Tangier. A hundred years later Muslims from the light-filled cities of Al-Andalús, Seville, Cordoba, and Granada joined the tapestry. Pilgrims came from Bhopal, Samarkand, and Kandahar. In the 1500s ships brought Muslims from Malaysia and neighboring countries farther east and south. By the 1860s more than half of all Hajjis came from European colonies around the world. The French, British, and Dutch issued passports, visas, and health certificates before transporting pilgrims to the Hijaz via steamship through the newly opened Suez Canal. Caravan traffic dwindled after the completion, in 1908, of the Ottoman-financed rail line from Damascus to Medina (Wolfe, 197).

England's legendary Sir Richard Burton, whose *Personal Narrative* published in 1855 remains the only full-length Hajj account widely available in the West today, was one of myriad pilgrims who wrote about the journey (see essay *Richard Burton: An Englishman at Mecca and Medina in 1853*). Other famous writers are Ibn Jubayr of Spain in 1183; Ibn Battuta of Morocco in 1326; Her Highness Sikandar, the Begum of Bhopal, India, in 1864; and Michael Wolfe of California in 1993. Wolfe's *The Hadj: An American's Pilgrimage to Mecca* is testimony not only to his personal journey, but also to the increasing numbers of non-European Western pilgrims now heading for Mecca each year.

A million people live in Mecca full time. It is a year-round destination for pilgrims – who come to perform the lesser pilgrimage or *umra* at any time. But only during the final month of the Islamic calendar is the Hajj – or greater pilgrimage – performed. And Mecca is just the beginning. Iranian philosopher and revolutionary Dr. Ali Shariati (1933-1977) noted in his passionate treatise on Hajj, "Deciding to go to Mecca is not the total actualization of Hajj nor are Ka'ba or Qibla the goals of Hajj. These are misunderstandings on your part. The leader of monotheism (Abraham) teaches you that Hajj does not end in Ka'ba, but begins the moment

Fig. 2
Travelers in the Middle East in the 1840s
David Roberts, *The Holy Land: Syria, Idumea, Arabia, Egypt and Nubia. From Drawings made on the Spot by David Roberts*, with Historical Descriptions by the Rev George Croly, Lithographed by Louis Hage. London, F. G. Moon, 1842-1849.
John JoBurns Library at Boston College

Fig. 3
The Hajj Terminal at King Abdul Aziz International Airport, Jeddah, Saudi Arabia, opened in 1981 and can accommodate up to 80,000 travelers per day. The soaring, tent-like design, reminiscent of the tents used by Hajjis by Skidmore, Owings and Merrill, won the 1982 Agha Khan Award for Architecture.
Photograph Jay Langlois/Owens-Corning Fiberglass

you leave the Ka'ba. It is not your destination but the point from which you start!" (Shariati, 48).

CHANGE IS IN THE AIR

"And pilgrimage to the House is a duty unto Allah for mankind, for him who can find a way thither."

Quran 3:97 (Pickthall)

Mankind has been finding a way thither since 632 CE, making Hajj one of the most colorful gatherings of people on the planet. Men and women from Africa wearing brightly patterned *boubous* with headpieces to match. Persians draped in black *chadors*, the men in turbans of black or white. Indonesians and Malaysians in groups of pink or white or blue. Turks in olive green uniform. Afghan women in blue *burkas* and Saudi men in starched white *distashas* with red and white headscarves called *kaffiyehs* held perfectly in place by black rope called *aghal*.

In the 20th century the numbers ballooned.

The biggest change in Hajj traffic came with the jumbo jet. With air flight, people could come from farther away, faster, more frequently, and in previously unfathomable figures. Where tens of thousands of people had amassed in the 19th century, there were two million by the end of the 20th. As pilgrims came to Mecca more quickly and easily, not only did their numbers grow, but the experience of Hajj itself was transformed.

Without long overland travel, pilgrims no longer met other people – Muslim or non-Muslim – nor encountered new cultures along the route to Mecca. Ibn Battuta, traveling from Morocco through Alexandria in 1326, "went to visit the Pharos lighthouse and found one side of it in total ruin." Nearby he met Shaykh al-Murshidi, a sage and a hermit, whose food was considered blessed by villagers. Today most contact with the global community of Muslims takes place in Mecca itself or in Medina, the City of the Prophet, located in an oasis about 250 miles north of Mecca. These two holy cities host a growing "global convocation where strangers of every background" mix, with international visitors arriving on seventy-five to eighty-five flights a day at the state-of-the-art Hajj Terminal at King Abdul Aziz International Airport in Jeddah.

Hajj Terminal opened in 1981 and can accommodate some eighty thousand people for a day at a time if need be. Designed by Skidmore, Owings and Merrill, the terminal won the 1982 Agha Khan Award for Architecture (Fig. 3). In 2000, plans to renovate the terminal were already under way, anticipating the arrival of up to 9.2 million pilgrims for the Hajj by 2025.

Arguably there are benefits to faster travel. But now pilgrims come for a shorter stay, and during much of it they are dizzy with jet lag – a condition unknown to travelers wending their way to the Arabian Peninsula over the course of weeks or months. "Everybody's off their sleep pattern," said Fidelma O'Leary, an American pilgrim, on her Hajj in 2003. "I don't know anybody that's had a good night's sleep for seven or eight days" (Bredar & Mehdi, *National Geographic*).

When pilgrims arrive at Hajj Terminal, tour group leaders manage their logistics. The vast majority of pilgrims travel today in tour groups; rarely does a pilgrim come on his or her own anymore to perform Hajj. Tour guides are responsible for accommodations, travel arrangements, and food for the pilgrims in Mecca, at Mina, and at Arafat – the three principle destinations of the Hajj (Wolfe, 246). Hurdles to smooth journeying are utterly predictable: traffic jams, over-sold hotel rooms, limited supplies of food, and pilgrims getting lost, left behind, or boldly venturing off on their own.

CHANGE IS ON THE GROUND

"Wherein are plain memorials of Allah's guidance; the place where Abraham stood up to pray; and whosoever entereth it is safe."

Quran 3:97 (Pickthall)

Managing the whereabouts of pilgrims during the events of Hajj is a colossal undertaking for the Saudi Ministry of Hajj. In order to keep track of more than two million people, the ministry catalogues pilgrims according to national origin. At the tent city of Mina, for example, pilgrims are assigned

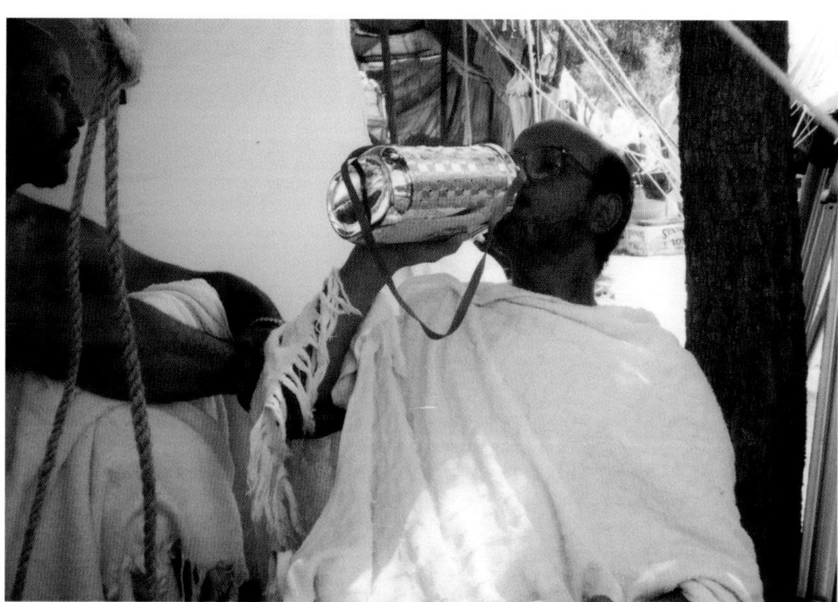

Fig. 4

Abdul Alim Mubarak made the Hajj in 1998, and, like most pilgrims, wore an identification bracelet in Arabic. Pilgrims often keep the bracelet as a memento of the experience.

Photograph © Anisa Mehdi/Whetstone Productions

Fig. 5

One of the great delights of performing the Hajj is meeting pilgrims from around the world. Abdul Alim Mubarak made the most of this opportunity on the Day of Arafat in 1998, turning strangers into friends.

Photograph © Anisa Mehdi/Whetstone Productions

quarters based on country of embarkation. Mina is about two square miles divvied into sections for Indonesians, Malays, Turks, South Africans, non-Arab Africans, Iranians, and so on. Pilgrims wear identification bracelets indicating the area of Mina to which they are assigned. Although effective, this approach is a shortcoming in the context of Hajj as a whole.

In order to fulfill one important aspect of the Hajj, Muslims must break away from the limits of the Saudi system. The opportunity of Hajj – indeed the mandate – is to meet Muslims from other places, to appreciate the diversity of the *ummah* or global community of Islam, and to see that there is no single interpretation of the faith.

During his Hajj in 1998, Abdul Alim Mubarak of Maplewood, New Jersey, positioned himself near the Mount of Mercy (*Jabal Rahma*) on the day of Arafat, and introduced himself to others approaching the hillock where Muhammad the Prophet gave his farewell sermon to pilgrims in 632. "Hi, I'm Abdul Alim from the US," he greeted them. "Where are you from?" Smiles lit up around him. In conversation with me ten years later, Mubarak recalled, "It was a meeting of different worlds, different peoples, under the banner of brotherhood. That is the whole meaning of Arafat, to get to know one another" (Figs. 4-5).

Pilgrim safety is key for the Kingdom of Saudi Arabia. The Kingdom is also the primary financial beneficiary of the annual event. After petroleum, pilgrimage is the Kingdom's second economic backbone. In 2004-2005, private sector revenues from the Hajj industry reached almost $4 billion (Fakar, *Arab News*).

But the government also gives back. The Kingdom has responded to rising numbers of pilgrims with major capital improvements, easing access to the holy sites and safeguarding the health and welfare of its guests.

When the Hajj Terminal opened in 1981 it was the world's fourth-largest air terminal. Within twenty years it was being upgraded. Currently it welcomes and processes up to 3800 pilgrims per hour (Abdullah, *Arab News*).

In the 1980s the Saudi government began a major expansion of the *Masjid al Haram*, or Noble Sanctuary, that surrounds the Ka'ba, Islam's central symbol. Modifications to the sanctuary date back to the 7th century, under direction of the second Muslim caliph, Umar. By the 1990s, close to a million people could worship in the renovated mosque and on the nearby plaza at any given time. On the third floor of the sanctuary is a television studio that broadcasts daily prayer at the Ka'ba.

The Saudi government has also modified the tent city of Mina where pilgrims stay for the several nights they are outside of Mecca. Tents had formerly been set in traditional fashion: sheets and carpets hung from rods with rugs laid below for sitting and sleeping. Tragically, Mina has been the site of fatal fires caused by cook stoves. In 1997 more than three hundred people died in fires at Mina. Subsequently, fireproof tents made of Poly Tetra Fluoro Ethylene (PTFE) replaced traditional tents. It was the biggest PTFE project in history. The total PTFE fabric used (7.16 sq. km) was one and a half times the size of the Mina Valley. A quarter of all tents were completed in time for the Hajj of 1998 (Bukhary, 31).

Another place where disaster routinely struck was the Jumrat, the place of the stoning ritual. For centuries three stone pillars sufficed for the tossing and pilgrims passed from one to the other as prescribed by tradition. But as crowds grew, pilgrims too often were suffocated or crushed in the crowd as people rushed to complete their obligations.

In the 1990s the Saudis built a two-tiered pedestrian walkway – a kind of spiritual superhighway – to ease access (*National Geographic*). Within a decade traffic was again too great, and now a new design graces the Jumrat. It is a trio of elliptical walls past which pilgrims flow as they throw stones against temptation (Fig. 7).

Alterations and improvements are imperative for safety and comfort. In addition, to control the numbers of pilgrims, the Saudi government imposes quotas on how many people may come from each country. The process for approval and distribution of Hajj visas is complex. Quotas stand at one thousand pilgrims for every million Muslims in any single country (*Islamicvoice.com*). There are an estimated five million to seven million Muslim Americans. In 2003 about seven thousand Americans made the Hajj.

PILGRIMAGE TODAY

"Then hasten onward from the place whence the multitude hasteneth onward, and ask forgiveness of Allah. Lo! Allah is Forgiving, Merciful."

Quran 2:199 (Pickthall)

There is electricity in this verse. It is animated, purposeful. Hasten. Ask forgiveness. 21st-century Muslims are eager for this absolution and favor from God. Life among the comfortable as well as life for the poor is taxing. We are not always as grateful or generous as we might be. Hajj is a route to our celestial and spiritual roots.

Today's pilgrims perform the same series of rituals described and demonstrated by Muhammad, the Prophet of Islam, in 632 CE. In taking these sacred steps Muslims believe they are obeying an even earlier command from the Creator to Abraham – Abraham, as he is called in Arabic, who called people to come and worship at this special spot. Why Mecca? The 2003 National Geographic documentary special *Inside Mecca* explains:

> *"At the heart of Islam there is a story about a place that always was. The story holds that long before the great Prophet Abraham, before Adam and Eve, even before creation, there was a holy place, the celestial house of God. It is called the Ka'ba. And its replica on earth remains today in the center of Mecca."*

Muslims don't worship the Ka'ba; they worship what it represents – the One God. The *tawaaf* or circumambulation of the Ka'ba proceeds on all three floors of the elegant and mammoth mosque. From above, it resembles a galaxy swirling counterclockwise around a heavenly center.

Circling of the Ka'ba creates a sense of communion among humans with the Almighty. For Ali Shariati, the Iranian philosopher, the experience is transcendental. "Come on – perform the Hajj! Join the river of circumambulating people by circumambulating too! After an hour of swimming in this 'stream of love,' you will abandon your 'self-centered mortal existence' and adapt to a new life among the people's 'eternal existence' on the 'eternal orbit' of Allah" (Shariati, 35).

But the pilgrimage itself is not achieved in the eternal orbit or by coming to Mecca alone. The Hajj pilgrimage begins in Mecca and climaxes at Arafat, an arid valley eighteen miles farther east.

In essence the pilgrimage dramatizes pivotal moments in the life of the family of the prophet Abraham. These stories are recounted throughout the Quran and in the Bible (Gn 16, 17, 21,22). The relocation of Abraham's second wife, Hagar, and their son, Ishmael, to a desert land far from their Palestinian home. Hagar's faithful search for water in that desert and her reward – the spring of Zamzam. God's terrible command that Abraham sacrifice his son to prove his faith, and Abraham's victory over temptation and ultimate reward – ram to sacrifice instead. The Quran further describes the relationship between Abraham and Ishmael in preparing the House of God (the Ka'ba) together for pilgrims to come. "And when We made the House (at Mecca) a resort for mankind and a sanctuary, (saying): Take as your place of worship the place where Abraham stood (to pray). And We imposed a duty upon Abraham and Ishmael, saying: Purify My House for those who go around and those who meditate therein and those who bow down and prostrate themselves in worship" (2:125).

Pilgrims come to try to build a House of God within themselves, to seek absolution and invite favor. They test themselves, asking: Is my faith on the scale of Abraham's and Hagar's? How far would I go to show my allegiance to God? Would I be willing to sacrifice my son? Do I have the strength to continue these many repetitions and long walks? How can I hasten my step when there is no space on the ground to fit my foot?

Each part of the Hajj is designed to stimulate piety, generosity, gratitude, and connection among people. In the fast-paced, consumer-oriented 21st century, these are essential tools for the seeker of inner peace and outward sustainability.

THE RITES AS TRANSFORMATIONAL EXPERIENCE

"And for every nation have We appointed a ritual, that they may mention the name of Allah over the beast of cattle that He hath given them for food; and your God is one God, therefore surrender unto Him."

Quran 22:34 (Pickthall)

Hajj is the ritual appointed to the Muslim nation. Once during his or her lifetime every Muslim who is physically and economically in a position to do so is expected to journey to Mecca, where God's climactic revelation was first disclosed. The basic purpose of the pilgrimage is to heighten the pilgrim's devotion to God and his revealed will, but the practice has fringe benefits as well. It is, for example, a reminder of human equality (Smith 247).

Preparation

To make sure the rituals are pertinent to 21st-century life, many pilgrims today embark on a study of the Hajj long before they embark on the journey itself. Some of the groups are ad hoc; many take place in mosques among congregants who will travel together. They study the Quran and the events in which they will participate. They look at maps of the landscape and peruse hotels on the Internet. Malaysia provides its pilgrims with guidance on saving money for the journey under the auspices of the Tabung Haji, Malaysia's official Hajj operation.

Classes may continue throughout the journey. In one classroom in Medina in 2003, an American instructor discussed the dress code, the *ihram*. For women it is simple, modest attire, hair covered. For men there is a greater challenge because upon reaching Mecca, male pilgrims remove their normal attire, which may carry marks of social status, and don two simple sheet-like garments. All people approaches Islam's earthly focus wearing the same thing; they are indistinguishable. Americans in the Medina class were accustomed to wearing suits and ties or jeans and tee shirts; some were ill at ease in the *ihram*, one sheet wrapped around the shoulders and the other tied from the waist down (Fig. 6). "Keep your shoulders covered," the instructor scolded his male

Fig. 6

Ihram is a state of ritual sanctity for each and every pilgrim on the Hajj. Pilgrims eschew gossip, short tempers and bad thoughts, and exercise acts of kindness. The men are required to dress in a particular manner as well. The two pieces of unstitched cloth they wrap around themselves is also called *ihram*.

Photograph © Anisa Mehdi/Whetstone Productions

students, "you must be modest." Was the men's discomfort due in part to the absence of earthly distinction as a sign of merit? Were they feeling the impact of true equality? The individualism of the late 20th century collides here with the community spirit that preceded it.

Circumambulation

Seven times pilgrims circle the Ka'ba, in the tradition of Muhammad the Prophet. Scholars don't know the origin of that tradition. The number seven holds power and mystery in other religious traditions and in numerology. Seven heavens. Seven days in a week. Pilgrims circle the Ka'ba and make the *sayee* seven times when they first arrive in Mecca, and seven times again after completing the Hajj rituals at Arafat and the Jumrat. Circling the Ka'ba is difficult in a crowd. When Abdul Alim Mubarak made his pilgrimage in 1998, the month of Hajj was coincident with March. It was hot. Mubarak toiled six hours to complete the *tawaaf*. "This was six grueling hours, and I was out in the blazing sun, and I had no cover on my head. I was dripping, soaking wet with sweat. You wouldn't do this for an ordinary man, you only do this for Allah, you know. So you go through this process because you know that you're doing it for Allah, and Allah will reward you for it."

The 20th-century Iranian philosopher Ali Shariati had no doubt about the reward. "After completing the seventh round of circumambulation, the state of *tawaaf* ends. Seventh? Yes! It is not simply the sum of six plus one, but it is a reminder of the seven layers of heaven. *Tawaaf*, your sacrifice for people, is an eternal movement on the path of people!" For Shariati, Hajj goes far beyond the physical journey. "It is Hajj and NOT a pilgrimage. Isn't this a genuine demonstration of existence? Isn't this the actual translation of *Tawheed* (the principle of the Oneness of God) and its true interpretation?!!" (Shariati, 33).

Sayee

Then pilgrims make the *sayee*: seven jaunts back and forth on a straight course between two small hills encased within the structure of the Noble Sanctuary. The hustle between these hills recreates Hagar's desperate search for water for her son after Abraham left them at the site that became Mecca.

Who is Hagar for the contemporary Muslim? She proves the worth of women and the high place held by mothers. She commands the respect of the entire community by dint of her strength, courage, conviction, and faith. All pilgrims, male, female, young, and old, retrace her steps in an effort to achieve a sense of her humility.

"Hagar was an example for humanity," writes Ali Shariati in his awe of Hagar's submission to God's will. "Allah, the great love and ally of man, ordered her to leave her home with her nursing child. She was told to go to the fearful valley of Mecca where no plant, not even thistles, will grow. Out of love for Allah, she understood and accepted this order. All of this because Allah wanted absolute reliance upon Him! Oh lonely maid, a helpless nursing mother, you and your child must rely upon Allah. Feeling secure with love, rely upon Him!" (Shariati, 32).

In a commentary on the *sayee* for National Public Radio that was broadcast in 2005, I tried to put myself into Hagar's sandals. "I wanted to have just a scrap of her kind of faith. I wanted to approximate her anxiety as she looked for water. I wanted to feel her female power, the kind a mother has when her child is in danger and those primal instincts rise to save the day." Hagar, who started her life as a slave, holds a high bar for all of today's Hajjis.

Arafat

Pilgrims must reach this plain east of Mina on the tenth day of *Dhul Hijjah* (the month of Hajj) and remain within its clearly marked boundaries or their Hajj may not count. Muslims believe that Adam and Eve found each other here after they were expelled from Eden. The day is spent in contemplation, prayer, and petition. The "Standing" at Arafat is seen as an earthly rehearsal for the Day of Judgment. And there is more.

The pilgrim's connection to the broader communion of Muslims becomes unambiguous at Arafat. The area is about six miles by four miles, jam-packed with people sharing a commitment that transcends national and ethnic loyalties. This is indeed part of the heart of Hajj. It affirms Surah 49, verse 13 from the Quran: "Oh Humankind! Lo! We have created you male and female, and have made you nations and tribes that ye may know one another. Lo! The noblest of you, in the sight of Allah, is the best in conduct. Lo! Allah is Knower, Aware" (Pickthall).

In an age of splintering nation-states, of ethnic ties and ethnic cleansings, of linguistic groupings and rigid definitions of patriotism, the experience of connection at the level of species and spirit is profound.

Back in New Jersey a decade after his Hajj, Abdul Alim Mubarak, whose Hajj I covered for PBS, still feels the influence of his encounters at Arafat. "I met some Palestinian brothers at Arafat and today, when Palestinians are being slaughtered in their homeland, I can feel with them," he reminisced with me. "That seed that was planted ten years ago has germinated and has grown in terms of concern for my fellow human beings. And you don't have to be Muslim to be part of my concern. They happened to be Muslim during the Hajj, but I know they represented other human beings from everywhere on Earth. It's an experience of shared humanity."

Muzdalifa

In the dusk following the long day at Arafat, pilgrims scrounge on the ground at a way station called Muzdalifa en route to Mina for pebbles to use in the next ritual: the Jumrat or stoning of the devil. The devil is represented by columns, and more recently, by the elliptical wall built in 2006 to ease access to the event (Fig. 7). Most people will sleep here under the stars, resting up for the strenuous activity of the day to come. In the busy daily lives of many Muslim professionals, the lesson of Muzdalifa is in girding one's strength.

Fig. 7

The stoning at Jumrat is facilitated by the elliptical wall built in 2006. Pilgrims throw stones at the wall in remembrance of Abraham's three temptations by Satan.

Photograph Courtesy Ministry of Hajj, Kingdom of Saudi Arabia

Jumrat

The stoning of the devil is another reenactment from the drama of Abraham. When God asked him to sacrifice his son, Abraham obeyed (Gn 22). According to various Islamic tellings of the story, Abraham leads his son up a hillside, explaining to him what is about to pass. The son, as faithful as his father, says he willingly submits to God's command. But Abraham remains distraught and the devil steps in to lure him away from God's plan.

"He started having some doubts and he realized that these doubts were really coming from the whisperings of Satan," explains Daisy Khan, executive director of the American Society for Muslim Advancement on the National Geographic documentary *Inside Mecca*. "We don't know exactly what Satan would have said, but it was something like, 'what do you think you're doing killing your son? Are you crazy?'"

Abraham gets angry and throws stones at Satan and gets rid of him once. Satan returns because it's his job to misguide people. Three times Satan taunts Abraham and three times he is repulsed with stones. The Jumrat constitutes the three stoning points

"As a ritual it has tremendous power," says Fidelma O'Leary, an associate professor of biology at St. Edward's University in Austin, Texas. "The more ways – physically, mentally, spiritually, verbally – the more ways that you try to contain the evil and the temptation then I think the more effective it's bound to be. I thought from a scientific point of view that that was a really good ritual" (Bredar and Mehdi).

The Sacrifice

Of course, the sacrifice of the son is aborted. At the last minute a ram comes on the scene and Abraham interprets this as a substitute, a redemption, from God. The ram is blessed and slaughtered. In the 21st century, this becomes what is considered the world's largest ritual sacrifice of animals. It is also an enormous, communal act of charity. Although pilgrims do not perform the sacrifice hands-on as they did in the past, they pay for the animal and for the services of the butcher. The pilgrim is apportioned some of the meat, but the bulk is processed, packaged, and sent to hungry people around the world.

Eid al Adha: The Feast of the Sacrifice

Following the final Jumrat event, all pilgrims trim their hair in a show of new birth and humility; male pilgrims change back into street clothing. Although there are still several rounds of stoning to complete, the *Eid al Adha* is under way. This is the feast celebrating the end of Hajj, the redemption of Abraham's son, and the prophet's extraordinary show of faith. Pilgrims also return to circle the Ka'ba. On her final round in 2003, Fidelma O'Leary reflected, "When you really want to go on Hajj you feel you've been invited. God wants me! And it's a really good feeling. And then you get here and you look around and you see there are millions of other people and you are like an ant and your significance is suddenly down to zero. It's a paradox, but it's a good paradox (Bredar and Mehdi). People celebrate *Eid* worldwide, with Muslims everywhere feasting – or fasting – in solidarity with the pilgrims in Mecca. This is a spiritual and celestial connection" (Fig. 8).

RETURN AND RENEWAL

The Hajj pilgrimage is one of the preeminent ways for Muslims and non-Muslims to appreciate what is at the heart of Islam. It is a quest for identity and absolution; it is an adventure for the body and soul. It is a drama based on a story known to many; it offers personal transformation in an age of skepticism and resignation.

In a modern world, the implications of this experience are as diverse as the personalities and the cultures of the Hajjis themselves. The results of performing pilgrimage may be personal, but they also touch one's wider world. To be a better Muslim means to live more authentically the precepts of Islam in daily life. Ismail Mahbob, a Malay pilgrim featured on *Inside Mecca*, promised to be "a better father, better worker, better leader, better subordinate." Mahbob's employer in Kuala Lumpur's financial sector was so impressed with his worker's professional performance on his return from the Hajj that he promoted Mahbob shortly thereafter. Subsequently, Mahbob started his own business. As a result of having been featured on a national television program, Abdul Alim Mubarak finds himself invited to give talks on Islam at conferences, churches, and schools.

Fig. 8
Fidelma O'Leary of Austin, Texas, completed her Hajj in 2003. Her journey was the subject of a National Geographic documentary film. This Muslim of Irish descent joins an increasing number of people from non-Muslim-majority countries participating in the Hajj each year.
Photograph © Reza/Webistan

A professional television news editor, he offers feedback to colleagues and provides resources and new sources to advance more accurate coverage of events relating to Islam and Muslims.

For O'Leary, Hajj stimulated a shift in attitude. "If I lined up my priorities before going to Hajj they were much more worldly: my profession and so on. Now I look for more time to read and study," she told me six years after her pilgrimage. "My understanding of Islam has deepened. And the first step for approaching that was humility – accepting the fact that I didn't really know as much as I thought." In addition she is more relaxed. "Instead of trying to manipulate everything in my world, I leave the big things to God."

Pilgrims return refreshed and cleansed to circumstances that are unchanged: home, work, school. But having experienced forgiveness on the plain of Arafat, many find it easier to forgive others. Tuning in to the *tawheed*, the Oneness, at Arafat creates a connection with humankind that will at least challenge, if not transcend, the biases and stereotypes about others that remain imbedded in their home cultures. Mores of the twenty-first century can be balanced against enduring traditions uplifting community, humility, and simplicity.

Pilgrims still carry canteens to collect the waters of Zamzam, both to drink at Arafat and to bring home and savor, but the flasks are more than likely made in China. Trinkets like prayer beads and remembrances like little stones from Muzdalifa will decorate lacquered office desks where once they adorned wooden chests inlaid with mother-of-pearl. The pilgrim has faced adversity and has conquered. He knows he is beloved of God and also utterly inconsequential to his Maker. She is at peace with paradoxes of life and faith though they still perplex. Hajjis share an unbreakable connection across humanity's timeline with those who have journeyed before and those who will travel in the years ahead. And they know the search for the sublime goes on.

See further reading on page 344

Details of Fig. 2

Personal Reflections of a Hajjah and Others

Najah Bazzy

THE MIGHTY MATRIARCH SITTI – THE FIRST GENERATION – 1972

I remember quite vividly the tears and hugs at the Detroit Metro Airport as we bid our grandmother farewell for her journey to Hajj in 1972. A good-bye in those days could have been a good-bye forever, as many who left for the journey of Hajj did not return but rather traveled to their eternal abode. Sitti (grandmother) was in her seventies. It was quite typical that only the elderly would make the journey to Hajj. She hugged each of us as though it was her last hug. She took in all of our scents as though to carry her last breath of us with her. She clung to my mother and aunts, entrusting them with all kinds of advice. "Be good, forgive me, I forgive you, remember to pray for me, I will pray for you and your children, don't forget the orphans in our family, be good to your spouses." So on went the motherly words to the generations that watched her embark upon this journey. I knew this was a monumental time. The airport was filled with families shedding tears as others bid their loved ones good-bye. I was only twelve years old at the time.

My only understanding of Hajj came from the brochure that I'd read over and again to my unlettered Sitti as she had prepared for this journey. Pictures of the cubic black structure called the Ka'ba, and names of stops along the way were mapped out for her to take on her journey. I remember Sitti packing her travel items, and explaining to me what these special items were. A bag for her pebbles with which she would pelt Satan, which I imagined was like a passage out of *The Wizard of Oz*; a pouch for her passport; and special white clothing that she later asked my mother to bury her in. Sitti seemed so old to me at the time and I remember thinking to myself that I would go to Hajj when I was thirty-six years old! My mother was thirty-six and the ideal robust energetic women who would certainly return to her children, something I was not sure my grandmother would. Sitti would comfort me by saying, "I am visiting Allah's home on earth and He is the best host. I am His guest and He has the right to return me home or take me to Him. Don't worry about me, whatever Allah wishes for me Insha'Allah (God willing) will happen."

When my Sitti returned home safely the celebration was so big it resembled a wedding feast. She filled my mind with images and stories that I would carry in my heart and soul for years to come. She still looked like Sitti, but somehow she was wiser, and more content with the opportunity to meet her Maker. Her eyes held more meaning and she looked radiant with contentment although her wrinkled face bore a resemblance to that of a tired, desert-baked shepherd. She and I shared a bed, and through her new enchantment with her Lord, I learned her prayers as she whispered them in the dark of the night. I too began to build the foundation of my own relationship with God through her whispered worship.

THE SECOND GENERATION – 1982

A decade later the scene would repeat itself, except this time my mother, at the age of fifty-two, would make her journey. She had been a toddler when her family moved from the United States to Lebanon and Syria; she returned when she fifteen without having attended school. By now I was twenty-two and a nurse, yet the child in me still worried that mama may not come home, this time due to the political tensions in Saudi Arabia. Once again I read to an unlettered woman the colorful brochure that mapped out the journey beginning with the arrival in the Holy City of Medina, where the Prophet Muhammad (peace be upon him) is buried. Once again I stood near my mother's side as she packed the important and vital items that she would need, a pouch for the pebbles, white clothing called her *ihram*, a hide-away zippered undershirt to conceal her money from opportunists, her passport pouch, and more. Tears streamed down our faces as she began to feel the time approach to leave. The airport scene was once again filled with emotion and tears. The litany of pledges and promises began as she clung to each of us, whispering in our ears the words of a mother. Be good, take care of your father and brothers, pray for me. Her oral last will and testament began to flow from her speech as we listened and cried. There is no way to describe the emotions felt by someone leaving on Hajj. No matter how many times the journey is made, there is a feeling of excitement bundled with a submission and surrender of the soul that cannot be captured in words. My mother returned from Hajj safely and again we witnessed a celebration with flowers, banners, and hand waving. Screaming family members waited at the doors of international arrivals for just a glimpse of the new Hajjis getting their baggage cleared.

Indeed, mother's stories carry on till this day and she frequently breaks into tears when speaking to her grandchildren and great grandchildren of her journey. With satellite now broadcasting from around the world, she stays tuned to the Saudi Channel, which shows the daily activity of Mecca and Medina. When the call to prayer occurs in Mecca, mom can be found glued to the T.V. with a smile and sense of peace upon her face. She prays daily with hands lifted to the heavens that God will return her to Hajj one more time before she leaves this earth.

Fig. 1

Michigan Pilgrims on Hajj in Saudia Arabia

Photograph Najah Bazzy

Fig. 2

Prayer rug, open, showing images of the Kaba of Mecca and the Mosque that contains the Tomb of the Prophet Mohammed in Medina

THE THIRD GENERATION – 1996

At the age of thirty-six I would find myself on my first independent journey to make my Hajj. By this time in life, I was an accomplished nurse and a busy mother of four children between the ages of four and eleven. It was April 19, 1996, and I rushed home after taking my last final exam to complete a second college degree. My mother was packing my suitcase. The difference was I was able to take my Holy Quran in English, CDs, and a journal to document my trip, not to mention a video camera of course. It was a *deja vu* moment as she packed my white clothes, a pouch for the pebbles that I would gather in the valley called Muzdalifa, and the necessities she felt I must have with me. My mother fought back tears in between packing items. She reminded me of all the safety tips: "Keep your picture I.D. on you at all times, never stray from the group, be careful what you eat, drink only bottled water, give alms to the poor but be wary of opportunist beggars in the streets, pray for everyone." She could not understand my desire to go at such an early age while leaving behind young children. She both approved and disapproved, but recognized my calling. The beckoning or invitation from God seems to be a call that comes as a whisper in the depth of one's soul. The journey returns the pilgrim to his or her primordial self, to the land of Adam and Eve, and the footsteps of the Prophets of God. I would make the Hajj six more times as of this writing, between 1996 and 2008. However, for the past five years I have gone in the capacity of Senior Advisor to an aspiring youth group called the YMA (Young Muslim Association), of the Islamic Center of America, in Dearborn, Michigan.

THE FOURTH GENERATION – 2005

The YMA began in 1999 with a core group of American Muslim youth congregates, organized by two American-born Senior Advisors and led by Imam Sayed Hassan Al Qazwini, the director of the Islamic Center of America. From 2001 to 2004, the YMA took smaller groups, ranging in age from sixteen to sixty, to Hajj. The YMA provided the opportunity to both youth and adult American Muslims who spoke English as their primary language. The number of YMA pilgrims grew from ten to almost sixty in three years (Fig. 1). In 2005 and 2006 I would have the opportunity to accompany two of my own children, Nadia and Tarik Bazzy, and two of my younger brothers, Reyad and Adnen Mallad. Nadia and Tarik were both eighteen when they made their first Hajj, half my age when I first accomplished the pilgrimage. My brothers were thirty-five and forty-three, both younger than our mother was when she made her first journey. There has been a steady and increasing phenomenon of younger Muslims throughout the world making their Hajj (Figs. 2-4).

Fig. 3
Guidebooks in English for the Hajj; clay prayer beads; clay pressed into a round tablet

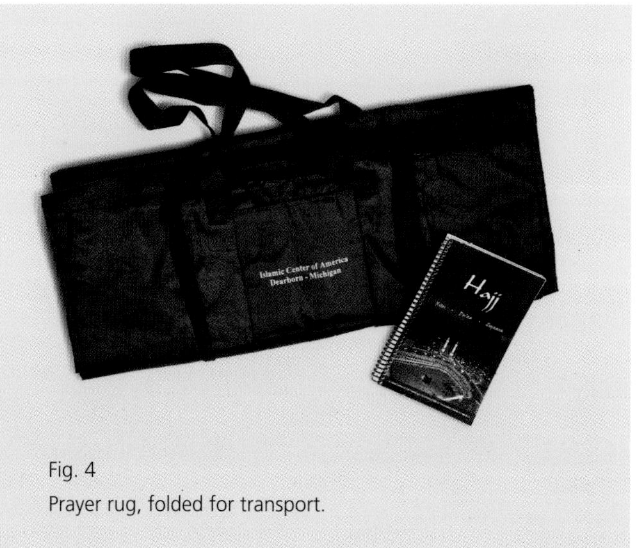

Fig. 4
Prayer rug, folded for transport.

From 2006 to 2008, the Hajj fell between Christmas and the New Year, thus giving high school and college students an opportunity to make the two- to three-week journey. I cherished hearing their reflections, as exemplified by Amenia, age twenty: "Millions of people are walking in *tawaaf* (circling the Ka'ba), different colors, sizes, shapes, and languages. Each is having a spiritual experience within a human existence. I am reminded of a verse from the Holy Quran (Surah 49:13): 'God says, I have created you nations and tribes that you may come to know one another.' Truly God is central to our existence and the act of circumambulation reflects the message that all things rotate around God, the spiritual orbit of humankind."

As I looked upon the two-and-a-half million pilgrims, I saw that many had faces of the younger generations from all around the globe. Hajj had broken through the generation gap. It was no longer the traditional trip of the aging, but the vigorous trip of the young as well. We labor to bring these young people to affirm their faith and to see their responsibilities toward others. I recall a conversation under the stars with YMA pilgrims in the Valley of Muzdalifa (between Mina and Arafat where pilgrims sleep out of doors and where they gather stones to throw the next day at Satan symbolized by the pillars of Mina): "Muzdalifa is like a human homeless camp of spiritual refugees, who have left their homes in search of God," one young pilgrim said. "It is fitting that your mattress is the earth, your roof is the starlit heavens, and the company around you is the world. In Muzdalifa it is said that Allah orders out the creatures and inhabitants to protect the Hajj visitors. They become homeless, that we find our home that night in safety and security. It is not a valley that the eyes would behold with beauty, but rather something the soul beholds with beauty. We feel one with the deprived in the world, the homeless, helpless, cold, and destitute."

Emann Allebban, age twenty, replied to my request to describe an incredible moment in Hajj with the following: "I'm at a loss. The right thing to say is: every moment was incredible. And while that is true in some sense, my most honest answer is that I had no truly incredible moment. I had no profoundly religious experience, no miracles or visions, no instant spiritual rebirth and transformation which was everything I was expecting going in, at least this is what I think many of us are led to believe. And so I walked the marble floors of the Great Mosque, looking down on the Ka'ba from the second floor, with unease: 'God, what am I doing wrong? What am I suppose to learn here?' It wasn't until after returning from Hajj that I came to understand that there may not be any one incredible moment at Hajj, but there's not supposed to be. God was teaching me that my growth in this life isn't so easily achieved by taking a trip for a couple of weeks. Rather, it's acquired and sustained by what I bring home from those couple of weeks to implement every day of my life." Such reflections encourage me to believe that these young Muslims who begin their adult lives with Hajj will become spiritual brokers for peace, justice, and equity in the human family.

Acknowledgments

Many people have contributed to this effort. Dina Bangdel and Virginia C. Raguin in consultation with Anisa Mehdi began initial discussions in 2007; a number of scholars, most represented in the catalogue, were contacted. In early 2008 F. E. Peters joined the project. We want to express our deepest thanks for the support from the National Endowment for the Arts and from private donors among them Cornelius B. Prior and John V. Raguin.

Our four venues:

College of the Holy Cross
Roger Hankins, Director of the Iris and B.G. Cantor Gallery; Paul Rosenblum, Administrative Assistant, Iris and B.G. Cantor Gallery; Timothy Johnson, Independent Preparator; Thomas Landy, Director of the Center for Religion, Ethics, and Culture; Charles S. Weiss, Director of Grants and Corporate and Foundation Giving; Barbara Burke, Assistant Coordinator of Grants and Corporate and Foundation Giving; The Committee on Faculty Scholarship; The Marshall Fund, administered by the Center for Interdisciplinary and Special Studies; Cassie Murphy, Administrative Assistant, Department of Visual Arts; Margaret Nelson, Academic Computing Support Specialist, Educational Technology; Nancy Andrews, Director of Montserrat; Faye Caouette, Administrative Assistant, Montserrat. Our special thanks to Rev. Michael C. McFarland, S.J., President of the College of the Holy Cross.

Loyola University Museum of Art
Pamela E. Ambrose, Director of Cultural Affairs; Jonathan P. Canning, Martin D'Arcy Curator of Art; Andrew Cunningham, Exhibits Manager; and Ann Meehan, Curator of Education. From the faculty: Dr. Theresa Gross-Diaz, History Department; Dr. Marcia K. Hermansen and Dr. Tracy Pintchman, Theology Department; and Dr. Eileen M. Daily and Dr. William S. Schmidt, Institute of Pastoral Studies.

University of Richmond
From the museum: Mr. Richard Waller, Executive Director of the University Museums, and his staff; from the faculty: Dr. Stephen Addiss, Tucker-Boatwright Professor of Humanities-Art and Professor of Art History; Dr. Elena Calvillo, Assistant Professor of Art History; Dr. Margaret Denton, Associate Professor of Art History; Dr. Olenka Pevny, Assistant Professor of Art History; and Dr. Miranda Shaw, Associate Professor of Religion; from the administration: Dr. Edward L. Ayers, President; Dr. Stephen Allred, Provost and Vice President for Academic Affairs; and Dr. Andrew F. Newcomb, Dean of the School of Arts and Sciences. University Museums acknowledges funding from the University's Louis S. Booth Arts Fund and the Cultural Affairs Committee. Dina Bangdel has worked closely with the museum. At Virginia Commonwealth University, our special thanks to Dr. Richard E. Toscan, Dean of the School of the Arts and Vice-Provost for International Affairs, and Dr. Fredrika Jacobs, Chair of the Department of Art History.

Rubin Museum of Art
Rubin Museum of Art, New York, Martin Brauen, Chief Curator, and Becky Bloom, Assistant Curator.

Our lenders:

Art Institute of Chicago: Dr. James Cuno, Director; Jay Clarke, Former Associate Curator of Prints and Drawings; Christina Nielsen, Assistant Curator for Medieval Art, Medieval Art; Suzanne McCullagh, Anne Vogt Fuller and Marion Titus Searl Curator of Prints and Drawings.

Boston College, John J. Burns Library: David E. Horn, Head, Archives & Manuscripts; Barbara Adams Hebard, Conservator.

Boston Public Library: Prints and Drawings: Karen Shafts, Curator; Rare Books and Manuscripts: Susan Glover, Keeper of Special Collections.

College of the Holy Cross: Karen Riley, Acting Director, Dinand Library.

Harvard University Art Museums: Mary McWilliams, Norma Jean Calderwood Curator of Islamic & Later Indian Art; Francine Flynn, Senior Associate Registrar.

Loyola University Museum of Art: Jonathan Canning, Curator of the Martin D'Arcy Collection.

Rubin Museum of Art New York: Martin Brauen, Chief Curator; Becky Bloom, Assistant Curator.

Metropolitan Museum of Art: Department of Medieval Art: Peter Barnet, Michel David-Weill Curator in Charge; Christine Brennan, Collections Manager; Department of Asian Art: Alison Clark, Collections Management Associate

The Newark Museum: Katherine Anne Paul, Curator of the Arts of Asia; Amber Germano, Associate Registrar

Library of Virginia, Richmond: Tom Camden, Director of Special Collections

Private Lenders: Sylvan Barnet and William Burto, Najah Bazzy, Elizabeth ten Grotenhuis; Robert and Marilyn Hamburger, Anisa Mehdi, and additional private lenders

It has been a privilege to work with all the contributors to the catalogue: Dina Bangdel, Virginia Commonwealth University; Najah Bazzy, Canton, MI; Martin Brauen, Rubin Museum of Art; Kerry Lucinda Brown, Virginia Commonwealth University; Megan Foster Campbell; Edward Holgate, Albuquerque, NM; Krisadawan Hongladarom. Chulalongkorn University, Thailand; Toni Huber, Humboldt Universität, Berlin; Susan L. Huntington, The Ohio State University; Paula Gerson, Florida State University; Oleg Grabar, Institute for Advanced Study, Princeton; Mitzi Kirkland-Ives, Missouri State University; Jennifer Lee, Indiana University Purdue University, Indianapolis, IL; Amanda Luyster, College of the Holy Cross; Alex McNair, University of Wisconsin-Parkside; Mika Natif, College of the Holy Cross; David M. Perry, Dominican University, River Forest, IL ; Frank. E. Peters, emeritus, New York University; Virginia C. Raguin, College of the Holy Cross; Kathryn M. Rudy, Koninklijke Bibliotheek, The Hague, The Netherlands; Elizabeth ten Grotenhuis, emerita, Boston University.

Advice and material support came from many sources: We want to thank George D. Greenia, Editor at Large, La corónica, College of William & Mary, Williamsburg; John C. Huntington, The Ohio State University; Todd Lewis, College of the Holy Cross; William Shea, Former Director, Center for Religion Culture and Ethics, College of the Holy Cross; Bieito Pérez Outeiriño, Director; Isabel Pesquera Vaquero, Conservadora de museos, Área de Documentación, Museo das Peregrinacións, Sanitago, Compostela; Rebecca Nichols.

Photographs and diagrams:

Individuals: S. M. Amin, Sanu Bajracharya, Lain S. Bangdel, Cathleen A. Cummings, Abdullah Y. Al-Dobais, Dr. Kurt Gitter and Ms. Alice Yelen, Toni Huber, Eric R. Huntington, John C. Huntington, Nicole Lawrence, Bill Lyons, Samia El-Moslimany, Toni Neubauer, Michel Raguin, Rachel Raguin, Norma Schulz, David Shankbone, Katrina Thomas, William Tracy, David H. Wells, Stuart Whatling, Mark A. Wilson, Wonderlane, and our authors.

Institutions: Archnet; British Library Board, London; Koninklijke Bibliotheek, The Hague; Jay Langlois/Owens-Corning Fiberglass; Huntington Archive, The Ohio State University; Ministry of Hajj, Kingdom of Saudi Arabia; Museum of London; Museo das Peregrinacións, Sanitago, Compostela; Oxford, Bodleian Library; Philadelphia Museum of Art; Queen of the Americas Guild; Réunion des Musées Nationaux/ Art Resource, NY; Reza/Webistan; Royal Ontario Museum; *Saudi Aramco World*; Swami Nardanand, Siddha Ashram; Virginia Museum of Fine Arts; and the lending institutions.

We are grateful for our visually elegant design to Serindia Publications: Shane Suvikapakornkul, editor; Lisa Graziano, text editor.

List of Contributors

EDITORS

Virginia C. Raguin is Professor of Art History, College of the Holy Cross. She has published widely on material culture, stained glass, and architecture, including *Display and Destruction: Art and Piety in Christian Religion, 1500-1700*, editor (Ashgate Publishing, 2010); *Stained Glass from its Origins to the Present* (Harry Abrams and Thames and Hudson, 2003), and *Artistic Integration in Gothic Buildings,* editor (Toronto University Press, 1995). She has also curated exhibitions on stained glass and piety, including *Catholic Collecting, Catholic Reflection 1538-1850: Objects as a measure of reflection on a Catholic past and the construction of recusant identity in England and America*, 2006 (distributed by The Catholic University of America Press).

Dina Bangdel is Associate Professor of Art History, Virginia Commonwealth University. She specializes in South Asian and Himalayan Art. In 2004 she received the Gorakha Dakshina Bahu VI (Nepal's highest honors for the arts). With John C. Huntington, she curated the exhibition *Circle of Bliss: Buddhist Meditational Art*, organized by the Los Angeles County Museum of Art and the Columbus Museum of Art. The catalogue (Serindia Publications, 2003) was a finalist for the 2005 Alfred Barr Jr. Award from the College Art Association. She is also the editor of *Sculpture of King Jayavarma and the Varma Dynasty of Nepal* (Mandala Publications, 2005).

with Francis E. Peters. Professor Emeritus of Middle Eastern and Islamic Studies at New York University. Peters interests are wide ranging, dealing with Christians, Jews, and Muslims in the Middle East. His many publications include a series with Princeton University Press: *The Children of Abraham* (1982; new ed. 2004); *The Hajj: The Muslim Pilgrimage to Mecca and the Holy Places* (1995), *Judaism, Christianity, and Islam*: 3 volumes (1990), *Jerusalem: The Holy City in the Eyes of Chroniclers, Visitors, Pilgrims and Prophets from the Days of Abraham to the Beginnings of Modern Times* (1985; paperback edition 1995); and recently *The Voice, the Word, the Books, the Sacred Scripture of the Jews, Christians, and Muslims* (2007).

CONTRIBUTORS

Najah Bazzy lives in Michigan and is a Transcultural Nurse involved with Arab and Muslim patients. Her work has been featured in *The New York Times* and *USA Today*. In 2007, she completed her fifth pilgrimage of the Hajj, and during the past three years has, mentored nearly 100 young men and women who were making their own Hajj. Bazzy is founder and director of Zaman International – Hope for Humanity, a humanitarian service organization.

Martin Brauen is chief curator of the Rubin Museum of Art, New York and has organized multiple exhibitions on Asian culture in Europe and the United States. His books include *The Mandala: Sacred Circle in Tibetan Buddhism*, trans. Martin Willson (Random House, 1997) and, in collaboration with Renate Koller and Markus Vock, *Dreamworld Tibet: Western Illusions* trans. Martin Willson (Orchid Press, 2004).

Kerry Lucinda Brown is a doctoral candidate in the Department of Art History at Virginia Commonwealth University. She specializes in South Asian and Himalayan Art, and has spent significant time over the last ten years researching and traveling in India and Nepal. Her current research focuses on Dipankara Buddha in Nepal and the practices of gift-giving in South Asia.

Megan Foster-Campbell, received her Ph.D. from the University of Illinois at Urbana-Champaign. Her dissertation examines pilgrims' badges, as actual souvenirs or as painted representations, in devotional manuscripts of the15th and early 16th centuries. Her research thus addresses religion in public pilgrimage and in private contemplation through prayer books.

Edward Holgate received his MA from Brown University and is an expert on Christian Folk Art of Europe and the Americas. He is owner and director of *Saints & Martyrs*, an art and antique gallery in Albuquerque, New Mexico The gallery is one of the few specializing in devotional antiques from Europe and the Americas, including santos, milagros, paintings, folk art, pilgrimage mementos, ex votos, and Spanish Colonial art.

Krisadawan Hongladarom, Ph D. Indiana University, is a specialist in Tibetan language and culture. She is an Associate Professor of linguistics at Chulalongkorn University, Thailand and has conducted numerous research projects on Tibetan dialects, particularly Kham Tibetan. In 2004 she established the Thousand Stars Foundation to promote understanding of Tibetan culture and to foster education and Dharma practice for children, nuns and retreatants in Tibet.

Paula Gerson is Professor of Medieval Art at Florida State University. She was formerly the Executive Manager of the International Center of Medieval Art at the Cloisters in New York City. Her major fields are Romanesque and Gothic Art and Architecture; she has published widely in these fields, including such books as *The Pilgrim's Guide to Santiago de Compostela: A Gazetteer* (Harvey Miller Publishers, 1995) and "Body-Part Reliquaries and Body Parts in the Middle Ages," with Caroline Bynum, *Gesta* 36 (1997).

Oleg Grabar is Professor Emeritus at the Institute for Advanced Study in the School of Historical Studies, Princeton. He has been a major force in the development of scholarship on Islamic Art and is the author of eighteen books, including *The Shape of The Holy: Early Islamic Jerusalem* (1996) and *The Mediation of Ornament* (1992), both by Princeton University Press, and *The Dome of the Rock* (Harvard University Press, 2006), as well as more than 140 articles.

Toni Huber, Humboldt University, Berlin, is a prolific author concentrating on anthropology and cultural history of Tibet and Himalayan areas. Among his works are *The Cult of Pure Crystal Mountain: Popular Pilgrimage and Visionary Landscape in Southeast Tibet* (Oxford University Press, 1999) and *The Holy Land Reborn: Pilgrimage and the Tibetan Reinvention of Buddhist India* (Chicago University Press, 2008).

Susan L. Huntington is Distinguished University Professor in the Department of History of Art, The Ohio State University, Columbus, Ohio. With John C. Huntington she is the co-founder of the Huntington Photographic Archive of Asian Art, housing approximately 300,000 photographs. Her publications include *The Pala-Sena School of Sculpture* (1984), *Art of Ancient India* (1985), and *Leaves from the Bodhi Tree: The Art of Pala India and its International Legacy* (1990).

Mitzi Kirkland-Ives, Ph. D. University of California, Santa Barbara, is Assistant Professor, Department of Art and Design, Missouri State University. She has published articles on Early Modern devotional art, including "Theme and Variation in Early Modern Stational Devotions" in *Viator: Medieval and Renaissance Studies* 40 No. 1 (2009). At present she is preparing a book on narrative performance and devotional experience in the art of Hans Memling.

Jennifer M. Lee is an Assistant Professor of Art History at Indiana University Purdue University, Indianapolis. Her publications include "Searching for Signs: Pilgrims' Identity and Experience Made Visible in the *Miracula Sancti Thomae Cantuariensis*" in *Art and Architecture of Late Medieval Pilgrimage in Northern Europe and the British Isles*, Sarah Blick and Rita Tekippe, eds. (Brill Publications, 2005).

Amanda Luyster teaches Art History at the College of the Holy Cross. She has published articles on artistic interchange in both the Christian and the Islamic medieval worlds, including cultural exchange in Papal Avignon and a study of the Alhambra. Most recently she has edited, with Alicia Walker, *Negotiating Secular and Sacred in Medieval Art: Christian, Islamic, and Buddhist* (Farnham, Surrey, England; Burlington, VT: Ashgate, 2009).

Alexander J. McNair is Chair of the Department of Modern Languages at the University of Wisconsin. He specializes in literature of the Golden Age of Spain and has published literary criticism in the form of essays and reviews in journals such as *Hispanic Review, Romance Notes, Calíope: The Journal of the Society for Renaissance and Baroque Hispanic Poetry, Explicator,* and *Renaissance Quarterly*.

Anisa Mehdi is an Emmy Award -- winning journalist. She received critical acclaim for producing and directing *Inside Mecca*, a documentary film on the pilgrimage for National Geographic Special, premiering on PBS in 2003. Mehdi also produced an award-winning series on the Hajj for PBS's "Religion and Ethics Newsweekly" in 1998. In 2002 she won the Cine Golden Eagle Award as executive producer of the PBS "Frontline" special *Muslims*.

Mika Natif, Ph.D. Institute of Fine Arts, New York University, is the Mellon Post-Doctoral Fellow in the History of Art at the College of the Holy Cross. She has been a visiting lecturer at Princeton University and a Hagop Kevorkian Fellow at the Metropolitan Museum of Art. Among her publications is "The Zafarnama [Book of Conquest] of Sultan Husayn Mirza" in *Insights and Interpretations*, Colum Hourihane, ed. (Princeton University Press, 2002).

David M. Perry received his Ph.D. in 2006 and is Assistant Professor in the Department of History at Dominican University, Ohio. His research focuses on the Crusades and relics and his publications include "St. Simon and the Seven Thieves: A Venetian Fourth Crusade *Furta Sacra* Narrative and the Looting of Constantinople" in *The Fourth Crusade: Event, Aftermath, and Perceptions*, Thomas Madden, ed. (Ashgate Publications, 2008).

Kathryn M. Rudy is the Keeper of Illuminated Manuscripts at the Koninklijke Bibliotheek in The Hague. She works primarily on devotional art in Northern Europe of the 14th through 16th centuries, in particular Middle Dutch manuscripts. Among her publications is *Weaving, Veiling, and Dressing: Textiles and their Metaphors in the Late Middle Ages,* edited with Barbara Baert, Medieval Church Studies, vol. 12 (Brepols, 2007).

Elizabeth ten Grotenhuis is Professor Emerita at Boston University. She has extensive experience in translating and editing as well as curating exhibitions on Japanese art and culture. Her publications include *Japanese Mandalas: Representations of Sacred Geography* (University of Hawai'i Press, 1999) and *Along the Silk Road* (Arthur M. Sackler Gallery and University of Washington Press, 2002).

Further Reading

BUDDHISM

Relics, Pilgrimage, and Personal Transformation in Buddhism

Huntington, John C. "Sowing the Seeds of the Lotus: A Journey to the Great Pilgrimage Sites of Buddhism," part 1 [Lumbini and Bodhgaya], *Orientations* 16, no. 11 (Nov. 1985):46-61.

_____. "Sowing the Seeds of the Lotus: A Journey to the Great Pilgrimage Sites of Buddhism," part 2 [Rishipatana Mrigadava], *Orientations* 17, no. 2 (Feb. 1986):28-43.

_____. "Sowing the Seeds of the Lotus: A Journey to the Great Pilgrimage Sites of Buddhism," part 3 [Shravasti and Sankashya], *Orientations* 17 no. 3 (March 1986):32-46.

_____. "Sowing the Seeds of the Lotus: A Journey to the Great Pilgrimage Sites of Buddhism," part 4 [Vaishali and Rajagriha], *Orientations* 17, no. 7 (July 1986):28-40.

_____. "Sowing the Seeds of the Lotus: A Journey to the Great Pilgrimage Sites of Buddhism," part 5 [Kushinagara, Appendices, and Notes], *Orientations* 17, no. 9 (Sept. 1986):46-58.

_____. "Pilgrimage as Image: the Cult of the Astamahapratiharya," part 1, *Orientations* 18, no. 4 (April 1987):55-63.

_____. "Pilgrimage as Image: the Cult of the Astamahapratiharya," part 2, *Orientations* 18, no. 8 (Aug. 1987):56-68.

Huntington, Susan L. "Early Buddhist Art and the Theory of Aniconism." *Art Journal* 49/4 (Winter 1990):401-408.

Huntington, Susan L. "Aniconism and the Multivalence of Emblems: Another Look." *Ars Orientalis* 22 (1992):111-156.

"The Obama Effect," In "Best and Worst of 2008," *People* (December 29, 2008):63.

Rhys-Davids, Thomas W., trans. 1881. *Buddhist Suttas, Sacred Books of the East*, vol. 11. Pt.1 The Maha-parinibbana Suttanna. Oxford: Clarendon Press.

Strong, John S. 2004. *Relics of the Buddha*. Princeton: Princeton University Press.

Trainor, Kevin. 1997. *Relics, Ritual, and Representation in Buddhism*. Cambridge: Cambridge University Press.

Willis, Michael. 2000. *Buddhist Reliquaries from Ancient India*. London: British Museum.

Tracing the Footsteps of the Buddha: Pilgrimage to the Eight Great Places (*Ashtamahasthana*)

Aitken, M. 1995. *Meeting the Buddha: On Pilgrimage in Buddhist India*. New York: Riverhead Books.

Guy, J. 1991. "The Mahabodhi Temple: Pilgrim Souvenirs of Buddhist India," *Burlington Magazine* 133 (1059):356-68.

Huntington, John C. "Sowing the Seeds of the Lotus: A Journey to the Great Pilgrimage Sites of Buddhism," part 1 [Lumbini and Bodhgaya], *Orientations* 16, no. 11 (Nov. 1985):46-61.

_____. "Sowing the Seeds of the Lotus: A Journey to the Great Pilgrimage Sites of Buddhism," part 2 [Rishipatana Mrigadava], *Orientations* 17, no. 2 (Feb. 1986):28-43.

_____. "Sowing the Seeds of the Lotus: A Journey to the Great Pilgrimage Sites of Buddhism," part 3 [Shravasti and Sankashya], *Orientations* 17 no. 3 (March 1986):32-46.

_____. "Sowing the Seeds of the Lotus: A Journey to the Great Pilgrimage Sites of Buddhism," part 4 [Vaishali and Rajagriha], *Orientations* 17, no. 7 (July 1986):28-40.

_____. "Sowing the Seeds of the Lotus: A Journey to the Great Pilgrimage Sites of Buddhism," part 5 [Kushinagara, Appendices, and Notes], *Orientations* 17, no. 9 (Sept. 1986):46-58.

_____. "Pilgrimage as Image: the Cult of the Astamahapratiharya," part 1, *Orientations* 18, no. 4 (April 1987):55-63.

_____. "Pilgrimage as Image: the Cult of the Astamahapratiharya," part 2, *Orientations* 18, no. 8 (Aug. 1987):56-68.

Huntington, S. L. and J. C. Huntington, 1990. *Leaves from the Bodhi Tree: The Art of Pala India (8th-12th Centuries) and its International Legacy*. Seattle: University of Washington Press.

Leoshko, J. 1988. *Bodhgaya the Site of Enligtenment*. Bombay: Marg Publications.

Huber, T. 2008. *Holy Land Reborn: Pilgrimage and the Tibetan Reinvention of Buddhist India*. Chicago: University of Chicago Press.

Pilgrimage Traditions in Nepal

Buffetrille, Katia. 2000. *Pelerins, Lamas et Visionnaires: Sources Orales et Ecrites sur les Pelerinages Tibetains*. Arbeitskreis für Tibetische und Buddhistische Studien: Vienna.

Dawa-Samdup, Kazi, ed. 1987. *Shri-Cakrasamvara-Tantra: A Buddhist Tantra*. Tantrik Texts, vol. VII., 1919. New Delhi: Reprint. Aditya Prakashan.

Dowman, Keith. 1995. *Power Places of Kathmandu: Hindu and Buddhist Holy Sites in the Sacred Valley of Nepal*. Rochester, VT and London: Inner Traditions International and Thames & Hudson.

Gellner, David N. 1992. *Monk, Householder, and Tantric Priest: Newar Buddhism and Its Hierarchy of Ritual*. Cambridge: Cambridge University Press.

Huntington, John, and Dina Bangdel. 2003. *Circle of Bliss: Buddhist Meditational Art*. Serindia Publications: Chicago.

Lewis, Todd. 2000. *Popular Buddhist Texts from Nepal: Narratives and Rituals of Newar Buddhism*. State University of New York Press: Albany, NY.

Gyatso, Janet. 1999. *Apparitions of the Self: The Secret Autobiographies of a Tibetan Visionary by Jigme Lingpa, Jigs-Med-Glin-Pa Ran-Byun-Rdo-Rje*. Princeton: Princeton University Press.

Gutschow, Niels. 1997. *The Nepalese Caitya: 1500 Years of Buddhist Votive Architecture in the Kathmandu Valley*. Stuttgart and London: Ed. Axel Menges.

Roerich, George, ed. 1959. *Biography of Dharmasvamin (Chag lo tsa ba Chos-rje-dpal): A Tibetan Monk Pilgrim*. Patna: K. P. Jayaswal Research Institute.

Slusser, Mary S. 1979. "Serpent, Sages, and Sorcerers in Cleveland." *Bulletin of the Cleveland Museum of Art* 66, no 2:67-82.

_____. 1982. *Nepal Mandala*. Princeton: Princeton University Press.

_____. 1985. "On a Sixteenth-Century Pictorial Pilgrim's Guide from Nepal." *Archives of Asian Art* 38:6-36.

Vergati, Anne. 2004. "A Newar Pilgrimage to the Lake of Gosainkund." In *Nepal: Old images, new insights*. Pal Pratapaditya, ed. Bombay: Marg Publications, 115-128.

Pilgrimage and Gift-Giving in Newar Buddhism

Allen, Michael. 1992. "Procession and Pilgrimage in Newar Buddhism." *The Australian Journal of Anthropology* 2, no. 3:130-43.

Brown, Kerry Lucinda. 2003. "Dipankara Buddha in Nepal: A Contextualization of the Newar Buddhist Iconography and Iconology." MA thesis, The Ohio State University.

Findley, Ellison Banks. 2003. *Dana: Giving and Getting in Pali Buddhism*. Delhi: Motilal Banarsidass Publishers.

Heim, Maria. 2004. *Theories of the Gift in South Asia*. New York: Routledge.

Lewis, Todd T. 2000. *Popular Buddhist Texts from Nepal: Narratives and Rituals of Newar Buddhism*. Albany: State University of New York Press.

Owens, Bruce McCoy. 2000. "Envisioning Identity: Deity, Person, and Practice in the Kathmandu Valley." *American Ethnologist* 27, no. 3:702-35.

Vergati, Anne. 2000. *Gods and Masks of the Kathmandu Valley*. New Delhi: D. K. Printworld.

_____. 1995. *Gods, Men and Territory*. Reprint. New Delhi: Manohar Publishers.

_____. 1982. "Le culte et l'iconographie du Buddha Dipankara dans la vallée de Kathmandou." *Arts Asiatiques* 37:22-27.

Pilgrimage in Tibet

Bernbaum, Edwin. 1982. *Der Weg nach Shambhala – Auf der Suche nach dem sagenhaften Königreich im Himalaya*. Hamburg: Papyrus Verlag.

Buffetrille, Katia. 2000. *Pèlerins, Lamas et Visionnaires. Sources Orales et Écrites sur les Pèlerinages Tibétains*. Wien: Arbeitskreis für Tibetische und Buddhistische Studien Universität.

Ekvall, Robert. B., and James F. Downs. 1987. *Tibetan Pilgrimage*. Tokyo: Institute for the Study of Languages and Cultures of Asia & Africa.

Ferrari, A. 1958. *mK'yen-brtse's Guide to the Holy Places of Central Tibet*. Roma: IsMEO (*Serie Orientale Roma*, XVI).

Huber, Toni. 1999. *The Cult of Pure Crystal Mountain: Popular Pilgrimage and Visionary Landscape in Southeast Tibet*. New York: Oxford University Press.

_____, ed. 1999. *Sacred Spaces and Powerful Places in Tibetan Culture: A Collection of Essays*. Dharamsala: Library of Tibetan Works and Archives.

_____. 2000. *The Guide to India. A Tibetan Account by Amdo Gendun Chöphel*. Dharamsala: Library of Tibetan Works and Archives.

_____. 2008. *The Holy Land Reborn: Pilgrimage and the Tibetan Reinvention of Buddhist India*. Chicago: University of Chicago Press.

Jest, Corneille. 1985. *La turquoise de vie: un pèlerinage tibétain*. Paris: Métailié.

Johnson, Russell, and Kerry Moran. 1989. Kailas: *On Pilgrimage to the Sacred Mountain of Tibet*. London: Thames and Hudson.

Large-Blondeau, A. M. 1960. "Les pèlerinages tibétains." In *Les Pèlerinages*. Paris: Editions du Seuil (*Collection Sources Orientale*, 3), 199-246.

Macdonald, A. W., and Dvags-po Rin-po-che. 1981. "Un guide peu lu des lieux-saints du Népal – 2eme Partie." In *Tantric and Taoist Studies in honour of R. A. Stein*, vol.1. Michel Strickmann, ed. Bruxelles: Institut Belge des Hautes Etudes Chinoises (*Mélanges chinois et bouddhiques*, vol. XXII), 237-73.

McKay, Alex, ed. 1998. *Pilgrimage in Tibet*. Richmond: Curzon Press.

Newman, J. 1996. "Itineraries to Shambhala." In *Tibetan Literature. Studies in Genre*. José I. Cabezón and R. R. Jackson, eds. Ithaca NY: Snow Lion, 485-99.

Tucci, Giuseppe. 1940. *Travels of Tibetan Pilgrims in the Swat Valley*. Calcutta: The Greater India Society.

Pilgrimages to Paradise

Aris, Michael. 1975. "Report on the University of California Expedition to Kutang and Nubri in Northern Nepal in Autumn 1973." *Contributions to Nepalese Studies* 2:45-87.

_____. 1979. *Bhutan, the Early History of a Himalayan Kingdom*. Warminster: Aris and Phillips.

Bacot, Jacques. 1997. *Le Tibet révolté: vers Népémakö, la terre promise des Tibétains 1909-1910*. Paris: Phébus.

Bernbaum, Edwin. 1980. *The Way to Shambhala*. Garden City NY: Anchor Press.

Damdinsüren, Cėdėm. 1977. "Sambala, the Happy Land of the Legend." *Zentral-asiatische Studien* 11.

Evans-Wentz, Walter Y. 1960. *Tibetan Yoga and Secret Doctines*. 2nd edition. London: Oxford University Press.

Gerber, Peter. 1975. *Die Peyote-Religion nordamerikanischer Indianer*. Zollikon: A. Wohlgemuth.

Grünwedel, Albert. 1915. "Der Weg nach Sambhala (Samb'alai lam yig) des dritten Gross-Lama von bKra sis lhun po bLo bzang dPal ldan Ye ses." *Abhandlungen der Königlichen Bayerischen Akademie des Wissenschafte*, 29/3.

La Barre, Weston. 1971. "Materials for a History of Studies of Crisis Cults: A Bibliographic Essay." *Current Anthropology* 12/1 (February):3ff.

Laufer, Berthold. 1907. "Zur buddhistischen Literatur der Uiguren." In *T'oung Pao*, vol. 8, 2nd series. London.

Mühlmann, Wilhelm E. 1961. *Chiliasmus und Nativismus, Studien zur Psychologie, Soziologie und historischen Kasuistik der Umsturzbewegungen*. Berlin: D. Reimer.

Müller, F. Max, trans. 1972. Sukhavativyuha-sutra, in Buddhist Mahayana Texts: Sacred Books of the East, vol. 49. Oxford, 1894; reprinted, Delhi.

Oppitz, Michael. 1974. "Shangri-la, le panneau de marque d'un flipper: Analyse semiologique d'un mythe visuel." *L'Homme*, 14/3-4 (July-December):59-83.

Reinhard, Johan. 1978. "Khembalung: the Hidden Valley." *Kailas*, 6/1.

Schwieger, Peter. 1978. *Ein tibetisches Wunschgebet um Wiedergeburt in der Sukhavati*. St. Augustin: VGH Wissenschaftverlag.

Talmon, Y. 1962. "Pursuit of the Millennium: The Relation between Religious and Social Change." *Archives européennes de sociologie*, III.

Thrupp, Sylvia L., ed. 1970. *Millenial Dreams in Action: Studies in Revolutionary Religious Movements*. New York: Schocken Books.

Wylie, Turrell V. 1962. *The Geography of Tibet according to the 'Dzam-gling rgyas-bshad*. Rome: Istituto italiano per il Medio ed Estremo Oriente.

Saikoku Pilgrimages: Japanese Devotees Search for Kannon

del Alisal, Maria Rodriguez. 2007. "New Forms of Pilgrimage in Japanese Society." In *Pilgrimages and Spiritual Quests in Japan*, Maria Rodriguez del Alisal, et al., eds. London and New York: Routledge, 74-83.

Bambling, Michele. 1996. "The Kongô-ji Screens: Illuminating the Tradition of *Yamato-e 'Sun and Moon' Screens." Orientations* (September):70-82.

Inoue, Yasushi. 1981. "Passage to Fudaraku." *Lou-lan and Other Stories*. James T. Araki, trans. Tokyo, New York, and London: Kodansha International.

Katô Bunnô, et al. 1975. *The Threefold Lotus Sutra*. New York and Tokyo: Weatherhill/Kosei.

Moerman, D. Max. 2005. *Localizing Paradise: Kumano Pilgrimage and the Religious Landscape of Premodern Japan*. Cambridge, MA, and London: Harvard University Asia Center,.

Rimer, J. Thomas. 1988. *Pilgrimages: Aspects of Japanese Literature and Culture*. Honolulu: University of Hawai'i Press.

Statler, Oliver. 1983. *Japanese Pilgrimage*. New York, Morrow.

ten Grotenhuis, Elizabeth. 1999. *Japanese Mandalas: Representations of Sacred Geography*. Honolulu: University of Hawai'i Press.

Usui, Sachiko. 2007. "The Concept of Pilgrimage in Japan." In *Pilgrimages and Spiritual Quests in Japan*. Maria Rodriguez del Alisal, et al., eds. London and New York: Routledge, 27-38.

Yü, Chün-fang. 1992. "P'u-t'o Shan: Pilgrimage and the Creation of the Chinese Potalaka." In *Pilgrims and Sacred Sites in China*. Susan Naquin and Chün-fang Yü, eds. Berkeley and Los Angeles: University of California Press, 190-245.

CHRISTIANITY

Christian Pilgrimage in the Middle Ages and the Renaissance

Brewyn,William. 1933. *A Fifteenth Century Guidebook to the Principal Churches of Rome*. C. Evenleigh Woodruff, trans. London: Marshall Press Limited.

Capgrave, John. 1911. *Ye Solace of Pilgrimes: A Description of Rome circa A.D. 1450 by John Capgrave, an Austin Friar of King's Lynn*. C. A. Mills, ed. London: Oxford University Press.

Caviness, Madeline. 1977. *The Early Stained Glass of Canterbury Cathedral: 1175-1220*. Princeton: Princeton University Press.

Elsner, Jaś. 2009. *The Oxford Handbook of Byzantine Studies*. Oxford: Oxford University Press.

Frugoni, Arsenio, ed. 1998. *Rome: The Pilgrim's Dream*. Florence: Giunti.

Furnivall, Frederick J., ed. 1867. *The Stacions of Rome* (Vernon Ms). London: Early English Text Society.

Head, Thomas. 2005. *Hagiography and the Cult of Saints: The Diocese of Orléans, 800-1200*. Cambridge: Cambridge University Press.

Hillgarth, J. N., ed. 1986. *Christianity and Paganism, 350-750*. Philadelphia: University of Pennsylvania Press.

Jones, Pamela M. 2008. *Altarpieces and Their Viewers in the Churches of Rome from Caravaggio to Guido Reni*. Visual Culture in Early Modernity. Aldershot: Ashgate Publishing Company.

Kühnel, Bianca, ed. 1987/88. *The Real and Ideal Jerusalem in Jewish, Christian and Islamic Art*: The Hebrew University of Jerusalem. *Journal of the Center for Jewish Art* 23/24.

Love, Nicholas. 2004. *The Mirror of the Blessed Life of Jesus Christ*. Michael G. Sargent, ed. Exeter: Exeter Medieval Texts & Studies Series.

Morris, Colin. 2005. *The Sepulchre of Christ and the Medieval West from the Beginning to 1600*. Oxford and New York: Oxford University Press.

Nichols, Francis Morgan, ed. and trans. 1986. *The Marvels of Rome, Mirabilia Urbis Romana*. New York: Italica Press.

Osborne, John, ed. and trans. 1987. *The Marvels of Rome*. Toronto: Toronto University Press.

Ragusa, Isa and Rosalie Green, eds. and trans. 1961. *Meditations on the Life of Christ*. Princeton: Princeton University Press.

St. John Damascene. 1898. *On Holy Images*. Mary H. Allies, trans. London: Thomas Baker, 10-17.Internet Medieval Sourcebook, ©Paul Halsall, Feb 1996.

The Relics of the Infancy of Christ at Rome's Santa Maria Maggiore

Brewyn, William. 1933. *A Fifteenth Century Guidebook to the Principal Churches of Rome*. C. Evenleigh Woodruff, trans. London: Marshall Press Limited.

Capgrave, John. 1911. *Ye Solace of Pilgrimes: A Description of Rome circa A.D. 1450 by John Capgrave, an Austin Friar of King's Lynn*. C. A. Mills, ed. London: Oxford University Press.

Furnivall, Frederick J., ed. 1867. *The Stacions of Rome* (Vernon Ms). London: Early English Text Society.

Kessler, Herbert L., and Joanna Zacharias. 2000. *Rome 1300: On the Path of the Pilgrim*. New Haven: Yale University Press.

Nichols, Francis Morgan, ed. and trans. 1889. *The Marvels of Rome*. London: Ellis and Elvey.

Rome's Santa Croce in Gerusalemme and Relics of the Passion of Christ

Baert, Barbara. 2004. *A Heritage of Holy Wood. The Legend of the True Cross in Text and Image*. Lee Preedy, trans. Leyden: Brill.

Brewyn, William. 1933. *A Fifteenth Century Guidebook to the Principal Churches of Rome*. C. Evenleigh Woodruff, trans. London: Marshall Press Limited.

Catholic Encyclopedia. 16 vols. New York: Robert Appleton Company, 1907-1914. http://www.newadvent.org/cathen/.

Fabri, Félix. 2003. *Les errances de Frère Félix, pélerin en Terre sainte, en Arabie et en Égypte (1480-1483)*. Vol. 2, *Troisième et quatrième traités*. Latin text with introduction, translation and notes made under the direction of Jean Meyers and Nicole Chareyron. Montpellier: Publications de l'Université Paul-Valéry et du CERCAM. Visit to church of the Holy Sepulcher, 165-91.

Furnivall, Frederick J., ed. 1867. *The Stacions of Rome* (Vernon Ms). London: Early English Text Society.

Krautheimer, Richard. 1980. *Rome, Profile of a City, 312-1308*. Princeton: Princeton University Press.

Saint Peter's in Rome and the Relics of Veronica's Veil

Belting, Hans. 1994. *Likeness and Presence: A History of the Image before the Era of Art*. Chicago: University of Chicago Press. Chapter 11 and Appendix 27.

Brewyn, William. 1933. A *Fifteenth Century Guidebook to the Principal Churches of Rome*. C. Eveleigh Woodruff, trans. London: Marshall Press.

Capgrave, John. 1911. *Ye Solace of Pilgrimes: A Description of Rome circa A.D. 1450 by John Capgrave, an Austin Friar of King's Lynn*. C. A. Milles, ed. London: Oxford University Press.

Furnivall, Frederick J., ed. 1867. *The Stacions of Rome* (Vernon Ms). London: Early English Text Society.

Kessler, Herbert, and Gerhard Wolf, eds. 1997. *The Holy Face and the Paradox of Representation*. Bologna: Nuova Alfa Editoriale, esp. Gerhard Wolf, "From Mandylion to Veronica: Picturing the 'Disembodied' Face and Disseminating the True Image of Christ in the Latin West," 153-79.

Relics Defined: Discoveries on Site, Invention, Translation, and *Furta Sacra*

Aigrain, René. 1953. *L'Hagiographie: ses sources, ses methodes, son histoire*. Poitiers: Bloud and Gay.

Brown, Peter. 1981. *The Cult of the Saints: Its Rise and Function in Latin Christianity*. Chicago: University of Chicago Press.

Dooley, Edward. 1931. "Church Law on Sacred Relics." Ph.D. diss. Canon Law. [Washington, D. C.]: The Catholic University of America.

Geary, Patrick. 1994. "Sacred Commodities: The Circulation of Medieval Relics." In *Living with the Dead in the Middle Ages.* Ithaca NY: Cornell University Press, 177-93.

_____. 1978. *Furta Sacra: Thefts of Relics in the Central Middle Ages.* Princeton: Princeton University Press.

Heinzelmann, Martin. 1979. *Translationsberichte und andere Quellen des Reliquienkultes.* Turnhout: Brepols.

Monk of S. George. 1877-1904. "Translatio corporis beatissimi Pauli martyris, de Constantinopoli Venetias." *Exuviae Sacrae Constantinopolitanae.* I. P. Riant, ed. Paris: E. Leroux, 141-49.

Cloistered Women's Strategies for Taking Mental Pilgrimages in Northern Europe

Carls, Wieland, and Felix Fabri. 1999. *Die Sionpilger* (*Texte des späten Mittelalters und der frühen Neuzeit,* 39). Berlin: Erich Schmidt Verlag.

Gonnet, C. J. "Overwegingen op het lijden des Heeren: voor degenen die in den geest de heilige plaatsen willen bezoeken." *Bijdragen voor de Geschiedenis van het Bisdom van Haarlem* 11 (1884):324-43.

Miedema, Nine. 1998. "Following in the Footsteps of Christ: Pilgrimage and Passion Devotion." In *The Broken Body: Passion Devotion in Late-Medieval Culture.* A. A. MacDonald, H. N. B. Ridderbos, and R. M. Schlusemann, eds. Groningen: Egbert Forsten, 73-92.

Müller, Wolfgang. 1982. "Die Villinger Frauenklöster des Mittelalters und der Neuzeit." *200 Jahre Kloster St. Ursula Villingen,* 14-31.

Rudy, Kathryn M. 2000."Den aflaet der heiliger stat Jherusalem ende des berchs van Calvarien: Indulgenced Prayers for Mental Holy Land Pilgrimage in Manuscripts from the St. Agnes Convent in Maaseik." *Ons geestelijk erf:* 75:211-54.

A Souvenir on Your Hat: Medieval Christian Pilgrims' Badges

Blick, Sarah, and Rita Tekippe, eds. 2005. *The Art and Architecture of Late Medieval Pilgrimage.* Leiden: Brill.

Bruna, Denis. 1996. *Ensignes de pèlerinages et ensignes profanes.* Paris: Musée National du Moyen Âge.

Grabar, André. 1958. *Ampoules de Terre Sainte* (*Monza-Bobbio*). Paris: Librairie C. Klincksieck.

Kicken, Dory, ed. (Medieval Badges Foundation) http://www.medievalbadges.org.

Kühne, Hartmut, Lothar Lambacher, and Konrad Vanja, eds. 2008. *Das Zeichen am Hut im Mittelalter: Europäische Reisemarkierungen.* Symposion in Memoriam Kurt Köster (1912-1986) und Katalog der Pilgerzeichen im Kunstgewerbemuseum und im Museum für Byzantinische Kunst der Staatlichen Museen zu Berlin [exhibition: Berlin: Staatliche Museen zu Berlin] Frankfurt am Main. New York: P. Lang.

Lee, Jennifer. 2003. "Signs of Affinity: Canterbury Pilgrims' Signs Contextualized, 1171-1538." Ph.D. Diss. [Atlanta] Emory University.

Lightbown, Ronald. 1992. *Medieval European Jewelry.* London: Victoria and Albert Museum.

Spencer, Brian. 1998. *Pilgrim Souvenirs and Secular Badges. Medieval Finds from Excavations in London* 7. London: Stationery Office.

Spencer, Brian. 1990. *Salisbury and South Wiltshire Museum Medieval Catalogue: Part 2, Pilgrim Souvenirs and Secular Badges.* Salisbury: Salisbury and South Wiltshire Museum.

"Pilgrimage on a Page": Pilgrims' Badges in Late Medieval Manuscripts

Bruna, Denis. 1998. "Temoins de dévotions dans les Livres d'Heures à la fin du moyen âge." *Revue Mabillon* 9:70, 127-61.

Koldeweij, A. M. (Jos). 1991. "Pilgrim Badges Painted in Manuscripts: A North Netherlandish Example." *Masters and Miniatures: Proceedings of the Congress on Medieval Manuscript Illumination in the Northern Netherlands.* Koert van der Horst and Johann-Christian Klamt, eds. Doornspijk: Davaco, 211-18.

Köster, Kurt. 1984. "Gemalte Kollektionen von Pilgerzeichen und Religiösen Medaillen in Flämischen Gebet- und Stundenbüchern des 15. und Frühen 16. Jahrhunderts." *Liber Amicorum Herman Liebaers.* F.L.J. Vanwingaerden, ed. Brussels: Crédit Communal de Belgique, 485-535.

_____. 1979. "Kollektionen Metallener Wallfahrts-Devotionalien und Kleiner Andachtsbilder, Eingenäht in Spätmittelalterliche Gebetbuch-Handschriften." *Das Buch und Sein Haus.* Vol 1. Rolf Fuhlrott and Gerhard Liebers, eds. Wiesbaden: Otto Harrassowitz, 77-130.

_____. 1965. "Religiöse Medaillen und Wallfahrts-Devotionalien in der Flämischen Buchmalerei des 15. und Frühen 16. Jahrhunderts." *Buch and Welt.* Hans Striedl and Joachim Wieder, eds. Wiesbaden: Otto Harrassowitz, 459-504.

Medieval Christian Pilgrims' Guides and Pilgrims' Texts

Aronstam, Robin Ann. 1975. "Penitential Pilgrimages to Rome in the Early Middle Ages." *Archivum historiae pontificiae* 13:65-83.

Birch, Debra J. 1998. *Pilgrimage to Rome in the Middle Ages.* Rochester, NY: Boydell and Brewer.

Bordeaux Pilgrim. http://www.christusrex.org/www1/ofm/pilgr/00PilgrHome.html.

Davidson, Linda K., and Maryjane Dunn-Wood. 1993. *Pilgrimage in the Middle Ages: A Research Guide.* New York: Garland Publishing, Inc.

Hoade, Eugene. 1993. *Western Pilgrims, 1322-1392.* Studium Biblicum Franciscanum, no. 18, 1952. Rpt. Jerusalem: Franciscan Printing Press.

Hunt, E. D. 1982. *Holy Land Pilgrimage in the later Roman Empire, AD 312-460.* Oxford: Clarendon Press.

Kempe, Margery. 1994. *The Book of Margery Kempe.* B. A. Windeatt, trans. New York: Penguin Books.

Mapping Margery Kempe: Web site administered by Virginia C. Raguin and Sarah Stanbury. http://www.holycross.edu/departments/visarts/projects/kempe/.

Nichols, Francis Morgan, ed. and trans. 1986. *The Marvels of Rome, Mirabilia Urbis Romae.* New York: Italica.

Palestine Pilgrims' Text Society (London, England). 1971. *The Library of the Palestine Pilgrims' Text Society.* Rpt. 13 vols. in 11. New York: AMS Press.

Shaver-Crandell, Annie, Paula Gerson, and Alison Stones. 1995. *The Pilgrim's Guide to Santiago de Compostela: A Gazetteer.* London: Harvey Miller Publishers.

Sumption, Jonathan. 1975. *Pilgrimage: An Image of Mediaeval Religion.* Totowa, NJ: Rowman and Littlefield.

Wilkinson, John. 1977. *Jerusalem Pilgrims before the Crusades.* Warminster: Aris and Philips Ltd.

_____. 1981. *Egeria's Travels to the Holy Land.* 1971. Rev. ed. Jerusalem: Ariel Publishing House.

Wilkinson, John, Joyce Hill, and William F. Ryan. 1988. *Jerusalem Pilgrimage, 1099-1185.* Works issued by the Hakluyt Society, 2nd series, no.167. London: Hakluyt Society.

St. James: The Eternal Pilgrim

Ashley, Kathleen, and Marilyn Deegan. 2009. *Being a Pilgrim: Art and Ritual on the Medieval Routes to* Santiago. Farnham, England, and Burlington, VT: Ashgate.

See also works listed for the preceding essay, *Medieval Christian Pilgrims' Guides and Pilgrims' Texts*

St. James as Pilgrim or Moorslayer in the *Poem of the Cid*

Bailey, Matthew. 2008. *Cantar de mio Cid.* Digital ed. Austin: The University of Texas. Last accessed 1 February 2008. http://www.laits.utexas.edu/cid/.

Barton, Simon, and Richard Fletcher. 2000. (Intro and trans). *The World of El Cid: Chronicles of the Spanish Reconquest.* Manchester and New York: Manchester University Press.

Berceo, Gonzalo. 2003. *Obras completas.* Jorge García López and Carlos Clavería, eds. Madrid: Biblioteca Castro.

Bishko, Charles Julian. 1975. "The Spanish and Portuguese Reconquest, 1095-1492." *A History of the Crusades* 3:396-456. Harry W. Hazard, ed. Madison: University of Wisconsin Press.

Blackburn, Paul. 1966 rep. 1998. *Poem of the Cid.* Norman: University of Oklahoma Press.

Castro, Américo. 1971. *The Spaniards: An Introduction to Their History.* Willard F. King and Selma Margaretten, trans. Berkeley and Los Angeles: University of California Press.

Coffey, Thomas F., Linda Kay Davidson, and Maryjane Dunn. 1966. *The Miracles of St. James: Translations from the Liber Sancti Jacobi.* New York: Italica.

Domínguez-García, Javier. 2008. "Simbología jacobea en el imaginario medieval: Iacobus Apostolus en la crónica *Psuedo Turpín* y Santiago Matamoros en el *Diploma de Ramiro I.*" *La Corónica* 36.2:295-311.

Fletcher, Richard. 1984. *Saint James's Catapult: The Life and Times of Diego Gelmírez of Santiago de Compostela.* Oxford: Oxford University Press

_____. 1990. *The Quest for El Cid.* New York: Alfred A. Knopf.

_____. 2003. *The Cross and the Crescent: Christianity and Islam from Muhammad to the Reformation.* New York: Viking.

Hamilton, Rita, and Janet Perry, trans. 1984. *Poem of the Cid.* London: Penguin.

Lowney, Chris. 2005. *A Vanished World: Muslims, Christians, and Jews in Medieval Spain.* Oxford and New York: Oxford University Press.

MacKay, Angus. 1977. *Spain in the Middle Ages: From Frontier to Empire, 1000-1500.* New York: St. Martin's Press.

Menéndez Pidal, Ramón. 1969. *Cantar de mio Cid: Texto, gramática y vocabulario.* 3 vols. 1908-1911. 4th ed. Madrid: Espasa-Calpe.

_____. 1969. *La España del Cid.* 1929. 2 vols. 7th ed. Madrid: Espasa-Calpe.

Merwin, W. S. 1959. *The Poem of the Cid.* New York: Random House.

Michael, Ian, ed. 1984. *Poema de mio Cid.* Madrid: Castalia.

Montaner, Alberto, ed. 2000. *Cantar de mio Cid.* Barcelona: Crítica.

Moore, John K. 2008. "Juxtaposing James the Greater: Interpreting the Interstices of Santiago as Peregrino and Matamoros." *La Corónica* 36.2: 313-44.

O'Callaghan, Joseph F. 1975. *A History of Medieval Spain.* Ithaca NY and London: Cornell University Press.

_____. 2003. *Reconquest and Crusade in Medieval Spain.* Philadelphia. University of Pennsylvania Press.

Raulston, Stephen B. 2008. "The Harmony of Staff and Sword: How Medieval Thinkers Saw Santiago Peregrino and Matamoros." *La Corónica* 36.2:345-67.

Reilly, Bernard F. 1988. *The Kingdom of León-Castilla under King Alfonso VI: 1065-1109.* Princeton: Princeton University Press.

Salvador Miguel, Nicasio. 2003. "Entre el mito, la historia y la literatura en la Edad Media: el caso de Santiago guerrero." *Memoria, mito y realidad en la historia medieval.* José Ignacio de la Iglesia Duarte, ed. Actas de XIII Semana de Estudios Medievales, Nájera 2002. Logroño: IER, 215-32.

Sánchez-Albornoz, Claudio. 1975. *Spain, a Historical Enigma.* Colette Joly Dees and David Sven Reher, trans. 2 vols. Madrid: Fundación Universitaria Española.

Simpson, Lesley Byrd. 2007. *The Poem of the Cid.* Berkeley and Los Angeles: University of California Press.

Smith, Colin, ed. 1976. *Poema de mio Cid.* Madrid: Cátedra.

Such, Peter, and John Hodgkinson, trans. 1987. *Poem of My Cid.* Warminster: Aris & Phillips.

Paths through the Desert: Hispanic Pilgrimage Experiences in Mexico City and Chimayó

Guadarrama, Jorge, exhibition curator. 1996. *La Reina de las Americas: Works of Art from the Museum of the Basílica de Guadalupe.* Chicago: Mexican Fine Arts Center Museum.

Gutiérrez, Ramón A. 1995. "El Santuario de Chimayó: A Syncretic Shrine in New Mexico." In *Feasts and Celebrations in North American Ethnic Communities.* Ramón A. Gutiérrez and Genevieve Fabre, eds. Albuquerque: University of New Mexico Press.

Howarth, Sam, and Enrique R. Lamadrid. 1999. *Pilgrimage to Chimayó: Contemporary Portrait of a Living Tradition.* Santa Fe: Museum of New Mexico Press.

Quiroz Malca, Haydée. 2000. *Fiestas, peregrinaciones y santuarios en México.* México, DF: Consejo Nacional para la Cultura y las Artes, Dirección General de Culturas Populares.

Schneider, Luis Mario, and Guillermo Tovar de Teresa. 1990. *México peregrino: diez santuarios procesionales.* México, DF: Banca Cremi.

Treib, Marc. 1993. *Sanctuaries of Spanish New Mexico.* Berkeley, CA: University of California Press.

Zarebska, Carla, ed. 2005. *Guadalupe*. English language edition. Jaqueline Robinson López, trans. Albuquerque: University of New Mexico Press.

ISLAM

The Pilgrim, the Image, and the Word in Islam

Allen, Terry. 1988. "Aniconism and Figural Representation in Islamic Art." In *Five Essays on Islamic Art.* Terry Allen, ed. Michigan: Solipsist Press, 17-37.

Blair, Sheila S., and Jonathan Bloom. 1994. *The Art and Architecture of Islam 1250-1800.* New Haven: Yale University Press.

Flood, Barry Finbar. 2002. "Bamiyan, Islamic Iconoclasm, and the Museum." *Art Bulletin* 84/4:641-59.

Grabar, Oleg. 1977. "Islam and *Iconoclasm*." In *Iconoclasm*. A. Bryer and J. Herrin, eds. Birmingham, England: Centre for Byzantine Studies, University of Birmingham, 45-52.

Irwin, Robert. 1997. *Islamic Art in Context: Art, Architecture, and the Literary World.* New York: Harry N. Abrams, Inc.

The Hajj Today – Connecting the Global Village

Books

Belt, Don, ed. 1991. *The World of Islam.* Washington, DC: National Geographic Society.

Kaïdi, Hamza, in collaboration with Nadjm Oud-Dine Bammate and El Hachemi Tidjaniate. 1980. *Mecca and Medinah Today.* Paris: les éditions j.a.

Peters, Frank E. 1994. *The Hajj: The Muslim Pilgrimage to Mecca and the Holy Places.* Princeton: Princeton University Press.

Shariati, Ali. 1993. *Hajj.* Ali A. Behzadnia, M.D., and Najla Denny, trans. Costa Mesa, CA: Jubilee Press.

Smith, Houston. 1991. *The World's Religions: Our Great Wisdom Traditions.* New York: HarperCollins.

Wolfe, Michael. 1993. *The Hadj: An American's Pilgrimage to Mecca.* New York: Grove Press.

_____. 1997. *One Thousand Roads to Mecca.* New York: Grove Press.

Articles

Abdullah, Wael. 2007. "Governor Inspects New Haj Terminal." *Arab News,* December 12. *http://www.arabnews.com/?page=1§ion=0&article=104526&d=12&m=12&y=2007&pix= kingdom.jpg&category=Kingdom.*

Al-Nagur, Dr. Ali Hassan. 2007. The Economy of Hajj and Umrah. Quoted in Arab News, December 12, in "Economic Impact of Pilgrimage Huge: Study" by Galal Fakar. *http://www.arabnews.com/?page=1§ion=0&article=104533&d=12&m=12&y=2007.*

Bukhary, Saleem. 2002. "Mina Fire Proof Tents Project Biggest in History." *Haj & Umra: A Monthly Published by Ministry of Haj.* 57, 2 (June-July):31.

Khan, Fouzia. 2008. "KAIA Haj Terminal Is Bigger and Better." From *Saudi Gazette*, December 30. *http://www.saudigazette.com.sa/index.cfm?method=home.regcon&contentID=2008112522946.*

Madani, Iyad Amin. 2002. "Amongst Hajis and Umra Performers: A Personal Note." *Haj & Umra: A Monthly Published by Ministry of Haj.* 57, 2 (June-July): 3.

Documentary Films

Bredar, John, and Mehdi, Anisa. 2003. "Inside Mecca." *National Geographic.* Washington, DC: NGT, Inc.

Mehdi, Anisa. 1998. "An American Hajj." 3-part series for Religion and Ethics News Weekly. PBS.

Websites

History of Jeddah. *http://www.hajinformation.com/main/h301.htm.*

Hajj Terminal. *http://www.archnet.org/library/sites/one-site.jsp?site_id=294.*

Hajj quotas. *http://www.islamicvoice.com/september.98/letters.htm.*

Bibliography

GENERAL AND COMPARATIVE

Colman, Simon, and John Elsner. 1995. *Pilgrimage Past and Present in World Religions.* Cambridge, Massachusetts: Harvard University Press.

Esposito, John, Darrell J. Fasching, and Todd Lewis. 2005. *World Religions Today.* 2nd ed. Oxford and New York: Oxford University Press.

Morinis, Alan, ed. 1992. *Sacred Journeys: The Anthropology of Pilgrimage.* Foreword by Victor Turner. New York: Greenwood Press.

BUDDHISM

Aitken, M. 1995. *Meeting the Buddha: On Pilgrimage in Buddhist India.* New York: Riverhead Books.

Bernbaum, Edwin. 1980. *The Way to Shambhala.* Garden City NY: Anchor Press.

Buffetrille, Katia. 2000. *Pèlerins, Lamas et Visionnaires. Sources Orales et Écrites sur les Pèlerinages Tibétains.* Wien: Arbeitskreis für Tibetische und Buddhistische Studien Universität Wien (*Wiener Studien zur Tibetologie und Buddhismuskunde,* Heft 46).

DeCaroli, Robert. 2004. *Haunting the Buddha: Indian Popular Religions and the Formation of Buddhism.* New York: Oxford University Press.

Dowman, Keith. 1988. *The Power Places of Central Tibet: The Pilgrim's Guide.* London: Rutledge and Kegan Paul.

_____. 1995. *Power Places of Kathmandu: Hindu and Buddhist Holy Sites in the Sacred Valley of Nepal.* Rochester, VT: Inner Traditions.

Eckel, Malcolm David. 1994. *To See the Buddha*: Princeton: Princeton University Press.

Ekvall, Robert B., and James F. Downs. 1987. *Tibetan Pilgrimage.* Tokyo: Institute for the Study of Languages and Cultures of Asia & Africa.

Epprecht, Katharina, ed. 2007. *Kannon, Divine Compassion: Early Buddhist Art from Japan.* Zurich: Museum Rietberg.

Findley, Ellison Banks. 2003. *Dana: Giving and Getting in Pali Buddhism.* Delhi: Motilal Banarsidass Publishers.

Germano, David. 2007. *Embodying the Dharma: Buddhist Relic Veneration in Asia.* Albany: State University of New York Press.

Gutchow, Niels, Axel Michaels, Charles Ramble, and Ernst Stienkellner, eds. 2003. *Sacred Landscape of the Himalayas.* Vienna: Austrian Academy of Sciences Press.

Heim, Maria. 2004. *Theories of the Gift in South Asia.* London and New York: Routledge.

Huber, Toni. 1999. *The Cult of Pure Crystal Mountain: Popular Pilgrimage and Visionary Landscape in Southeast Tibet.* Oxford and New York: Oxford University Press.

_____, ed. 1999. *Sacred Spaces and Powerful Places in Tibetan Culture: A Collection of Essays.* Dharamsala: Library of Tibetan Works and Archives.

_____. 2008. *The Holy Land Reborn: Pilgrimage and the Tibetan Reinvention of Buddhist India.* Chicago: University of Chicago Press.

Huntington, John C. "Sowing the Seeds of the Lotus: A Journey to the Great Pilgrimage Sites of Buddhism," part 1, *Orientations* 16 no. 11 (Nov. 1985):46-61; part 2, *Orientations* 17 no. 2 (Feb. 1986):28-43; part 3, *Orientations* 17 no. 3 (March 1986):32-46; part 4, *Orientations* 17 no. 7 (July 1986):28-40; part 5, *Orientations* 17 no. 9 (Sept. 1986):46-58.

_____. "Pilgrimage as Image: the Cult of the Astamahapratiharya," part 1, *Orientations* 18 no. 4 (April 1987):55-63; part 2, *Orientations* 18 no. 8 (Aug. 1987):56-68.

Huntington, Susan L., and John C. Huntington. 1990. *Leaves from the Bodhi Tree: The Art of Pala India (8th to 12th Centuries) and Its International Legacy.* Seattle and London: Dayton Art Institute in association with University of Washington Press.

Inoue, Yasushi. 1981. "Passage to Fudaraku." *Lou-lan and Other Stories.* James T. Araki, trans. Tokyo, New York, and London: Kodansha International.

Johnson, Russell, and Kerry Moran. 1989. *Kailas: On Pilgrimage to the Sacred Mountain of Tibet.* London: Thames and Hudson.

Leoshko, J. 1988. *Bodhgaya the Site of Enligtenment.* Bombay: Marg Publications.

Lewis, Todd T. 2000. *Popular Buddhist Texts from Nepal: Narratives and Rituals of Newar Buddhism.* Albany: State University of New York Press.

Katô Bunnô, et al. 1975. *The Threefold Lotus Sutra.* New York and Tokyo: Weatherhill/Kosei.

Moerman, D. Max. 2005. *Localizing Paradise: Kumano Pilgrimage and the Religious Landscape of Premodern Japan.* Cambridge, MA and London: Harvard University Asia Center.

Pratt, James Bissett. *The Pilgrimage of Buddhism and a Buddhist Pilgrimage.* New Delhi, India: Asian Education Services.

Reader, Ian. 2005. *Making Pilgrimages: Meaning and Practice in Shikoku.* Honolulu: University of Hawai'i Press.

Rimer, J. Thomas. 1988. *Pilgrimages: Aspects of Japanese Literature and Culture.* Honolulu: University of Hawai'i Press.

Strong, John S. 2004. *Relics of the Buddha.* Princeton: Princeton University Press.

Swearer, Donald K. 2004. *Becoming the Buddha: The Ritual of Image Consecration in Thailand.* Princeton: Princeton University Press.

ten Grotenhuis, Elizabeth. 1999. *Japanese Mandalas: Representations of Sacred Geography.* Honolulu: University of Hawai'i Press.

Trainor, Kevin. 2007. *Relics, Ritual, and Representation in Buddhism: Rematerialising the Sri Lankan Theravada Tradition.* Cambridge: Cambridge University Press.

Usui, Sachiko. 2007. "The Concept of Pilgrimage in Japan." In *Pilgrimages and Spiritual Quests in Japan.* Maria Rodriguez del Alisal, et al., eds. London and New York: Routledge, 27-38.

Where the Buddha Walked: A Companion to the Buddhist Places of India. 2003. Pilgrimage & Cosmology Series: 5. Indica Books: Varanasi, India.

Yü, Chün-fang. 1992. "P'u-t'o Shan: Pilgrimage and the Creation of the Chinese Potalaka." In *Pilgrims and Sacred Sites in China.* Susan Naquin and Chün-fang Yü, eds. Berkeley and Los Angeles: University of California Press, 190-245.

CHRISTIANITY

Ashley, Kathleen, and Marilyn Deegan. 2009. *Being a Pilgrim: Art and Ritual on the Medieval Routes to Santiago.* Farnham, England and Burlington, VT: Ashgate.

Baert, Barbara. 2004. *A Heritage of Holy Wood. The Legend of the True Cross in Text and Image.* Lee Preedy, trans. Leiden: Brill.

Belting, Hans. 1994. *Likeness and Presence: A History of the Image before the Era of Art.* Chicago: University of Chicago Press.

Birch, Debra J. 1998. *Pilgrimage to Rome in the Middle Ages: Continuity and Change.* Woodbridge, Suffolk, and Rochester, NY: Boydell Press.

Blick, Sarah, and Rita Tekippe, eds. 2005. *The Art and Architecture of Late Medieval Pilgrimage.* Leiden: Brill.

Brown, Peter. 1981. *The Cult of the Saints: Its Rise and Function in Latin Christianity.* Chicago: University of Chicago Press.

Bruna, Denis. 1996. *Ensignes de pèlerinages et ensignes profanes.* Paris: Musée National du Moyen Âge.

Caviness, Madeline. 1977. *The Early Stained Glass of Canterbury Cathedral: 1175-1220.* Princeton: Princeton University Press.

Davidson, Linda K., and Maryjane Dunn-Wood. 1993. *Pilgrimage in the Middle Ages: A Research Guide.* New York: Garland Publishing, Inc.

Duggan, Anne. 2005. *Thomas Becket.* Oxford: Oxford University Press, a Hodder Arnold Publication.

Dyas, Dee, ed. 2007. *Pilgrims and Pilgrimage. Journey, Spirituality and Daily Life Through the Centuries. An Interactive DVD.* Nottingham: University of York.

Elsner, Jaś. 2009. *The Oxford Handbook of Byzantine Studies.* Oxford: Oxford University Press.

Frugoni, Arsenio, ed. 1998. *Rome: The Pilgrim's Dream.* Florence: Giunti.

Geary, Patrick. 1994. "Sacred Commodities: The Circulation of Medieval Relics." In *Living with the Dead in the Middle Ages.* Patrick Geary, ed. Ithaca NY: Cornell University Press.

_____. 1978. Furta Sacra: *Thefts of Relics in the Central Middle Ages.* Princeton: Princeton University Press.

Gingras, George E., trans. and ed. 1970. *Egeria: Diary of a Pilgrimage.* New York: Newman Press.

Howard, Donald R. 1980. *Writers and Pilgrims: Medieval Pilgrimage Narratives and their Posterity.* Berkeley: University of California Press.

Howarth, Sam, and Enrique R. Lamadrid. 1999. *Pilgrimage to Chimayó: Contemporary Portrait of a Living Tradition.* Santa Fe: Museum of New Mexico Press.

Hunt, E. D. 1982. *Holy Land Pilgrimage in the Later Roman Empire, AD 312-460.* Oxford: Clarendon Press; New York: Oxford University Press.

_____, Joyce Hill, and William F. Ryan. 1988. *Jerusalem Pilgrimage, 1099-1185.* Works issued by the Hakluyt Society, 2nd series, no.167. London. Hakluyt Society.

Kempe, Margery. 1994. *The Book of Margery Kempe.* B. A. Windeatt, trans. New York: Penguin Books.

Kessler, Herbert L., and Johanna Zacharias. 2000. *Rome 1300: On the Path of the Pilgrim.* New Haven: Yale University Press.

Morris, Colin. 2005. *The Sepulchre of Christ and the Medieval West from the Beginning to 1600.* Oxford and New York: Oxford University Press.

Palestine Pilgrims' Text Society (London, England). 1971. *The Library of the Palestine Pilgrims' Text Society.* Rpt. 13 vols. in 11. New York: AMS Press.

Ryan, William G., trans. 1995. *The Golden Legend: Readings on the Saints: Jacobus de Voragine.* Princeton: Princeton University Press.

Rudolph, Conrad. 2004. *Pilgrimage to the End of the World: the Road to Santiago de Compostela.* Chicago: University of Chicago Press.

Shaver-Crandell, Annie, and Paula Gerson. 1995. *The Pilgrim's Guide to Santiago de Compostela: A Gazetteer with 580 Illustrations.* London: Harvey Miller Publishers.

Swatos, William H. Jr., and Luigi Tomasi, eds. 2002. *From Medieval Pilgrimage to Religious Tourism: The Social and Cultural Economics of Piety,* Westport, CT: Praeger.

Turner, Victor, and Edith Turner. 1978. *Image and Pilgrimage in Christian Culture: Anthropological Perspectives.* New York: Columbia University Press.

Vauchez, André. 1993. *The Laity in the Middle Ages: Religious Beliefs and Devotional Practices.* Margery J. Schneider, trans. Daniel E. Bornstein, ed. South Bend IN: University of Notre Dame Press.

Webb, Diana. 1999. *Pilgrims and Pilgrimage in the Medieval West.* London and New York: I .B. Tauris.

Wroth, William. 1991. *Images of Penance, Images of Mercy: Southwestern Santos in the Late Nineteenth Century.* Published for Taylor Museum for Southwestern Studies, Colorado Springs Fine Arts Center, by University of Oklahoma Press.

PEOPLE OF THE BOOK: JEWS, CHRISTIANS, AND MUSLIMS

Fletcher, Richard. 2003. *The Cross and the Crescent: Christianity and Islam from Muhammad to the Reformation.* New York: Viking.

Kühnel, Bianca, ed. 1997/98. *The Real and Ideal Jerusalem in Jewish, Christian and Islamic Art:* The Hebrew University of Jerusalem. *Journal of the Center for Jewish Art* 23/24.

Lowney, Chris. 2005. *A Vanished World: Muslims, Christians, and Jews in Medieval Spain.* Oxford and New York: Oxford University Press.

Matar, Nabil, ed. and trans. 2003. *In the Lands of the Christians – Arabic Travel Writing in the 17th Century.* London and New York: Routledge.

O'Callaghan, Joseph F. 2003. *Reconquest and Crusade in Medieval Spain.* Philadelphia: University of Pennsylvania Press.

Peters, Francis E. 1985. *Jerusalem: The Holy City in the Eyes of Chroniclers, Visitors, Pilgrims, and Prophets from the Days of Abraham to the Beginnings of Modern Times.* Princeton: Princeton University Press.

_____. 1982. *The Children of Abraham: Judaism, Christianity, Islam.* Princeton: Princeton University Press.

ISLAM

Adle, Chahriyar. 1972. "Un disque de fondation en céramique, 711/1312." *Journal asiatique* 260:277-97.

Aksoy S., and Rachel Milstein. 2000. "A Collection of Thirteenth Century Illustrated Hajj Certificates." In *M. Ungur Derman 65th Birthday Festschrift.* Irvin Çemil Schick, ed. Istanbul, Sabanci Universitesi: 101-134.

Armstrong, Karen. 1993. *Muhammad: A Biography of the Prophet.* San Francisco: Harper.

Blair, Sheila, and Jonathan Bloom, eds. 1991. *Images of Paradise in Islamic Art.* Hanover, NH: Hood Museum of Art, Dartmouth College.

Bianchi, Robert. 2004. *Guests of God: Pilgrimage and Politics in the Islamic World.* New York: Oxford.

Bredar, John, and Anisa Mehdi. 2003. *Inside Mecca* National Geographic Special, premiered on PBS.

Burton, Richard F. 1856. *Personal Narrative: Pilgrimage to Al-Madinah and Meccah.* London: Longman, Brown, Green and Longmans.

Encyclopaedia of Islam, 2007 (and earlier editions) edited by P. J. Bearman, Th. Bianquis, C. E. Bosworth, E. van Donzel and W. P. Heinrichs. Leiden and Boston: Brill.

Ettinghausen, Richard, Oleg Grabar, and Marilyn Jenkins-Madina. 2001. *Islamic Art and Architecture 650-1250.* New Haven: Yale University Press.

Eickelman, Dale F., and James Piscatori, eds. 1990. *Muslim Travellers: Pilgrimage, Migration and the Religious Imagination.* Berkeley: University of California Press.

Esposito, John L., ed. 1995. *The Oxford Encyclopedia of the Modern Islamic World.* vols. 1-4. New York: Oxford University Press.

_____, ed. 2000. *The Oxford History of Islam.* Oxford and New York: Oxford University Press.

Gibb, Sir Hamilton, ed. 1958. *The Travels of Ibn Battuta.* [The Hakluyt Society] London: Cambridge University Press.

Grabar, Oleg. 1992. *The Mediation of Ornament.* Princeton: Princeton University Press.

_____. 2005. "The Umayyad Dome of the Rock." In *Jerusalem.* Oleg Grabar, ed. Farnham, Surry: Ashgate Variorum, 1-19.

Haneef, Suzanne. 1996. *What Everyone Should Know About Islam and Muslims.* Chicago: Kazi Publications.

Hisham Ibn-al-Kalbi. 1952. *The Book of Idols by Hisham Ibn-al-Kalbi.* Nabih Amin Faris, trans. Princeton: Princeton University Press.

Lane, Edward W. 2003. *An Account of the Manners and Customs of the Modern Egyptians: The Definitive 1860 Edition.* Cairo and New York: American University in Cairo Press.

Le Strange, Guy, trans. 1971. *Al-Muqaddasi. Description of Syria, including Palestine.* Palestine Pilgrims Text Society Reprint. vol. 3, New York: AMS Press.

Milstein, Rachel. 2006. "Futuh-i Haramayn: Sixteenth-century Illustrations of the *Hajj* Route." In *Mamluks and Ottomans: Studies in Honour of Michael Winter.* David J. Wasserstein and A. Ayalon, eds. London and New York: Routledge.

_____. 1999. "The Evolution of a Visual Motif: the Temple and the Ka'ba." *Israel Oriental Studies* 19:23-48.

_____. 2001. "Kitab Shawq-nameh, an Illustrated Tour to Holy Arabia." *Jerusalem Studies in Arabic and Islam* 25:275-345.

Mujir al-Din, 1876. *Histoire de Jérusalem et d'Hébron depuis Abraham jusqu'à la fin du XVe siècle de J.-C.: Fragments de la Chronique de Moudjir-ed-dyn.* Henry Sauvaire, trans. Paris: Leroux.

Nasir-I-Khusrau. 1971. *A Journey through Syria and Palestine.* Guy Le Strange, trans. Palestine Pilgrims Text Society, London, 1895; Reprint New York: AMS Press. vol. 4.

Nasr, Seyyed Hossein. 1987. *Islamic Art and Spirituality.* Albany: State University of New York Press.

_____. 2001. *Ideals and Realities of Islam.* 2nd ed. Chicago: Kazi Publications.

Peters, Francis E. 1994. *The Hajj: The Muslim Pilgrimage to Mecca and the Holy Places.* Princeton: Princeton University Press.

Rauf, M. A. 1964. *The Life and Teaching of the Prophet Muhammad.* London: Longmans, Green & Co.

Renard, John. 1998. *Windows on the House of Islam.* Berkeley and London: University of California Press.

Roxburgh, David J. 2008. "The Pilgrimage City." In S. Jayyusi and others, *The City in the Islamic World.* Leiden. Brill. vol. 2, 753-74.

Shariati, Ali. 1993. *Hajj*: High Wycombe (Bucks). Jubilee Press.

Sourdel, Dominique, and Sourdel-Thomine, Janine. 2006. *Certificats de pèlerinage d'époque ayyoubide: contribution à l'histoire de l'idéologie de l'Islam au temps des croisades.* Paris: Académie des inscriptions et belles-lettres.

Strike, Vincenzo. 1976. "A Ka'bah Picture in the Iraq Museum." *Sumer* 32:195-201.

Wolfe, Michael, ed. 1997. *One Thousand Roads to Mecca: Ten Centuries of Travelers Writing about the Muslim Pilgrimage.* New York: Grove Press.

Glossary

BUDDHISM

Avalokiteshvara "Lord who gazes down (with Compassion)": The Sanskrit name of the Bodhisattva of Universal Compassion. The most popular of the celestial Bodhisattvas, able to hear all cries of sentient beings, he appears in multiple forms, and both genders. Called Kannon in Japan, Chenrizi in Tibet, Karunamaya in Nepal and Guanyin in China.

Bodhgaya: the site in India where Shakyamuni Buddha achieved enlightenment under a tree. Buddhists today revere this species of tree (*Ficus religiosa*) planted at monasteries and pilgrimage sites.

Bodhisattva: an individual who has achieved the perfections of enlightenment but who still postpones release from *samsara* into *nirvana* to stay in this world to help other sentient beings. In the Mahayana tradition, all individuals should consider themselves Bodhisattvas and aspire to become Buddhas.

Buddha: one who has "awakened"; one who is freed from the cycle of birth and rebirth; able to enter nirvana.

circumambulate: to walk around something sacred. Buddhist practice encourages the ritual of circumambulation around natural landscape features as well as buildings in a clockwise direction. Muslims circumambulate sites, such as the Ka'ba in Mecca, in a counterclockwise manner.

darshan: literally means "seeing," and refers to the physical act of seeing an important person, image, tree, relic, or other worthy objects. Through sight, the mind is potentially transformed by the holy.

dana: selfless giving, the most honored of the six perfections to be cultivated as a means of self-transformation.

Dharma: the Buddha's teaching, referred to by Buddhists as one of the three refuges, along with the Buddha and the Sangha (the monastic community). See also Three Jewels.

Eight Great Places: pilgrimage sites associated with major events of the Buddha's life: Lumbini, the place of his birth; Bodhgaya, place of enlightenment; Sarnath, the deer park where he first taught; and Kushinagara, the site of his death, with four additional sites of miracles. At Shravasti, he produced the "Twin Miracle", reconciling water and fire: flames emanated from the upper part of his body and water from the lower. At Rajagriha, he subdued an enraged elephant; at Sankashya he descended from heaven after visiting there for three months to teach his mother; and at Vaishali he received an offering of honey from a monkey.

Eightfold Path: the eight qualities needed to reach enlightenment: right views, right intention, right speech, right action, right livelihood, right effort, right mindfulness, and right concentration.

enlightenment: a state achieved by individuals who have purified their minds of all passions such as desire and anger. They will undergo death, but then enter a transpersonal state for all eternity, escaping the cycles of rebirth.

Gau: a container, usually made of metal, that is worn as an amulet. The Gau most commonly contains written mantras, tsa-tsas (small clay sculptures), or other mementos of pilgrimage or devotion.

Kannon: see Avalokiteshvara.

Karma: "action," from the verbal root *kr*, which means "do": refers to everything one has thought and done, whether virtuous or not, including, most fundamentally, adherence or non-adherence to the teachings of Shakyamuni Buddha.

***Lotus Sutra*:** one of the earliest and most influential Mahayana Buddhist texts, which reveals the cosmological nature of a Buddha and the universal character of Buddhist truth.

Mahayana: the branch of Buddhism called "Great Vehicle" that was until the present dominant in Nepal, Tibet, and East Asia. The Mahayana school recognizes Buddhahood incipient in all sentient beings and envisions the universe populated by innumerable Bodhisattvas. Often, like Avalokiteshvara, they are the subject of intense affection and ritual veneration.

mandala: a geometric layout with a sacred being at the center. The systems of supportive divinities, usually arranged concentrically around the focal figure, are seen in most mandalas. By visualizing the mandala in detail, including turning it into a three-dimensional space in the mind, advanced Buddhist practitioners seek to "assume the divine mind" of the Enlightened Buddha or Bodhisattva, and reach enlightenment.

mantra: a short formula of sacred words given by a Buddha or Bodhisattva, with powers to heal, cleanse, or open the mind to spiritual truth.

nirvana: literally "to extinguish." Release from the cycle of rebirth and death after attaining enlightenment. Final cessation and last rebirth of an enlightened being. See enlightenment.

punya: merit, or good karma. Punya is earned by following Buddhist moral and spiritual teachings, and doing rituals such as pilgrimage. Individuals practicing circumambulation and prostration focus their minds on Buddhist spiritual ideals.

prayer wheel: container for mantras (prayers) printed or written on slips of paper that are wound around a cylinder that spins around an interior axle. The container is then spun around coinciding with the multiple replications of the mantra recitations in the mind of the worshipper. Prayer wheels can be small enough to carry in one's hand; larger wheels, resembling drums, are installed at major monasteries and temples.

Pure Land: rebirth realms as defined in Mahayana Buddhism. Buddhas and advanced Bodhisattvas are able to create a place where humans can be reborn; those within the pure lands are able to progress more easily towards certain enlightenment.

relic: tangible mementos of a holy person. In Buddhism, the term for relic is *dhatu*. Somewhat like Christians, Buddhists recognize a three-fold hierarchy: 1) bodily relics (*sharira*) such the ashes of a cremated body; 2) locations (*paribhogika*), literally "places of pleasure," implying the places of action and objects of use associated with the Buddha, and 3) images and representations, (*uddeshaka*) meaning "point to" or "illustrate," that are reminders of the Buddha. All can be objects of pilgrimage.

***samsara*:** the cycle of transmigration to which all living beings are bound. Buddhists hold that while each of our lives ends in death, death in turn results in rebirth. This is true not only for humans but for all sentient beings.

sangha: the Buddhist monastic community of monks and nuns.

stupa (also **chorten):** a dome-shaped monument, used to house Buddhist relics or to commemorate significant places/events of Buddhism or Jainism. The dome is surmounted by a pole and umbrella. Miniature models of these structures are frequently used as devotional objects. The stupa becomes the pagoda in East Asia.

Theravada: the branch of Buddhism now dominant in South and Southeast Asia. It is dominated by the monastic community who consider their tradition the most traditionalist.

Three Jewels (Triratna): refer to the Buddha, the Dharma, and the Sangha in which every Buddhist takes mental refuge during all rituals.

tsa-tsas: sacred images made most commonly of clay, popular in Tibetan Buddhism. They are produced in molds as part of group or individual ritual and also serve as empowered mementos for pilgrims. Sometimes made as part of meditation practice.

Vajrayana: one of the three branches of Buddhism. The path of esoteric Buddhist practice, now dominant in Nepal, Tibet, and Japan.

CHRISTIANITY

Catholic: those churches that base their governance on apostolic succession.

Christ: from the Greek, meaning "messiah" or "anointed one." This was applied to Jesus of Nazareth, traditionally referred to as Jesus Christ.

Corporal Works/Acts of Mercy: seven injunctions for charitable actions: feeding the hungry, giving drink to the thirsty, clothing the naked, giving shelter to the homeless, ministering to the sick, visiting the imprisoned, and burying the dead.

Gospel: from Old English, "good news." The term used for the four accounts of Christ's life in the New Testament.

grace: the concept that divine love and assistance flows to humans through the boundless mercy of God; it is given freely, not earned, since human actions can never constrain the divine.

heresy: a term used to designate beliefs which deviate from what a group deems to be orthodox teaching. The "orthodox" teaching generally refers to theological doctrines such as the Trinity, nature of Christ, the power of God over all creation, the Virginity of Christ's mother, etc.

Incarnation: the taking on of flesh by the Second Person of the Trinity (Jesus Christ) through his birth from Mary.

justification by faith: Martin Luther, one of the principal leaders of the Protestant Reformation, asserted that humans are saved by faith alone. They do not gain salvation through good works. Thus concepts of gaining merit though pilgrimage or indulgenced prayers were rejected.

Mass: the ritual commemoration of the Last Supper of Christ. For Catholics, it denotes the sacrament of the Eucharist when the priest transforms the bread and wine of the offering into the sacramental body and blood of Christ that is received by the faithful.

monasticism, monastery, monk: referring to a way of life adopted by both Christians and Buddhists, a withdrawal from normal society to practice bodily mortification (such as fasting and sexual abstinence) and intense prayer. Both men and women, living in separate communities, have been drawn to such a life. In the Middle Ages, monasteries were among the most powerful social institutions in both Eastern and Western Europe and were vital parts of the cult of relics and pilgrimages.

original sin: the taint on the human soul due to the disobedience of the first parents, Adam and Eve. Christians believe that this affected all human beings by damaging their will so that they are easily corrupted.

pardon or **indulgence:** The medieval Church developed a reward called an indulgence, forgiveness for the "temporal punishment" after death that was due for various types of transgressions or sins. The indulgence's power was based on the belief in the superabundance of merits established by Christ that could be dispensed by his representative, the pope. These were part of the belief system that focused on earning merit, akin to Buddhist beliefs that also supported pilgrimage. Indulgences became increasingly current in the 12th century and developed into a standard aspect of piety associated with designated prayers before a venerated image. In the 14th century indulgences became linked to special years when the faithful were encouraged to visit Roman holy places.

pope: the bishop of Rome, regarded by Roman Catholics as possessing authority over all other bishops, and thus as the supreme head of the Church.

Protestant: churches that reject the descent of authority through apostolic succession. Ministers are often selected by the community. For most of these churches, worship is grounded in the belief in a direct personal relationship with God in Christ, rejecting elaborate ritual. Reading of the Bible and preaching are prioritized. Thus the intersession of saints and veneration of relics are rejected and pilgrimages to shrines other than the Holy Land are discouraged.

purgatory: a time/place anticipating entrance to heaven. At death, most people (saints are an exception) are condemned to a period of attendance and suffering in a location called purgatory. There they expiate the penalties of sin (see also **pardon** or **indulgence**).

Redeemer: Christianity accepts that as a result of the sin of the first couple, Adam and Eve, the human race was estranged from God and at the mercy of evil in the form of Satan. The sacrifice of Christ was a redemptive death, making up for transgressions and bringing humanity back to its closeness to God. Thus he is the Redeemer.

relic and **reliquary:** tangible reminders of the dead. These objects (relics) were invariably encased in containers (reliquaries) of precious materials that were executed with great artistic skill. Like Buddhism, Christianity cherished many kinds of relics, building churches over the remains of holy individuals and even dividing their remains as a means of disseminating sanctity. Before the Reformation of the 16th century, the cult of relics permeated pious practice.

sacraments: outwards signs that relate to God's promise of grace. Ritual action, such as the pouring of water at Baptism or the speaking of a promise at Marriage, is said to impart grace to the participant. Roman Catholics recognize seven sacraments, Baptism, Eucharist, Reconciliation, Confirmation, Marriage, Holy Orders, and Last Rites, in general necessitating the actions of ordained clergy.

saint: an individual who lived so commendable a life that he/she moved directly to union with God after death. Manifestations of this circumstance are usually attested to by miracles. In early medieval times, saints were more popularly acknowledged; in the present, for Roman Catholics, designation is rigidly controlled by papal commissions. Saints are seen as intercessors, bringing the prayers of their admirers to God. They are also seen as models of an exemplary life.

Trinity: the Christian faith in a triune God, defined as Father, Son, and Holy Spirit. The Trinity shares a single divine nature, and is thus not seen as a statement of multiple deities. The Nicene Creed of 325 CE defines "One God" the Father, the maker of heaven and earth; the Son, eternally begotten of the Father; and the Holy Spirit, emanating from both Son and Father.

two natures, one person: Christ, because of his birth from Mary, has two natures (divine and human). He is fully human in all things except sin; he is fully divine, enjoying the same fullness of God as does the Father and the Holy Spirit.

ISLAM

Allah: God

Arafat: an area with a small hill, called the Mount of Mercy, about fourteen miles from Mecca. Pilgrims must reach Arafat on the tenth day of the Hajj. The day is spent in contemplation, prayer, and petition, and seen as an earthly rehearsal for the Day of Judgment.

Eid al Adha: The Feast of the Sacrifice. Following the Jumrat, pilgrims on the Hajj sacrifice an animal to commemorate Abraham's sacrifice of a ram sent by God as a substitute for his son.

hadith: the report by others of Muhammad's sayings and actions. The collected texts are highly revered as a study for decisions in the Muslim community.

Hajj: annual pilgrimage to Mecca, one of the Five Pillars of Islam. It comprises a circuit of travels with prescribed rituals from Mecca, to Arafat, and return by Muzdalifa and Mina; of great antiquity, even predating Islam.

Five Pillars of Islam: Every Muslim assumes a fivefold religious obligation, first to proclaim that there is no god but Allah and that Muhammad is the messenger of God. There follow four prescribed ritual acts: prayer five times daily; the payment of an annual alms; dawn to dusk fasting during the lunar month of Ramadan; and, finally, the performance, at least once in a lifetime, of the Hajj or pilgrimage to Mecca, if physically and financially able.

haram al-sharif: meaning "noble sanctuary"; the area built on top of the temple mount in Jerusalem, containing, among other edifices, the Dome of the Rock and the Al Aqsa mosque.

hijra: migration. In 622 Muhammad fled from Mecca to Medina, an event referred to as the *hijra*. The event marks the first year of the Muslim lunar calendar.

ihram: ritual state of sanctity during the Hajj. Men are required to proclaim ihram through their dress. During the Hajj they wear two pieces of unstitched cloth that they wrap around themselves, also called *ihram*.

Islam: submission or surrender to God.

jumrat: ritual of stoning Satan. As pilgrims leave Arafat to return to Mecca, they stop to recall an event from the life of Abraham. When asked by God to sacrifice his only son, Abraham is tempted by the devil three times. Each time Abrahams throws stones to banish the tempter. Pilgrims on the Hajj reenact this event in a ritual Stoning of Satan, casting pebbles at stone pillars located at Mina.

Ka'ba: meaning "The Cube" (al-ka'ba). The small structure, now surrounded by a great mosque, is revered as a house of prayer built by Abraham and his son Ishmael. *And when We made the House (at Mecca) a resort for mankind and a sanctuary, (saying): Take as your place of worship the place where Abraham stood (to pray). And We imposed a duty upon Abraham and Ishmael, saying: Purify My House for those who go around and those who meditate therein and those who bow down and prostrate themselves in worship*" (Quran 2:125).

Kiswa: the fabric covering of the Ka'ba. It is made of silk, now black but formerly in various colors, and elaborately embroidered with designs and with verses from the Quran.

masjid: "place of prostration," a mosque; Muslim place of worship and prayer.

Medina: site of Muhammad's tomb: In 622, confronted by opposition in Mecca, Muhammad fled to Medina with his followers, an event known as the *hijra*. In 630, he returned with an army and conquered Mecca. In 632, he returned to Medina and died. The site is revered throughout the Muslim world and a large mosque surrounds his tomb.

minbar: pulpit in the mosque from which the Friday sermon (*khutba*) is preached.

mohr or **turbah:** Shi'ite Muslims cherish the practice of praying by touching the forehead to a small piece of clay called a *mohr* or *turbah* from the Holy City of Karbela. These small tablets vary in shape but generally carry some inscription commemorating Muhammad, his son-in-law Ali, and his grandsons, Hasan and Husayn.

mosque: see *masjid*

muezzin: the person who issues the external call to prayer in the mosque.

Muhammad's Night Journey (*Isra*) and Ascent to Heaven (*Miraj*): A tradition cited in the Quran (17:1): in which the winged steed Buraq brings Muhammad from Mecca to Jerusalem where he prays with others, then remounts Buraq to ascend to the heavens where injunctions concerning the Muslim faith are revealed.

People of the Book (*Ahl al-Kitab*): generally meaning Jews and Christians as well as Muslims. These religions each possess not only a revealed scripture from God, but correspondences among the three revelations.

qiblah: direction that should be faced for Muslim prayer. Muslims originally prayed toward the Noble Sanctuary in Jerusalem; in 623, while in Medina, Muhammad changed the direction to Mecca. Most mosques contain a niche indicating the quiblah.

Quran: meaning "The Recitation," the revelation given to Muhammad by Gabriel, the angel of Allah. Its authentic form is in Arabic.

Ramadan: the lunar month of fasting, the ninth month of the Muslim calendar when from dawn to dusk Muslims refrain from food, drink, tobacco, and also acts/thoughts of violence or anger.

salat: each Muslim is enjoined to offer official prayer performed five times each day.

shahadah: declaration of Muslim faith: "There is no god but God and Muhammad is His Messenger".

sharia: Islamic law, which takes as its authority the Quran and the hadith.

Shi'a: meaning partisan or follower; Muslims who follow the leadership of Ali. Muhammad's daughter Fatimah married Ali, who thus became the prophet's son-in-law. For the Shi'a, the leadership of the Muslim community should belong to Muhammad's descendants. Ali's burial place in Najaf, Iraq, is now surrounded by a great mosque and is the site of fervent devotions.

Sunnah: "example" referring to Muhammad's example. The term Sunni is derived from this word.

Sunni: the term for those who prioritize "example" over the blood lines in determining Muslim leadership. The Sunni accept the historic succession of the Caliphs while the Shi'a support the descendents of Muhammad. Sunnis comprise the majority of the Muslim community.

surah: the term given to a chapter of the Quran.

umrah: the circumambulation of the Ka'ba (*tawaf*), the fast-paced transit between the hills of Safa and Marwah (*sayee*), and finally a ritual cutting of hair, in commemoration of Abraham, Hagar, and their son Ismael. These rituals can be performed at any time but are invariably incorporated with the yearly performance of the Hajj.

ziyara: "pious visits." Such pilgrimages are practiced beyond that to Mecca during the time of Hajj. Muslims visit Mecca at other times of the year, the Prophet's tomb at Medina, the Dome of the Rock and other sites around the Haram al-Sharif on the Temple Mount in Jerusalem, as well as Islam's hundreds of other tomb shrines, like those at Karbela and Najaf in Iraq and Mashhad in Iran.

Index